THE RED
and the
BLACKLIST

Also by Norma Barzman

Rich Dreams

THE RED
and the
BLACKLIST

THE INTIMATE MEMOIR OF A
HOLLYWOOD EXPATRIATE

Norma Barzman

Thunder's Mouth Press / Nation Books
New York

PS
3503
.A754
Z476
2003

THE RED AND THE BLACKLIST: *THE INTIMATE MEMOIR OF A HOLLYWOOD EXPATRIATE*

Copyright © 2003 Norma Barzman

Published by
Thunder's Mouth Press/Nation Books
161 William Street, 16th Floor
New York, NY 10038

Nation Books is a copublishing venture of the Nation Institute and Avalon Publishing Group Incorporated.

Library of Congress Cataloging-in-Publication Data
Barzman, Norma
   The red and the blacklist: *the intimate memoir of a hollywood expatriate*/ Norma Barzman.
   p. cm.
   Includes bibliographical references and index.
   ISBN 1-56025-466-1
   1. Barzman, Norma. 2. Screenwriters--United States--Biography. 3. Journalists--United States--Biography. 4. Hollywood (Los Angeles, Calif.)--Biography. 5. Motion picture industry--United states. I. Title.

PS3503.A754 Z476 2003

                                                                              2002075072

9 8 7 6 5 4 3 2 1

Book design by Paul Paddock

Printed in the United States of America
Distributed by Publishers Group West

For Ben
with whom I shared forty-seven years,
seven beautiful children, thousands of stories and
a rich, exciting life.

The compensation of growing old was simply this: that the passions remain as strong as ever, but one has gained—at last—the power which adds the supreme flavour to existence, of turning it round, slowly, in the light.

Virginia Woolf
Mrs. Dalloway

CONTENTS

ACKNOWLEDGMENTS

A couple of months before he died, Abe Polonsky was hollering at me. This was an almost daily occurrence during that period, and there were times when he talked very, very softly, but this was not one of them. "I toldja! You've got to write your memoir! You don't have a choice. Whyncha listen to me? You've gotta stop talking about it and get to work." His voice was rising in pitch. "And you either do it honestly—or you don't do it at all!"

"Oh, I'll do it honestly," I chirped, wondering if I could do that.

Abe wasn't alone in recommending honesty. Gore Vidal, in his admirable memoir *Palimpsest,* reminded me that a memoir is "how one remembers one's own life. An autobiography is history and requires much research. In a memoir it isn't the end of the world if your memory tricks you and your dates are off by a week or a month as long as you honestly try to tell the truth."

"Honesty," however, didn't seem adequate. I could try to be honest but as I jotted down events in my life, I began to see that I often succeeded in hiding the truth from myself.

On September 26, 1999, in the *Los Angeles Times Book Review,* I read Vivian Gornick's critique of Edward Said's memoir, *Out of Place.* I felt, as Coleridge wrote, "like some watcher of the skies when a new planet swims into his ken."

"A memoir," writes Gornick, "is a work of sustained narrative prose that, though it originates in actuality and not invention, bears the same responsibility as does all writing: to shape a piece of experience, transform a set of events, deliver a bit of wisdom. The reader must always be persuaded that the narrator is speaking the truth, that she or he is *honestly working hard to get to the bottom of the experience at hand in order to better understand one's own self.* [my italics] A novel has many agenda, a memoir only one: self-definition. . . . The question being asked in the exemplary memoir is: 'Who am I?' On that question, the writer of memoir must deliver. Not with an answer but with depth of inquiry."

Over a burger at Hamburger Hamlet on South Beverly Drive a few blocks from Abe's place in Los Angeles, I read the Vivian Gornick piece aloud to him. "Exactly!" Abe cried. "You have to wrestle with yourself!"

He grinned. "You. Not me. I don't have to. I know who I am. 'I' am in everything I've ever written."

Once I embarked, I understood what Gornick meant by an idea of self being worked out on the page. Lately, since the long rough draft has been completed and I am in the process of revising, insights I have kept deeply buried are beginning to surface. During the almost three years that I've been writing the memoir, it has not become easier to tap into areas I shied away from and successfully avoided in my psychoanalysis.

Abe, I am beholden to you for your love and encouragement. I thank Vivian Gornick and my dear friend Mollie Gregory, and all those who helped me to see that this memoir could have value only if I dug down where it hurts.

I am grateful, too, for having had available to me Ben's journals, in which he wrote with zest and humor about many of our shared adventures, and without which it would have been almost impossible to reconstruct our life. I have relied on his accounts of his heroic making of the key to the mysterious locked room of our Boulogne house; his losing my passport when it was returned to me after seven lean passportless years; the John Wayne stories; and other delicious anecdotes. I can still hear him telling his stories.

I don't know how to thank Larry Ceplair and Paul Buhle for their encouragement, or friends from Betsy Blair to Pierre Rissient, whom I phoned in England and France at all hours of the day and night to verify data, or those who simply shared nostalgia with me.

I do know that extra-special thanks and love are due my Mollie, my lovely agent, Julie Popkin, who brought this manuscript to Nation Books, and to my most wondrous and delightful of editors, Carl Bromley.

NORMA BARZMAN
Los Angeles
August 17, 2002

BEFORE THE TITLES

Monday, March 22, 1999, the day after the Oscars. The phone rang. It was Sophia. What other Sophia was there?

She said, "Norma, I saw you on television and you were beautiful."

I said, "Sophia, I saw you on television and you were beautiful."

Sophia Loren became our close friend in 1960 in Madrid when my husband, Ben Barzman, was writing El Cid *straight for the camera.*

Laughing melodiously, Sophia said, "I'm calling because you did a wonderful job. Only about a third of the audience stood and applauded Kazan."

In less than five weeks, those of us blacklisted writers who were still alive had organized a protest against the Motion Picture Academy of Arts and Sciences granting a lifetime award to informer Elia Kazan.

We opposed the award because during the frenzy of Cold War McCarthyism, Kazan, a distinguished New York theater director, in order to continue to work in films, became a star witness for the House UnAmerican Activities Committee (HUAC) and named as Communists some of his closest friends. To most blacklisted writers, his "lifetime achievements" were not only his films, for which he had already received two Oscars (Gentlemen's Agreement *and* On the Waterfront) *but also the destruction of lives.*

"I had pity for the old man," Sophia went on, "but I sat quietly and did not applaud. Next to me, Benigni. In front of me, Spielberg. Tom Hanks. Geffen. Sherry Lansing. All sitting. I turn around. In back of me, every row down. At home later, I looked at the tape. A small group led by Charlton Heston was standing as if they were everyone in the audience, applauding loudly. But I was there. What was shown on TV was not what I saw or heard. Most people were seated. Applause was slight. You know, Norma, I am not political. But this—! How could the Academy do it? I do not understand."

I didn't understand either. I am still trying to understand what began on my twenty-first birthday, September 15, 1941, the day I arrived in Hollywood. Or did it really begin one year later, with a cross between a boy-meets-girl screwball comedy and a fighting love story?

PART ONE

HOLLYWOOD
IN THE '40s

1

Boy Meets Girl

The Time: Halloween, October 31, 1942. A party for Russian war relief.

The Place: The Beverly Hills home of writer-director Robert Rossen (*Body and Soul, All the King's Men, The Hustler*). One sweeping wall of the beige sunken living room opened, as you would expect, on a brightly illuminated azure swimming pool.

"What's a nice girl like you doing with a shit like him?" was The Boy's opening gambit.

The Boy was in his early thirties. His skin was well tanned, his hair black and curly, his brown eyes twinkled playfully. A mustache covered his upper lip. Although he was wide-shouldered and broad-chested, he was short. (In later years, he resembled Prince Rainier.) Not handsome, I decided, magnetic. Perched on a fuzzy white armchair, he was casually cleaning his fingernails with his Phi Beta Kappa key.

I was The Girl, generally considered a dish, either because I was so young and already divorced, or because of my big boobs, at that moment plainly visible under a pink cashmere pullover. The frames of my harlequin eyeglasses matched my pink sweater. My long brown hair turned under in a pageboy like the model on the cover of *Mademoiselle's* 1942 "College Issue."

Moments passed before I realized with astonishment that "What's a nice girl like you doing with a shit like him?" was directed at me because I'd been trying to impress a top Hollywood agent.

The Boy was waiting for me to approach.

I took a few steps forward, defensively sticking out my chin. "I'm not with him, just talking to him."

"Stage direction, flirtatiously—"

I angled my chin from defensive to assertive. "I may need an agent."

"Not that one." His warning was issued in a deliciously warm voice with an accent I couldn't recognize, not New York, Western, Midwestern, or Southern, though it was almost a drawl. The way he spoke reminded me of J. M. Barrie's definition of char-r-rm in *What Every Woman Knows*—more about how one sounds than how one looks. "You want to know just what kind of a shit he is?" he went on as I came closer. "He was going to New York for a few months. Would I take his apartment? I said I couldn't afford it. He insisted his place would make me look good. Shortly after I moved in, his landlord came by. I discovered my agent-friend was paying fifty bucks a month and charging me seventy-five when he knew I was broke and out of a job."

The Boy put away his Phi Bet key, got up, drew his five feet four up to the tallest possible, brushed imaginary fuzz from his sloppy-in-the-right-way English flannels.

"What kind of job you looking for?" he asked.

"Eventually I want to write and direct."

He had a trick of narrowing one eye. "Direct? Nobody starts out that way. Later maybe, if you're an actor or a cutter or a frustrated screenwriter—"

"Uh-huh. Like my cousin Henry who complains that the shit he turns out never reaches the screen."

"Henry? Henry Myers? He's written some great comedies!"

"*Destry Rides Again. Million Dollar Legs.*"

Henry Myers. Screenwriter, novelist, playwright. My idol. Henry was why I wanted to be a writer, why I'd come to Hollywood. My cousin Henry. My mother's sister's son. My first love. When I was thirteen, he took me to lunch at Sardi's, sat me down under a caricature of himself.

Already under the spell of his Byronic regard, romantic limp, his long wavy musician's hair and sideburns, I hadn't needed Sardi's or his witty stories of the literary mighty for my seduction to be complete.

"Henry doesn't write 'shit,'" The Boy objected. "Anyway, 'shit' is a lousy word."

"Why is it all right for you to say it?"

"It just doesn't sound right coming from you. So you're the little cousin from the East. Norma. A movie name. Norma Shearer. Norma Talmadge."

"My mother named me after the opera *Norma*."

"By Bellini," Henry supplied right on cue, offering two glasses of bubbly. "I see you've found each other. If I weren't twenty-seven years older—" He lifted his circumflex eyebrows mischievously and disappeared.

The Boy went right on as if Henry had not interrupted, "Last week I sold my first story to the movies—"

I knew who he was. Ben Barzman. *True to Life*, $30,000 for an "Original Story for the Screen," not a screenplay. After the agency took their 10 percent and the money they'd loaned him to live on, the $30,000 had to be split three ways between Ben, his brother Sol,[1] and Bess Taffel, who had collaborated with him. Paramount was going to make it with Mary Martin, Victor Moore, Franchot Tone, and Dick Powell.

"*I've* directed stage musicals," he continued. "*Labor Pains.* The International Ladies Garment Workers Union (ILGWU) show? But *I* don't think about directing. What makes *you* think—?"

My pink cashmere was suddenly too hot.

"I've written a—a screenplay," I stammered, "and made drawings of what the film should look like."

One eye narrowed again, this time in real disapproval. "A storyboard stops actors from coming up with anything."

"It's a method used by some distinguished filmmakers. Hitchcock. Minnelli. Milestone—"

"I've tremendous respect for Millie. He works closely with his art director. I trust actors. I directed my own play for the Federal Theatre—"

"You sound as if *you* want to direct."

"I'm afraid your drawings—" His speech was becoming more and more clipped.

"Are you British?"

"No," he replied, not missing a beat, "just affected." His timing was fabulous. He gave me a moment to laugh, then he, too, laughed. His ability to laugh at himself, I concluded, was what saved him. He leaned toward me, as if he were going to make another great admission, but said only, "Why don't we have some dessert?" and started heading for the buffet.

As I followed him, I became aware of the others at the party: at the piano, rosy, rotund Jay Gorney, the composer of "Brother Can You Spare a Dime?," accompanied Henry, who was singing his lyrics from *Meet The People,* a political musical revue that had opened in Los Angeles and had gone on to New York to become a hit.

> I shot grouse
> With Oscar Strauss
> And lived upon women and wine.
> Ausgezeichnet! Donnervetter!
> Life vas perfect, even better
> Than a Schubert operetta
> In that Mittel Europa
> Of mine . . .

Near the piano, our hosts, Bob and Sue Rossen, were looking on, pleased with themselves. Bob was chunky, built like a prizefighter, and Sue was one of those innocuous wives Hollywood men acquired in the early New York phase of their careers.

On the sofa, Gordon Kahn, my screenwriting teacher from the School for Writers, was wedged between Paul Jarrico and Ring Lardner, Jr. Paul's screenplay *Tom, Dick and Harry* had been nominated in 1941 for an Oscar. Ring had won the Oscar that year for his screenplay *Woman of the Year.*[2] Gordon Kahn, a B screenwriter, was noted for his coverage of the 1930s Lindbergh kidnapping when he was a reporter on the *New York Mirror*. The three men could not have been more dissimilar. Paul's open, bright-child's face radiated good fellowship. Ring's fine features, as well as his shyness, were hidden by thick-lensed horn-rimmed eyeglasses. To support a weak eye muscle, Gordon wore a monocle, which gave him the demeanor of a Prussian officer. But he was so small—sitting on the sofa, his feet didn't touch the floor—that he was not threatening.

Near the trio of writers, on a loveseat, B director Bernard Vorhaus sat close to his bawdy Welsh wife, Hetty. Known for bringing in his eight-day wonders on schedule, Bernie was good-looking despite his occasional lip-pursing tic. Sunk in a huge armchair, Abbott and Costello comedy writer Bobby Lees looked like a collar ad with Valentino patent-leather hair. His snub-nosed, freckled, adorable wife, Jeannie, cuddled in his lap.

I recognized many of the other guests from a recent projection of *Chapayev* I'd attended with Henry. He'd introduced them to me en masse as "the Hollywood Progressive Community": gravel-voiced Lionel Stander, who'd made over fifty films but is remembered for his role as "Max" the chauffeur in the popular TV series *Hart to Hart;* handsome John Garfield, the star who didn't win the Oscar for *Body and Soul* and usually looked as if the world was against him; Gene Kelly and his wife, actress Betsy Blair;[3] gangster-faced Edward G. Robinson; suave Paul Henried; 1932 *Scarface* star Karen Morley; pompous Herbert Biberman,[4] who was about to direct *The Master Race,* and his Oscar-winning actress wife, Gale Sondergaard, who looked just as she did in pictures—exotic.

Within a few years, most of the people in that room would be summoned before the House UnAmerican Activities Committee to be asked about their membership in the Communist Party.

But on that evening, I was dazed by the star-studded room. It took me a moment to remember who was at my side.

"Ben," I tried out his name. "How did you get started?"

"Standing on my feet in an Oregon cloak and suit factory for ten years, paying my way through college. Reed. Who put this writing-directing bee in your bonnet?"

I hesitated. "The curator of MOMA's film archive."

Ben looked puzzled.

I quickly calculated how much I should tell him. At the end of my sophomore year at Radcliffe, I'd run away to France, where I met a fellow who'd just graduated from Yale. A scion of a Jewish St. Louis shoe-manufacturing family, he'd refused to go into the business. He knew what he wanted to do. Since film schools, as such, did not exist,[5] he'd invented a new métier for himself. He was the first person I heard speak of film as art. He'd spent every summer in France, was knowledgeable about European cinema, talked by the hour about a Russian woman director who was, in his view, on a par with Eisenstein.

I returned to Radcliffe for my junior year, married Claude Shannon, an MIT PhD who became known as the Father of Information Theory.[6] I left Claude in June 1941, bumped into the Yale grad. He had acquired an MFA and had just been hired by the Museum of Modern Art to assist Luis Buñuel, who was editing anti-Nazi films for Nelson Rockefeller.

"Why do you have to think about my question so hard?" Ben asked me, as he took his place in the line for dessert.

I grinned. "A friend of mine at MOMA showed me pre-1900 Gaumont films—Meliès, Alice Guy—"

"Who?"

"Alice Guy Blaché. Monsieur Gaumont's secretary. He gave her his first shorts to write and direct."

"The first film director was Meliès," Ben said flatly.

"Blaché was the first director to bring narrative film to the screen."

"Films are more complex now, technically way too tough for a woman."

"Dorothy Arzner directs top stars."

"I said 'woman.' "

"That's a lousy thing to say."

Ben looked me over. I had that uncomfortable feeling of being cased by a man who just wanted to get in my pants. "Henry says you've been out here a year. A pretty bright college girl like you—what have you been doing with your time?"

"Learning to write."

"No such thing. You write."

"I *am*. I'm writing."

"When I drop you home, you can give me your script. I promise to read it."

His assumptions and his condescending attitude grated on me.

Jeannie Lees was next in line for dessert. She reached for a plate, handed it to Ben, turned away, and gave herself a slice of cake.

Ben bent over the buffet, trying to decide between the cheesecake, the devil's food, and the lemon meringue pie. He didn't ask me which I wanted. He smiled and held out a large portion of beautiful squooshy meringue pie.

"Mabel Normand?" I said. "Y'know? The silent film star?" To this day, I don't know why I did what I did. Intuition? Self-preservation? I took the plate of meringue from him. "Mabel Normand was also a director for Mack Sennett. It was *she* who invented"—I pitched the pie into his face—"pie-throwing!"

His face was covered with sticky goo. Creamy stuff dripped onto his impeccable navy-blue blazer. He reached out blindly.

I handed him two napkins. With one, he wiped the meringue out of his eyes, with the other, out of his nose.

The more I tried not to, the harder it was for me to keep from laughing. I spluttered.

Under the white froth, I saw that he, too, was laughing—ripples, then tides of wild deep-down laughter.

I looked around to see if anyone had noticed.

Jeannie Lees, next to Ben, had seen the whole thing but tactfully turned away. Bob Rossen, the host, had noticed something and was dancing toward us like a boxer, sparring with the air. Jeannie grabbed her husband, Bobby, and together, they blocked the view of Ben from everyone.

"Ben spilled a little meringue on himself," Jeannie explained calmly to Rossen.

"Sue!" Bob called his wife, who was immediately at his side. "Honey, get the cleaning fluid!"

The Rossens looked as if they were afraid they would be sued.

Bob put his arm around Ben and danced him through the doorway to the hall.

Had it happened to someone else, Ben would have jumped on it, molded it into a gorgeously hilarious tale. A great raconteur, he had a way of taking even the smallest incident, dressing it up, polishing it until it glittered. (In later years, I came to resent his appropriating events that happened to me and telling them better than I.)

The story of our first encounter did not enter his repertoire. It was too humiliating. Out of deference to him, I have never told it until now.

That night, Ben, angry about the meringue cream pie incident, did not take me home. The agent asked if he could accompany me, but, warned by Ben, I declined.[7] Henry had brought me. Henry took me home.

I lived next door to him and his domineering mother, my aunt Muzzy. My mother, Muzzy's younger sister, had bought our house, three curves up the road from the Sunset Strip, the year before, when she and I tired of living at the Beverly Wilshire Hotel.

Mother had grown up wealthy, the daughter of a woman who had founded a pincushion-and-comforter factory in Chicago in the late 1860s. My maternal grandmother married a ne'er-do-well Shakespearean actor who, at age eighteen, had found gold in California a year before the Gold Rush and gambled it away. He returned to Chicago, married my grandmother, fathered three children, then disappeared, never to be seen again.

My mother, Muzzy, and their brother inherited enough from the pincushions to be quite comfortable. To my father, Sam, who had been bankrupted by his crooked partner, Mother must have looked rich. He had worked his way up from office boy to president of a textile-import firm, and after he got rid of the partner, he handed out red and green Eversharp pencils printed with his logo, SAMALONE. In 1920, at the end of World War I, he brought Swiss fabrics back to America, heavenly voiles, chiffons, organzas, dotted Swiss. By 1928, he retired with his first million and took his family to France to live.

Mother had married my father to escape Muzzy's tyranny, so it was difficult to understand why Mother bought a house right next door to her. Of course it was also next door to Henry. She got the price down from $20,000 to $18,500, paid cash for it, put it in my name, and, to keep things equitable, promptly sent my older sister Muriel, a New York lawyer, a check for the same amount.

When Mother and I moved into 1290 Sunset Plaza Drive in March 1942, I pruned, raked, hoed, weeded, and wrote a novel. At night, I dated junior writers and attended a screenwriting class. But for several days after meeting Ben, I didn't engage in any of these activities. I sat near the phone, reading John Howard Lawson's *Theory and Technique of Playwrighting.*

When Ben finally called, his impersonal voice came quickly to the point. "I make a good eggplant thing. I think it's Romanian. I marinate cheap cuts of steak, then sauté them in mushrooms."

Mother was hovering over me. "What shall I bring?" I asked.

"Your script."

"No, I mean, should I bring . . . " Dessert came to mind, but after what I'd done with the last one at the Rossens' party, I rejected it. "Wine?"

"Red."

I knew we would get along.

"A man who cooks!" Mother exclaimed. "Better hang on to him."

Ben's Hollywood apartment was easy to find, the upper floor of a small Spanish two-story job with a lot of iron grillwork. It was on Vista, down the street from the School for Writers.

The baked eggplant, chopped fine with sweet onion, seasoned with oil, vinegar, salt, and pepper, was already well chilled.

Nervous, I said its French name, *Caviar d'aubergines.*

"You have a fine accent," he observed stiffly.

"I lived there when I was little."

We eyed each other.

Vodka warmed, the eggplant soothed. After a few mouthfuls of each, we hopped into bed, where we stayed for the next three weeks, except for tennis next door at Plummer Park, and my Thursday night class. Occasionally, I went home for fresh clothes. Mother smiled, made no comment.

Ben was the first man with a mustache I'd ever kissed. I hadn't expected to like it. But I did. I enjoyed the prickles. I liked his smell. Physically, I liked everything about him.

After we made love, he was still and silent. I was at my most talkative but tried not to say too much about my childhood. I encouraged him to tell me about growing up in a Russian-Jewish family in the Canadian Northwest. "Bossy Man" became my favorite story and would eventually become our children's favorite. Ben's storytelling, seductive, hypnotic, could have charmed the wolves in the forest. And, since he never revealed his feelings, it was only from his stories that I knew what he really felt but could not say.

Bossy Man was a Chinese vegetable vendor who made his rounds of Vancouver in a horse and wagon. Ben overheard his parents having a late-at-night, worried-about-money discussion. He wanted to help but what could an eight-year-old do?

Ben noticed that every time Bossy Man came by, he and Ben's mother went to the back door. With a pencil she listed the prices paid for the day's vegetables on the wooden doorjamb. At the end of the week, she added the amounts and paid him.

The day before the end of the following week, Little Ben dragged a chair up to the door, got on it, carefully erased what was scribbled there, and wrote in amounts half as big.

Later, Ben's mother and Bossy Man added up the numbers. Worried, she asked if he was absolutely sure the total was correct: the amount seemed too small to her. Bossy Man insisted in broken English that the list written on the doorjamb was what she owed.

After a couple of weeks of Ben's 50 percent reduction of the vegetable bill, his mother and father suspected something. They surprised him as he stood on a chair, erasing the true amounts.

Grim, unsmiling, his father explained to Ben that he had committed a serious injury. Bossy Man was saving to smuggle in his wife and two sons from China. This expensive subterfuge was necessary since the Oriental Exclusion Act made it illegal for Chinese women and children to immigrate to Canada.

A few months later, in the middle of the night, Ben's father woke him and took him in his butcher's truck to the seaside. They waited a long time on a dark, lonely stretch of beach, taking turns swinging a lantern. At last, they saw a blinking signal from a ship offshore.

Eventually, a rowboat bearing a young woman and two boys about Ben's age appeared. Ben's father paid off the two "people smugglers," then hid the Chinese family in the back of his truck under several animal carcasses.

As they approached the outskirts of Vancouver, the Royal Northwest Mounted Police stopped them. Ben's father managed to convince them that he and his son were on a cattle-buying trip.

When they pulled into a farm where a group of anxious Chinese farmers waited, Bossy Man ran to the truck to embrace his wife and children. Ben remembered seeing a tear rolling down his father's cheek.

"When my father died," Ben told me, "my mother wanted me to 'sit Shiva,' to remain with the dead and say prayers." Ben already knew that although I was Jewish on both sides, I'd had no religious training, didn't know any Hebrew or Yiddish, or even what the holidays were or when they fell.

"My father was an atheist," Ben continued, "an old-time socialist who hated my mother's religious ways. To say those prayers over him was against everything he stood for. I couldn't do it. Instead, I wrote a play, *Shiva*. It won the Federal Theatre Play Contest and was put on in Portland. It was too short to fill an evening so I wrote a curtain-raiser, a comedy about an Orthodox young couple who, because of the stringent religious laws regulating when you can or can't, never manage to have sex. And when they can, either he's angry at her or she's angry at him."

"That's not our problem, is it?" I said cheerily.

"What? We don't get angry with each other? I'm still mad as hell at you. Hey! What was all that shit about Mabel Normand?"

I jumped out of bed. "From 1913 on, before Charlie Chaplin even came to America, Mabel Normand was using entire routines that we think Chaplin invented."

"The pie!" His eyes were fierce. "Why did you do it?"

"You were being an insufferable male chauvinist!"

"Am I any different now? Three weeks later?"

"No, but now I know what it comes from. A mother who serves you, who doesn't sit down when you eat. You've been brought up with a bad attitude toward women. I would have a hard time—"

"You won't have to endure my male chauvinism forever," he snapped. "I'm waiting to be sent overseas. High blood pressure stopped me last time. Next time I won't drink coffee."

"You may want someone to come back to."

"I'd make a terrible husband." His arms were around me. "But I like you more than any girlfriend I ever had." Suddenly, he was kissing me with a new urgency, pulling me back onto the bed, enveloping me. "This isn't intermission," he said, "just a lowering of the curtain to denote the passage of time."

Since the start, we'd had neither a "before" nor an "after," only lulls followed by surges I'd never dreamed existed.

Later, at home, I took a bath and put on clean everything.

Mother looked at me quizzically.

"I'm going to marry him," I told her.

"Has he asked you?"

"No."

"It's only been a year since your divorce. I thought you wanted to write."

"I'll never find anyone this right for me."

"You don't have to get married again. You have a handle to your name." Mother meant I was Mrs., not Miss.

"I want to have kids—lots of them."

"Why?"

"Because I was like an only child—with an older sister who was a second mother."

Mother turned away. "At least he cooks."

I didn't tell her that he hadn't cooked since the eggplant.

The School for Writers (soon to be on the Attorney General's List of Subversive Organizations) was a couple of blocks from Ben's apartment on Vista.

Around 8 P.M. on a night in November of 1942, I arrived for class. The school was dark. A notice tacked on the door read: GORDON KAHN IS SORRY. HAS FLU. WILL BE HERE NEXT THURSDAY.

I left my car parked in front and walked down Vista to Ben's apartment house. I rang the bell. He didn't answer but I could see he was there. His lights were on. I rang again.

Finally he came running downstairs in his shirtsleeves, disheveled, breathless. He took my arm forcefully, piloted me back up the street, away from his place.

"Get lost, darling," he commanded, "for about two hours. I can't explain."

"I'll get lost—for two—lifetimes!" I turned on my heel, tears in my eyes. I didn't look back. When I did, he was out of sight.

I cried most of the night. In the morning, Mother woke me with a dozen long-stemmed roses.

"He means business," she said, handing me the card. MEET ME FOR BREAKFAST AT THE DERBY AT TEN. BEN.

Not "Love, Ben," I noted.

I hadn't yet gotten over Los Angeles. I still smiled at The Tail of the Pup, a shack shaped like a giant hot dog, and the famous derby-shaped Brown Derby Restaurant. But that morning I couldn't smile. I was angry and suspicious. Why had he rushed me away from his apartment? Was it a blonde or a redhead? Or Bess, his girlfriend-collaborator who'd been vacationing in New York?

Sitting alone in a big round leather booth, reading *Variety*, Ben was nonchalantly sipping orange juice. He popped up when he saw me, pecked my cheek, pulled me down close to him, and whispered, "It wasn't a girl. It was a meeting. In Hollywood, the Communist Party is underground."

2

Girl Gets Boy

During the year I lived in L.A., before I met Ben, Henry, a founder of the Screenwriters Guild, had been briefing me on Hollywood politics.[1]

In 1933, the Academy of Motion Picture Arts and Sciences, which embraced producers, directors, actors, writers, and technicians, approved a 50 percent pay cut for everybody working in the industry— except the stars, those luminaries whose contracts guaranteed their names above the title, star billing. The Academy, a company-formed union created by Louis B. Mayer in 1927, had already approved numerous 10 percent pay cuts during the five years it had successfully forestalled any real labor organizing. That Academy is the same one that on Oscar night, March 21, 1999, seventy years later, honored Elia Kazan.

The 50 percent pay cut came in the middle of the Depression, when most businesses were in trouble. The film industry in the United States was one of the few, besides steel and automobiles, that was thriving. The cut was initiated to save profit margins and huge executive bonuses. The Academy, Jack Warner later admitted, had "arranged" a decision, which the studio executives had reached unilaterally, to reassess the practice of giving actors and writers long-term contracts, their one area of security.[2]

Screenwriters and actors were enraged, especially after a government report indicated motion pictures had not only survived the Depression but also, through the policy of wage slashes, were doing better than other entertainment industries. The salaries of Hollywood employees had declined about 16 percent.

Labor fought the pay cut. The studios gave in to the International Alliance of Theatrical Stage Employees (IATSE), the technicians' union, since their salaries were only a small fraction of production costs. Producers strongly opposed the formation of talent guilds, particularly a writers' union.

At that time, the treatment of screenwriters in Hollywood was blatantly unfair: no minimum wage, medical insurance, or pension plan; residuals had not yet been invented;[3] writers were discharged without advance notice, laid off without pay while under contract, had no certainty of receiving credit, and often discovered additional writers had been hired to rewrite their scripts without their knowledge.

Writers who had won a fair Dramatists Guild contract in New York helped organize the Screenwriters Guild in 1933. In retaliation, the producers founded a company union, the Screen Playwrights, which lasted four years until the Supreme Court decision of 1937 upholding the National Labor Relations Act (NLRA). The NLRA guaranteed the right of workers to form unions and to engage in collective bargaining. Even after four hundred screenwriters voted overwhelmingly for the Screenwriters Guild, the producers kept trying to bludgeon them into accepting the company union. Finally, the National Labor Relations Board issued citations to the producers and threatened legal action.

The studio heads branded the "militant" founders of the Guild as "Red" although many writers became politicized only during the fight for a union, and didn't join the Communist Party until years later.

I was not surprised Ben was a Communist. I was astounded that the meetings were secret.

"The Communist Party is *legal!*" I cried, outraged.

The two women eating breakfast in the booth next to ours at the Derby looked at me suspiciously as if I were an international spy.

"Sssh!" Ben whispered. "None of us would have a studio job if they knew we were in the Party."

"I don't like that it's underground here. It makes it seem subversive. In New York, you can walk right into C.P. meetings. They welcome you—"

"Not the radio and theater branches. They're underground there, too."

"If they found out you were a Communist, you'd never get work?" He nodded. "Then you're risking a lot."

"I grew up during the Depression. Communists led the struggle for the unemployed. They unionized workers. They fought for Negro rights and against injustice wherever it existed."

I rose, reached for a chair from the other side of the table, pushed it at him. "Your soapbox."

He laughed. "The American Communist Party is not revolutionary. Nobody wants to overthrow the government with force or violence." One of the two women choked on her bacon. "It's just the best, most organized way I know to fight Fascism and imperialist war and to aid the colonial peoples in their struggle for freedom."

I started to reach for the chair again.

The woman who wasn't choking smiled at us. "*I* know," she said. "You're rehearsing!"

"Ben," I asked, "you were already radical in college, but what made you join the Party?"

"When I got to Hollywood, I wrote a couple of sketches for the ILGWU revue called 'Labor Pains,' a sort of West Coast 'Pins and Needles.' I was a garment worker myself—sweated it out for ten years in the Beaver Cloak and Suit Factory in Portland. That's probably one of the reasons they dumped the whole show in my lap to write, direct, produce, train the dancers, coach the actors—and all with nonprofessional people. Garment workers.

"They wouldn't take no for an answer. It was such an opportunity to get started that I agreed, then found myself drowning. Suddenly, as if a fairy godmother waved her wand, into the theater trooped three men and a woman, Jacobina Caro, a great choreographer with flame-colored hair and a cape to match. The three men were your cousin Henry, Eddie Eliscu, and Jay Gorney. They watched the rehearsal quietly. At the end, they asked if they could be of assistance. I knew who they were, of course, and how many thousands of dollars they made every week. "We'd love to have some help but we can't afford you," I told them.

"'It won't cost you anything,' Henry said. 'We just want to see a labor show be the best possible.'

"I wanted to make sure I understood their offer," Ben went on. "I made them repeat it. Then I said, 'Even if it's a hit, you won't make a dime out of it. There's a long line of people who have to be paid first.'

"At that point, Jacobina took off her cape and began showing the girls on the stage how to walk, sit, stand, move, and how to do exercises at their machines. Most of the girls were still working half-time in a garment factory. Jay sat down at the piano and went over the songs. Henry and Eddie worked with the actors.

"Afterwards, I asked them again how they could be so generous with their time. They said they were Communists. It was a pleasure to do anything to destroy Fascism and make a better society. Well—it was simple for me. I'd never seen selfless people doing hard work they didn't have to do and weren't getting paid for. I said, 'Gee, guys, can I join, too?' Norma," Ben said, very low, "I'm not trying to recruit you. I don't want you coming in because of me."

"Don't worry," I replied. "If I come in, it'll be because I want to."

"But you must have objections, things that stick in your craw, like the trials, the purges?"

"I suppose the people who were executed were traitors. They were threatening the existence of the first socialist state. I just wish Stalin hadn't had them killed. . . . Okay," I confessed, "One thing does trouble me."

"What's that?"

"Force or violence."

"That's what *they* say about us," he cut in. "If the majority voted democratically to have socialism, the haves would use force and violence to keep their property." He stared at me. "How did someone with your background go so far to the left?"

I mulled the question over. "First, there was Henry, who was a radical. Then my sister went to Columbia Law School, which was half Trotskyites, half Communists—"

The waitress served Ben a white telephone. "Mr. Goldwyn on the line," she said, plugging it in.

I had never seen one of the Derby's famous white phones in real life. But Ben acted as if he received calls on white telephones from Samuel Goldwyn every day of the week.

"*Swing Shift*? I'd love to work with you, Mr. Goldwyn. But don't you think the war may be over soon? Oh, thanks. I'll keep that in mind." Ben hung up. "Goldwyn was angry. But he liked my honesty. I could tell. He'll hire me sometime for something else. Why are you laughing?"

"You and I were so serious until the comedy relief à la Lubitsch arrived—the white telephone—"

"Lubitsch! Jeesus! I forgot! Lubitsch is shooting *To Be or Not to Be* on the Goldwyn lot! I could have watched him direct."

"I thought you didn't want to direct."

He gave me a look. "Let's get back to 'serious.' Weren't you upset by the charges of Russian anti-Semitism?"

"Russia has always been anti-Semitic even though the Soviet constitution expressly forbids anti-Semitism."

"You're not bothered by those who say the Soviet Union is totalitarian?"

"Maybe that's temporary, while the whole world is gunning for them."

"And the Nazi-Soviet Pact?"

"At Radcliffe I majored in government. For years before 1939, Russia was trying to get France and England to join them to stop Hitler. I read a white paper about it. Anyway, Russia wasn't ready to fight Germany alone. They needed time to arm themselves. Look how they're beating back the Nazis."

"Listen, nothing says you have to join. But we're making a difference. We influence producers to make pictures about real people. About women. We keep out the 'Stepin Fetchit' characters. Movies are less bad because of us."

"Couldn't you do all that without being 'in'?"

"We can do it better collectively. We learned that during the Depression. Strikes, immigrant labor, civil rights, miners, children."

"I'm glad you brought that up."

"What?"

"Children. I think we should have at least two, although I'd like more."

"Holy Christ! I told you I'm not a marrying kind of guy. Can't we just go on being happy?"

"Happy? Wondering when it will be over? I'm leaving. They say it's beautiful in Palm Springs in December."

The two women in the next booth were preparing to go. The woman who'd choked smiled at us. "What a sweet couple!" she murmured to her companion.

Mother and I spent Christmas and New Year's in the desert. Nothing is quite as depressing as hotel gaiety over the holidays. Ben knew where I was, but didn't even send a Christmas card.

"Ultimatums are a bad policy," Mother said, "unless you're certain of the outcome."

We'd been back over a week when Ben's best friend, screenwriter Adrian Scott, who would play an important role in our lives, called at two in the morning. One of the Hollywood Ten[4] who later went to jail for refusing to say whether he was or was not a Communist, Adrian was the only unfriendly witness who defied HUAC in a soft voice. He used that same voice to me that night on the phone.

"I just can't listen to Ben any longer. He's been going on about you for weeks. Will you talk to him?" Adrian asked.

"Hmmm."

"How are you?" Ben said, using his phony New York stage voice.

"I'm okay." I lied. "How about you?"

"My blood pressure is up without coffee. They made me 4F."

I said nothing.

"This makes me think of an old joke," he said. "A young man goes to the rabbi. 'If I get married, I'll be unhappy. If I don't get married, I'll be unhappy. What should I do?' The rabbi says, 'Get married and be unhappy like everybody.' "

"I don't get it."

Another silence. "This is a proposal."

"I don't like it but I accept."

On a chilly, rainy Monday morning in January 1943, a defrocked rabbi in penny loafers and a chamois jacket married us.

Ben Lowell had been the rabbi of a wealthy reform temple in Montgomery, Alabama, when he heard about the Scottsboro Boys, whose case became a cause célèbre championed by the Communist Party. In 1931, nine young black men were accused of the rape of two white women on a freight train. After nearly being lynched, all were tried and convicted, with only the youngest escaping a death sentence. At the jail where they were being held, Ben Lowell presented himself as their spiritual adviser and was permitted to see them. The following Sunday, he told his congregation he was convinced they were innocent. A mob literally tarred and feathered him, chased him out of town, and threw him on a train headed north.

In New York, an old college friend, a Communist, introduced him to someone at Sovexportfilm, a distribution company that offered him a job. Soon afterward, he fell in love with a renegade Lowell, of the Lowells who speak only to Lodges. Rabbi Ben Goldstein didn't want anything to do with his old identity. When he married Juliet Lowell, he took his wife's name.

"Did you find out if he has the right to marry us?" I asked.

"Oh yes. A rabbi retains the right to marry."

"How'd you find out?"

"I asked him," Ben replied.

"Oh!"

Mother never did believe we were married.

Looking back, I wonder how Ben and I could have been so insensitive. We didn't ask our mothers to the wedding. Instead, we enlisted only the necessary two witnesses, both of them Ben's friends, one his ex-girlfriend Bess Taffel.

"We had better do it now, before we're inebriated," Ben Lowell said solemnly, "in which case it could be declared null and void." We put down our glasses. He intoned, "According to the laws of the state of California and the customs of mankind, I pronounce you man and wife."

Several days before our wedding, Mother had packed her bags and called for a taxi to take her to the Ambassador Hotel.

"Mother! Why won't you let me drive you?"

"It feels good to be doing things on my own again."

"But Mother, I feel awful, you moving out and Ben moving in."

"It couldn't have come at a better moment. I was up to here"—she gestured to her tiny, carefully lipsticked Cupid's bow mouth—"with my big sister."

She knew I understood. I had a big sister, too.

Without a honeymoon or even a wedding breakfast, Ben and I drove home in his pale green Chrysler convertible. The rain beat hard on the canvas top.

Ben had been to the house once to visit Mother. He'd never been upstairs. I'd been sleeping in the middle of a king-size bed in my bedroom. I gave Ben the side near the windows, which I would always do wherever we were. The other side felt more protected.

"There are two bathrooms upstairs," he observed. "Should we both use the big white one?"

"We could each have our own."

"Fine. As long as I don't have to have the black bathroom."

The next morning I woke up early and drove down to Sunbee Market. I loved the way Californians made up names: Sunbee, Sunset and Larrabee, the Wiltern Theatre, at the corner of Wilshire and Western.

The war caused meat and gasoline shortages. The War Rationing Board doled out supplies to wholesalers and retailers and issued coupons to individuals to provide a fair distribution of scarce products. Immediately, a black market in meat flourished but Mother and I never bought any. This morning was different. Ben and I had something to celebrate.

On my return, Ben was dressed, casual but dressed. In forty-seven years, I never saw him lolling around the house in pajamas or robe. He said they made him feel like a sick child.

He sat down at the table, which I had already set with juice, coffee, and a creamy winter rose from the garden. He picked up the *Los Angeles Times,* handed me the *second* section, and began to read.

Suddenly I knew I was married.

After a few moments, he peered over the top of the newspaper, saw our plates loaded with beautiful, thick filet mignon steaks and fluffy eggs, did a huge take and uttered a heartfelt, "My God! What did I marry!"

Six months later, I heard that line once more.

Ordinarily, we wouldn't have gone to an art auction, but the *New Masses,* the Communist review on the order of the *Nation,* relied on an annual art auction to make up its financial deficit. Social Realist painters like Jack Levine and Joseph Hirsch donated their work, and wealthy progressives frequently lifted oil paintings from their walls to be auctioned off, all in the effort to keep the *New Masses* rolling one more year.

Ben was sitting in a front row; I was standing in the back next to Jeannie Lees, who was in charge of the event. Diego Rivera's painting *The Card Players* was up for auction. A slender, well-dressed man started the bidding by holding up three fingers. I held up four. He, five. I, six. He, seven. I, eight. He, nine. I took a deep breath and said in a tiny voice, "One Gee!"

Ben's head swiveled around. Apoplectic, he cried again, "My God! What did I marry!"

He needn't have worried. The man bidding against me went higher. The auctioneer pronounced it "Sold!" We learned later that the bidder was commissioned to buy the Rivera at whatever price for Cecil B. DeMille. That painting today must be worth well over a million dollars.

After three or four dinners of take-home chicken or cold cuts, Ben shouted, "Delicatessen psychology!"

The following evening, I made lamb chops, baked potatoes, salad. The response was the same, "Delicatessen psychology!"

"But that's not deli," I protested.

"You didn't put any thought into it."

I phoned Mother. "Buy an earthen pot," she said, "and a recipe book called *Casserole Cookery.*" The next day I set to work. When Ben came home, he savored the aroma, spooned himself a mouthful of the "lamb casserole," narrowed one eye, searched for a place to spit it out, motioned for me to listen: "Three friends, hunters, go on a camping trip. One of them will have to stay behind at the campsite, be responsible for the food. They draw lots. The two tell the unhappy loser the next trip one of them will cook and he can hunt. Finally, he gives in, but *no* complaints or he'll quit. That night, he over-salts everything. The two hunters eat avidly nonetheless. The second night, the cook empties the sugar into the stew but the other two eat with gusto. The third day he goes looking for moose droppings, sautés them with onions and potatoes. At supper, he waits expectantly for reactions. One hunter takes a big mouthful, chews slowly, looks wild-eyed. 'Hey, this is *shit!*' he says, then, catching the other hunter's eye, adds quickly, 'But *good!*' "

Storytelling was also Ben's way to avoid issues he didn't want to address. The "shit but *good!*" story came in handy in show business.

One night soon after, Ben came home to find no dinner and no me, just a note: "COME TO GUS BERKSON'S."

Gus Berkson's was a deli, across from Schwab's Drugstore on Sunset Boulevard near Laurel Canyon. Students, teachers, and others from the Actors Lab congregated there in noisy convivial groups. Founded in 1941, the Lab was made up mostly of Group Theatre actors. It was at the Actors Lab that I first saw Jack—John Berry[5]—in *All You Need Is One Good Break,* a social drama about tenement life by Arnold Manoff. Jack directed it and played the main role with the same larger-than-life dynamism he had offstage.

The Lab flourished for nearly ten years, mounting old and new plays, performing shows in Army camps, hospitals, and overseas bases, running an acting school called The Workshop, until 1951, when the House UnAmerican Activities Committee decimated it.

Canada Lee, the great black actor who'd come to L.A. to play the lead role in the Lab's production of Richard Wright's *Native Son,* had been refused service at Berkson's when he and his friends dropped in for a bite. Within an hour, a hundred pickets were milling around on the sidewalk in front of Berkson's.

Helen Levitt, secretary of the Lab, had asked me to call five people. I phoned Jeannie and Bobby Lees and four others, and asked them to make five calls. Trudging along the sidewalk were Morris Carnovsky, Stella Adler, and the others of the Group Theatre who had founded the Lab. It looked like a performance of Odets's *Awake and Sing.*

As I walked up and down in front of Berkson's carrying a sign ("UNFAIR"), I worried that Ben might construe my note to mean I'd decided not to cook anymore for the duration! We had not been picketing long when Gus Berkson himself appeared. "We'd be glad to serve Negroes," he apologized.

Too little and too late. We continued to picket. By the time Ben arrived, the crowd of pickets didn't need the four of us. Bobby and Jeannie and I took Ben off to dinner at Canter's on Fairfax Avenue. He seemed fated to eat deli. But two weeks later, Los Angeles had one less deli—Gus Berkson's closed.

July 18, 1999.

An obituary in this morning's *Los Angeles Times* reads: "Lupe R. Leyvas, 100, mother of a defendant in the 'Sleepy Lagoon' murder case.

"Leyvas was born in Chihuahua, Mexico, but crossed the border into El Paso at the age of sixteen after Pancho Villa's forces destroyed her family's bakery. She married, settled in East Los Angeles, and became an American citizen. In 1943, her nineteen-year-old son Henry was one of a dozen young men convicted of murder. An appeals court eventually overturned the conviction and reprimanded the judge for 'his prejudice and hostility toward the defendants.'"

• • •

Girl Gets Boy

The *Times* obituary reminded me of my first Communist Party branch meeting. Despite months of classes in Marxism, I was very nervous when Ben and I arrived at the comfortable old frame house on Franklin Avenue in Hollywood where the meeting was to be held.

Dan James stood in the doorway. Well over six feet, lanky, ruddy, easy-moving, he had a wide, warm, reassuring grin on his face. Dan had scripted Charlie Chaplin's films *Modern Times* in 1936 and *The Great Dictator* in 1940. He still played tennis with Charlie. The great-nephew of Jesse James, Dan had come from a well-to-do Kansas City family, and, I suspect, never had to worry whether he earned a living or not. Leading the meeting, he slouched in a deep oversize armchair, his long legs folded out of the way. Screenwriter Paul Jarrico recalled much later that "we [Communists] never overcame our male chauvinism. The chairmanship of the branch tended to go to a man, and the organizational secretaryship tended to go to a woman."[6]

Pauline Townsend, a public relations person who later named Ben and me, was "Org. Sec." She wrote for film magazines but was in a Writers Branch[7] because she was the wife of screenwriter Leo Townsend.[8]

Dan had been quiet during the "Educational," which, I recall, was a discussion of Stalin's pamphlet *Nationalism*. When he announced that it was time for "Good and Welfare," Dan, flushed and seething with outrage, suddenly took the floor himself. New troubles between zoot-suiters and Anglo teens backed by sailors had broken out in Venice.

During the Depression, second-generation Mexican-American Angelenos, known as *pachucos* because of their pleated, peg-topped, high-waisted trousers and the drape-like shape of their long, loose, wide-shouldered coats, were beginning to be noticed outside the *barrios*. To the police, the zoot suit was a means of identifying young gangsters, whom they rounded up from time to time and worked over.

In August 1942, when the body of a youth was found near an abandoned gravel pit christened "Sleepy Lagoon" by a reporter, police arrested twenty-four young Mexican-Americans, including two who had signed up with the United States Navy. In January 1943, twelve of the defendants were found guilty of murder and five of assault. Their convictions were overturned because of the incessant courtroom struggle between the prosecutors and progressive lawyers, as well as pressure from liberals, left-wingers, and Communists. But eight of the young men would serve nearly two years before they were released.

Dan spoke slowly, trying to contain his intense feelings. "Sailors have been invading the *barrios*. Four Mexican kids were killed. Nine sailors were arrested but no charges were brought. Soldiers, sailors, Marines stormed downtown, arms linked, four abreast. Several thousand servicemen and civilians halted streetcars, broke into theaters, dragged out *pachucos*, stripped them naked, and beat them senseless. Only the *People's World* [9] has been really following it. Police did nothing or joined the mob."

Dan's wife, Lilith, graceful and feline, with slanting tigress eyes and a long black plait held in place by Mexican silver combs,[10] cried enthusiastically, "We must organize a protest march!"

"There's a war on," George Sklar cut in.[11] An outstanding Social Realist playwright of the thirties who headed the Party-run Writers' Clinic, George was unpretentious, kind, and known for his wisdom. "These were servicemen," George went on. "Many are kids from the backwoods. They need to be taught. We're writers. We should combat racism with words."

Guy Endore, author of numerous books including *The Werewolf of Paris,* mumbled, "I'll write a leaflet." Guy was pale and lean, ate only nuts and fruits, and stood on his head every morning for five minutes.

"We've got to write letters to the mayor," cried Bobby Lees, "to the City Council—"

"And the newspapers," added Pauline Townsend.

Most of the people there were about ten years older than me. I glanced at Ben, wondering if he'd think what I was going to say was silly. My heart was beating wildly as I put up my hand. Dan nodded to me.

"The Sleepy Lagoon boys are still in jail," I said. "They must feel abandoned. Do you think we could write to them?"

"They may be allowed only one letter a week," Dan said, "in which case they probably want to hear from their families. If not, it's a great idea."

Girl Gets Boy

I had a long correspondence with one of them, Bob Telles. On the back of his picture, he had scribbled, "To Mrs. Barzman, to whom I am grateful for life. P.S. I'm 19 now. How old do I look?"

One thing became clear to me after our branch meeting. Why did I love Ben so much? I'd loved my first husband but my feelings for Ben were quite different. What was the difference?

It sounds silly and maybe that's why no one mentions it. Hollywood Communist couples had a romantic notion of themselves as the ideal young man and young woman surging forward with the Red flag, the logo of Artkino (Soviet films). Each of those couples saw themselves as a tiny collective that would go out and make the world better. Together, Dan and Lilith took upon themselves a social worker's task to teach and to help Latinos in the barrio. Bob and Jeannie Lees brought long hoes and shovels to the Salinas Valley Filipino lettuce pickers, who were breaking their backs with short-handled tools.

To be together in this enterprise of making the world better brought with it a chest-bursting pride, a heady elation, a belief in the gloriousness of life, which was an integral part of Communist love between a man and a woman. It was so strong and all-pervasive that the ordinary trials of everyday married life became small and unimportant. Ben screamed at me and tried to make me into a housewife, but in the larger picture, his actions seemed of little consequence. My love for him during these years was unconditional because the basis for it was grand and invincible.

Late one night, not long after our wedding, Ben and I found Adrian Scott sitting on our doorstep.

My friend, actress Betsy Blair, once said of him: "He was like the doctor in a small town, a really gentle American fellow."

Occasionally a wisp of fine, wavy hair would stray to his thoughtful forehead, now creased in anxiety. "Could I stay with you?" he asked quietly. Before he stood, he picked up his shoes, wiggled the toes of his argyle socks, and said, "Dorothy doesn't seem to want me around anymore."

We both loved Adrian.

I soon learned his presence brought me an advantage: Ben didn't complain about food when Adrian was around. However, I hadn't counted on my jealousy of their friendship. I was deeply in love with Ben and not at all sure of his love.

A former editor of *Stage Magazine,* a sophisticated publication devoted to the New York theater, Adrian eyed the Hollywood scene critically and knowledgeably. Ben and Adrian spent most of the time passionately discussing what Adrian thought was badly needed, inexpensive films with good stories, "the terrific little pictures" that Adrian would produce at RKO in the late 1940s with such success: *Murder, My Sweet, Cornered,* and *Crossfire.* They spoke in a kind of shorthand, like an old married couple. Although Adrian always said sweetly, "Norma, leave the dishes," and Ben added, "Wait. We'll help you," they didn't really mean it. Off I'd go while they enjoyed each other.

Ben had given a blanket invitation to his ex-girlfriend collaborator, Bess Taffel, to come to dinner anytime. She arrived whenever she had a story problem, which was frequently. To stop her from kvetching about unemployed women screenwriters, I suggested she tell us about Salka's, where she spent most Sundays. Actress-writer Salka Viertel, Greta Garbo's best friend, joined the MGM story department in the early thirties and worked closely on all Garbo's major films. In Germany, Salka had founded an avant-garde theater and married an Austrian stage director, Berthold Viertel. With the rise of Hitler, they came to the United States. The Viertel home, 165 Mabery Road, Santa Monica Canyon, became known as a literary salon where outstanding exiled European intellectuals met—Thomas Mann, Feuchtwanger, and Brecht as well as some of the British stars, Charles Laughton and Charlie Chaplin. Christopher Isherwood lived over the Viertel garage.

Actively engaged in liberal causes, though not a Communist, Salka Viertel found herself blacklisted by the studios during the McCarthy period. No longer able to work in Hollywood and with most of her family in Europe, she applied in 1953 for a passport, which the State Department denied. Salka got a lawyer and swore she was not a Communist. When she was confronted with her signature on a clemency

Girl Gets Boy

petition for the Rosenbergs, she denied following any "line" but admitted she was against capital punishment. After prolonged questioning, the interrogator gave her a passport with a four-month time limit, which permitted her to see her new granddaughter. She left New York the next day, January 1, 1954. The night before, New Year's Eve, she and Greta Garbo drank vodka and toasted each other.[12]

I tried pairing off Bess with Adrian to no avail. She was dating a married man, Sidney Buchman, who'd written *Mr. Smith Goes to Washington* and was, at that time, executive head of Columbia.[13] Adrian fell in love with Anne Shirley, a bright, neurotic young actress who looked like Olivia de Havilland, and whose first good role as an adult was in *Murder, My Sweet,* which Adrian produced from Raymond Chandler's *Farewell, My Lovely.* Pushed by her mother into being a successful child star (*Anne of Green Gables*), Annie still threw up before each of her scenes.

Jobless when we married, Ben was in the middle of writing a play. I wasn't used to a man about the house and was elated the one day a week I had an excuse to leave early and stay away late. Since Mother didn't drive, she was virtually a prisoner of the posh Ambassador Hotel district. I loved sailing down Wilshire Boulevard past the gorgeous Art Deco structures, the black-and-gold Security Pacific Bank and the sea green Wiltern Theatre, to pick up Mother and head for an even more exciting Art Deco building, the Bullock's Wilshire department store.

The jewelry department, surrounded by vaguely Cubist wall reliefs on tropical woods, was the first thing we saw when we entered the store. Mother barely looked at the jewelry (Mother's came from Van Cleef and Arpels, where Father had always bought her extravagant presents when he'd been unfaithful on business trips). In the perfume hall, where mottled marble panels had been set in diagonal slabs across the walls, Mother replenished her supply of Chanel No. 5.

White-gloved boys opened the monumental elevator's heavy metal doors, embellished with brass inlays and overlays, manipulated the lever as if for takeoff, shot us up five floors to the tearoom-restaurant, which had a panoramic view of the city. Similar in style to the entrance downstairs, bronze-framed Art Deco panels screened fluorescent lighting that lit a complex array of mirrors, Lalique glass, and marble.

One day, over chicken à la king, Mother asked, "Are you happy?"

Her question was my cue to complain.

"He's impossible! When I'm half out the front door, he says pitifully, 'I'll just open a can of soup.' Mother! He wants me to feel guilty for not staying home with him."

"They're all like that," she said with a tight little smile.

3

Girl Gets Job

Ben's play, *Ridin' on His Pony,* was a comedy about an entrepreneurial young businessman. He suspects there is molybdenum (a metal needed to toughen alloy steels, important for the war effort) beneath a national monument, a colonial village like Williamsburg. An old senator blocks excavation. The senator's Katharine Hepburn–like daughter backs her father until she falls in love with the Spencer Tracy–like businessman.

Through Bess, Ben and I had become friends with Harold Clurman and his wife, Stella Adler. Harold asked Ben to let him read *Ridin' on His Pony.* The phone rang the next day. In her stagey voice, Stella Adler told Ben that Harold had given her the play. "I'm looking for something to direct. I like it immensely. Can we talk?"

That evening, Harold turned up unexpectedly, picked Ben up, drove him to the chic, very red-velvet Regency Apartments, where the Clurmans were staying.

Harold opened the apartment with his key. When the door was barely ajar, a frighteningly loud, raging, stormy tirade burst forth from Stella: "Harold-you-dirty-lousy-no-good-son-of-a-bitch-fucking-god-damn-bastard!"

The door opened a trifle more and Stella could see that Harold was not alone but with Ben, the man whose play she wanted to direct.

In the blink of an eye, her frenzied anger fell away and her expression became angelic. "How lovely that you could come, Ben," she said softly, graciously.[1]

Meanwhile, Ben's agent, George Willner, famous for claiming that a Communist could become a Hollywood agent and still remain "idealistic and honest," showed the play to Theron Bamberger, producer of the Broadway hit *Tomorrow the World,* presenting film director Mike Gordon, whom George represented, as part of the package.[2] Bamberger sat right down and wrote out a check for five hundred dollars to bring Ben and Mike Gordon to New York for casting.

What is more fun than showing someone you love your old hometown? Except . . . except . . . in New York, I realized that I'd concealed some of my background from Ben because he resented my comfortable childhood. He made me ashamed of having American-born, well-to-do German-Jewish parents without accents.

On the way back from the Cloisters, we got off the bus at the Metropolitan Museum. I pointed out the apartment house across the street where I'd lived during high school—1016 Fifth Avenue. He stared hard at it. "I always suspected something like that about you," he said, accusingly. Nevertheless, I was nostalgic for that time. I wanted to see my father's place of business, but when the taxi skidded around Grand Central into Fourth Avenue, the continuation of Park Avenue, I knew I was not going to be able to tell Ben about the magic Saturdays I sat alone on the backseat of the chauffeur-driven Pierce Arrow with the Brewster body, all the way from our home in Westchester into the city to lunch at Lüchow's with my father.

Wherever Ben and I went in New York, we froze. Walking around the Central Park reservoir, Ben said between chattering teeth, "This is why we left Canada." California had spoiled us. No matter what time of day, when we were too cold, we'd rush back to our tiny dusty steam-heated hotel room and make love.

The only good thing about our crummy hotel, the Wellington on Seventh Avenue, was the newspaper kiosk at the corner. A big, soulful-eyed, shaggy, blue-gray dog guarded it. Every morning we bought our paper there, admired the dog. "A Hungarian Puli," the news vendor said proudly, "rare."

One night, we came back late after the theater. Our news vendor was still there.

"Anything new in the papers?" Ben asked.

"For two cents, I should give you a résumé?"

Since I was a big admirer of left-wing, best-selling author Howard Fast (*The Last Frontier, Freedom Road*), Mike Gordon took us to Howard and Bette's Central Park West apartment for drinks.[3] Although I liked Bette immediately, I was upset when the three men separated themselves from us. Gender segregation was common in the 1940s but less so in Communist homes.

After Mike departed, I overheard Howard ask Ben if he'd be interested in adapting Howard's book *The Maccobys* for the screen. Ben wasn't sure *The Maccobys* would be good film material. The book was the saga of a Jewish dynasty of patriots, high priests, and kings of the first and second centuries.

"We can always distort history to fit our needs" was Howard's incredible reply.

However, from further talks with Howard, I believe he had a double standard: *books* had to be historically accurate, but in *movies,* history could be "shaped."

In New York, Mike Gordon also arranged for us to meet his best friend, brilliant Social Realist artist Joseph Hirsch. Joe would become famous for his logo for *Death of a Salesman,* Willy Loman hefting his suitcases. At MOMA, Ben and I had just been moved by Joe's powerful painting of a black organizer proselytizing a white worker.

At the Hirsch's, I admired the portrait of their redheaded baby boy, thinking Joe had done it. But it turned out to be by Arbit Blatas, a Lithuanian who'd lived in Paris and painted his friends, the Montparnasse artists Fujita, Soutine, Modigliani, Giacometti.

The Hirsches became our dearest friends. Joe's wife, Ruth, a choreographer who'd worked with Martha Graham, was not only stimulating but an important influence on my life. She would lead me from my narrow view of art as an instrument of revolution to an appreciation of abstract painting that made up most of her and her second husband, Leonard Bocour's, fine collection.

The evening we all met, Joe came out to dinner with us and seduced us with his intellectual playfulness. Ruth didn't come along but the next day took us to the studio of Arbit Blatas.[4] The first painting we saw was an enormous oil, an interior of the studio, rich and dark. The figure of his little daughter, Dorothée, wearing a red velvet dress was the only bright touch.

Arbit watched us. "You both love it. Take it with you, back to California. When you have the money, you will send it to me."

Just before we arrived at Arbit's studio, Theron Bamberger had told us that his backers thought *Ridin' on His Pony* was a Communist play showing the bankruptcy of capitalism. Our prospects to get the play mounted seemed as bleak as the bilious New York sky outside.

We hugged the painting to us, kept it in our compartment on our westward-bound Super Chief, returned home broke and with no prospects for work. Weeks went by, then months. George, Ben's agent, wasn't hopeful. I wrote letters applying for a job to the four Los Angeles metropolitan dailies. When I was nine, I'd been impressed by a movie in which Bebe Daniels played a newspaper reporter who, in the pursuit of a story, leaped from one spike to another around the head of the Statue of Liberty.

"I think we're jinxed," Ben said. "We've got to get rid of that painting. We're never going to get jobs with that painting in the house." I used my last cash to send it back to New York.

The following morning, I received a phone call from the city editor of the *Los Angeles Examiner*. "That true? What you wrote me?" Jim Richardson began gruffly. "You write like a commando fights." He bellowed with laughter. "You want to come down here and see me?"

"Today?" My hair didn't look great.

"Yeah. Now." The phone clicked.

"Ben!" I moaned, "I told him I had experience!"

• • •

Girl Gets Job

On the corner of South Broadway and Eleventh Street, I looked up at the prodigious *Los Angeles Examiner* building, designed in 1914 by Julia Morgan. Its colorful Mission Revival architecture, Spanish-tiled roof, graceful arches, and ceramic tiled domes and cupolas so delighted Hearst that he'd commissioned Julia Morgan to design his castle at San Simeon. Although I had seen Orson Welles's newly released *Citizen Kane* and had been brought up believing Hearst was ready to plunge the country into war just to sell newspapers, his taste and willingness to hire a female architect at that time convinced me that he couldn't be all bad.

I entered the City Room and, shaking, marched myself over to James Hugh Richardson, who had a reputation for being "the lone survivor of the old fire-breathing city editors." Every paper in the country had fired him for drunkenness.

Jim had a glass eye. I wondered if he'd lost it in a drunken brawl. The eye was half-closed in a perpetual squint which made him look as cynical as he actually was. He'd seen too much. But, like many rehabilitated drunks, he was also a true believer. Whatever he believed in, he believed in firmly. In a room full of Roosevelt-haters, Jim was the only man wearing a Roosevelt button. It was the size of an orange and he wore it over his heart.

As much as he detested the idea of a "girl" in the city room, he was not going to train one more young man only to have him drafted.

"Take that desk," he ordered. "Our Long Beach man'll dictate the story."

To be the only female in that smoky, jokey sea of macho required the courage of Richard Lion-Heart, the diplomacy of Anthony Eden, the poise of Sarah Bernhardt, and a strong stomach.

I made my way to a long double bank of desks whose occupants spat, farted, belched, and made lewd gestures to make me uncomfortable. I wedged myself between two of them in the spot Jim had pointed out, and struggled with the earphones.

Unaccustomed to the constant deafening din of a city room, I couldn't hear the Long Beach man over the noise. Desperately I screamed into the phone, "What? What? What?" Everyone knew in the first five minutes that I'd never been near a newspaper.

I would have loved to tell Ben I got the job, rejoice that I was a reporter, which I'd always wanted to be, and that my salary, though small, would be money coming in. But how could I?

The scrawny rewrite man next to me interrupted my reverie. "Can you write a story?"

I hesitated. "No."

"I give you a week," he said.

The next to last night of my first week (my shift was 1 P.M. to 10 P.M.), I went to supper as usual across the street from the paper. I was too anxious to eat. I was sure Jim was going to fire me the next day.

When I came out of the café I saw a boy and a dog, the only humans on dark deserted South Broadway. I watched them wearily plodding along the pavement, the dog behind the boy as if each step was their last. What was a little boy doing alone in downtown L.A. at night? I stopped him.

"I came by bus from Santa Monica," the boy said, "to get my dog out of the pound. But we can't ride back. Buses don't take dogs."

"How come they took your dog away?" I asked.

"My mom works in a war factory. Our neighbor was supposed to look after the dog." His voice was barely audible. "My father was killed overseas."

I understood then why they called my profession "sob sister."

"You come with me," I said. "When I get through work, I'll drive you home."

On his way downstairs from work, the late Jim Murray, Pulitzer Prize–winning *Los Angeles Times* sportswriter, then an *Examiner* cub reporter like me, blocked my way. "What the hell you doing bringing that mangy dog in here?" He continued down the stairs, called back, "Barzman—don't you know you're hanging by a thread?"

Abby, an inside photographer, the only one who'd befriended me during that awful first week, put the boy and the dog on a long table and covered them with a blanket.

I asked mild, easygoing Harry Morgan, the night editor, if, after writing the boy-dog story, I could leave. When I put it on Harry's desk, he glanced at it cursorily, grunted. I drove the boy back to Santa Monica, went home, and fell into bed, trying not to wake Ben.

The next day at 1 P.M. when I opened the door to the city room, I was greeted by Richardson's loud angry bark, "Barzman!"

He pointed to the chair on the other side of his desk.

I sat.

He threw a telegram at me: GIVE THE BOY DOG STORY A BYLINE. Jim threw a second telegram at me. GIVE THE BOY DOG REPORTER A BONUS TELL HIM I AM WATCHING HIS CAREER. A third: TELL HER I AM WATCHING HER CAREER. A fourth: TAKE CARE OF BOY AND DOG STOP GIVE THEM WHATEVER THEY NEED. All four telegrams were signed THE CHIEF.

"Do you realize what that means? Mr. Hearst taking a personal interest in you? I was going to fire you today. Now I'm stuck with you! But I can make your life a holy hell. And I will! I'll give you every boy-dog girl-cat story until you quit in despair!"

With that, he hurled the newspaper at me. "You don't even read the goddamn paper!" he shouted.

Abby's blown-up photograph of the boy and the dog asleep on the table covered the top half of the front page of the second section. Beneath it, the headline "THE BOY AND THE DOG." My story, headed by my byline, "By Norma Barzman," occupied the bottom half of the page. Not one word had been changed.

I called Ben and told him about it proudly. He congratulated me, said he too had good news: he'd been hired to write a John Wayne picture. "You see," he said, "we just had to get that painting out of the house!"

When I hung up, I caught Hearst's mean-faced special investigative reporter watching me intently. As he whipped around and disappeared into the managing editor's office, I caught sight of two holstered revolvers strapped on his hips beneath his jacket.

4

Feudal Lords

Los Angeles had been particularly dear to me since I was ten years old.

In 1928, Father sold his business and retired; the suburban New York home I'd grown up in was also sold. We moved to France. Two years later, my sister, Muriel, twenty, having been "finished" by a Swiss boarding school, acquired a penniless baron. Afraid she would elope with him, my parents packed up and rushed us back to the States with no plans about where we would live. They knew they'd miss the Deauville Casino and Racetrack but they had heard of Agua Caliente. They finally settled on California—the climate was good and its "easy lifestyle" appealed to them. Besides, my cousin Henry Myers was under contract to Paramount Studios, which made the glamour of Hollywood seem accessible. My parents didn't ask if Los Angeles was the right place for Muriel or me.

Henry recommended we stay at the Hollywood Knickerbocker, one of the few apartment hotels in town, which he knew of because screenwriters had met there to organize the guild. The Knickerbocker, on Ivar Street, was one block from Hollywood and Vine. I literally jumped up and down when I found a miniature golf course across the street. Henry and I left my parents and sister to cope with the luggage while we played a quick nine holes.

Feudal Lords

Henry was thirty-seven, and, like me, growing on eleven. But in those days in Hollywood, everybody was a child. Movie people played tiddledywinks, charades, camouflage, made you guess "handies," and played practical jokes. Didn't Carole Lombard have an elephant delivered to Clark Gable for his birthday? The stars sat in front seats at the circus and rode the carousel on the Santa Monica Pier.

Even then, the city had attracted me: the rolling yellow-white sand covered in pinkish moss sloping down into the Pacific Coast Highway; yellow cherimoya and lavender jacaranda trees bending over the streets; ridiculous tiny-headed giraffe palm trees; pumping oil wells; canyon houses on stilts; the illuminated Van De Kamp Bakery windmill that I could see from my hotel window, revolving till after midnight; searchlights of gala premises sweeping the night skies; Orange Julius stands selling frothy orange malteds on deserted sidewalks; Olvera Street and the modest hacienda that was the first house in Los Angeles; Sunset Boulevard, an old curvy wagon road that started downtown, wandered west, skirting the uneven line of the foothills for miles to the sea where "weenie bakers," L.A.-speak for hot dog barbecues, were the night scene on the beach, and where, under a full moon, tiny grunion came on shore in spring high tides.

When Ben and I returned to Los Angeles from our New York trip in January 1944, we were where we wanted to be and we were both finally working. But anxiety kept us from settling down to a normal life. Hearst's top Communist investigator was developing too big an interest in me, and Ben was about to do a film with John Wayne, Hollywood's biggest anti-Communist star.

Nineteen forty-four was too early to worry about such things, although the Hearst press continued to run anti-Red stories all through the war, even after General MacArthur's Message to the Red Army: "The world situation at the present time indicates that the hopes of civilization rest on the worthy banners of the courageous Russian Army." The general's words were set to music by Jay Gorney and Henry, and sung at mass meetings and "cause" parties (Russian war relief or the Joint Anti-Fascist Refugee Committee).

During the war, Red-baiting in the motion picture industry abated. In 1938, the Dies Committee (the House UnAmerican Activities Committee) had attempted to investigate Hollywood. One year later, Walt Disney "inspired" Jack Tenney of the California legislature's Committee on UnAmerican Activities to launch an assault on "Reds in Hollywood." A united front of liberals and progressives effectively squelched the attack, but an underground stream of anti-Communism running through the movie and newspaper worlds broke to the surface once the war had been won. A renewed fight against Communists would mean we'd be the first to be Red-baited and fired.

The worst part of my growing anxiety at this time was that I'd fallen in love with my job and wanted to keep it. I was even getting used to Jim Richardson's sarcasm.

"You think you're getting the hang of it, Barzman?" he'd say, not expecting an answer. He would adjust the phone that was perpetually wedged between his shoulder and ear, and shift his ever-present cigarette from one side of his mouth to the other.

"Our man in the sheriff's office is on the line," he said to me one day, adding sarcastically, "Would you like to have a go at it?"

I wrote it up and put the story on Jim's desk. A second later, Jim boomed "Barzman!" waving my pages in the air. "Why do you always begin your stories at the end?"

I stood there, looking and feeling like a naughty little girl.

"Most stories don't begin at the beginning," he said in a confidential tone. "Right now I can only think of two stories that do. One is Genesis, which starts 'In the beginning God created Heaven and Earth.' Now that's the only way that story could have been written. That's the only lead paragraph the Bible could have had."

"What's the other?" I asked timidly.

"The other story that begins at the beginning is the birth of the Prince of Wales. He's heir to the throne the moment he's born. Nothing more important than that can happen to him. His story begins when the doctors bend over and take a look and out goes the bulletin 'It's a boy,' and the guns start booming and the people start dancing in the streets.

See what I mean?" He picked up the story I'd just written and shoved it under my nose. "Why do you write your stories upside down?" he hollered. "Here you have a story about a gal in court for being drunk. And what does she say? She says that the liquor the cops say they smelled on her breath was not from drinking but from the sherry in the lobster Newburg she ate. That's the first time anybody ever came up with an excuse like that." Then he whispered, " *That's* what makes a story. That's your lead paragraph, sticking its finger right in your eye. And you've got it buried down in the last paragraph. Understand?" He capped his lesson by screaming at me, "No more once-upon-a-time stuff! Okay?"

I tried to do what he said but my stories kept bouncing back. From time to time, Jim rose from his desk and stretched. He'd walk the length of the city room. When he passed me, he'd look down and announce loudly to everybody, "Barzman's legs are tight together. The story she's working on will bounce back as fast as it hits my desk." Sometimes, on his walk, he'd stop, bend down, and peer at my legs beneath my desk. "They're wide apart," he'd bellow. "Maybe there's some hope!"

His salvos were hailed by a surge of heavily sexual male guffaws flooding the city room. My cheeks burned. I sweated. I never got used to the ridicule.

But I was learning from the best goddamn teacher in the business. He started sending me out on some good assignments: MRS. PEETE ON DEATH ROW; LUPE VELEZ'S SUICIDE; THE STRUGGLE FOR POWER WITHIN THE AIMEE SEMPLE MACPHERSON CHURCH. I covered L.A. from the DIS-APPEARANCE OF AN HEIRESS in Pasadena to A FORTUNE-TELLER'S SCAM in Southgate.

In Jim Richardson's language, I was "getting the hang of it." A sure sign of my improvement came when my paycheck doubled. I thought it was a mistake, but Jim sidled by, whispered, "You earned it." I'd been there five months.

I used the raise to buy myself two cool suits for work, a checked gingham, gray, black, pink, white; and a plaid gingham, navy, green, red, yellow; and a small black straw hat with a turned-up brim. (See photo insert). In those days, women had to wear hats.

I never tired of driving. The War Rationing Board gave reporters all the gasoline we needed. I drove hundreds of miles a day. I felt like Philip Marlow. Adrian had given me one of Raymond Chandler's books to read and I was hooked. My peregrinations took me past shrubbery Chandler had mentioned, deodars, white acacias, grevillea trees. His acerbic observations of every level of Southern California life, boulevards and alleyways, crooked cops and heiresses, made me look at L.A. in a new way.

RKO had hired Ben to write the screenplay of a John Wayne film, but first he was obliged to do two "chores": first, rewrite a Claire Trevor movie while it was shooting, and, second, hang around the set of another picture to keep the erratic director, Irving Reis, from going over budget.

Ben was elated when he finally set to work on the new Wayne film, *Back to Bataan.*

Three days after their attack on Pearl Harbor, on December 10, 1941, Japanese troops landed in the Philippines. General MacArthur's American forces defended the islands, but were soon forced to abandon Manila. They withdrew to the Bataan Peninsula, where the wounded, starving, disease-ridden men withstood the Japanese for three agonizing months. MacArthur decamped precipitously in late April 1942, promising, "I shall return." Colonel Clark, the technical adviser for Wayne's film, who had been on Bataan, described the general's departure from Corregidor by submarine, accompanied by another submarine full of his furniture, rather than fighting men. According to Colonel Clark, after MacArthur left, a group of guerrillas badly in need of guns and ammunition got word that a sub would land them supplies. With great anticipation, they tore apart the first crate that came ashore on a rubber raft. It contained no guns or bullets, only cartons of cigarettes, each one emblazoned with the slogan: "I shall return."

Many of us in the States doubted that President Roosevelt had actually ordered MacArthur to Australia. Others believed the general was saving himself for a victorious return, which would give him appeal as a presidential candidate. But the fact is MacArthur abandoned 75,000

American troops. They were forced to surrender, though some held out a few more weeks on Corregidor Island. On May 6, 1942, the Japanese brutally herded their prisoners across the Philippines, a sixty-five-mile forced march to jungle prison camps. That travail became known as the Bataan Death March. Thousands died.

Americans were so outraged at the ruthless and inhuman treatment that the U.S. Navy decided to invade the Philippines sooner than planned.

"Believe it or not," Ben told me, "RKO is going to synchronize the release of the film with the invasion."

"Holy mackerel!" I exclaimed. "You don't want to know a top military secret like that! Tell them you don't want to know!"

"I did. I did. They're giving me a bare five weeks to write a script and Eddie Dmytryk ten weeks to shoot! You just have to add—"

I put my hands over my ears. "I don't want to know!" I thought a minute. "Hey, why such a long shooting schedule?"

"The script has to be rewritten during shooting from news stories, bits and pieces of underground information, and developments as they actually occur on the Philippine front. And there are a lot of dangerous and difficult action sequences that have to be figured out on the set. Don't you want to know what the Duke is like? He's nice."

"*Nice?*" I squawked. John Wayne was one of the few Americans against Women's Army Corps (WACS) and Women Accepted for Volunteer Emergency Service (WAVES) and women in war factories, against spending on health and education. "He can't get further right. How can you say that?"

"I just mean he's—personable," Ben said lamely.

"Yeah! He's an actor."

The Duke, Ben explained, was a feudal lord surrounded by a permanent retinue of a dozen technicians, makeup, wardrobe, and lighting pals who went wherever he went.

"One of them," Ben said, "is his own 'personal screenwriter,' a guy named Peter Paul Fix a.k.a. Peepee a.k.a. Slippers, who's going to collaborate with me. I met him today when he came to my office. You'd recognize him from Wayne's westerns—tall, sandy-haired, about my age, a nice smile, wears chaps and cowboy boots."

"How is he as a writer?"

"Not sure. He doesn't have any ideas. When I come up with one, he wrinkles his forehead and looks uncomfortable. I guess we have to get used to each other."

Peepee was a mine of juicy John Wayne gossip, which Ben recounted no matter how late I got home from the paper. According to Peepee, the Waynes weren't getting along. He'd married a wealthy society woman who admired his "wicked thighs." The Duke had a mistress, an actress named Ella Raines, whom he had nicknamed "The Bitch." She sent him his favorite Delhaven cheesecake, perhaps to remind him of her succulence. The Duke and Peepee each had a slice. "Why don't you take the rest over to Mrs. Wayne?" the Duke said. "She's in bed with a sore throat. This would slide down easy. . . . " Unfortunately, when Mrs. Wayne opened the cake box from Delhaven's, she saw on the back of the top flap a scrawled billet doux: "Don't eat it all. Save a little for sucking. Signed, THE BITCH." Mrs. Wayne sued for divorce.

"I've figured out the character for the Duke," Ben reported. "He'll play the real-life American colonel who organized the guerrillas into a regiment of United States Filipino Scouts." Ben was excited. "We'll have the Filipino Scouts led by the Duke join up with U.S. forces to liberate our death march survivors from the prison camps!"

"Did Peepee come up with this?"

"No. Our collaboration was one of the shortest in film history. I tried out a couple of ideas on him. He looked as if he had some kind of intestinal pain. He was pale. Huge beads of sweat formed on his forehead. I said, 'Peepee, you okay?'

" 'Is this the way you guys write a story?' he asked in disbelief.

"I said, 'Yes. How do you guys write for the Duke?'

"Peepee's pallor disappeared. He sprang to his feet, paced, and dictated a screenplay to me. 'We usually begin with "Exterior. A wild countryside. The Duke on a horse at sunset. Shot of stagecoach—" No, change that to a wagon. It careens wildly across the screen. Close shot. The girl in a bonnet is screaming, trying desperately to control the run-away horses. Shot of the Duke as he hears screams and the horses neighing in panic. Sounds of a wagon crashing. Cut to the Duke as he spurs his horse to a gallop. Shot of the Duke on his horse looking at— we see what he sees—the wagon girl sitting in the creek, water up to her waist. Shot of the Duke looking at the girl. He's puzzled. The girl, as if in answer to the Duke's unasked question, lifts her hands out of the water. For the first time, we see the handcuffs on her wrists.'

" 'How do you like it?' Peepee asked me.

" 'It's great,' I said. 'But we're not doing a western. We're doing a war story.'

"Peepee sighed deeply. 'Yeah, I know.' Suddenly he scooped up his pencils and notebook. 'Listen, pal,' he said, 'call me if you need me. I mean it,' and ran out of my office."

I thought a minute. "Does this mean we won't be getting any more of those spicy stories? Once you're shooting, if there's ever anything exciting like you said there would be, let me know, I'll call in sick."

"I thought you hated the Duke."

"I hate his politics. But I'd like to see him up close."

A few weeks later, director Eddie Dmytryk told Ben, "I want you on the set every day. You'll have to rewrite as we go along. From day to day, there'll be developments coming out of the Philippines."

Eddie was the person who, more than any other, would influence our lives. Ben had met him the previous year, 1944, when Adrian produced *Murder, My Sweet,* which Eddie directed and Johnny Paxton scripted.[1] Ben, Adrian, and Johnny Paxton hung together at RKO. Although Johnny and Ben were not fond of Eddie, they worked well with him, used the same phrase to describe him: "a good technician," which meant he wasn't creative.

Dmytryk was born in northwestern Canada of poor Ukrainian immigrant parents. When Eddie's mother died, he was shunted to foster homes until his "cruel" father and new stepmother brought him to Los Angeles. In 1922, when he was fourteen, he ran away "with only $30 in my pocket, to escape mistreatment and exploitation."[2] He got a part-time job at Famous Players Lasky Studio while he went to high school, then worked as a messenger at Paramount, where he learned to cut film. He became an editor, then moved into directing B films (*Emergency Squad, Sweetheart of the Campus*) from 1935 to 1943.

Adrian, Johnny, Ben, and I were all put off by Eddie's steely eyes and the streak of cruelty we sensed in him. Eddie just wasn't "our kind of guy." He never cracked a book, except for science manuals; he became a member of the Communist Party with little understanding and no study, telling us he'd joined "because the Party was for the underdog and I feel like one."

On the set, the Duke was constantly feuding with Ben, and roared with laughter when the Filipino actors mispronounced Ben's dialogue. Every time Ben came on the set, he heard hissing whispers of one of the lines he'd given to a Filipino actor: "With knifessss and bolossss against massssine guns?"

Ben whirled around, seeking the culprit, but saw only innocent faces. As Ben slunk away, their barely suppressed laughter followed him. Sometimes, Wayne baldly baited Ben. "You know what each of these cigarettes cost me?" he'd say, "on account of *your* man in the White House? Two dollars apiece!"

The Duke had a reputation for being a good chess player. He challenged Ben to a game. Ben won. "A fluke," Ben told me. "I'm no good at the game. He just got rattled by the dumb way I played. He wants a return match. I won't give it to him. So he puts me down whenever he can in front of everybody."

"Everybody? Hundreds of Filipino extras?"

"Plus the liege lord's vassals, twelve strong, whose raison d'être seems to be to make fun of me."

Back at the paper, I was feeling sorry for myself because Jim wasn't giving me top assignments. I was a reasonably good reporter by then and wanted to go out on the best story of the year, "The Black Dahlia." Instead, Jim sent Jim Murray to Santa Ana and used me as a decoy to keep the *Times* reporters busy in the wrong place so they wouldn't know what we were up to. One day, Jim called me over to his desk. In a hushed tone I'd never heard from him, he said, "the *Examiner* is Mr. Hearst's favorite paper. All the reporters are obliged at one time or another, to do a favor for him or for Miss Marion Davies. No reporter is too mighty. Understand?"

I understood. Whatever the errand or favor, its purpose was to remind us that we owed fealty to our liege lord, William Randolph Hearst, just as the Duke expected fealty from his vassals and, I suppose, from Ben.

"This happens about once a year," Jim continued softly. "It's your turn, Barzman. The Rolls is waiting downstairs with the chauffeur. He'll tell you what she wants. Do it. And take the rest of the day off. Go!" It may have been true that every reporter had to do a favor for Mr. Hearst or Miss Davies, but no male reporter was ever asked to shop for hair dye or bobby pins.

A few weeks later, I was astonished when Miss Davies called Jim. She wanted me to do her another "favor." The chauffeur told me that she would like to see some barrettes. At the Broadway Downtown department store, near the paper, I bought a selection of barrettes I thought would look good with blond hair, and handed them to the chauffeur.

"You can present them to Miss Davies yourself," he said. "We're on our way up there."

San Simeon is on the coast midway between Los Angeles and San Francisco. Today, it is just off the U.S. 101, but then the freeways hadn't been built. The first one finished was the Hollywood Freeway in 1948. I looked at my watch. We wouldn't get to San Simeon until after nightfall, too late to drive back.

I shivered with anticipation. I'd be invited to stay overnight, surrounded by Hearst's fabulous art collection, for which his experts combed the far corners of the earth. He had so many great paintings that when decorator William Haines said admiringly of a portrait, "What a fine Goya!" Hearst, surprised, replied, "I didn't know I had a Goya," and took it off the wall to hang elsewhere.

I imagined Hearst had invited his favorite celebrities—David Niven,

Rosalind Russell, Cary Grant, Gary Cooper—to a dinner party. I'd heard they dined at a baronial refectory table set with antique silver, Blue Willow china, crystalware, and oddly, paper napkins, ketchup bottles, and pickle jars! Mr. Hearst wanted to create the atmosphere of "a ranch," his name for the castle. My heart hammered. In those days, everyone prayed to be invited to Hearst's castle. When George Bernard Shaw visited, he is reputed to have said, "This is probably the way God would have done it, if He'd had the money."

The drive on the narrow, curling road north seemed endless. We stopped once for a hamburger and a shake.

On "The Enchanted Hill," the chauffeur slowed to five miles an hour. "The animals roam freely," he explained. "One has to be careful not to hurt them." Sure enough, around the next curve, the car's headlights picked out a giraffe and another animal the chauffeur confirmed as a yak. I recalled Hearst had the largest private zoo in the world. Most of them were grazing animals, sacred white deer from India, llamas from Peru, water buffalo, Arabian camels, and from Australia, emus and kangaroos.

As we drove higher, the castle loomed over us like an illustration from a book of fairy tales. At the main portico, a footman in full regalia led the way up the marble stairway. Glowing globes of alabaster lit the fishpond, where a sculptured Grecian goddess reclined on a dolphin. Below the illuminated medieval stone facade, statues of St. Peter and St. Paul guarded the exquisite Spanish wrought-iron gates. Above, a Gothic Madonna and Child gazed down at me.

The footman ushered me into a tiny two-seater elevator that took us to the Celestial Suite on the fourth floor. A maid showed me to Miss Davies' "apartment." At the end of the tapestry-lined hall, sculpted doors opened into a sitting room whose walls were hung with gold damask.

In daylight, the bank of windows on one side must have had a sweeping view of the Pacific. Far off, a few lights twinkled. I knew a bit about the castle from a biography of its architect, Julia Morgan. Mr. Hearst had scribbled on a reproduction of one of her beautiful plans: "I don't know what this wall will do to the arch effect but the view from the sitting room would be much better if the sitting room should be extended beyond the bedrooms and occupy the space now given to the porch."[3]

In 1894, the University of California had no School of Architecture. Julia Morgan was obliged to attend its School of Engineering. Later, in Paris, she studied architecture at the Ecole des Beaux Arts. But her engineering skills came in handy. Everyone had despaired of transporting matériel up "The Enchanted Hill." Morgan directed, that a wharf be built on the shore at the bottom so everything could be shipped in by boat, to be sent up by funicular.

From the Baroque ceiling of the room, painted seraphs and cherubs smiled coyly down at me. I gazed at an elegant Tiffany lamp with flounces of Alençon lace skirting its shade. I'd read that Mr. Hearst's mother had had a penchant for Art Deco. She had taken ten-year-old Will to Europe to inculcate in him a love of art. I wondered if the eclectic taste on display belonged to Miss Davies or whether she'd been forced to keep some items already collected. Or had she wandered the castle picking out what she wanted?

At last, a small bubbly blonde appeared. Despite her fortyish figure, Davies was sexy. Her baby-blue eyes exuded humor.

"Was it an awful ride up? I can't offer you a drink-drink." She giggled, and I remembered she had a drinking problem. "But would you like something?"

I declined. I presented her with the paper bag full of barrettes.

She spilled them over the marble-topped Louis XV table, stirred the barrettes, touched each one, picked out two, and, like a teenager, skipped to a gold curlicue mirror to try them on.

"Did they have any tortoiseshell lighter than this?" she asked.

"No." I wished I could think of something bright to say.

"You've been to other shops?" she pursued. "Is there anywhere else I could get them to match a bunch of different outfits?"

"I could try—"

"I'll let you know," she said vaguely. "Brennan will drive you back. Isn't he a dear? And doesn't he drive well?"

"Yes," I agreed weakly.

I never told this before because I was vaguely ashamed of aspiring to hobnob with film celebrities and then of not being accepted by them. I didn't even tell Jim. I came close to it once when he was telling me about his game "Stinkers," in which each player tried to outdo the others by telling a bigger "stinker," a story of how utterly shameful he'd been. Jim won with a high school tale. "I was at a girls' prom. The boys were mostly bound for Harvard or Yale. One pimply-faced boy asked me, 'What prep school did you say you attended?' The only prep school whose name I could remember was one advertised in the education pages of a magazine. S-T-A-U-N-T-O-N.

"Staunton," Jim had replied, pronouncing it "Stawnton" as it is spelled. The pimply-faced boy looked at Jim in disgust. "You never went there," he said, "or you'd know it's pronounced Stanton."

I could identify with Jim's shame. How often did I pretend?

5

The Honeymoon Is Over

The Duke had proudly proclaimed he never used doubles, that he'd begun his career as a stuntman and had played All-American football. Hating Wayne's reactionary politics and seeing an opportunity, Eddie and Ben invented stunts they hoped would make the Duke cry uncle and ask for a double.

Ben thought Eddie should have canceled one tricky stunt that seemed a needlessly dangerous risk. Eddie had a special harness custom-tailored for the Duke. Slender but strong wires attached the harness to a complicated crane, the controls of which were at a crazy height in a tower above camera range. The technicians set an explosive charge next to the Duke; at the exact second the explosion blew, the crane would snatch Wayne high in the air and then drop him just a few inches from the ground, making it look on-screen as if Wayne had been blown sky-high by the shell. If the crane worked with precision, the Duke would not get hurt and they'd have a sensational shot. But if the crane were a few inches off or a second late, he could be smashed to earth and seriously injured.

I took the day off for this shot and went out to the location set with Ben. "Dress warm," Ben counseled. It turned out to be one of the coldest, clearest days we'd ever had in Southern California history. As we drove far out into the valley to the RKO ranch, which had been dressed by the scenic designers to look like rice paddies in the Philippines, I saw the ponds were frozen over. Where they were shooting, a man wearing a plaid hunter's cap with earmuffs and a fur jacket was bending over a strange contraption. I didn't recognize him. It was Eddie.

"Hope you wore your woolen undies," he greeted me.

"Hi, Eddie," I said. "What's that you're doing?"

"Testing the Duke's harness," he replied, grinning mischievously. "I designed it. You're just in time to see it used."

John Wayne was surrounded by his vassals when Ben presented me.

"Any wife of our boy genius is welcome." He shook my hand, almost breaking it.

"She's press," Ben said proudly.

"Then she shouldn't be here," the Duke retorted, smiling his special crooked smile.

Peepee whisked the Duke off to the harness. He was strapped in and the wires were attached to the crane. A pyrotechnic expert set the explosives almost directly beside him. The crew took shelter behind a metal bunker.

Eddie gave the signal. A terrifying explosion erupted. Rocks and debris showered us. Lifted by the crane, the Duke shot high in the air and came slamming down. A breathtaking moment of silence seemed like a year while we waited for the smoke to clear. We sighed in relief as the tall figure pulled himself to his feet, staggered, found his famous gait, moved away.

Eddie cupped his hands and yelled, "That was great, Duke! You okay?"

The Duke signaled, somewhat unenthusiastically, that he was.

Eddie shouted, "Let's do it again! We need a protection shot." We all looked at him, astounded.

After a moment, the Duke gestured reluctantly: okay, a second take. While the crew set up the explosives, Peepee hurried over to Eddie. "The studio'll go nuts. You sure the insurance covers a second take?"

Eddie looked at Peepee coldly. "I've got a hunch this shot is going to be spectacular."

The Honeymoon Is Over

As Eddie predicted, the second take *was* spectacular. Later, when I saw the film, I would never have believed that Wayne hadn't been blown sky-high but had survived without injury because he was so tough.

I thought the day's work was done, but Eddie and Ben had cooked up another whopper.

Ben had discovered that the real Filipino Scouts in the real war had devised an ingenious way to evade Japanese patrols. Hotly pursued by heavily armed soldiers, a trapped scout quickly made for a jungle pond, snatched a long reed, and, holding it in his mouth, leaped into the water, sank to the bottom, and sucked air through the reed. The scout could stay submerged until dark, then silently slip away into the night.

Ben suggested Eddie use it toward the end of the picture when the Duke and his Filipino lieutenant, played by Anthony Quinn, elude a Japanese patrol. Eddie loved the idea. "It'll give stature to the Duke's character, show him ready to submit to hardships himself."[1]

No matter how weary everyone was, Eddie was determined to shoot "the reed trick."

Anthony Quinn ambled over. He was almost as big and brawny as the Duke, but there the resemblance ended. Tony, whose father was a cameraman of silent films, claimed his mother was Mexican-Indian and that he got his looks from her: strong features, bushy black eyebrows, dark skin. Tony's father-in-law, Cecil B. DeMille, never helped him get better roles. Until 1951, when Dino De Laurentis brought him to Italy, where he was "discovered" by Fellini, Tony had been a supporting actor playing, usually, Indians. Tony's versatility enabled him to play a great variety of roles, from the mentally weak strongman in *La Strada* to *Zorba the Greek*.

Tony appreciated the role Ben had written for him. In the film, Tony, the Filipino lieutenant, has a romantic relationship with a Filipina. It was the first time that a love story between persons of color was shown on the screen.

Tony and I joined Ben, who was suggesting to Eddie that they do the "reed trick" in an indoor pool dressed to look like a jungle pond.

"No," Eddie said.

"But the location ponds are icy."

"No matter what you do to an indoor pool, it'll always look fake," Eddie replied. "We're going to have to shoot it here and now."

"I'm game," said Tony, assuming they were waiting for him to speak up.

I squeezed Ben's arm. He thought I meant he should do something. "Hey, Eddie," he said, "why can't we use a couple of doubles for this one? It's freezing."

"Oh, fuck it!" the Duke said, looking daggers at Ben. "I'm not going to start using a double at this stage of the game."

Eddie shouted, "Let's go, guys. One fast take."

A crewman quickly broke the ice on the pond and carried away the cracked pieces. The Duke and Tony, in thin summer fatigues suitable for hot, steaming jungle, made for the pond, pursued by the Japanese patrol. Each grabbed a reed and—*whammo*—without hesitation, took flying leaps into the freezing water.

Eddie had at least four cameras to cover all the angles so there'd be no possible screw-up. A retake was unthinkable. The cameras rolled furiously as the Japanese burst onto the scene. For a moment, the scene seemed perfect, until the Duke and Tony rose slowly to the surface in full sight of the Japanese extras standing around the pond.

"Cut!" Eddie screamed.

The crew yanked Wayne and Quinn out of the ice-cold water, stripped off their wet fatigues, threw blankets over them, and gave them huge swigs of whiskey.

Almost dark. The temperature was dropping. Urged by Peepee to grab hold of anything on the bottom of the pond, the Duke and Tony, in dry fatigues, plunged into the freezing pool. Inexorably, they rose to the surface. Plunge after plunge, the Duke, his lips blue, huddled in blankets, his hair spiky. He looked at Ben and said through chattering teeth, "This better not be something you dreamed up out of your little head as a goddamned parting gift."

Eddie came up just in time. "Peepee and I figured out how to do it."

The Duke extended his arm as though to punch Ben, but Ben put the bottle of whiskey in his outstretched hand. The Duke took a swig and passed it back.

Wayne and Quinn dived in again. A couple of the Duke's guys raced up, put heavy rocks on their backs. The cameras rolled and the two bodies stayed down long enough for the take to be successful.

When they were both in their blankets drinking whiskey, Eddie solemnly said, "I want to thank you. If I had them, I'd give you both Purple Hearts."

"I've already got purple lips," Wayne said. "That's good enough for me."

I giggled, and the Duke flashed me another of those dazzling crooked smiles.

He shook hands all around, even with Ben. "You were right, kid," Wayne said. "It's going to look great on film."

It did. The film was finished on time and released right after the invasion in March 1945. The Navy camera crew went into the Philippines with the forces, and filmed our G.I.'s as they were freed from the prisoner-of-war camp. They walked toward the camera, each with a sign giving his name, rank, and place of origin, the perfect ending for *Back to Bataan*.

At the 1945 New Year's Eve party in the home of Bob Fellowes, producer of *Back to Bataan,* Ben and I were toasting John Wayne and his new darling Mexican bride, Chotta. The Duke and Ben were both wearing dark suits, not tuxedos. "You really look good, Duke," Ben said. "That's a magnificent tie."

Wayne undid Ben's tie, removed his own, adjusted it around Ben's neck. It hung down to his crotch. "It was made to order," the Duke explained, "on account of my height." Then he put his arms around Ben and embraced him with fervor. "You goddamned Communist!" he accused, lovingly.

Ben hugged him back. "You goddamned Fascist!"

Spring 1945.

I was sitting at my desk in the city room when the tape came through that Roosevelt had died. The room erupted with celebration. Booze was passed around in lily cups. I wept openly. Jim seemed close to tears. He turned away from everyone and stared out the window. With his back to us, he called, a tremor in his voice, "Barzman, better go home."

Still weeping, I pulled the car into our driveway. I saw and heard our reactionary neighbors, in the house catercornered to us on Belfast, whooping it up.

Ben was already home. His eyes were bloodshot. "You know what Adrian said?" Ben whispered hoarsely. " 'This is very bad for the world.' "

What we thought would happen, happened. Hearst's "special" investigative reporter went to the managing editor, Van Ettisch, with a well-documented report about Ben and me being well-known Hollywood Commies. Van ordered Jim to fire me. Jim got through to The Chief. "She's one of my best reporters," Jim said. "If she goes, I go."

Jim told me later that Mr. Hearst had said in his highest, most piping voice, "I don't care if she *is* a Red. I don't care *what* she is. I never fire a good reporter."

I don't think that prompted Mr. Hearst to visit the *Examiner*. But soon after that he came down to Los Angeles. Jim presented me as the girl reporter whose work Mr. Hearst admired, to which he replied in his high-pitched voice, "I particularly appreciated your piece on the bigamist. The Trolley Car Troubadour, was it?" He shook my hand and went on to the next reporter.

Jim called RKO to tell Ben that he'd saved my job and invited us to Sunday dinner at "Happy Ending," the Richardson home in Arcadia Oaks, where he lived with his lovely fourth wife, Maggie, former *Examiner* women's page editor. The rambling ranch house actually had a white picket fence with red roses pushing through the pickets.

As we got friendlier with Jim, he was always trying to give us the best seats for ball games, the opera, the Rose Bowl. One day Jim said, "Barzman!" (He still called me "Barzman." He called Ben "Ben.") "There's going to be a big event in this town. I want you and Ben to go. Our society editor is covering it. And our music critic. All you've got to do is enjoy. Toscanini's always refused to come out here. He thinks Los

Angeles is a hick town. Somehow or other, Mr. Hearst and some of his society friends convinced the Maestro that Los Angeles is growing up. So Toscanini's agreed to play a concert for war relief. Guess another reason he said yes is he wants to show he isn't pro-Mussolini."

That night, thousands of Angelenos dressed up and filled every seat in the immense Shrine Auditorium. I looked at the program. "Toscanini's playing down to us," I said to Ben. "No Brahms, no Beethoven, no Mozart. He still has contempt for Los Angeles. Look, the first piece is 'Invitation to the Dance.'"

Arturo Toscanini came out on the podium and bowed. The whole audience got to their feet and bowed back! Then the Maestro turned to the orchestra, tapped his baton. The audience listened in rapt silence to the heavenly, liquid notes.

Suddenly, from the wings a woman in a black leotard danced onto the stage. At first, the orchestra didn't see her. She was actually quite good, quite professional. I had a fleeting thought that Toscanini had arranged the dance as a sign of his contempt for Los Angeles. As the dancer pirouetted across the stage, members of the orchestra who could now see her, did a take and left off playing. Toscanini's back was to her. He did not see her as she floated across the stage behind him, but he began to sense something was wrong. More and more musicians, incredulous, stopped playing. By now the audience was aghast.

Toscanini, amazed his orchestra had stopped playing, turned and saw the young woman execute a rather good entrechat. He jumped and almost fell off the podium, regained his balance, shook himself, and left the stage. Two men, not in white jackets, glided up to the leotarded figure and firmly danced her into the wings. After a long wait, Toscanini resumed conducting the orchestra as if nothing had happened, finishing with Tchaikovsky. The audience cheered. The concert was a triumph.[2]

Toscanini granted me a brief interview in his dressing room. "You are just not ready for great art," the Maestro said. "Los Angeles is a cultural desert." It was the first time anyone had used that phrase.

• • •

As soon as Jim became bosom buddies with Ben, he put me on the day shift, nine to six, and gave me to understand, if there was nothing important, I could leave early. Every night I got home in plenty of time to prepare dinner.

Nevertheless, Ben grumbled. He wanted the little woman at home, feelings hard for a Communist to admit, especially one who had just spent the weekend at a meeting on "The Woman Question" where they discussed whether to pay wives a salary. In theory, the Party was dedicated to equality for women. In practice, most Communist men, especially those in Hollywood, did not behave according to their tenets.

Instead of asking me forthrightly to quit the paper, which I would have refused to do, he used a Machiavellian ploy to keep me at home. "I never see you anymore," he said. "If we worked together at a studio, we'd see each other all the time."

"Uh-huh."

"If we collaborated on a story, we could get a job together writing the screenplay."

"Uh-huh. Funny, I just happen to have a good movie idea. I was thinking of working on it myself in my spare time."

"You don't have any spare time. It would never get done. Maybe you should quit your job, and concentrate on the story."

"I wouldn't dream of giving up my job."

"Well, maybe we should work on it together. What's the idea?"

"A couple are divorcing," I said. "Their nine-year-old daughter can't bear their splitting up. The father, a man-about-town, doesn't take marriage seriously, wants to go out all the time, never helps in the house, spends no time with the daughter. When he moves out, the little girl decides to make her father jealous. She sends a photo of her mother in a bathing suit to a Marine overseas. He's a handsome young guy and comes back on furlough. He cooks, fixes things in the house, helps the little girl with her homework, takes her to the zoo, and falls in love with the wife."

"That's a helluvan idea!" Ben enthused. "Very saleable. Timely. We have to hurry to get it done while they're still thinking 'war.'"

I remained on the paper; Ben and I worked on my story idea every moment we had. We enjoyed working together, acted everything out, and quickly wrote a long treatment almost as full as a screenplay. Ben's agent, George Willner, surprised us with an immediate offer for *Never Say Goodbye* from Warners. Errol Flynn wanted to do a comedy. "But," said George, "they want Ben to write the screenplay with S. K. Lauren. He has a reputation for witty dialogue."

I grabbed the phone. "George, it's my story. We did the whole thing so that Ben and I could work on the screenplay together at a studio. We told you."

"You risk losing the sale," Willner replied, coldly.

"We really need the money," Ben said to me.

"I can borrow from Mother."

"It's bad enough we live in *your* house," he said.

"If they want Sam Lauren that bad, I could collaborate with the two of them," I told George.

"Warners wouldn't hear of it," George said.

"*Ben . . .* " I appealed to him.

"I don't think we can take the chance."

Ben didn't fight for me. I felt betrayed, but I didn't fight for myself either. I gave in. That night I realized how much my feelings toward Ben had changed in two and a half years. In bed, for the first time, I pulled away.

6

Reel Life

Spring 1945. A tumultuous upheaval rocked the Party. In April, the political journal *Cahiers du Communisme* published French Party leader Jacques Duclos's famous or infamous piece, rumored to have come straight from Stalin. It stated that "Browderism" was an error. Browder's ideas had coincided with mine, that in the United States, the Party, unlike the European Parties, was not revolutionary and should take its place as a political party like the Democrats or Republicans. I'd welcomed Browder's dissolution of the CPUSA in May 1944, replacing it with the Communist Political Association. That seemed to me to be an outgrowth of the Popular Front, the period from 1936 to 1939 during the Spanish Civil War when liberals and Communists alike saw democracy threatened by Fascism.

New Yorkers and the Hollywood film community, already politicized by the fight for the Guilds, spurred liberals and Communists to come together in mass organizations like the Joint Anti-Fascist Refugee Committee. This Popular Front had lasted until the Nazi-Soviet Pact in 1939.

Two years later, June 22, 1941, the Nazis invaded the Soviet Union. The Russians counterattacked fiercely. Once again liberals and Communists saw the necessity of uniting to fight Fascism. A second Popular Front was born. Due to the war and the alliance between the USSR and the

U.S., the American Party had grown enormously by opening its doors to liberals and progressives. We thought the Party might achieve social, economic, and political gains and a lasting peace in the postwar world.

However, when the war was over, the United States denied the Soviet request for a loan to aid their domestic reconstruction while, at the same time, organizing Europe under the Marshall Plan as a bulwark *against* the Soviet Union. That killed the American Party's chances to have a broad alliance with liberals and progressives.

The Duclos letter was published in the *Daily Worker* on May 24, 1945. Two months later, the Communist Political Association re-formed into the Communist Party of the United States. Earl Browder was replaced by a new leader, William Z. Foster, who returned to the principles of the class struggle, as Duclos had recommended. The old-timers like George Sklar and Gordon Kahn, who'd been "in" since the thirties, had never been comfortable with the association that let in many people without education or training in Marxism.

After one meeting, I asked Ben why he wanted the return to being a party. "If you didn't agree," he snapped, "why didn't you speak up?"

"I don't know enough . . . "

"Goddamn right! You never read a fucking thing!"

I felt cowed, but the truth is that Ben and I read completely different things—I read books and plays, he read newspapers.

At a dinner party at our house, Lester Cole held his glass high and said jokingly, "Now we can toast the revolution again!"

On another evening, it had been a different story. Ben and I were having dinner at the Cloverdale apartment of Pauline Lauber, an active militant, whose husband, Aubrey Finn, later one of the leading attorneys for those who ran afoul of HUAC, was still in the Army.

I admired Pauline. She had tremendous assurance and was one of the few women of the Left who was articulate and never hesitated to speak up or debate with our most distinguished theoreticians—John Howard Lawson, Johnny Weber, and Abe Polonsky.

Abe had arrived in Hollywood earlier in the year when he left the Office of Strategic Services, the OSS (which gave him the right to brag about his exploits as an American "spy"). Brilliant and politically experienced, Abe took over the *Hollywood Quarterly* from Jack Lawson after only a few months in town.

Abe and his wife, Sylvia, showed up late at Pauline's. "We're in time," Abe said, peering through his thick glasses at the dessert. His voice, so very Bronx, sounded like my old CCNY boyfriends. Thin, wiry, and intellectual-looking like them—he'd been a professor of English at the College of the City of New York—his sharp, quizzical face and his humor commanded attention. Sylvia sat down, saying little but keeping track of everything.

Abe's lively eyes jumped around the room and lit on my belly. "What *is* it with this town? Everyone's pregnant. Must be the climate." Given to outrageous remarks, fifty-four years later Abe said at a dinner party at his son's house, as he put his arm on my shoulder, "Seven—each by a different genius. How come they all look like Ben?"

That night in 1945, he quickly got down to what was on our minds—the changes going on in the Party. Why was Earl Browder, heralded for his leadership during the war years, out? The French Party's "Duclos Letter"—approved by Stalin—scolded the American Party for revisionism. The Party leadership in New York had accepted the criticism as if it were the Sermon on the Mount. "I never liked Browder's extreme positions," Abe said, "but this kind of abrupt about-face makes us look ridiculous."

Pauline Lauber agreed. "You'd think the leadership would have learned from the last time."

"Right!" Abe chimed in. "Instead of being blindly pro-Russian at the time of the Nazi-Soviet Pact, the American Party should have had its own independent anti-Fascist position."

"It was idiotic," Ben said, imitating Herbert Biberman slavishly echoing the leadership's position, pounding on the table and insisting, "'We'll be for peace until the cows come home!'"

"Idiotic!" Pauline repeated, "to think we could be for peace when Hitler was taking over Europe."

Abe chuckled. "The cows came home early! In a year, Hitler invaded Russia and we American Communists were left with the leadership's idiocy. We had to correct a position that lost us more than half our membership and the support of the liberals."

Delighted by the camaraderie of Abe and Pauline, I saw that he respected her brain and treated her as an equal. The other thing that amazed me was that they were openly critical of the Party leadership and talked freely and with humor of what we all took so seriously.

Sylvia, who'd been quiet, waited for the end to add in her small voice, "The cows came home and fought off the Nazis at Stalingrad."[1]

When William Z. Foster himself came out to California to explain the necessity for the change, many screenwriters, as Ring Lardner, Jr., pointed out, were "flattered" that the Eastern hierarchy recognized the importance of the Hollywood section.[2] But none of us realized at the time the implications of the changeover.

I was preoccupied with other matters. Every day before going off to the studio to work on my story, Ben told me what a nice guy his collaborator was. He also volunteered that Errol Flynn had offered him "some hot women." I felt like vomiting. I felt like vomiting anyway. I was still so angry with Ben that I didn't tell him I suspected I was pregnant. I couldn't shut the plackets of either the pink, gray, black, and white checked or the navy, red, green, and yellow plaid ginghams. Ben noticed before I announced it. Jim Richardson did, too.

"Don't worry, Barzman," Jim whispered. "I'll take it easy on you. You're my best rewrite man. I won't send you out on any story unless you're dying to go." He sidled by, mumbled very low, "You'll be the first Hearst reporter on *paid maternity leave.*"

I was glad when Warners fired Ben off my story and put I. A. L. Diamond on the screenplay.[3]

The summer of 1945 was hot. Then, Hiroshima, August 6, 1945. Unbearable. I kept thinking: men make war, women make babies. I began to focus on the life in my belly. Even though I almost never went out on stories, I was weary after a day's work on the paper. I fell asleep every night reading Grantley Dick Reade's *Painless Childbirth* and Gesell's *The First Five Years of Life.*

The Big Moment arrived on a sunny Sunday morning, January 6,

1946. Our pale green Chrysler convertible, top down, sailed along Sunset Boulevard. I was in labor. I breathed. No pain. When we arrived at the old Cedars Hospital, they couldn't get me to the delivery room fast enough.

No one yet in America was using the Lamaze method of painless childbirth (without anesthetic). Although it had originated in the Soviet Union, we learned later that it was practiced in only one big polyclinic in Moscow, for the wives of apparatchiks. For Luli, my first child, I prepared with the exercises and breathing. My obstetrician, Dr. Melinkoff, insisted on giving me a caudal, a spinal that puts to sleep the lower half of the body. I was conscious. The delivery was a joy. Holding out my arms for the pink bundle, I half-sang, "Come to me, my Melinkoff baby."

Meanwhile, in the fathers' waiting room, our friend movie star John ("Julie") Garfield had been waiting all night for his beautiful wife, Robbie, to deliver. A few minutes after Ben joined Julie, a nurse entered, carrying the small pink bundle. "Which of you is Mr. Barzman?"

Ben couldn't believe his ears. Silently, he pointed to himself.

"Mr. Barzman, it's a girl," she said, holding the baby close to him. "See? She's pretty. They don't all have hair. She has hair."

"Shit!" cried Garfield. "Not fair. I've been pacing for eighteen hours. You've only been here fifteen minutes." Ben said nothing because he knew Julie's nine-year-old daughter had died only nine months before. The new baby was a replacement. (Ben told me later he couldn't help but think of my mother's agony at having lost an eight-year-old daughter nine months before I was born. I had been a replacement, too.)

Julie was shouting, "You got the girl! Now we don't have a chance!" But Robbie did give birth to a girl, whom the Garfields named Julie after her father.[4] A few years after she was born, John Garfield died of a heart attack shortly before he was to testify before the House UnAmerican Activities Committee.

We named our daughter Elizabeth because that would give her many nice nicknames to choose from, although we knew already we were going to call her "Luli" after the daughter of Spanish aristocrat Constancia de la Mora,[5] who joined the Loyalists (those loyal to the democratic republic of Spain).

Reel Life

• • •

Luli. Our daughter Luli. I had never held a baby before. Ben and I looked at her in wonderment. How could someone so marvelous come out of us? She was a delicious baby. From birth, she had enough hair to make a curl on the top of her head around which we tied a ribbon; we called it "the fountain." Luli grew into a scrumptious little girl. Aside from a few adolescent years when she slammed the door on me, she turned into a fine young woman and a good screenwriter.

I was enjoying Luli thoroughly but I was anxious to get back to the paper. Ben wouldn't hear of it. Never mind that an excellent nurse, a housekeeper, and my mother could look after the infant. He'd objected to my being away from the house even when there was no baby. Now he said, "You cannot leave the baby" and right after that pronouncement, persuaded me to leave the baby to take "the Mexican honeymoon" we'd never had.

In Acapulco, Ben started off by buying a huge sombrero. We had one glorious day together, walking arm-in-arm through the quaint town, swimming in warm waters, covering each other's toes with white sand, sharing the shuttered torrid coolness of "afternoonsies." He photographed me with my arm around a little Mexican boy who worked the beach, selling coconut juice, *muy frio*. We didn't want any but the boy said *no madre, no padre* and Ben gave in. The kid climbed a tall palm tree, brought back a coconut he broke with a hammer and poured its juice into a lily cup. "*No frio*, not cold," Ben complained.

"*Si, muy frio*," the boy insisted. "Very cold!" chorused his little brothers and sisters. Giggling, they followed us as we realized the "orphan" was one of a big family.

Ben and I chartered a boat, caught a big bonito. In the evening, the hotel grilled it. We soared on margueritas, rhumbaed under the milky starlight. Ben didn't like to dance but was so high on tequila that he did the box step, which, with his black hair, black mustache, and intense eyes, looked authentic.

Suddenly, Ben excused himself, left me at our table on the dance floor. I could see by his pallor as he left that Montezuma was having his revenge. The minute Ben was gone, a handsome young American, the kind we used to read about in women's magazines, appeared. With a big smile, he took my hand and piloted me out onto the dance floor into a flawless rhumba.

George Peabody Gardner was a Peabody, as in the museum in Cambridge, Massachusetts, and a Gardner as in Mrs. Gardner's Museum, Boston. He was a John P. Marquand character: Back Bay, Choate, Harvard, a couple of trust funds, an overbearing, straitlaced family, and, like Marquand protagonists, trying out his wings in New York as a junior editor at Putnam. I felt the most eligible and desirable young man I could have dreamt up was testing me.

When Ben didn't return, George took me over to his table and introduced me to his sister, Belle, and her husband, a Chicago Jewish stage photographer named Maurice Seymour.

"Nosey Bellikin," as George called his older sister, was shockingly outspoken. "George wants to do what I did," she explained laughingly. "Marry someone unsuitable. *De préférence,* Jewish. Totally unacceptable to the family."

I felt myself turn crimson. "I have a new baby!" I gulped.

"Ah!" George sighed. "That explains the radiance."

"I'm married," I said stiffly.

George laughed with the same abandon as his sister. "You didn't say 'happily.' "

George's brother-in-law, a lot older than his wife, was black with sunburn except for his nose, which was pink where the skin had peeled off. What was left of his dark hair stood up like horns. He threw his head back and laughed. "These two are impossible," he said, glaring at them. "I never know what they're going to come up with next. But don't be afraid. They're harmless."

Ben was searching for me. I excused myself, hurried to his side. He was weak from the runs, hardly knew how he could make it back to our room. After a terrible night, he wanted to sleep the next day. George and his sister and brother-in-law invited me on a drive to "the morning beach" for a swim and lunch.

At first, Ben was relieved to get rid of me. Though I felt guilty, the same words kept running through my head: *Serves Ben right.* He should have let me go back to work. He shouldn't have tempted me with a tropical paradise. After a week, when Ben felt better, he began to complain about how much time I was spending with George. Ben was jealous! Ben, who'd never said he loved me and who, from the way he'd proposed, had left the question of "love" unclear.

George had a lot to offer. He wasn't macho, was attractive intellectually as well as physically, hadn't picked up his considerable literary knowledge from cocktail party chitchat, had really read the criticism of Walter Benjamin. I reasoned it was good for Ben to see that someone like George, desirable on all counts, not a Communist but extremely liberal, wanted to be with me. But I didn't want to let it get out of hand. "George," I said, "You're acting like a moron. We've only known each other a week."

"I know precisely what I want," he answered forcefully. "You. Bright. Open. Eager. Full of life. On top of that, I'm in love with you." He kissed me. We did kiss romantically several times but never went to bed. Looking back now, I think George was looking for a wife. As his sister had said, he wanted to do what she had done. Marriage in defiance of the family would help free him from their values and constraints. He was working up the courage to approach Ben. I'd heard George rehearsing: "Why not admit it? You two don't love each other." He was going to ask Ben as if he were asking my father for my hand in marriage. "I will cherish her—and the baby girl . . . " I had to forestall it. I told him that I would never leave my husband.

When Ben announced, "No more!" I agreed. I had chosen to love Ben. With all his faults, he was the man I wanted to make my life with. I needed to be strong, learn to stand up to him. "We're leaving!" Ben cried. "The afternoon plane." It was not a coincidence that our friends film and stage actor Lee J. Cobb,[6] who would become famous playing Willy Loman in *Death of a Salesman,* and his wife, actress Helen Beverly, were staying at our Mexico City hotel. Bobby and Jeannie Lees had recommended it to us and to them.

When we were alone together, Ben brooded about what had just taken place in Acapulco. "I know you didn't do anything," he said, "but you led the guy on." The Cobbs turned out to be a blessing. With them along, Ben couldn't bring up what he called "my little Acapulco adventure," which later became the launchpad of my story *The Locket*.

Recovered from dysentery, Ben wanted to see the city. Delighted, Lee and Helen accompanied us everywhere, to the corrida, the markets, down the narrow canals of Xochimilco in a flower-decked barge, me sneezing all the way. At the thieves' market, Lee Cobb noticed with satisfaction that a man was staring at him. Lee strutted like a peacock. "How nice it is," he said, all puffed up, "to be recognized. Even in Mexico, I'm a star." As the man approached, Lee murmured, "I guess he wants my autograph."

The man gazed at Lee appraisingly. "*Bist a Yid?*" he asked. "Are you a Jew? Even from a distance," the man continued in Yiddish, "I could see that you were." He looked around, then leaned confidentially toward Lee. "Mexicans!" he whispered. "A *vilde volk!* A primitive people! How long since you had a morsel of good Jewish food in your mouth?" He held out a card to Lee. "Here. Let me give you the address of my restaurant."

The next day, while Lee and Helen napped, Ben and I rushed to the Bellas Artes to see the work of the great muralists, Rivera, Orozco, and Siquieros, which the Cobbs had already seen before. In front of the immense Diego Rivera mural, which had been in Rockefeller Center, we noticed a large barefoot Mexican-Indian family—father, mother carrying the baby, sons and daughters, each about nine months younger than the last one. They stood quietly facing the Rivera mural for some time, studying it. After that, they made a little circle and with gestures, argued about what it meant, then returned to gaze at it again. They were the answer to a "*vilde volk*," a primitive *cultured* people.

Like good parents, we booked our return flights on two separate Clippers. Ben's arrived without mishap. My plane, after many delays and detours, got back two days later. By that time, Ben was in the thick of "the Maltz controversy" that had begun after we left L.A. Albert Maltz's article "What Shall We Ask of Writers?" had been published in the *New Masses* on February 12. It demanded that works of art be judged by their creative contributions rather than their political positions.

Ben was upset that he hadn't been able to join Abe Polonsky, Johnny

Weber, Phil Stevenson, Henry, Bess, and the others who had met in Morris Carnovsky's basement to defend Albert's position. Ben had had the disheartening experience of bringing his own beautiful play *The Factory* to Jack Lawson and being told, "It's a good play, but do you want to be just another Odets?" which Ben interpreted to mean "Your play is not revolutionary. Do you want to be just another bourgeois playwright?"

Ben became convinced the Party didn't really understand art, that anything writers could do to educate the Party hierarchy in the East was to the good, and that Maltz was completely in the right since the editor of the *New Masses* had invited writers "to express all viewpoints."

In February, while we were in Mexico, Browder, who had promised creative freedom, was thrown out of the Party. In 1934, he had declared: "We believe that the overwhelming bulk of fine writing has political significance . . . that fine literature must arise directly out of life, expressing not only its problems, but, at the same time, all the richness and complexity of life itself." From 1935 on, there had been the unstated assumption that the goals of proletarian literature and Party literary criticism were inappropriate to the American cultural scene.[7]

Maltz's article said in effect that until Browder's declaration of creative freedom, the early 1930s Party position, envisioning art as a weapon in the class struggle, was "a vulgarization of the theory of art" and a "strait-jacket for the writer." Maltz added, "In order to write at all, it has long been necessary for me to repudiate this view and abandon it."

The Party seized upon Maltz's article as heresy. A March 1945 *Daily Worker* called him "a revisionist." He had "let the luxury and phony atmosphere of Hollywood poison him."

On the first Sunday we were back, Ben telephoned to assure Albert of our support. He suggested that Ben and I come to see him. On the way to their home, Ben tried to prepare me for Albert, whom I barely knew, though I admired his novels, which included *The Cross and the Arrow*, and his short stories, especially *The Happiest Man in the World*. "Albert is . . . " Ben searched for words, "deliberate, over-serious, even slightly pompous. But you mustn't be put off by his manner. He's a helluva good guy—"

"What's the 'but'? You're one of his tennis buddies."

"With Albert, you don't say 'buddies.' 'Tennis partners.' The first time I played with Albert, he asked me at the outset, 'How do you play?' 'Oh, pretty well,' I replied. 'I've been playing since I was a kid.' Albert said, 'Oh, I meant, Do you play to win? Or for the exercise?' 'I play for fun,' I answered. And Albert said, 'Oh!' and didn't smile."

When we arrived, a distraught Margaret Maltz was turning the house upside down looking for their son Peter. "He's not inside," Albert said stiffly. "I've combed the upstairs, the downstairs, and the cellar." He spoke slowly, carefully, as if he were calculating. "Peter must have gone out."

Ben had not exaggerated. Albert was borderline pompous ass and had the long unemotional face of a fine horse. I'd just finished his moving novel, *Underground Stream*. It was difficult to imagine this man writing it.

Ben and I accompanied Albert around the block. He walked cautiously, at a snail's pace, searching bushes, hedges, doorways. When we'd completed the tour, Ben asked, "Why don't we look for Peter across the street?"

"Oh, no," Albert replied. "I've rejected that possibility. Peter is not psychologically equipped to cross the street."

"Let's look anyway." Of course, that's where Peter was. He had crossed the street.

Peter and his sister had been adopted when they were tiny babies. The Communist Party had a flirtation with Soviet biologist Lysenko's doctrine of "acquired characteristics," which stressed the importance of environment over heredity. Many good Party people, out to prove that environment was more important than heredity, adopted children from Appalachia—not quite the Jukes and the Kalikaks (those mountain families that intermarried so much that their children had genetic deficiencies). Nonetheless, there'd been a lot of intermarriage and recessive traits surfaced. Our friends the Maltzes and Herbert and Gale Biberman, a plastic surgeon and his wife, were some of the couples who adopted babies from that area. From time to time, years later, we'd hear bulletins: the son of one took a shot at the president of Mexico, the daughter of another was a prostitute in New Orleans. But it was hearsay. It may or may not have been true.

Reel Life

After the ruthless attacks on him, Albert had begun to feel that maybe he had not fully considered the balance of forces in the world. Not long after, without letting his supporters know, Albert hied himself downtown to California Communist Party headquarters and recanted. In the *New Masses* of April 9, 1946, he acknowledged that the piece he'd written was "revisionist thinking" and "distorted Marxism." The truth may well have been that he was afraid of being expelled from the Party. Thirty years later, he said, "I felt the Party was the best hope of mankind; that it would be the force which moved the world to brotherhood. I was truly in a state of shock over the accusations that I had taken an anti-Party and anti-Marxist stance."[8]

Gerda Lerner told me that Albert also said the whole episode had been "the most unsettling experience of my life, infinitely worse than going to prison; nothing compared to it."[9]

I had time to write but I wasn't writing. Haho, the Welsh nurse we'd inherited from the Vorhauses, divided child care and housekeeping chores with me. I felt empty, not in the belly, but in the head. I wasn't used to staying home. Angry and frustrated that I had neither a studio job nor a job at the paper, I reasoned that if having a big family was what I wanted—and I was *sure* I did—then I should get the baby part over with early. Soviet educator Makarenko advised spacing a large family so that the older children could take care of the younger ones. Together, the children would make an effective collective. Ben said it was his experience that siblings close in age had a better time growing up, and if we were lucky, we could hang on to Haho. I stopped using a diaphragm and became pregnant immediately.

Lester Cole, soon to be one of the Hollywood Ten who later went to jail, was collaborating with Ben on an original comedy about "the Hungarian Invasion," the stream of Hungarian playwrights who came to Hollywood when Hitler overran Europe. I didn't think the idea funny.

Ben and Lester were working in the living room. One floor directly above, in the just-as-large master bedroom, I was struggling with a story about marriage. (I always wrote in the bedroom, frequently in my nightgown, as many women writers do.) Lester's loud rasping voice climbed through my open window. He'd pounce on what Ben said, shred it, relinquish it. Another flow of quiet words from Ben. Lester leaped on them, chewed them, spit them out, winding up with "D'ya know?"

As a result of the New York news vendor's lovely Hungarian Puli, Ben and I had bought a Kerry blue terrier. Naming him Kerry, I felt, displayed a remarkable lack of imagination on our part especially since next door lived Henry's Scottie, Lord Byron, and his black dachshund, Poe. Kerry couldn't be named Sean O'Casey or James Joyce. He was too foolish. We decided to give him away as soon as we had a baby, although that seemed like betrayal. We took him to dog-training school where the teacher confided that the Kerry blue is not the brightest of breeds. Oh, why couldn't Kerry be like Pushkin, Bobby and Jeannie Lees' black standard poodle, who pranced or danced, didn't walk or run, and stood guard over their babies?

While Ben and Lester hammered out their story in the living room, Kerry, above them on the balcony outside our bedroom, jumped up and down, searching for a dog. When he spotted one, he yapped his head off and tried to leap over the balcony wall. One day, he yelped wildly. Ben screamed, then Lester's raucous voice, "It wasn't Norma!"

Ben came running upstairs. They had both seen a body fall from the balcony. Kerry had made an excellent ski jump. He'd landed on the front lawn on all fours and kept running until he caught up with the dog down the block, a fierce caramel-colored chow.

"What did you think?" I demanded. "That I committed suicide?"

Haho, Luli's Welsh nurse, had heard the scream. Perspiring, wisps of hair straggling over her misty rimless glasses, she stuck her head in and pronounced, "That dog doesn't deserve a good home!"

I'm not sure what resolved me, maybe just Lester's voice, but in minutes, I had flown the coop too. I was driving up steep curves high in Laurel Canyon; 2101 Stanley Hills Drive felt far, far out in the hinterland with its orchard of fruit trees on one side of the house and a field of long grass on the other. From a distance, I could see the two little Stevenson boys, Joe and Teddy, in a tree's top branches.

Reel Life

Hearing my car, Janet emerged from the house wearing a carpenter's apron, holding a hammer. Although she was not very big, Janet Stevenson exuded strength.[10] She had an angular jaw, a determined chin, thin lips, piercing eyes, and delivered her penetrating wit through what seemed like clenched teeth. Her pale complexion and no-nonsense short dark hair, fastened tightly at the side with a barrette, didn't soften her sharp features. "I've been expecting you," she said.

"How could you? I just came on the spur of the moment."

"Not exactly," she observed dryly. "A while back, I told you to come over when you were ready. I calculated that by now you'd be ready."

We had run into each other at the farmers' market. She'd remarked that I didn't seem my exuberant self. "I'm always like that when I'm not working," I'd said.

"You're not alone. Most women screenwriters are unemployed. Phil and I have been a writing team for years. He's working at a studio and I'm not. Why don't you write with someone else?" she'd asked.

"Would you work with me?"

"Depends on the project."

"I have the beginnings of an idea."

"Come over when you're ready and we'll talk about it."

It had taken me two months to get up the courage. I liked Janet and respected her work. She was older than me, already had a reputation as a writer. "Well, here I am," I said. She led me into the garage remodeled into her office. "Don't you have to keep an eye on the boys?" I asked.

"Oh, you'll hear the screams soon enough. So what's this idea of yours?"

I told her the story, about a couple who had married for love, have a boy and girl, eight and six, and everything to make them happy. But they are not happy. The wife has become completely dependent on him, can't do anything for herself anymore. When the successful businessman husband wants her to entertain his associates, she goes to pieces. Nor can she cope with the children. The husband thinks he and his wife just need a vacation alone together. At the last moment, the husband is delayed by an important business deal. He tells his wife to drive north, gives her minute directions; he'll take a plane and meet her. She's hesitant. He always does the driving on long trips. Eventually, tense and full of fears, she pulls the car out of the driveway, clasps the steering wheel so tightly that her wedding ring hurts. She takes it off.

At that moment, Janet's telephone rang. "Just a moment." She put her hand over the mouthpiece. "It's Ben."

"I didn't tell him where I was. I told Haho but said not to call unless she really needed me."

Janet handed me the phone. "Hi," I said.

"What's up?" he asked.

"Nothing's up. I'm working."

Long pause. "I just needed to know," he said, "Are we going to Bobby and Jeannie's tonight?"

"You know it's next Monday. Jeannie makes beef and barley soup for us every Monday night. We play games or go to the movies. Why do only I know that?"

"Oh, sorry. I forgot." He hung up.

Janet laughed again, but this time, it was a knowing laugh. "Go on with the story—working title: *With This Ring.*"

"The wife is caught in a storm, runs the car into a ditch. A truck rolls up. The driver asks if she needs help. He can't extricate her car but gives her a lift to the next town. Now what I want to happen," I explained, "is that during the next few days while the car is being fixed, the young man treats her as an equal, assumes she'll help him with his work—I don't know exactly what the work is—but something where she can be of real assistance. It's hard to believe but she was once a teacher."

Janet cut in, "He could be with the Department of Agriculture, assigned to a community where he has to convince the farmers to use better methods of soil conservation."

"That's good. She could really help him on his rounds, talk to the farmers' wives—"

The phone rang. Ben again. He wanted to know where his gray suit was. "You told me to take it to the cleaner," I said. "You hardly need it right now to work with Lester."

"He went home," Ben replied sheepishly. "When are *you* coming home?"

"I just got here."

"Okay. G'bye."

"D'you think if we write this together," I asked Janet, "it will always be like this?"

"Yes," she answered. "Ben will desperately need his green tie even if he doesn't have one."

Janet and I worked for eight or nine weeks. Despite Ben's frequent phone calls, the story was taking shape and the screenplay was being written.

In the story, the husband can't get away from his business as soon as he expected. When her car is repaired, instead of continuing on, the wife decides to remain in the agricultural district. By the time the husband is ready to meet her, she's developed a relationship with the soil conservationist, she's studied his book, mastered erosion theory, and has been instrumental in converting a number of farmers to the new methods. To find out why she refuses to come back, the husband goes to the little town where she's living in a motel. There he encounters a completely different woman from the one he knew. No longer weak and helpless, she explains that she could never be happy living with him as they did in the past. The husband argues. When the young man champions her, she realizes that he, too, has a distorted view of her. She's a better, more competent woman but that's not necessarily who she is or wants to be. She's been molding herself into what each man wants! Janet and I opted for an unconventional ending, though we were sure no producer would go for it—the wife wanting time on her own to find out who she is. We gave the screenplay to our friend Tom Chapman, the Warners story editor. He read it. "This is just what Milton Sperling is looking for. Let me set up an appointment."

Soon after, we were ushered into the offices of Warner son-in-law Milton Sperling, who blurted out, "I read *With This Ring*. I like it. And I want to buy it." What a miracle! Then he said, "Only it doesn't have any jeopardy." As he went on, we both realized he was a bundle of uncertainty. "I see it in the snow in the mountains. Something that will give it jeopardy. Mountain climbing. Skiing. Bob Prick, excuse me, is a ski instructor—"

"The point," Janet cut in acidly, "is that *she* works at something that gives her self-esteem, that brings back her confidence in herself." I began to worry. Janet was turning him off.

"Of course," he agreed. "For example, she could ski for help when he breaks his leg. Or she could substitute for the ailing teacher of the mountain village school—"

Janet showed her impatience. "Why don't you give the agricultural community a whirl?"

"Smacks too much of Roosevelt. No one cares about soil conservation. Nothing exciting visually—and there's no jeopardy!"

He had a point, I thought. Years later, in Paris, when Tammy Gold[11] and I rewrote the basic idea for *Orient Express,* an American TV series, we gave it jeopardy and put a man's life in the balance. "Mr. Sperling," I said, "maybe an avalanche? They can't get back, she's good at survival—"

"Norma!" Janet said tightly. "He doesn't like our story."

"Fucking right! Excuse me," he apologized. "Prick" and "fuck" weren't used in front of women then, one reason men didn't like women around. "I see the husband battling a snowstorm to get to them. There hasn't been a good snowstorm since *The White Hell of Pitz Palu.*"

Janet tried to say something but it was too late. He didn't like the way she stood up to him—like a man. She wouldn't compromise. I shivered. We were two unemployed women writers who finally had a chance to write a major film at a major studio. I wanted to go for it. Janet tried to say something but he drowned her out. "The mountain is there," he boomed. "You defy it because it's there! Bob Prick is a mountain guide. By the time the husband shows up, the wife has scaled the Matterhorn!"

The next thing I knew we were in the Warner parking lot. Janet was no paler than usual. I felt faint. I had a right to. I had missed a period. But it wasn't that. In Milton Sperling's office, I'd had an epiphany. *I* must climb a mountain—or see a shrink. Which gave me a Story Idea!

7

Galileo

Our son, John Barzman, stuck his head out into the world on January 21, 1947.[1] We were the ideal American couple, with a son and a daughter. On the surface, all was well, but Ben wasn't working. Our agent, George Willner, suggested he write a play based on Ruth McKenny's short stories about her grandfather, *The Loud Red Patrick*. After the success of *My Sister Eileen*, Ruth McKenny had become one of the top clients of the Nat Goldstone Agency, of which George was now a partner.

Ben's first experience with Broadway had been bad, George explained, but this time Herman Shumlin, one of the great established theatrical producers, was going to finance Ben's dramatization of the McKenny stories. Because Shumlin would have a financial stake in it, *The Loud Red Patrick* would most certainly go into production if Ben did a good job.

When George Willner said something, you believed him. He had small, well-tanned, unremarkable features, a pleasant, soft-spoken manner, and he was a likable fellow everyone respected. He was one of the few Hollywood agents reputed to be honest.

His wife, Tiba, more than ten years older than me, was formidable.

Tiba is Hebrew for "dove." Tiba Willner was loud, aggressive, domineering, and often angry. She laughed only at her own jokes, told partially in Yiddish, which I didn't understand.

Old-time, militant, hardworking Communists from the East Coast, a different breed from "Hollywood artist lefties," the Willners were revered by the Party in the West. In New York, George had been a furniture salesman, and he carried a thousand-dollar bill in his wallet that he let people see, until he became the business manager of the *New Masses*. Tiba's family ran a socialist camp in the Catskills. George and Tiba, sent to California to supervise the first *Masses* art auctions, liked it so much they moved to Hollywood with their teenage children. They arrived at the tail end of the Depression; George could only find a job as a used-car salesman.

Lester Cole and nine other Communist clients of the Goldstone Agency approached Nat Goldstone and told him how knowledgeable George was, that they trusted him, and Nat should let George represent them. Nat couldn't say no. The agency grew because of George, and Nat offered him a partnership. When George was later named at the HUAC hearings, he was forced to sell his $750,000 interest in the agency for $25,000.[2]

In winter, Ben and I once made the mistake of going to Arrowhead for a few days with the Willners. The weather was bad. It developed into a poker weekend. I had never played. "Oh, that's all right," Tiba said, handing me a little card indicating that a flush beat a straight and four-of-a-kind beat whatever. I was seated between Tiba and George. They bumped and raised me over and over. When I lost, they laughed and Ben shouted at me. Back in town, one of the poker players, Jay Gorney, came to see Ben. He hoped Ben didn't treat me the way he had at Arrowhead. I was humiliated and Ben furious. I blamed Tiba for egging me on, George for going along with her, and myself for having played with them.

Tiba, I assumed, knew I would have liked to spit in her eye. I was greatly surprised when she asked if they could borrow our house for their twentieth-anniversary celebration. "Our place is tiny," I said.

"It's centrally located," she countered.

"The garden's too small," I protested.

"It's not so small without that one big tree."

"That's our only tree," I cried, horrified. "I love that tree. It's an avocado."

"You'd think," her eyes flashed murder, "now you have two small children, you wouldn't want your garden full of guacamole. If the tree weren't there, you could have a sandbox and a slide." She managed to make me feel like a bad mother.

"The roots of the tree aren't doing your house any good either," she added.

"I'd never cut down that tree!"

She pulled me over to the side of the house, where she pointed to a crack. "You'll have to sometime." She smirked. "I'm just suggesting you do it sooner."

She kept bullying me until, finally, in tears, I said, "Do what you like—"

She did. She had my beautiful avocado cut down.

I caved in. I was weak, not only with Ben. I didn't fight for what I wanted or believed in. The Willners had their party.

A week later, when two men were unloading the redwood sandbox I'd bought, I saw Ben, rushing off to his car, muttering, "George has done a terrible thing!"

George had made the following deal with Shumlin: Ben was to receive a minimal payment on signature. He promised to deliver Act One and an outline of the rest of the play by a certain date. On delivery, he was to be paid a second small payment. If McKenny approved, Ben would write the rest of the play and receive a substantial amount, making it worthwhile to have worked on another writer's material.

Thrilled that George got him a second chance at Broadway, this time with a prestigious producer like Shumlin, Ben quickly wrote a wonderfully funny first act. The outline took longer because he had to come up with a plot. *The Loud Red Patrick* was a collection of short stories. The date he was to turn in both to McKenny for approval was approaching. Ben asked if, along with Act One, he should hand in the outline as it was, pretty much notes to himself, and meet the date of the contract.

George answered, "Turn in Act One. Make the outline the best you know how. Don't worry about the date."

Ben did as George told him, gave the agency the first act, and, taking his time, structured the play. He did a splendid outline but, of course, it took nearly a month longer.

One week after Ben handed it in, he received a registered letter from an attorney declaring that Ben was in violation of the contract, that he had not met the provision of the deadline, and that all material reverted to Miss McKenny.

I was terrified that Ben would have a heart attack because he was always talking about his father dying young of heart failure. Ben tried to get George on the line. Dusty, George's secretary, said, "He's with a client." Ben tried again. Dusty said George was out. That was when Ben rushed to the agency.

Dusty, sitting outside George's office, was flustered to see him. "George is in a meeting," she said.

Ben tried to push past her, screaming, "They can't do this—"

Suddenly, George appeared. "It's not me, Ben. It's Nat. And Shumlin. And McKenny. They want to do the play. But without you. And they've got a legal right to get you out!" George strode past Ben. "I'll see you later."

Ben grabbed George. "No! Now!"

George shook himself loose and hurried away, calling out, "Dusty, show Ben the file!"

She handed Ben a thick dossier full of contracts and letters. Weak with anger, Ben sank into a deep armchair, the open file on his knee. He stared hard at the top letter from Ruth McKenny, the most recent of the sheaf of correspondence: "Bruce and I read it aloud and laughed ourselves sick. Barzman really caught the character of my grandfather, captured the atmosphere and turned the whole thing into something warm, funny, and irresistible. I can't understand why I didn't see the possibilities myself. Barzman makes me think it might turn out better even than *My Sister Eileen*.

"I know this is a bit late for me to decide that I want to do it myself," McKenny continued. "You *must* get it back from him, George. I don't care how you do it. If you never do another thing for me, and believe me, you never will if you don't do this. I must be the one to write it. After all, they're *my* stories. It's *my* grandfather."

Ben flicked through a note from George reassuring McKenny ("I'll do whatever is necessary") and a series of memos: from Nat to George ("If she wants it back, get it back! Just tell Ben he didn't meet the deadline"). From George to Nat ("I told Ben not to worry about the deadline"). From Nat to George ("In writing?"). From George to Nat ("No, not in writing"). From Nat to George ("Get him out! Or you're out!").

Deeply hurt, Ben left, and told George's other Communist clients what George had done. Many departed, and, like us, went over to the only other Communist literary agent, Johnny Weber at William Morris.[3]

Right after this, Haho announced that she was going to take her savings and travel. "But you and Mr. Barzman have been so kind, I want you two to take a long weekend while I'm still here before there are new people for Luli and Johnny." New people. She was right. She'd been doing the work of two.

A holiday was the last thing *we* wanted. Ben was suicidal about *The Loud Red Patrick*. I had never seen him this depressed. I took him to the movies to relax him. Unfortunately, the Rosalind Russell–Fred MacMurray comedy we saw would have made *me* almost suicidal had I been prone to depression. It had the same plot as *Justice Is a Lady,* which I'd written with Jay Gorney's wife, Sondra, a magazine writer, at the time Ben and I were married. The story of the new independent career woman, a domestic-relations court judge, who sits on a divorce case embodying her own troubles with her husband, was almost identical with our original, which had been circulated by George Willner to all the studios but not sold. Registration with the Guild rarely protected the material. Suing the studios was out of the question. If you did, as far as they were concerned, you were dead.

I don't know how I could have said no to Annie's invitation for us to join her and Adrian, publisher Bennett Cerf, and his wife, Phyllis, at La Quinta. I called Annie back. Bennett's repartee would distract us and the weekend would keep me from being alone with Ben's misery. Unfortunately, all I remember of La Quinta is Adrian, poolside, plucking hairs from Annie's legs with a tweezers, and me picking up a bee, throwing it out of the pool, and winding up with a 105-degree fever and a webbed thumb and forefinger' no space between them like a frog. I missed all of Bennett Cerf's wicked wit.

One morning, Adrian wandered by to see how I was doing. He stretched out on a striped chaise longue. "Ben," he began, "I've been thinking." Ben made an encouraging sound. "I've bought a short story that appeared in the Sunday magazine section of the *L.A. Times,* by a woman I never heard of." Adrian reached for coffee. "It's about a little boy whose hair turns green."

Ben swallowed. "What happens?"

"That's it," Adrian replied. "He wakes up one morning and his hair is green."

"I see," said Ben, not seeing at all.

"Are you curious?" Adrian asked.

"I am curious," I replied.

"When we went to England last year to do *So Well Remembered,* you know Annie and I brought back our adopted son Michael, a war orphan. He'd lost his parents in the London Blitz."

"I see," Ben repeated, seeing a great deal more than before. "If a little boy who is a war orphan suddenly has green hair, it might be for a reason."

"I want you to think about this seriously, Ben. We'll talk from time to time. RKO has a deal with Technicolor. Do you know Joe Losey? No? He's never directed a picture. I liked a play he did in New York. He's going to direct Brecht's *Galileo* here in Hollywood."

A glimmer of hope.

That was all we heard about *Green Hair* for a while. With no other job on the horizon, Ben suffered terribly. The George Willner–Ruth McKenny coup had left him in deep despair. With some trepidation, I suggested he "get some help."

Galileo

Now, the Communist Party had a rule against its members going into psychoanalysis. "Freud and Marx were regarded as antithetical," and, as my future analyst, Dr. Isidore Ziferstein, pointed out, "There were ideological reasons for feeling that being psychoanalyzed was not the Marxist thing to do: you were subjecting yourself to the propaganda of the enemy. Psychoanalysis is basically the tool of the class enemy to justify inequities of society by attributing them to flaws in personality rather than the system."[4] In *Naming Names,* Victor Navasky also commented: "So, the party had a double fear: that the analysand would be ideologically poisoned; and since it is a rule of psychoanalysis that the patient reveals everything, the Party's security as a secret organization would be compromised."[5]

This last was borne out when, during the hearings, the Party members who had consulted Phil Cohen, a Communist posing as an analyst with not even a psychologist's degree, were urged by him to name names.

Most of us stayed away from analysis or did not consult orthodox Freudians. The Los Angeles Psychoanalytic Society had split in two, the A Group of orthodox Freudians and the more liberal B Group.

When I suggested to Ben that he consult Dr. Isidore Ziferstein, a liberal analyst of the B Group, one of the few on whom the Party looked favorably, Ben howled at me: "*You* go! *You're* the one who needs it! You've got allergies and hay fever!"

In those days, we thought everything was psychosomatic. When my hay fever developed into asthmatic wheezing, I took myself to Dr. Ziferstein, instead of an allergist.

Mousy, huddled in a warm woolen shawl, Dr. Isidore Ziferstein received me at his home. At one point, I sat bolt upright. "You look like Elizabeth Barrett Browning!" I accused him. "I don't need someone weak and sniveling."

Another time, I complained of his wife's piano playing during my hour. Zif almost never made a comment. This time he said, "Have you asked yourself why you have so much fury against her?"

"Maybe," I said, "because my mother was always playing the piano when I was a child and wanted her attention."

I have no idea whether, when associating freely, I actually questioned why I had stopped writing. I do remember Zif's rare words, "If you worked, you could pay for your analysis."

The next thing I knew, I was writing a story, *The Locket*, which I didn't show to Ben and wouldn't have if it hadn't been for our Musso Frank lunch with our new agent, Johnny Weber, the head of William Morris's story department. We hoped he would find Ben a job.

"Adrian's got a project for me." Ben told him about *The Boy with Green Hair.*

"That won't be for some time," Johnny said. "Either of you two working on anything?"

"I've been puttering around with a psychological thriller," I answered. "A guy meets a girl in Acapulco. They don't know anything about each other. They fall in love—" Ben gave me a look. He was thinking of George Peabody Gardner. I went on, "They marry. When the bride brings her husband home, her mother looks at the two of them strangely.

"The heroine, Nancy, is a little off. Like me, Johnny. She steals—"

"Norma only steals ashtrays," Ben put in quickly.

"I made Nancy a kleptomaniac. She's not aware she steals. The husband returns the things she takes but her behavior threatens their marriage. He doesn't like the idea of psychoanalysis but finally, in desperation, gets her to a shrink."

Johnny grinned. "Psychoanalysis is 'in.' It wouldn't surprise me if the studios would go for something like that—"

"In a succession of distorted flashbacks," I continued, "one within another—"

Ben's voice was stern. "Flashbacks should only be used to advance the story—"

"Not these," I interrupted. "They're how she remembers. A defense. The work of a sick mind."

"Flashbacks," Ben said, "aren't—"

"Let her explore," Weber said. He looked from one to the other of us and laughed. "Why don't you two go home and work it out. Ben, 'putter around' with Norma, at least until I find you a job."

Galileo

"A gold antique locket," I said, "is the one tangible thing that finally convinces the husband that Nancy's delusions have a basis in reality."

Ben looked at me squarely, then turned to Johnny. "Johnny," Ben said, "if Norma and I write this, and William Morris sells it, will you for Chrissake see to it the two of us have a job writing the screenplay together?"

I had a moment of elation.

We went home. I read Ben what I'd written. But I felt so well disposed toward him that we didn't do much work on *The Locket* before we went up to bed.

My cousin Henry, who lived next door, was coming over to see us more often. We wondered if he wanted to escape the bullying of his new shrewish wife or if eighteen-month-old Luli and six-month-old Johnny had suddenly become "interesting."

On this particular visit, I suppose, he had come over to console Ben about *The Loud Red Patrick*. Henry confided that for years he himself had been so mesmerized by the theater that he'd invested his hardearned movie money in his own Broadway flops.

"You had one hit," I said, "before you came out to Hollywood."

"*The First Fifty Years.* Precursor of the grow-old-together plays. Only two characters. It's mentioned in almost every history of the American drama."

Both my mother and her sister, Henry's mother, Muzzy, daughters of a Shakespearean actor, were bitten by the theater bug. My mother ran away at sixteen to go on the stage. Muzzy lived vicariously through her son. She made him take a badly paid job press-agenting for the Schuberts so she'd always have house seats, then forced him to write a play a week. Monday, Tuesday, Wednesday, he wrote. Thursday, he gave it to her for suggestions, rewrote and had it on Lee Schubert's desk by Friday evening so he could read it over the weekend.

"I just remembered why I came over," said Henry absentmindedly. "I have two extra seats for tomorrow night's opening of Brecht's *Galileo*." For no apparent reason, Henry exploded with laughter.

"What's so funny?"

"Charles Laughton plays Galileo. It's years since he's acted on the stage. He's dreadfully nervous. Two nights ago at rehearsal he was so nervous that during the opening scene, he put his hands in his pockets and began playing with his genitals. Nobody had the guts to tell him to stop. So Weigel, Brecht's actress wife—she designed the costumes— decided she better do something about it. Yesterday, at the dress rehearsal, Laughton couldn't get his hands into his trouser pockets. Seething, he screamed, 'Who sewed up these pockets?' He chased and almost killed the poor wardrobe girl who had to undo Weigel's sewing, stitch by stitch."

"How in heaven did you get four tickets to opening night when everyone in Hollywood is clamoring for them?"

Henry drew himself up. "I," he said, "am a pillar of the theater in this town, the founder of the Hollywood Theatre Alliance. *Meet the People* is not the only show we produced."

I thought of Henry's courage after being crippled by polio, his wit, and all the things in his character that made me idolize him. Once Henry took me to a meeting where they were deciding what to do about a play that was losing money. Hour after hour people proposed ways of saving it. Leaflets. Skywriting. Near midnight, Henry put up his hand. Everyone turned, thinking he had the magic solution. Henry raised his triangular eyebrows and said carefully, "The trouble with this play is that people go to see it and don't like it and tell their friends. The thing for us to do is keep people from seeing it."

Aside from the birth of our son John, the high point of 1947 for me was the gala premiere of Brecht's *Galileo* at the Coronet Theatre on La Cienega Boulevard. The play was a symbol of the flight of art, culture, and intellect from Germany and the rest of Europe during Hitler's Third Reich. Brecht's radical influence on our theater and filmmaking was only one tiny part of the fabulous contribution brought to us by the many exiles from Thomas Mann to Einstein.

On the night of July 30, 1947, a stunning crowd pushed into the

Coronet: Salka Viertel, surrounded by Chaplin, Kurt Weill, and other artists who frequented her Sunday salon in Santa Monica; Hollywood stars Charles Boyer and Ingrid Bergman; and many of our friends— Gene and Betsy Kelly, John and Robbie Garfield, Jack and Gladys Berry, Tony Quinn, and other Actors Lab members.

It was an unbearably hot night to sit through a long play in a tiny jam-packed theater. Buckets of ice were placed at the sides of the stage and electric fans blew the cool air toward the audience. The night was hot in another respect. The parallel between HUAC's activities in Washington, D.C., and the Inquisition, which forced Galileo to recant in the seventeenth century, escaped no one. We'd been shutting it out of our minds, but only three months before, in May, HUAC had staged mock hearings in L.A. with fourteen "friendly witnesses" of the MPA, the Motion Picture Alliance for the Preservation of American Ideals, Robert Taylor, Ward Bond, Adolphe Menjou, Lela Rogers (Ginger's mother), and others who privately named Hollywood figures they imagined must be Communists.

Brecht was less interested in the Inquisition than he was in exposing the magnitude of Galileo's criminality in recanting when he knew his discoveries to be true. In Brecht's view, Galileo was an opportunist. Laughton seemed unable to play the role that way, and maybe, since he had taken a malicious pleasure in exposing Galileo's cowardice, he didn't want to destroy what he'd been building up, the character of a great man *and* his weaknesses. He seemed to want sympathy, or at least understanding for Galileo's frailties.[6]

On July 30, 1997, the fiftieth anniversary of the play's opening, Brian Dennehy acted Brecht's *Galileo* in a reading at the Coronet Theatre. Dennehy was superb. In the lobby hung a huge photo blowup of the first-night crowd fifty years earlier. I stood in front of it a long time, identifying Adrian, Annie, the Kellys, Ben, myself, and a host of others.

At the end of the 1947 premiere, Ben and I went backstage to congratulate the production designer, our friend John Hubley, who later created Mr. Magoo. He presented us to Faith Elliott, who would become Mrs. Hubley and would, when they were blacklisted, found with him an independent company that made animated surrealist-style films with philosophical, scientific, and political themes, honored at festivals around the world.[7]

Johnny then introduced us to a man who, from that time on, was to play an enormous role in our lives: Joseph Losey. Joe had a large, wide, florid Dutch face like those in Franz Hals portraits of wealthy burghers. Even in those days, when Joe's asthma was not supposed to be "so bad," he wheezed, gasped, and spritzed himself between his tirades. After he enumerated what had gone wrong during the performance, he carefully made a respectful allusion to Brecht.

For at least a year, Losey, in and out of Hollywood, under contract to MGM, where he was only allowed to direct shorts, had been preparing *Galileo*. He had interested the play's major investor and was responsible for putting the production together. Nominally, Joe was director, but research confirmed that Brecht really directed it with much "help" from Laughton.

We'd heard that during the stormy rehearsals, after much abuse from Brecht, Joe finally threw the script at him and walked out; Laughton had prevailed upon Joe to return, provided Brecht would apologize; the playwright had then sent Joe a message: "Brecht never apologizes." Joe went back anyway.

After we knew him better, we asked Joe, who was an important New York stage director, whether he'd been upset by Brecht's taking over the direction.

"It was hard," Joe admitted with a gorgeous smile, "but I was *with* Brecht."

8

The Shit Hits the Electric Fan

In September 1947, after the Los Angeles run of *Galileo,* our morning *Daily Variety* whacked us across the face with the headline: "HUAC ISSUES SUBPOENAS TO 19! Committee Will Question Them as to Their Political Affiliations."

Ben and I hadn't believed such a thing could happen. Even when it did happen, we couldn't imagine the catastrophic events that lay in wait for all of us.[1]

Tuesday, October 26, 1999.

Abe Polonsky died. Dear Abe, dear friend. Brilliant, talented, witty, often so ornery that few realized what a fine man he was. He cared about all things great and small; when he met someone, he asked questions, really wanted to know what they did, what they thought. He read endlessly for the joy of knowing, a curiosity that gave him the knowledge which his fine mind turned into wisdom.

The night before Abe died, I called him as I did almost every day with some inane question. I wanted to know about 1947. How could we have lived through eight months of the year without realizing what was happening? I couldn't fathom it. We lived as if nothing were wrong until September, when the subpoenas arrived!

"You were naive," Abe cried. "You were romantic! The way you always were about everything!" He was screaming at me. "You had only to look. The signposts were everywhere."

I understood what Abe meant because I'd just finished reading the chapter on 1947 in *The Inquisition in Hollywood*. But at the time, Ben and I had not paid any attention to Abe's "signposts": Up to 1947, the studios had stood firm against the government's Red-baiting, but feeling the squeeze of postwar economic recession, they needed government to keep European markets open to them, to subsidize new markets like Latin America, and to keep labor from making demands. In return for government intervention on their behalf, Eric Johnston, new head of the "U.S. Film Bureau," demanded that movies going overseas "reflect on the good name and reputation of this country and its institutions," which effectively made films like *The Grapes of Wrath* taboo.

Because of the postwar recession, the studios fired 12,000 workers, and cut in half the number of actors, writers, directors, and staff. By summer, only 440 of the 1,500 members of the Screen Writers Guild were working. Low employment and liberals joining arch-reactionaries in the anti-Communist crusade divided the membership of the Guild and rendered it impotent.

The Hollywood labor movement was a thing of the past. The studios had effectively paralyzed the Conference of Studio Unions (CSU), the progressive Sorrell-led union, by pushing it into a jurisdictional dispute with the corrupt, reactionary, studio-dominated IATSE technicians' union. Sorrell won the first eight-month strike from March through October 1945. I was pregnant with Luli at the time. Ben forbade me to go near Warners, where private studio police were using tear gas and hoses on the picket line, but he accompanied Henry, who, lamed by polio, used a cane, which he brandished at the worst of the goons. I collected money for the strikers, but when the strike was over they were blacklisted. Many lost their homes.

The succeeding CSU strikes couldn't be won because the Hollywood Left was weakened by the historical tides sweeping the world. The Russian

The Shit Hits the Electric Fan

takeover of Eastern Europe had begun. Churchill had given his Iron Curtain speech, quarantining Western from Eastern Europe. Under the Truman Doctrine, the U.S. furnished military aid to conservative governments that put down popular uprisings (Turkey and Greece); under the Marshall Plan the U.S. provided economic aid to countries that didn't vote Left. The Communist Parties of England, France, Italy, and Germany were gaining strength because Europeans believed that the war had been won by the Soviet Union and by the European resistance movements, mainly composed of Communists. It wasn't difficult to understand the anxiety of the average American drowning in Red Scare propaganda. Even Ben's "progressive" nephew David was terrified that his prosperous postwar sporting goods firm would be forced out of business. He was sure a united Communist Europe would not buy his skis and ice skates.

In January 1947, an anti-Communist liberal movement had been established, the ADA (Americans for Democratic Action), which Mrs. Roosevelt joined. It killed off the Hollywood Independent Citizens Committee of the Arts, Sciences and Professions, the leading Popular Front alliance of liberals and radicals in postwar Hollywood. If one listened, Abe punned, "one could hear the last Hiccasp."

Yet when the Ten went off to Washington to appear before HUAC, we still thought we could count on liberals to stand behind us, and so they did—at the beginning. Humphrey Bogart, Lauren Bacall, Rita Hayworth, Katharine Hepburn, Judy Garland, Frank Sinatra, and Groucho Marx thronged the home of lyricist Ira Gershwin, where they planned a radio program, "Hollywood Strikes Back," condemning HUAC. I helped Joe Losey organize a protest meeting at Shrine Auditorium, at which the massive audience sang "The Bill of Rights" set to music by my cousin Henry and Jay Gorney.

Amusing highlight: Jay and Sam Ornitz, who was to speak that night, were suddenly thrown together for the first time. Sam asked Jay what his name had been before it was Gorney. "Gornitzky," Jay said, "was just too long."

"Good heavens!" Sam exclaimed. "Our name was Gornitzky too. Where were you from?"

"The Ukraine," Jay replied.

93

"So were we. What town?"

They suddenly realized that not only did their families come from the same shtetl but they were first cousins. Their fathers were brothers! And, as I watched them embrace, I saw they had the same build and shared many features.

The mass meeting was a huge success, and the next day, October 27, director John Huston, who founded the Committee for the First Amendment, flew to Washington with a group of celebrities. He made one stipulation: no Communist Party members must come along because he had wangled an invitation to dine with President Truman in the White House. Lauren Bacall recollects how she and Bogey, Danny Kaye, and Gene Kelly were impatient to get to Washington. "Wouldn't it be incredible," she'd said, "if we really could make HUAC stop?"[2]

The stars delivered a petition and filed into reserved seats at the hearing, which was broadcast live across America. Ben and I listened proudly to the first of the witnesses, John Howard Lawson, defy the Committee. Chairman J. Parnell Thomas pounded his gavel and yelled at Lawson, "Stand away from the stand," to which Jack retorted, "I shall continue to fight for the Bill of Rights, which you are trying to destroy."

But the "performance" of Lawson and the witnesses who followed lost the invitation to the White House and much public support. It was unclear whether the Committee for the First Amendment began to fade because of the defiant attitude of the witnesses or because, on their return to Hollywood, the stars were called in by studio heads and threatened with suspension if they continued to support the Ten.

A minor casualty of that moment was the project on which I was collaborating with Max Welles (the ex-husband of my friend publisher Annette Welles, later a Universal VP). Max had sparked when, inadvertently, I came up with a title that practically dictated the story. "Once Upon a Timeclock" had to be a Tracy–Hepburn vehicle in which a woman efficiency expert drives an industrialist crazy with her innovative stunts to increase productivity.

We started to work. Then, during the hearings, I praised the stance of the Ten.

The Shit Hits the Electric Fan

Suddenly, Max jumped up from the typewriter as if he'd been shot. "You don't mean you really think they're doing the right thing—defying the Committee?"

Max was supposed to be progressive like Annette.

"Yes," I replied. "I don't think there's any alternative."

"I guess I should have known better than to work with you. I heard you were Mrs. Ironpants but it was hard to believe. You have such a soft exterior."

"Well, let's not discuss politics. Let's get on with the story."

"I don't think I can," he said, grabbing his hat and running out.

We never finished writing the story, although Johnny Weber pitched it to several producers who were receptive. Therefore, it wasn't surprising that we eventually saw our movie with Tracy and Hepburn but the genders reversed, Tracy as the efficiency expert and Hepburn, the business owner.

Constant rumors kept us in a state of anxiety, which was aggravated that summer by the hellish torture of L.A.'s very own fat-assed, stifling, unbearably hot wind, the Santa Ana. It is comparable to North Africa's Hamsheen, during which Arabs are permitted to murder their wives without facing criminal charges—or so my friend, the Algerian filmmaker Mohammed Lakhdar-Hamina told me.

I was so hot and miserable that I did something no sane Angeleno ever does. I plopped down on the front lawn, hoping for some wisp of cool breeze to soothe me until the nurse returned with Luli and Johnny from the beach, where I'd sent them, as the back of our house, now equipped with slide and jungle gym and the redwood sandbox, smelled of burning brushfire.

Ben arrived home from RKO first, and waved from the car. He reappeared in a flowered Mexican shirt and the sombrero he hadn't worn since our unmentionable Acapulco vacation. Grinning broadly, he flourished two tall glasses of gin and tonic. For a moment I was flooded with love. With the world turning against us, we were drawing closer to each other. Ben handed me a glass, kissed my upturned face enthusiastically, and settled down beside me.

It was at this point we realized there was a lot more going on before us than the usual screeching brakes and crazy driving. The drivers seemed to be looking for something, then stalled right in front of us.

Groucho Marx, who lived a few houses below us on the other side of the street, came by wearing his white pith helmet, chomping on a big cigar, his rump out, pushing a pram with his new baby daughter, Melinda.

He started to walk past us, then changed his mind, set the brake on the pram. "Yes," he said to no one in particular, "it's hot enough for me, my mother and my grandmother, God rest her soul, and Melinda, who you didn't even have the ordinary decency to ask me if it was hot enough for—" With a strained expression, he raised his eyebrows and rolled his eyes. "Of course, it's doubly hot for you—with two kinds of heat. But don't ask me for anything more than ice cubes, which is as far as my sympathies go."

With that, he released the pram's brake and continued on his mock-angry way.

"Hey, what was all that?" I asked puzzled.

I could see Ben was bothered, too. "He was trying to tell us something" was Ben's take.

Usually, when Groucho was out on his evening walk with the baby, he stopped and got off a funny monologue, like the night there was a spectacular meteorite display in the sky, he looked upward and said, "You think *that's* something. You should have seen the searchlights they had on Fairfax for the opening of Canter's. By the way, their pastrami is only so-so."

Suddenly, a huge white elderly Cadillac convertible, top down, careened into our driveway. In its driver's seat, a swirling mass of golden wind-tossed hair.

The engine died. The mass of blond hair subsided, revealing a lovely young girl in the act of deciding something.

She nodded to herself, got out of the car. As she smoothed her heat-sticky, crumpled dress, a most curvaceous body took form. She checked the house number, nodded again, and started toward us.

Ben got to his feet.

"It just hit me it might be fun here what with your sombrero and your sitting on the lawn with drinks?" she said. "I was going to the Minellis. They live just up the way with their new baby, Liza." She was not at ease. "They're having a party. My agent says it would be good for me to show myself, get exposure?"

It was obvious that she had something else on her mind. "Sit down," I said.

The girl nodded, sat down alongside me with the gracefulness of a flower opening in reverse.

"Hot," she said, subsiding on the grass.

"I'll get you a gin and tonic," Ben said. He usually let me get drinks for guests.

When he came back and gave her the drink, she sipped it tentatively. "I thought it was going to taste like medicine but I like it fine. I think I'll make it *my* drink. My agent says everybody in Hollywood has *his* or *her* drink. I mean, it gets to be known?"

"Yes," I agreed. "People remember and serve it up without you having to ask. Something's worrying you?"

"Well, yes," the girl said. "My mother always told me never to be the one to bring people unpleasant news. Murphy's Law?"

"Murphy's Law?" I repeated. That was the first time I'd ever heard of it.

"Murphy's Law says that if there's something unpleasant, don't worry, people will find out soon enough, don't you be the one to tell them. Like if a good or bad thing can happen, don't worry, the bad thing will happen? Now, what was I going to tell you?"

"You were trying to make up your mind whether or not to tell us something unpleasant?" I prompted.

"Don't you know?" she asked hopefully. We shook our heads. She took a deep breath. "There's a deputy sheriff's car with two cops at the bottom of this hill. They're stopping practically every car coming up the hill. There was this guy in front of me and the deputy stopped him so suddenly I almost hit him. I was really upset. Then I heard the deputy ask the guy where he was going? Was he going to your address by any chance?"

"Our address?" I asked incredulously.

"I heard it loud and clear. The guy said no and the cop waves him on. Then I drove up. 'You stopped that guy so suddenly I almost crashed him.' The cop says in that way I hate—I seem to bring it out in most guys—'Lady, I wouldn't have stopped *you*,' then he grins a big fat grin and says, 'I sure would've, if I had an excuse.' Well, to make a long story short, he leans over me, he's a really big guy, and says, 'You don't happen to be going to 1290 Sunset Plaza Drive?' "

I gasped.

" 'No, I don't,' " she said, "That's your number, isn't it?" It was. "What's going on? Is there a murder or something?"

The ground had slipped from under me in one of those neat Los Angeles land-shifts. I guessed what was coming.

The girl went on, " 'The sheriff's office is keeping an eye on the house. Subversive groups are meeting there.' Well, sir, I really blew. I said, 'Who the hell is this sheriff of yours? Hitler?' Gee whiz: Subversive? With that sombrero?"

I moved closer to Ben. "You mean he's told everybody on this hill we're subversive?"

"So what did the deputy sheriff do finally?" Ben asked.

"Oh, he gave me a ticket for obstructing traffic," the girl said. "My mother was right. There's no percentage in being the one who brings lousy news."

"I think I know why the sheriff's car is doing that," Ben said. "A bunch of us, screenwriters and directors, were going to meet to discuss what to do to help the Hollywood Ten. The Committee for the First Amendment—the one Humphrey Bogart resigned from? The meeting was called off this morning—"

"Somebody must have forgotten to call off the sheriff," the girl said. "I bet if you gave it a little thought, you could figure out who that was."

"Right now I don't want to know," I said. "It might be a friend."

The girl rose and stood there in an odd posture.

"My name is Norma," I said, getting up and extending my hand.

"Gee, my name is Norma, too," she said, and we shook hands all around. "I'm glad I stopped in on you guys. I mean, I hoped there was somebody kind of behind the scenes worrying about things, not just letting them get away with all the stuff they do to us. A struggling young actress like me knows about that. I'm real glad there's people like you trying to figure out ways of not getting pushed around. I don't care what you are. I like it that there's somebody watching the store. I think I'll sleep better tonight." She turned toward her car.

"Thanks," Ben called after her.

As she got into her elderly Cadillac, we saw my old maroon Mercury Coupe from my first marriage, waiting to turn into the driveway. The blonde backed out and sped up the hill. The Mercury pulled in. Ben and I ran to kiss the babies (a protective reflex after the warning we'd just received). They were asleep in the backseat, Luli clutching a pail of shells with her tiny chubby fist, Johnny snoring gently, his hat pulled down over his face.

I remembered Mother needed to be reassured and went inside to phone, leaving Ben outside to help with the children. I picked up the receiver and literally could not believe I was hearing a conversation I'd had with Jeannie Lees three days previously. I listened, as it repeated for the second time. I hung up, picked up the phone again. I heard a click.

Two years later, sitting with Ben at a café on the Champs Elysées, the shock was almost as great when he let out a yelp: "Hey! That girl!" He passed me the *Paris Herald Tribune.* "The blonde who warned us! Look at the photo!" It was Marilyn Monroe. "Remember? She said her name was Norma."

9

Not Enough Jeopardy

Like brushfires all around us, the blacklist was raging, subpoenas were out, the sheriff was watching us, and our phone was tapped. That seemed like enough jeopardy, but then our babies caught a virulent infection called Virus X, reputed to have killed several infants. Both Luli and Johnny had high fevers, threw up everything, and had continuous diarrhea. The nurse and the housekeeper walked out together.

Mother arrived in a taxi in time to see me miscarrying (in an early month) due to the virus. She took care of everybody and called the employment agency. Before the answering voice could finish, Mother said, "Send her over at once in a taxi."

Her name was Margaret Heatherington and she was sent from heaven. Large, strong, and graceful, warm and caring, she cheered me the moment I saw her beautiful dark features. She ministered to everyone, found time to make Mother a cup of tea, and, although it was only the last week in November, sang Christmas carols as she went about her work. (Years later, I discovered that when sculptor Beverly Pepper interviewed applicants for the job of housekeeper, she required that they sing for her and only hired them if their voices were pleasing and they were in the habit of singing at their work.)

Not Enough Jeopardy

Margaret's sweet soprano filled the house, drove away its hospital atmosphere. In no time, we were all well. But being ill had masked the events of the last month. Every night while I was sick, Ben came home from RKO with bulletins: On November 24–25, the studio heads met at New York's Waldorf Astoria. Although men like Zanuck, Mayer, and Dore Schary seemed determined to protect the "unfriendly" witnesses whom they had under contract, the New York–based executives, Skouras (Fox), Schenk (MGM), and Rathvon (RKO) had a view based on profit and loss. They insisted on firing "defiant" employees. They pointed to the American Legion's threat of boycott, newspaper editorials turning against the Ten, and the fact that an audience had actually stoned a film starring Katharine Hepburn, a staunch supporter of the Committee for the First Amendment. Of course, for legal reasons, the studios couldn't say they were firing the Ten because they were Communists, but simply that their behavior had brought public disapproval. Only Sam Goldwyn protested that these matters were "not weighty enough to justify a blacklist of ten screen artists."[1]

Dore Schary, who couldn't bear to do it himself, had another executive fire Adrian and Eddie. Zanuck's assistant dismissed Ring Lardner, Jr. By December 1, the five of the Ten who had been employed were as jobless as the other five who had no hope of finding work.

Ironically, Johnny Weber phoned to say he had an offer of $35,000 for *The Locket* from actor Hume Cronyn, who was thinking of producing it himself but had no definite plans. We were not offered a studio job to write the screenplay. Still, Johnny recommended we take the deal, since selling a story after the studios announced a blacklist was a terrific victory. I, particularly, felt heartened about my writing. *The Locket* was the second story for the screen I'd sold in two years.

Of course, I didn't know then that Hume Cronyn would sell it to RKO and that they would make it with top stars, Laraine Day, Robert Mitchum, Gene Raymond, and Brian Aherne. Nor could I guess that RKO would give credit only to Sheridan Gibney for the screenplay, as if the story had sprung like Athena from Zeus's head—or Sheridan Gibney's head. How in the world could I have dreamt that no matter how Gibney changed the story, what the critics liked about *The Locket,* and what made it a classic, was what I'd created and fought for?

"Consciously Freudian in its approach, *The Locket*'s source of continuing fascination is in its pattern of narrative construction that mirrors the heroine—a chronic and disarming liar. Flashbacks within flashbacks within flashbacks. Does the flashback provide an explanation for action or does it avoid an explanation for action? Each revelation of the past renders the present more opaque."[2]

We spent Christmas Eve with Adrian and Annie at the Lees' as we usually did, helping Bobby and Jeannie trim the tree. We weren't sad. We were defiant. Adrian was sure the Ten would win in the courts.

Ben couldn't stand the idea of a Christmas tree in our house. For him, it was like a crucifix. "Why don't we wear tiny guillotines or electric chairs on a chain around our necks?" he joshed. But gradually, I had accustomed him to the idea of a nice young Jewish couple, Bobby and Jeannie, having a tree. (Ben didn't care if I'd grown up with one every year, some in hotel lobbies.) Nineteen forty-seven was the first Christmas Ben permitted me a little tree on a table. He wanted to see the wonder in the eyes of Luli and Johnny. On Christmas morning, Margaret, Ben, and I got them up in their sleepers and showed them the shimmering tree surrounded by their presents, his on the right, hers on the left, and helped them open their gifts. Johnny loved the wrapping paper and ribbon as much as the toys. Luli, pleased with her gifts, took her father's hand and tried to lead him to the side of the living room. He didn't know what she was doing. She pulled him to the paneled door to the den and commanded him to open.

"There are no presents in there," Ben said, worried. "I'm sorry, Luli, that's all the presents there are, the ones you found under the tree."

"Open," she insisted, tugging at him. "Open, open."

Ben opened the door. My Christmas present to Ben was a completely and surreptitiously furnished den so he'd have an office and wouldn't have to work in the living room. Comfortable and tweedy, it had a divan with cushions for a nap, desk and desk chair, a big easy chair, lamps, bookcases, his books, and all around his favorite photographs . . . even one of his idol, Monty, the psych professor he'd had at Reed.

I could see Ben was moved. "Hell!" he said. "Maybe I'll wind up liking Christmas."

Margaret, warm and happy in the robe I'd picked out for her, asked with a wide grin, "The Missus really had you fooled, Mr. Barzman, didn't she?"

Ben and I greeted the New Year at a party for the Ten at Lucey's, the movie hangout near Paramount and RKO. It was mostly Party people, few of the old liberal friends. Nevertheless, that night we managed to raise several thousand dollars. Like Adrian, everyone was certain we'd win in the courts. We toasted 1948 with champagne.

Long before he was fired, Adrian had asked Ben if he wanted Al Levitt,[3] a new young writer, to collaborate with him on *The Boy with Green Hair*. Al, a sweet bright guy, had taught my class in story editing at the School for Writers when he was a story editor at Paramount.

At the beginning of their collaboration, they agreed that the boy, played by Dean Stockwell, should steal some apples. Ben suggested that they each go home and write the scene and bring it back the next day. Al had been brought up in New York City. In his scene, the boy passes the grocery store and steals apples from a crate. Ben, who was from the country, had the boy climb a tree and steal the apples from the low branches. They compared notes, had a good laugh, and were relaxed with each other after that.

Al didn't mind that Ben took the helm. He told me he enjoyed working with him. The script turned out well. They all liked it: the Technicolor executive who'd been hired to replace Adrian as producer; Adrian, no longer at the studio but to whom Ben brought each scene; Dore Schary; and Joe Losey, who was to direct.

It was Joe Losey's first film and he kept Ben on the set, asking his advice. Every day Ben came home with a tale of how Joe had angered the crew. The production manager complained, "There's this plastic runway that has to shine to show off Technicolor. There's Joe waving a mop to show the man who was supposed to be wielding the mop. The guy takes the mop and throws it at Joe. 'Here, you do it!' So Joe's mopping the goddamn runway and doing everything else there is to do."

Despite being unable to delegate any job, Joe got the film shot in thirty-four days, the fastest anyone had ever made a film in color. Joe told me afterward that one of the things that bothered him on the picture was that he had to be cruel to the boy to get him to cry. Yet all he did was get Dean to think about the saddest thing that had ever happened to him, which was the death of his kitten. It's interesting that Joe thought he was being cruel. Vittorio De Sica confessed to our daughter Luli, when she was working as his assistant, that he'd put a burning cigarette in the pocket of the boy in *The Bicycle Thief* to get him to cry.

While *The Boy with Green Hair* was shooting, eccentric Howard Hughes bought RKO and its theaters for $9 million. The result was disastrous both for the studio and for the film. Most of RKO's staff resigned. In the next six years, Hughes lost $40 million on the studio.

Hughes hated the pacifist message of *The Boy* and did what he could to sabotage it. At one point, he called Pat O'Brien and Dean Stockwell into his office. The child was terrified.

Hughes said to Dean, "Now listen, boy. You know where the orphan kid says to you that war's no good for children?"

Dean nodded.

"Well, I want you to say, 'And that's why America has gotta have the biggest army, and the biggest navy, and the biggest air force in the world!' You got that, boy?"

Dean thought about it for a couple of minutes, then said, "No, sir."

"No, sir!?" A twelve-year-old kid, to one of the most powerful men in the industry! When he couldn't sway the child, Hughes started to scream. O'Brien would have been willing to do anything, according to Ben. Not Dean. He damn well knew what the film was about, and believed in it. Ben said he and Joe pretended they were responding to Hughes's "directives" but that Joe was careful to shoot the picture in such a way that there was no possibility for change.[4]

Hughes remained unhappy with the result, spent $100,000 in an unsuccessful attempt to get the line that Dean wouldn't say inserted into the film, but couldn't; gave the film a token release, then withdrew it, and shelved it for six months to lose all the good of the publicity campaign.

The *New Yorker* critic and a few others didn't like the film's sentimentality but audiences loved *The Boy with Green Hair,* which became a classic.

In fall 1948, Ben was still working but the town swarmed with rumors of new subpoenas. One night, Ben and I heard strange sounds from the kitchen. Knowing Margaret had already gone off to bed, we nervously went together to investigate. The kitchen was empty and quiet, but we heard scratching on the back door. A U.S. marshal? A coyote? Ben pushed me back to shield me, opened the door slightly, and peered out.

Tense and agitated, and heavily into cloak-and-dagger, Bernie Vorhaus, with a three-day beard, looked around furtively. He was a tall, good-looking, nervous man with an impressive repertoire of tics, one causing his mouth to move in and out like a trumpet player doing lip exercises. When his lips were in a full-extended pout, he seemed to be asking for a kiss. Ben joked that this tic was pronounced when I was around. I didn't think Bernie attractive.

Bernie was a phenomenon of that period. A significant number of films produced consisted of B pictures that had to be made for under $100,000, no mean feat even then. The studios still owned separate strings of theaters where they distributed their own product. The $100,000 films had a guaranteed take of $125,000 no matter what. Thus, if a studio made forty B films a year, they had an annual profit of a million dollars, providing they were brought in on budget, which meant they had to be turned out in seven shooting days, a frantic, backbreaking pace. Men like Vorhaus, able to deliver these eight-day-wonders one after the other, were considered national treasures by the studios. Although most of these films were trash, a surprising number of Vorhaus's were good, like *The Spiritualist,* a film noir.

"Did something happen?" Ben asked Bernie.

"Not only has the shit hit the electric fan but it's aimed smack at us."

Bernie held up one long slender finger. "We've got to get over the feeling we're anointed."

Ben and I were baffled.

"Anointed," he explained, "that by some special dispensation, we will be spared. That it happened to Adrian and Eddie and Lester and Herbert, but that it won't happen to us. Well, it will. I've heard a whisper they're after us. You"—pointing to Ben—"and me"—pointing to himself. "You guys know how it works?" He sounded like an executioner about to explain to a condemned man how the electric chair worked. "A United States marshal suddenly pops up at the door, asks if you are you, you say yes, hands you a subpoena to appear—"

"Bernie, we know all that," Ben protested.

"Hear me out," he went on relentlessly. "Once the Committee has you, they question you. 'Are you now or have you ever been a member of the Communist Party?' Congress has passed the Smith Act. It makes membership in the Party illegal."

"The Act is unconsti—"

Ben cut me off. "Only when the Supreme Court says it is."

"They will," I said.

The Supreme Court did in fact declare the Smith Act unconstitutional, but not for another year.

"Refusal to present yourself will be considered contempt of Congress," Bernie continued. "One year in a federal prison. If you admit anything, like attending meetings, not only do you brand yourself subversive but from then on, the Committee has a right to demand you give them a complete list of all the people who were at those meetings."

"Either you turn stool pigeon or you lose everything," I said impatiently.

"People who refuse to answer and stand on the Fifth Amendment are immediately fired by the studios," Ben said thoughtfully. "Besides, that leaves the implication they were guilty of something—"

Bernie stared hard at us. Perhaps he felt we didn't look sufficiently scared. "Maybe you think you can simply refuse the subpoena?"

"That's a year in jail," I retorted. "You didn't stop by to scare the hell out of us. You must have some idea."

"Where was I?" Bernie asked.

"We were all doing a year in a federal penitentiary," I said.

"Let's say a marshal appears with one of those pink subpoenas and tries to hand it to me, and I say 'Who, me? You've got the wrong guy!' "

"One year in the federal can," Ben said. "We've been through that."

"No," Bernie said carefully, "maybe not."

"For heaven's sake, Bernie!" I was beginning to be angry. "Have you or have you not an idea?"

"You're sure you want to stand up to them?" Bernie asked. "It means your job, your house, the nursery school, your housekeeper, your cars. Most of your friends will leave you."

"We're always sounding off on high moral values," Ben said. "This is our moment of truth. Probably the one time in our lives we'll be put to the test. Why do I feel like I'm speaking my last words?"

"They may be," Bernie replied. "Last words as what you are. Well-paid, well-regarded members of the most glamorous community in the world."

"We haven't harmed anybody or anything," I burst out in frustration. "What the hell do they really want?"

"They want the spectacle, the fabulous publicity. Now they've even got television cameras. Think of the excitement watching an uncooperative witness being called a traitor, fired from a high-paying job, cast out of his community. If the Romans had had TV, what a spectacle that would have made. Christians being ripped apart by lions—or even a crucifixion."

"Bernie!" I had to call him back. He was in ancient Rome. "You have an idea how we can beat this?"

Bernie returned from the Coliseum. "I've met with others in the same situation. We concluded the thing for us to do is duck subpoenas. Give 'em as few victims as possible."

"Leave town?" I demanded.

"Hell, no," Bernie said irritably. "Give up without a fight?"

I picked up my favorite stolen ashtray, ready to hurl it at him. "Bernie—your idea?"

"Well, when the man comes to the door with that pink paper and asks you, are you Bernard Vorhaus, you naturally say 'No, I'm not Bernard Vorhaus'—which is the truth. Right?"

I wondered if Bernie was losing his marbles.

"But why in hell would a man with a pink paper knock on my door and ask me if I'm you?" Ben demanded.

"Or come to my door and ask me if I'm you?" Bernie went on.

"Right," Ben said. "Why?"

"Simple," Bernie said. "We change houses."

A big long heavy silence.

"Our houses are almost identical." Bernie began to itemize: "We have two kids, a boy and a girl, you have a boy and a girl, we have Lorraine (their black housekeeper), you have Margaret. You have a Kerry blue (Kerry had returned from his wanderings, older and wiser). We have a cocker spaniel. So you move into our house. We move into yours. Then when the marshal comes to your door and asks if we're you, we tell the truth. We say we're not."

Another heavy silence.

"You may have something there," Ben said thoughtfully. "They're not serving subpoenas on studio property."

"Why not?" I asked.

"Might make the studios part of a conspiracy to blacklist," Bernie replied. "They could be sued."

"What about phone calls?" I had already moved on and was facing practical contingencies. "We get your calls. You'll get ours. Our phones are tapped. What do we say?"

"Right, right," Bernie cut me off. "Just say I've gone location hunting. Leave a message. Mr. Vorhaus will call you back. All calls we get, we'll say you've gone to Arrowhead for a few days. If the man actually comes with the subpoena, we let each other know immediately."

"When do we make this move?" I asked.

"Tonight," Bernard replied. "Goddamn it! It's an emergency."

Ben thought a minute. "We could move at once—"

I shot him a look.

When we were ready, Bernie coached us, we were to ring three times and wait. He would ring us back three times. We would then start moving.

We exchanged keys. All at once, it became real and frightening.

Bernie said, "An ex-Cliffie like Norma must be good at throwing a few things together in a hurry. Like for a last-minute weekend—"

"Bernie!" I glared at him. "This is a far cry from Harvard-Yale weekend—"

"What I meant was," Bernie was fast on his feet, "this is good practice. From now on, we may be constantly moving in a hurry." All at once, he put down his drink and left.

"He seems to know what he's doing," I said.

"Bernie spent the war in the Army. They used to say of him, 'Major Vorhaus got on his horse and rode off in all four directions at once.' "

"What can we lose?" I said.

"Nothing," Ben replied. "We're in the middle of a hot spell and they have a pool."

Margaret Heatherington, obviously aware something was up, waited in the kitchen for us. "Kids just won't get to sleep. Nervous or something. Guess it's the heat and all."

"Maybe it's just as well they're awake. We're changing houses with the Vorhauses tonight."

Margaret didn't bat an eye. "How long will we be staying?" she asked.

"A few days," I told her casually, "a week. Maybe ten days."

"I'll get their stuff ready." Margaret went off without further comment.

"Maybe she understands," I said.

"It's probably not the first time she's changed houses. They're used to process servers."

Almost immediately, it was obvious that Ben, Bernie, and I had sorely underestimated the enormous strains involved in moving two small children, three adults, and a dog. The bare necessities turned out to be far from bare. Johnny needed Blinky-Blanket, Luli needed her doll Squeechy, but writers are the hardest to move. They never know what books, which scripts they will need.

"People will think we're escaping from the heat," I said as we all waited in the living room for Bernie's three rings. Uneasiness gave way to apprehension, which began to get through to the kids. Ben waited long after the third ring of three, made a dumb show of picking up the receiver. "Funny. No one there."

Margaret and I moved into action. Johnny, inexplicably, burst into frightened sobs. Margaret held him close and shushed him till he stopped crying and we climbed into our overloaded Chrysler.

In four or five minutes, we were on the Vorhaus hill, a few blocks farther up Sunset. Thirteen twenty-five North Wetherly Drive was the only house on the hill extravagantly illuminated. Bernie had left all the lights on for us. The unloading and settling were done quickly. The house had a pool, but the inside of the house was no cooler than ours.

The kids were finally persuaded to fall asleep in their new beds in a room almost identical to their own except that Gwynneth's first blobs of color had been framed in red whereas Luli's had been simply encased in glass. Hetty had provided the same toys for the boy as for the girl (dolls for both) as we had done. The disc player was exactly like ours; all the child had to do was slide in a record to play it. The same records, *Chirkendoose*—it's not a chicken, turkey, duck, or goose, it's a chirkendoose; and Nat King Cole singing "Kemo Kimo." Fortunately, we didn't bring the children's musical rocking chairs. Gwynny and David had them, too. The only difference seemed to be that instead of Guatemala hangings, they had Mexican folk art.

After the children were asleep, we explored. The pool was enclosed by a wire fence and a locked gate. It could be carefully watched from the kitchen. Hetty had posted a long list of no-no's, such as "no glasses at the pool"—which she'd signed forcefully with a flourish, Hetty Vorhaus.

As Ben and I took in the intimate details of their living arrangements, our picture of the Vorhauses changed considerably. The dressing room housed a small fridge stocked with ice cubes, cheese, caviar, candy bars, champagne, beer, and Coca-Cola. Between the king-size bed and the working fireplace stretched a tiger skin complete with head. A small table was invitingly set with two glasses, bottles of vermouth and gin, a jar of pickled onions. We first assumed it was a gesture of welcome from Bernie and Hetty (one that we'd neglected to make), but no, their Lorraine had simply gone through the nocturnal ritual of setting up their nightly martinis. Small bookcases, one on each side of the bed, overflowed with a selection of books about sex: *The Kama Sutra,* a beautifully illustrated Japanese *Pillow Book, Nights in a Perfumed Garden,* and a wide variety of sex manuals, several in Swedish.

"What if Bernie has to testify and reporters get into this place. Quite a story—no?"

"We have laws about privacy," Ben said smugly.

I shrugged. "Reporters never heard of them."

We had martinis. I wasn't counting. They were so conveniently located, and what with the frenzy of getting settled, later the sex manuals and related activities, I forgot to remind Ben to go down to the Strip and call his mother from a pay phone. I didn't have to worry about my mother. She would never call at night, and she slept late. I had plenty of time to phone her in the morning from Sunbee and tell her of the house-swapping.

That oversight about Mumma, Ben's mother, sent off a chain reaction of confusions. It had taken several years to know my mother-in-law. She was a quiet, retiring person with a lot of angst that she was entitled to. Russian-Jewish, she'd escaped from pogrom-ridden czarist Russia. Pogrom is a Russian word meaning "massacre," but for Mumma and thousands like her, it meant specifically the massacre of Jews by Cossacks. She managed to elude the Cossacks across most of western Russia and a good piece of Europe with two small children, a samovar, and almost no money, then cross the Atlantic and rejoin Ben's father, a trumpet player who deserted from the czar's army and got himself to Toronto.

Mumma had a deep mistrust of almost everything. Who would send her a telegram for other than a catastrophe? In Canada, she'd been right. Nor had she made her peace with the telephone; she'd worked out a way to live with it. Disuse. No long gossipy Angeleno calls for her.

Just as the Vorhauses were unloading at our house, the phone rang and their Lorraine, who loved to answer the phone, said, in a charming voice, "Hello, how may I help you?"

Isn't that what nurses say, thought Mumma, who decided there was something strange afoot and it was imperative to get to the bottom of it.

"I want to speak to my son."

"Who?"

"My son!"

Lorraine passed the phone to Bernie. "Who is it?" he asked in a hoarse whisper, which confirmed what Mumma feared, that Ben was sick with a sore throat.

"It's your mother."

"I have no mother."

Frantic burbles emanating from the receiver were Mumma imploring someone to speak to her.

Hetty grabbed the phone. "He's fine. We're all fine."

"You may be fine. It's my son I'm worried about."

"He's not home just now. He's been detained."

"He's in jail?"

"No, no, nothing like that."

Now Mumma was ready to settle for a major accident. There were, after all, good doctors. "What hospital is he in?"

"Oh, no. He's not in the hospital—"

"Why not?"

"Because he's not sick."

Bernie took the phone away from Hetty. "I'm a friend of the family."

"Who comes when there's a terrible accident or death," she asked, "but a friend of the family? Let me speak to my daughter-in-law."

"She's not here right now."

"Oh, my God! She was in the car too—and the children?"

"Car?"

"Accident car?"

Hetty picked up the phone again. "Your son is absolutely fine. He'll call you in three minutes."

Not Enough Jeopardy

Bernie then called Ben with a Russian accent, and Ben called his sister Anne and had her telephone their mother and reassure her all was well.

Ben told me that I snored through all this, but he couldn't get back to sleep, he was too caught up in *Straight Talk about Sex.*

Days went by. The hot spell kept up. We were enjoying the pool. Luli was learning to swim. Nobody was surprised when toward noon on one of the hottest days, Bernie and his son, David, were seen trudging up the hill to their house, which we were in. They didn't come by car for fear they'd be followed. Hot and weary, they came to the back door.

Bernie asked in a whimper, "Do you think we could have a swim?"

"Of course," I replied, "it's your pool."

In a few days, the heat had left us, the slim-jims hadn't come, and Ben said, "Maybe we should go home."

We packed carefully and were ready early, the children round-eyed and solemn, for some reason choosing to sit on their personal valises the way wartime refugees always seem to.

The only thing I stole from the Vorhauses' was one of the sex manuals, *Six Positions You May Not Have Tried.* I don't think many people tried them. They seemed to involve the risk of serious spinal dislocation.

We made the move with absolutely no incident. I doubt the Vorhauses' neighbors even suspected we'd spent a week there.

On Sunset Plaza Drive, we turned into our driveway. If anyone noticed the loaded car, it could have been our return from an impromptu vacation to escape the heat.

But that evening just as we'd finished unpacking, the doorbell chimed. Ben and I peeked out cautiously from our upstairs window. We descended slowly. Margaret stood hesitant. I said, "I'll get it, Margaret."

"Don't you do that," Margaret said. "Go out the back! I'll meet you later with my car. I can just say you're not here."

"No," Ben said.

I thought of Bernie and how he'd said it was dangerous to consider ourselves anointed.

"Is there an alternative?" I asked. "Take it. We'll get it over with. It'll be a relief."

"I'll be fired," Ben said. We'd heard dozens of desperate stories of unemployed friends trying to find any kind of work.

"I told you. We'll live through this."

The chimes rang again. Not too impatiently but with polite insistence. It was nine-thirty. They must have known we had small children.

Ben took a deep breath and opened the door.

A neat blue suit with a snap-brim and a slim-jim tie (he was almost exactly as I'd pictured he would be) stood there. The young man's face lit up as he saw Ben.

"I'm sure glad you came to the door in person," he said. "You and your wife looking us over from upstairs. We thought maybe—"

"Strangers seldom ring our doorbell at this hour."

"Oh, sure, sure," he said with the utmost friendliness, even smiled. "I don't mind telling you, you led us a merry chase. But we finally figured it out." He caught himself abruptly, obviously he was talking more than he needed to. "We've got something for you, Mr. Vorhaus."

We were stunned.

Several seconds later, Ben asked, "For whom?"

"Vorhaus," he repeated. "V-o-r-h-a-u-s." He reached into an inside pocket and pulled out a pink subpoena, which he handed to Ben ceremoniously.

Ben scrutinized it with great interest, read down to the place where it said "Bernard Vorhaus," then leaned over in a friendly way to the slim-jim. "You want somebody named Vorhaus."

"That's right," the slim-jim said.

Ben handed him back the subpoena. "I'm not Vorhaus."

At first, he wouldn't take it back.

"Are you claiming you're not Bernard Vorhaus?"

"Claiming?" Ben said irritably. "I'm stating. You've got the wrong man."

The slim-jim's face hardened. "We've wasted a lot of time on you. Now it happens, Mr. Vorhaus, it's a federal offense, one year in prison, to deny your identity to a U.S. marshal. I'm a U.S. marshal."

"I'm pleased to make your acquaintance," Ben said handing him the subpoena, "but it so happens that I'm not Bernard Vorhaus."

Not Enough Jeopardy

The young man's eyes swept over Ben from head to toe like a heavy-duty vacuum cleaner, then over at me. "You're not Bernard Vorhaus?" he demanded in outrage.

"Yes," Ben said, "I'm not Bernard Vorhaus," and started to close the door. The slim-jim stuck his foot in the jamb, consulted some notes. His companion got out of the car, joined him, pulled out a pencil-slim flashlight, and focused it on the notes. Ben turned on the outside light to help them. "You affirm you are not Bernard Vorhaus?" the first one asked.

"Yes, yes, I do indeed," Ben said, turning away from them and closing the door. Through the window we watched. The slim-jims got in their car, spoke a moment, and shot off. Ben and I hugged. "My God!" I said, "We won!"

"We don't know for how long. We've got to warn Bernie there's a sub-poena out for him—"

The slim-jims had thought we were living at Sunset Plaza Drive, then found we'd exchanged houses. They'd discovered the exchange just when we changed back. Perfect timing. One of the few plans Bernie ever conceived that worked. Possibly, just possibly, the slim-jims' confusion would make them think twice before trying again. And maybe Bernie was wrong. Maybe we *were* anointed.

10

They Went Thataway

When the slim-jims failed to reappear, we began to go about our normal lives.

Around 8:30 A.M. every weekday, Ben drove to RKO, where he was writing *The Boy with Green Hair* in collaboration with Al Levitt. (Adrian was no longer at the studio but Ben consulted regularly with him, not with the Technicolor executive who'd been hired to substitute for Adrian.) At 9 A.M. I delivered Luli to the psychoanalyst-run School for Nursery Years. Johnny, I took to a new modern house designed by a Neutra protégé who'd turned it over to our cooperative nursery group. His wife had the same problem as I, her eighteen-month-old wanted Mommy nearby at all times. I remained all morning, changed their pants, blew their noses, comforted them. Johnny didn't seem to mind as long as I was in view.

Early in World War II, before I even contemplated having children, the importance of good nursery education had become clear. Without it, women war workers would not have been able to do the job. Patsy Moore, radio writer Sam Moore's wife, and many other Communist women led the fight in Sacramento for Lanham Act Funds to pay for nursery care. The result of our struggle was twofold. We achieved model state-supported nursery schools and, more important, practically wiped out absenteeism from our war plants and shipyards. When Rosie the Riveter came to work knowing her child was well looked after, her productivity went up.

I was working on an original for the screen, *Amnesia.* I got the idea from a true story Dashiell Hammett told my cousin Henry. A safe falling from a great height to the sidewalk below lands only a few feet from a pedestrian. The man suddenly thinks: I could be dead. Is that all there is? Horrified by his average suburban life, nice house, nice wife, two nice children, and membership in the country club, he disappears and is not heard of for years, when he's found in another northwestern state in a nice suburban home with a nice wife, two nice children, and a membership in the country club.

If the safe had hit him but not killed him, I mused, he might have amnesia, and even with a second chance might not have the imagination to construct something different. What if he got knocked in the head again, came out of the amnesia, and discovered his folly? Now he's a man with two nice suburban families! That's both dramatic and comedic. When *Amnesia* didn't sell, I went to work on another original, *Young Woman with Ideas,* based on my sister's experiences as a young lawyer.

From the time Howard Hughes bought RKO, he made Dore Schary's life insufferable. Schary resigned to become head of production at MGM, and took Ben and Al Levitt with him to work on a Lana Turner vehicle, *The Wild Country,* from a mediocre Louis Bromfield novel. Ben accepted the assignment because it was for Dore and because Johnny Weber got him his first ever "thousand a week." Although Ben had agreed to collaborate with me on the original, he came home each night weary and irritable. One evening he came back from the studio, stared at my desk, where I'd been working all afternoon, and, like a B producer, queried, "Where are the pages?"

I laughed but Ben could see I was miffed. He invited me to lunch at the MGM commissary. It flashed through my mind that perhaps it was also because he would never again be able to ask me to lunch at a studio—that's how we were thinking in November 1948.

A receptionist at the entrance to the sepulchral Thalberg Building announced me. Ben came hurrying down and took me up in the elevator.

"I came down to get you," he explained, "because I wanted to show you the girl who sits opposite the third floor elevators."

"Look," he whispered when the elevator doors opened.

Across from us was the girl. She was beautiful, made up, coiffed and dressed as if about to have a screen test. She sat at a large, bare, circular desk decorated by a vase of flowers and nothing else.

Ben grinned. "You can't say she's a receptionist. She doesn't have a phone."

"What does she do?"

"Nothing," he replied. "She *must* do nothing. She's not even permitted to read a book."

"How come?"

"When Cedric Gibbons redecorated the Thalberg Building, he drew a desk here with a beautiful girl. She's part of the decor. You saw. The receptionist downstairs has the phone."

I watched the beautiful girl do nothing with style. "Poor thing!" I said.

"It's worse than that." Ben laughed. "When she goes to lunch, they replace her with another beautiful girl."

In those days, all major studios not only had a commissary where employees could have lunch but there was a special table for each of the major talents: a Directors' Table, a Producers' Table, a Writers' Table, and of course, a special Executive Dining Room off by itself where the top studio brass dined in isolated splendor.

"And over there," Ben said, "at the Producers' Table, Arthur Hornblow, Jr., has his chauffeur come in each noon with a special hamper of his own linens, silver, and wine, and an intricate contraption that keeps the wine at exactly the right temperature."

After being introduced, Mac Benoff, nicknamed "Jokes," who was hired to add some badly needed humor to an unfunny comedy (never made), leaned over to me, and asked with a wicked leer, "Do you think he inserts a thermometer into his wife to be certain she's the proper temperature before fucking?"

I didn't think that was funny. Neither did Marguerite Roberts. Maggie was one of the few successful women screenwriters and one of the best paid. She'd been under contract to MGM at a huge salary for thirteen years, writing hugely popular films like *Honky Tonk, Dragon Seed, Ziegfeld Girl*, and other moneymakers. Not part of a team, she'd collaborated on one film with her husband, novelist John Sanford, but he decided he preferred to stay home and write books. MGM gave her privileges writers rarely enjoyed: a six-week vacation with pay; she was shown "the rushes"; she was sent on location, attended executive meetings, and was consulted on casting and costume. She rarely lunched at the commissary so I was delighted she was there. I didn't know Maggie well but I knew Henry admired her. Known for her great sense of humor and her ability to get along with macho men, she didn't blush or tug at her skirts when they told their men's stories. Maggie's father was a sheriff and she liked to write westerns.

But very soon she was blacklisted and tossed out of the studio with no credit for scripting *Ivanhoe*. She didn't work again for over a decade. Maggie was admirably suited to write her comeback script, *True Grit*, starring John Wayne as an over-the-hill sheriff. Right-wing Wayne won his only Oscar for a film written by a blacklisted woman!

"I've always worked with men," she told me. "Gable liked my stuff because he didn't take himself seriously."

"Gee," I said, "any hope of Clark Gable turning up here today?"

"I wish he would," Ben said. "He's great. When your cousin Henry was a New York press agent, be discovered Gable, then a struggling actor. Henry and he are close, close enough so that when Henry taps a tooth, it's the cue for Gable to take out his false teeth, grin, turn to everybody, and say, 'See the great movie idol now!' "

"Oh, dear!" I murmured.

"For a while, after Carole Lombard was killed in the plane crash," Maggie said soberly, "Gable didn't make any pictures. He joined the Air Force."

"Norma, there's a movie star for you," Jerry Davis, a comedy writer, cried mischievously, pointing to Margaret O'Brien, then ten or eleven. She had just given one of the most charming performances I'd ever seen in *Meet Me in St. Louis.*

I adored Jerry Davis. He was so handsome nobody believed he was a writer. His actress wife, Nancy Davis, was a May Company heir. Later, when Jerry's Nancy was blacklisted, she, who would later marry Ronald Reagan, made a big stink. There'd been an awful mistake! She, Nancy Davis, couldn't possibly be blacklisted because she and her father were prominent members of the archconservative Birch Society. Apparently, Margaret O'Brien had been told it was a good idea to smile at the writers, so she dutifully stopped at our table and her face lit up. Jerry must have been brooding about the life of a child star because just as O'Brien flashed her ersatz smile, he stuck his tongue out at her. She hadn't been programmed for that. She looked around for help, then fled.

Suddenly, Clark Gable showed up. I throbbed as he approached a table only a few steps away, where, sitting unnoticed and half-hidden, was Spencer Tracy. Both were in their makeup and wore big fat sweaters.

Gable shouted at Tracy, "I hear you're about to make faces," Gable's way of saying the rumor was out that Tracy had finally read a script he liked. That meant the heart of every producer within hearing had stopped as he wondered whether it was the script he was developing.

In the long silence that ensued, Tracy answered, "It's possible, possible. What about you, King?"

Gable replied with a grimace, "It's possible, possible," so that no one was sure whether he meant it or had just been mimicking Tracy.

After my last commissary lunch for thirty years, well stuffed with stardust, I was ready to be whisked back to Ben's office, where he made me read some awful junk he'd just been writing.

The phone rang. Ben picked up the receiver. "Tell him to come up." To me he said, "It's Eddie Dmytryk. A wonder they let him in." Eddie had been fired from RKO a year earlier and was on the official studio blacklist.

Surprised I was there, and maybe none too happy about it, Eddie kissed me, shook hands with Ben, and put the book he was carrying on the desk with a flourish.

"*Christ in Concrete*," he said.

I'd read it when it came out in 1939, my sophomore year in college. My English prof had called it "one of the few American proletarian novels." Written by a young, unschooled Italian-American mason, Pietro di Donato, I remembered it as a savage, tender story of the life and death of the author's father and of the lives of di Donato's beloved *paesanos,* the newly arrived Italian immigrants of the 1920s. It was about the Depression and all the things that had made many of us turn to socialism; it was a cry of outrage against exploitation. Its lyricism and its fury gave the story stature.

"It's a beautiful book, Eddie," I said.

"Ben, read it," Eddie commanded. "I want you to adapt it—do a screenplay."

"How could I? I'm in the middle of a screenplay for Dore."

"Read it, Ben. You'll see that it will make a magnificent film."

"Impossible," Ben replied. "I don't have any time. It's all I can do to squeeze a movie out of this piece of shit."

"You'll do it nights and weekends," Eddie stated matter-of-factly. "We'll get it made in England. I have reason to believe that the British don't look favorably on the American political scene. I'm telling you." He turned to Ben and said with a kind of grim confidence, "Just read the book." Ben read the book, and, of course, loved it. I reread it and loved it more than ever. It would make an unusual and daring film that would say what needed to be said. But those were reasons why it would never be made, or so Ben thought at the time.

He wrestled with himself. I'd seen him struggle before on one or two occasions, but not quite like this. If it was made in Britain, it would be a minor victory. Yet defeating HUAC on any level was a major coup.

Ben was full of fears. Besides his theatrical superstitions—being anxious his hat might land on a bed—his mother's pessimism, superstitions, and apprehensions had infected him. I had seen how convinced he was that neither of us would get a job until Blatas's painting was out of our house. Years later, Ben was gratified to find Vittorio De Sica even more superstitious than he was. If someone wearing purple, which De Sica considered unlucky, came into sight, he had to excuse himself and squeeze his left testicle.

Ben's mother said *Kinnehora,* Yiddish for "no evil eye," after every other word. "What a beautiful child! *Kinnehora.*" When a kid graduated or a baby was born, *Kinnehora!* to take the jinx off the congratulations. Mumma and her children, especially Ben, lived in fear that anything good would be taken away. Ben could not admit to happiness because he believed the evil eye would see and destroy it. He tried to stay low profile. Years later, when hopes for socialism and a more equitable world were gone, for Ben it proved that even if you struggled for good, it wasn't worth it. It would be taken away.

The screenplay of *Christ in Concrete,* if he was to take it on, would be a tremendous responsibility and an enormous risk. We both saw the effort it would require and the miracles that would have to occur to take the book to the screen.

From time to time, Ben talked to me, thinking aloud. "Even if I did it, and I don't know how, but if I did, how can Eddie promote the money to make the film?"

"But if it *is* done," I said, "do you realize what that would mean? Blacklisted guys getting *Christ in Concrete* made? It's just about the best thing we could do for everyone. Not just for Eddie. For *everyone.* For ourselves too."

"You talk as if it could be done."

"I don't know any other way to think about it."

Most of the time, Ben was depressed and anguished. On rereading the book, he realized, as I had, that it was a series of vivid sketches, loosely strung together—vignettes of di Donato's father's life and of his mother's life after his father's brutal death. No story held it together.

"Ben," I said, "a very young man wrote about his father's agonizing death, which should never have happened. It appeared as a short piece in *Esquire* so beautifully written, so moving, that a publisher asked Pietro to lengthen it into a book. He didn't know how. But the strength of its being real and human made it into a classic. Instead of feeling sick about it, start thinking of a story. A lonely Italian worker in the States sends for a wife from the old country that he's never seen. A young woman leaves her home in Italy, takes a long voyage to the unknown to be wed to a man she's never met. They fall in love, have children. But disaster awaits them."

"That doesn't help," he groaned, picking up the book again.

That was late Friday night. The next morning, Saturday, Ben got up early, dressed, barely played with Luli and Johnny, went into the tweedy study, sat at his desk, stared at a sheet of blank paper, the lonely screenwriter, blocked.

When I brought Luli and Johnny back from the Beverly Park ponies (where the giant eight-story Beverly Center mall is now, on the edge of Beverly Hills), Ben was still staring at the same blank piece of paper. I didn't envy him. I wanted to write movies, but I was glad it wasn't me sitting there.

Sunday, Margaret's day off, I took the kids to Griffith Park, Johnny in his Taylor Tot, Luli walking stiffly at my side until, ready to drop, she climbed onto his buggy and I pushed the two of them.

On my return, Ben was still sitting there, a wild look on his face. "I can't do this," he screamed.

Luli and Johnny were so tired from the zoo, they fell asleep during Nat King Cole's "Kemo Kimo." When I came downstairs, Ben was pacing. "There's a man coming over," he announced. "Says his name is Rod Geiger and that he's going to produce *Christ in Concrete.*"

During World War II, Geiger, an American G.I. who had moved into Rome with the liberating forces and stayed on, was like a marvelous character in *All Quiet on the Western Front,* a sergeant who had a sixth sense for divining food, water, women, or shelter miles away.

Geiger happened to be in Rome when Roberto Rossellini was trying to shoot what became the classic *Open City.* World War II had just ended. Italy was short of everything, even raw film stock. Rod managed to get hold of enough odds and ends of unexposed film clips from the U.S. Signal Corps to keep Rossellini supplied with sufficient raw stock to shoot a film.

Rod also got his hands on enough lire to keep Rossellini and crew from starving. Because of the film shortage, Rossellini had been obliged to print his first take every time. Whatever he shot on his first take was it. Intentional or not, the film had a raw, overpowering, newsreel-like quality, superbly suited to the subject. Italian Neo-Realism had just been born.

Open City liberated the motion picture from the fantasized romance, which had been its stock in trade. Hollywood, with its emphasis on lighting, makeup, and artificial beauty, had been the chief culprit. *Open City* showed the world what film could communicate once it was released from the beauty parlor and went out into the real world.

After Ben's description of the sort of thing Geiger had pulled off, I expected someone slick. But no, the individual at the door was a rosy, moon-faced, angelic-looking chap with a few wisps of sandy hair smashed down diagonally on his forehead. He radiated confidence. It wasn't long before he was assuring us, "You'll lick this. We'll make this film." What endeared him to me immediately was his complete lack of machismo, probably due to his being married to one of the world's top designers, Katya of Sweden.

"Do you have the money to make it?" I asked.

"That's never worried me before," he answered. "All I need is a good script." He had us believing him.

He took out a many-paged contract. "It just says that if we get the money for the picture on the basis of your screenplay, you will have the same remuneration you are receiving from MGM—it's only fair. I asked Eddie what you were getting." Geiger took out a fountain pen and signed solemnly. "You can sign if you like," he said. "It won't mean anything unless we go into production."

It *was* a meaningless piece of paper, since it indicated no specific date by which Geiger would pay the money, but it was a generous contract and included all expenses.

Ben signed. I wondered if he would now, suddenly, be able to write the script.

Geiger left about 10 P.M. Ben went back to the study, and I, done in from the zoo, collapsed into bed. I slept for what I thought was several hours and woke with a start. Ben wasn't in the bed by my side. I looked at my watch. Four in the morning. I got up, saw a light, made tea, brought two cups of tea to his study. He was playing out a scene with himself, in the most god-awful, corny, broken English with a fake Italian accent like Chico Marx. "It'sa notta my fault. I tella you what. I'm notta thata kinda guy—"

"What are you doing?" I asked.

"I'm practicing talking like Pietro's characters."

"They don't talk like that," I said. "Pietro's characters are speaking Italian. He simply translated their language into poetic English: 'In the house of Geremio, there is no food.' "

"Oh, my God!" Ben exclaimed, and put his arms around me and kissed me. "They're talking Italian! Not some broken language. They're expressing themselves articulately and colorfully. I was thinking of them as speaking spaghetti English. I don't know why. Of course they're talking Italian. They're men and women of passion, dignity, courage, love, anger, humor—Italian. They're speaking Italian!" and he began to dance the gazotsky.

"It'll be hard," I said, "to convey the music of their native speech without making them seem silly—"

"Yes, that's what I have to do, let them express themselves naturally, avoid any Americanisms. You're right. Now, suddenly, I see them. I know what they're like."

He was excited. Rarely had I seen him so happy. He went back to his desk and began writing.

We didn't have much of a Christmas. I went alone to Bobby and Jeannie's to trim the tree. Adrian and Annie were there but they were very quiet.

In the morning, Ben watched while Luli and Johnny opened their gifts, then returned to his study to work. Margaret, in her new winter coat, and I played with the babies.

Ben wrote and wrote from the moment he came home from the studio until late at night. Yet he seemed less weary. Obsessed, he never talked of anything else. Anyway, there was no time to talk. Once in a while, he'd ask me what would a woman do if her husband stayed out all night, would Annunziata cry in the beginning and then grow strong as she looks at her children? What would I be like if there was no food for Luli and Johnny?

Ben finished the first draft screenplay in record time. He hardly went over it. I had been typing it but not until I read it through did I feel its splendor and its power. I wept softly, and when I'd finished, my weeping became uncontrollable. "It's so—passionate and human," I said, drained.

Ben telephoned Eddie and Geiger, told them to come over. Each sat reading a carbon copy. Neither made a comment, like "It's good," or "It's what we hoped for," or "It's lousy," or "You'll have to change so-and-so." Nothing.

At last Geiger said simply, "We've been sitting around waiting for this. Now we can move."

Eddie translated, "Rod means that now we will immediately fly to London—"

"And we'll give it to an English producing group," Geiger added, "and get their reaction."

Both Ben and I assumed it must be J. Arthur Rank and his large-muscled man striking the huge gong because that was the only "English group" we knew of.

Dmytryk and Geiger left right after Johnny's second birthday, January 21, 1949. Several weeks passed during which Ben tormented himself that they'd said nothing because the screenplay wasn't any good.

"I know *you* think it's good," he accused me, "but you're my wife!"

I understood his fear. It's hard for a writer to know whether what he or she writes is good or bad. "Ben," I said, "I don't tell you everything you write is wonderful. I'm tough!"

He paid no attention. "I'll tell you what went on with those guys," he said. "That script was all they had. They had to go with it. Only a nut like Geiger could dream up bringing a story about the American Depression to British producers."

• • •

Meanwhile, several of our friends had received subpoenas. Ben, sick with fear, was constantly on the lookout for the slim-jims. The joy and satisfaction he'd had while writing the screenplay had vanished. In its place were his usual anxieties. Something had to happen.

On the evening of the tenth of February, as Al and Ben were leaving the studio, Al pointed to two men getting out of an innocuous car. They fit the slim-jim description. Snap-brims. Young.

"Why don't you go back to the office and pretend you're working?" Al suggested. "If they follow me, I'll call you when I get home."

A moment after Ben reached his office, the telephone rang. It might be a trick of the slim-jims to see if he was there. Then they might lie in wait for him until, eventually, he would have to come out. Ben waited, but on the third ring, he picked up. A British operator was asking for him. Overseas calls were unheard-of then. It had to be Geiger. But even if it was good news, maybe the FBI guys were listening. Ben steeled himself. He better watch what he said. Suddenly, corroborating his estimate of the situation, came Rod's voice trying to be casual, "How's the weather?"

"You really want to know how the weather is here?" asked Ben in delight, knowing Rod expected him to say the sun was shining and Rod would be able to say it was raining in London.

"Yes," Rod answered cautiously.

Ben, jubilant, especially since this conversation would put anyone off, replied, "It's snowing. First snowfall in Southern California in thirty years."

Rod repeated, "S N O W?"

By that time, maybe Eddie had figured the FBI would have grown weary, because he came on the line, his voice one notch above casual, which was about as excited as he ever got.

"*He,*" said Eddie meaningfully, "and his associates read it and called us in. 'We want to do it,' he said. 'There's just one question I would like to ask—' I was ready to pee in my pants." Ben, too, at that point was ready to pee in his. "I was sure," Eddie went on, "that the sixty-four-dollar question was coming—Are you now or have you ever been—?

But no, the question was, 'Mr. Dmytryk, do you believe in God?' Well, I thought a moment, and then extending my hand, I replied, 'If I didn't, I do now.' " (When Ben told me what Eddie had said, I thought, Gee! That was the quickest conversion in history!) "At which point," Eddie continued, "he rose, shook my hand, and said, 'Then we shall do your film, Mr. Dmytryk.' "

"Great!" shouted Ben, who had been sweating. "Okay," Eddie had said to Ben. "But they won't do it unless *the writer* comes over here immediately and makes revisions they and the English censor want."

"Hey! I—uh—the writer is in the middle of an assignment."

"Dore will let him off," Dmytryk had shouted back.

"There are other problems. The writer's wife is pregnant. And her mother's not well—"

"Geiger will pay first class for everybody on the next sailing of the *Queen Mary*. Time is of the essence. People have been known to change their minds . . . " Eddie's voice faded away. The connection was gone.

Either Ben, Eddie, and Rod, in their flat-footed way, had fooled the slim-jims or they hadn't been listening. Ben came home without being followed and we talked all night.

To go off like this was crazy and risky. Was it really only for six or eight weeks? The children. How could we drag them out of their routine, away from what they knew, and give them instead instability? And me? Just beginning to make some headway with Zif. How hard would it be for me to travel pregnant? Was it fair to drag Mother around with us, use her as a sort of granny-nanny for the kids? But leaving her behind, alone, was worse. What about my career? I had two credits. No one knew me in Europe and no one would hire me. Ben had a reputation, but could he find film jobs in foreign countries? Worse, we would be deserting our comrades. Was that right? Not to stick it out with them? We had strong ties. Our fellow progressives were closer to us than our brothers and sisters. But how long could one hang around and hide from slim-jims? It was no way to live.

By morning we had decided to go. Ben would talk to Dore and we would each talk to our mothers.

It was not easy to face Dore Schary. He had been good to Ben and was a sympathetic guy. Dore had been a writer himself and he'd struggled, too. He'd started out as an actor in 1930, tried his hand at journalism and publicity, couldn't make it as a playwright, came out to the Coast to see if he could write movies. Finally, in 1938, he shared an Oscar for the original story of *Boys Town*. MGM made him a B producer but he resigned to join Selznick, then left when he was made executive in charge of production at RKO. Under Dore Schary, RKO had a phenomenal record of commercial and artistic successes.

Like many responsible filmmakers at the time, he resented the McCarthy invasion, but in the end, when the choice was between executive splendor or unemployment and community ostracism, he chose to remain an executive. When you make that choice, you change. And he did.

Ben explained that he needed to go to England to see that *Christ in Concrete* was made. It would help to break the blacklist.

"Now? In the middle of a film you're writing for me?"

"Dore, I don't like to leave you in the lurch this way."

"If you do," said Dore Schary, the executive, "even if you're not blacklisted, you'll never work in Hollywood again!"

Dore Schary himself would be brought down in the McCarthy furor. He was fired in 1956 after eight years as head of production at MGM. Eventually he went East and wrote a hit play about Roosevelt called *Sunrise at Campobello,* which won five Tony Awards.

I picked up Mother at the Ambassador Hotel. On the way to the elevator at Bullock's Wilshire, she started toward the perfume department. I stopped her. "You can get Chanel No. 5 in France without duty."

"I'm not going to France."

"Oh, yes, you are," I said. "We're going first to England to make a film and then to France for a vacation." It was the first time I'd articulated it.

"Is it this blacklist business?" she asked, her voice shaking.

"Yes. We can work in England and France. We probably won't be able to work here much longer."

"You're going for good?"

"I don't really know. Maybe for a few months, maybe a few years."

"Would money help?" she asked. "Do you want to fight it? A good lawyer? I don't like Communism but I don't like what's happening here any more than you do."

"Mother, we can't stay here. And I won't leave without you." She looked at me in wonder. She smiled and her face glowed.

"I don't consider it a hardship to go to Europe—with my kiddies." She giggled girlish giggles up and down the scale.

"The *Queen Mary* sails from New York Wednesday. We have to leave here on The Chief before the weekend, stay overnight in New York. Everything is paid for. You, too."

At once, it became real. We were going. Suddenly, all I was leaving was dear to me. Every pebble in our garden. The bush from which I'd picked the cream rose I'd set on the breakfast table the morning after we were married. Everything. The minuscule palm that had taken root between two garden stones. Wasn't there a big fat no-no to plants? And the Guatemalan fabric with the many-colored ducks and cats and little men? How would I live without it? It wasn't like moving to the Vorhauses for a few days. It was thousands of miles away, another continent. Zif. What would I do without Zif? I'd come to rely on Mondays, Wednesdays, and Fridays at three. And Margaret? What would Johnny do without Margaret's ample lap? Mother would have to be more grandmotherly.

"It will all blow over." "We'll win in the courts." None of that was true. Nothing was going to withstand this rising tide of terror. America was frightened of ideas! I shivered. They weren't going to win in the courts. We were never coming back. The den I'd made into Ben's tweedy study, he'd never use again.

My hands shook as I packed the hooded green wool snowsuit outgrown by Julie Payne, daughter of Anne Shirley and screen idol John Payne, who had given it to Luli for cold wet London.

We were leaving. We didn't know for how long. I was scared. My parents had moved because they liked to move. They never had to flee. I'd always wanted to stay in one place. Twelve ninety Sunset Plaza Drive was the closest I'd come to it.

They Went Thataway

The two unliftable Mark Cross suitcases that had accompanied me to France the summer of '39, when war broke out, stood in the hall, ominous. Ominous too, the passport already in my pocketbook, with a photo of me trying to smile, holding my arms protectively about Luli, clutching Squeechy, and Johnny, holding Blinky-Blanket.

Come on, Norma, I told myself, your father carried you through the catacombs when you were two. This is different. I don't want to go anywhere. I just want to live with my husband and my children in our house and not move. You have them with you, Norma, and one in the belly, and you have your mother, and enough money.

Margaret said, "Please, don't look like that, Miz Barzman. I'll pray for you."

I thought, It must be nice to have someone to pray to.

Ben met his mother at her favorite ice cream parlor, the Pig'n Whistle on Hollywood Boulevard next to Grauman's Egyptian Theatre.

I could visualize the meeting. When I saw Mumma for the first time, she'd conjured up a plucked pigeon feather, tiny, worn thin and so lightweight a soft breeze might blow her away. After a while, her bright intelligent eyes and decisive tone told me of the strength that had enabled her to escape from Russian pogroms with two babies, join her husband in Canada, then bring up their seven children when he was away most of the time and unable to support them.

Mumma could reach strong, decisive tones, but she usually began with a whiny kvetch. This time, when Ben didn't seem to know how to begin, she prompted with a half-kvetch. "Something to do with changing houses? Your sister Anne explained." Mumma didn't sound worried. Ben was not prepared for her calm. And she wasn't kvetching. "Now I understand," she said with a huge sigh of relief. "Your Cossacks have finally come for you. For years I knew they would."

"These are not Cossacks, Mumma. This is a Committee of the U.S. Congress—"

She paid absolutely no attention. "So, now the Cossacks are after *you*? I knew it. I knew all along one day they would come for you."

Ben tried to explain but instead she took his hand fondly, no longer a frightened, helpless woman. She was calm, confident. "Now you listen to me," she commanded quietly. "Danger is not always something you can see. It's more something you feel. The moment you feel it, never hesitate. Take Norma and the children and flee! Run! That's what the German Jews didn't understand. They waited."

"It's not at that point yet, Mumma," Ben protested. "No one knows for sure exactly whom they're after or what they really want."

"Naturally." She nodded knowingly. "That's the way they were with us too. Cossacks—who knew when they would strike? Or where? Or why? Your Cossacks, they're anti-Semitic?"

"It's not obvious."

"Up-to-date Cossacks." Mumma nodded. "Too smart to be openly anti-Semitic. Smart Cossacks are the most dangerous."

"Listen, Mumma," Ben said. "These are United States congressmen."

"Cossacks come in all shapes and forms," she replied. "Cossacks don't have to be on horses to be Cossacks . . . " Then, in a hushed tone, "But there may be another way. Sell your jewels."

"What jewels?"

"The family jewels. Then buy the Cossacks off."

"Buy them off?" Ben asked. "Elected representatives of the people?"

"Don't be shy." She was not in the least disturbed. "Offer them money. They take. Don't worry." After a moment, "You need money? I have a string of pearls, real pearls I've kept for emergencies. You take them. They're worth a couple of thousand dollars. Somewhere among the Cossacks, there's always at least one who'll take—"

Ben told me later that he'd suddenly remembered a few months before when he'd had a phone call from lawyer Martin Gang. "Ben," Gang said over the phone, "I have a matter which will be, I'm sure, of great interest to you." He called Ben by his first name although they'd never met.

Ben's curiosity was piqued and he made the long drive downtown to Gang's offices. "Mussolini Modern," Ben described the decor. "Colossal furniture to make you feel small, helpless."

At first, Gang made chitchat, crafted to show he knew a great deal about Ben. "These films you wrote at RKO. *Back to Bataan,* a terrific moneymaker. Sure, John Wayne's pictures always make money. But in the industry, they know. Ben Barzman—he can write action, he can write comedy. Didn't you do *True to Life* with Victor Moore? Funny!" He didn't wait for an answer. "When someone young comes along with that kind of talent, they watch you. They know you've got an exciting future. You're on your way to the top! That's why it's a shame if anything stupid gets in the way. Is there anything that could get in the way?"

Ben opened his mouth to speak but Gang went on relentlessly, "Because a certain congressman found out you were Canadian and only became a naturalized American a few years ago."

Ben cut in, "That's no crime. Sure, I became an American citizen during the war so I could join the Armed Forces—"

"Yeah!" said Gang, "but you didn't—"

"I tried," Ben said hurriedly, "they wouldn't take me. My blood pressure was too high."

"Yeah, I know. That's not the point. This congressman said it would be really regrettable if, because of your misguided interest in unpopular causes now on the attorney general's list, your career went down the tube. In fact, the congressman said you might even risk deportation."

After much circuitous talk, Gang finally let it out. For $16,000 the congressman would advise Ben how to avoid these dire consequences.

Ben told me he'd thought for a moment, then burst into laughter. "That's a funny amount. Why sixteen? Why not fifteen or twenty? Sounds to me like $15,000 goes to the congressman and $1,000 goes to you."

Gang pretended to be offended. "Think about it."

Ben did and the more he thought, the more he realized it really was $1,000 to the lawyer and $15,000 to Richard Nixon, our congressman, who was most certainly "the congressman." It seemed like small potatoes until Ben found out that Gang had called nine other screenwriters with a similar proposition. Ten times $15,000 was a tidy $150,000.

"So if you're not going to buy them off," Mumma had said to Ben, "you're leaving. When?"

"But we can't leave," Ben said. "Dore Schary doesn't want me to quit my job. There's the kids, the house—"

"Never mind all that," she said. She was now completely composed. "The job, the house, forget all that."

"We can't just pull out. If we do, we may not see each other for years."

"Leave that in God's hands. Sometimes He's smarter than we are."

"You mean—just go?" Ben asked incredulously.

"Not just go—*flee*. You'll drop me a line now and then, you'll send photos of the children. Don't be afraid to go out into the world. There will be jobs, houses. The world is full of people. Where there are people, there are friendly hearts. Go! Now! You'll find someplace where there's no Cossacks. There you'll stay."

PART TWO

EUROPE IN THE '50s

11

A Bit Soupy, eh Guv'ner?

In 1949, all that remained of posh, prewar, Fortnum and Mason, privileged, upper-class England was the *Queen Mary.* The First Class Dining Room overflowed with caviar, foie gras, Scottish salmon, and quail. The wines, I'm certain, were superior to any left in the cellars of the French aristocracy after the German Occupation. Breakfast was like an MGM movie—kippers, kidneys, sausages, and fluffy scrambled eggs in covered silver chafing dishes. The ship's library burst with British classics, Jane Austen, Agatha Christie, and the favorites of English public school boys, Jeeves and Aldous Huxley. The linens were impeccable, from sumptuous bath blankets and tiny finger towels to doilies of finest cotton from the far-flung, now lost, British Empire.

On one such doily, each morning at eleven, a steward brought me a cup of delicious beef bouillon and tucked me into my comfortable deck chair. I lay back, soothed. What is more amniotic than a sea voyage? But on this February journey, in contrast to the *Queen Mary'*s normal roll (a side-to-side motion), she pitched, rising and falling. In spite of having recently been equipped with a new technological advance, the gyro-stabilizer, the *Queen* was having herself a high old time.

We had just left Hollywood where Bobby, Jeannie, Adrian, and Annie had given us an exuberant going-away party. (See photo insert). Across the living room, they'd strung what looked like balloons but on closer examination turned out to be inflated condoms. For once, it had not been a "cause" party. We drank, danced, laughed, and shouted with our friends as if we were young, which we were! We had no idea that many of us would never meet again or that we'd see each other after youth had quietly slipped away and we were all grappling with midlife crises.

When Ben and I reached New York, Phil Brown,[1] a former actor with the Actors Lab, Eddie Dmytryk's assistant director on *Christ in Concrete*, met us at the Hotel Royalton on 44th Street. He was supposed to hand us our *Queen Mary* first-class tickets. "In London, Geiger gave me a check for a thousand," Phil said, "drawn on a Chinese bank. He told me to go back to New York and shoot the Lower East Side exteriors. Ben, you know as well as I, that didn't leave anything for your tickets." Even in those days, a thousand dollars was not enough to take care of a crew on location for a week.

"What are you talking about?" Ben demanded heatedly. "Geiger promised—"

"I just got a call from him," Phil said, defensively, "about your passage. I'll have to do a whole black-market operation."

"So what?"

"But I can't get your passage in time for the sailing tomorrow!"

"If you don't get those tickets, your life won't be worth much!" Ben was frightening when furious.

That week, Arthur Miller's play *Death of a Salesman* had rocked New York. Ben's argument with Phil continued across 44th Street past Broadway to the theater where Lee J. Cobb, playing Willy Loman, had left house seats for us. *Playbill* came with the tickets. Its cover, well known now around the world, showed Joe Hirsch's drawing of the salesman and his suitcases. Joe had scribbled on it, "See you in Paris."

Wildly, Ben wheeled about, and clutching our theater tickets in one hand, he grabbed Phil's wilted shirt front with the other. "Unless the *Mary* tickets are as firmly in my hand as these by tomorrow morning," he shouted, "I'll hold back the final script and there'll be no *Christ in Concrete!*"

Next morning, Phil handed us our tickets. We didn't listen carefully to his adventures of the previous night—getting the Chinese ambassador and various black marketeers out of bed, blackmailing a Hungarian travel agent who had no green card. We hurried to the wharf of the Cunard White Star Line. There, a scene from a long-gone era greeted us. Bands played, crowds waved bon voyage, confetti flew in every direction. We let Johnny throw some of the gaily colored wigglies at people on the pier below, which made his day.

Phil didn't see us off. The episode with him had dramatized the precarious nature of our undertaking. We couldn't trust Rod Geiger, yet we were putting our lives in his hands.

Lying on a deck chair, between two worlds, between two lives, I took stock. Twenty-eight, married, two children, and a third growing inside me. I was a journalist and a screenwriter, but the move to Europe probably wouldn't favor either career. Just to set up the living arrangements for a family with children and to accustom them to a new environment would be a full-time job for years. I had no illusions. Uprooted children would require more loving care than those in stable environments. Before having children, I'd never guessed how much they would mean to me, nor had I ever imagined a situation that would require a choice between children and career. I knew by now that I was married to an old-fashioned, chauvinistic man whose neurotic brilliance and talent were, in great measure, responsible for my loving him. I did not know that all these qualities would make life more difficult.

On a cold and murky morning, Eddie Dmytryk met us at Southampton.

"The Bank of England has refused to release even expense money for Americans in London," Eddie said, gloomily. "Geiger was supposed to have brought all the 'above the line' financing, an acceptable shooting script—all paid for—a director, two stars, and the leading secondary actors."

Geiger hadn't paid Ben, so he didn't have a signed release allowing him to use the screenplay, a document the bank considered critical. He'd given Dmytryk a down payment, but hadn't even made that to Sam Wanamaker, the star, or to Italian actress Léa Padovani, who was to play Annunziata. Until Geiger had a signed release from Ben declaring he'd been paid in full, the film would not roll. Ben and I stood on that dim, barren, bomb-shattered pier, glad we could not see each other's faces through the heavy fog.

"If I sign a statement saying I've been paid in full," Ben said, "I'll never be paid."

Eddie shrugged.

Our return passage was guaranteed but the prospect of crawling back to the States, where the Committee crouched in wait for us, was too demoralizing even to consider.

"You know they drive on the wrong side of the road here?" Eddie said, handing Ben a bunch of keys. He pointed to a forlorn wreck up ahead. "Sometimes the lights go out. It was the best we could do."

"Excuse me," I said, walking away from them into the fog so they couldn't see me throw up. They might have heard short coughing sounds. I wiped my mouth, returned to them, and began to laugh.

"You think it's funny?" Ben demanded.

"Don't *you*?" I said. "It's too small to be tragic."

"I was just thinking of that lovely blonde in the convertible," Ben said. "Murphy's Law? If a good or a bad thing can happen, don't worry, bad will happen." He hugged me and our bodies shook and I suppose the sounds we made could be called laughter.

Luli and Johnny hesitated to get into the dilapidated contraption but when their granny urged them to join her in the backseat, they clambered in and hung on to her for dear life. The car emitted an apologetic grumble, like someone with minor intestinal trouble, the motor caught, our lights jumped on. The right light died, the traffic side, the dangerous side, another perfect example of Murphy's Law. Fortunately, we met few oncoming cars in the thick haze.

Over four years had passed since the war had ended but the punishment

England had taken was far more terrible than anything we'd imagined. The outskirts of London were scarred and pitted by deep bomb craters. Rising above the city streets were mountains of tragic debris.

"Churchill lived around the corner," the Hotel De Vere receptionist proudly told us in Irish brogue. Facing Kensington Gardens, the small hotel had seen its best years during Queen Victoria's youth. Londoners joked that during the bombings the Albert Hall was the safest place to be because a bomb would never rid them of that monstrosity. The De Vere was like that. Having survived the V-bombs and doodle bombs, the hotel's dark redbrick ugliness had acquired a kind of nostalgic beauty.

Other than the Irish elf at the reception desk, the hotel was staffed by dubious stateless Poles who'd served in the Polish Free Forces and were waiting for fate and the United Nations to confer some sort of nationality on them. They wore tails, food-stained tuxedo shirts, and pale yellow ties. We handed over the ration tickets for fresh milk, eggs, and meat issued for me and the children but received only a chalky mixture supposed to be fresh milk, never saw whole eggs, just a powdery concoction served in a battered silver dish.

Early one morning after our arrival, Léa Padovani, the beautiful young Italian actress who was to play Sam Wanamaker's wife, showed up alone. She was exactly the Annunziata I had visualized, lovely, eager for life, direct, intense. (See photo insert). Ben, too, was immediately taken with her. She barely spoke. At first I thought she was self-conscious about her English, but as time went by and she didn't utter a word, I realized that the female lead spoke no English. My heart sank.

Léa took Ben's hand, looked into his face, and said slowly in mellifluous tones, "I've fallen in love with this role the way a woman falls in love with a man." She had taught herself to say that line and said it so perfectly, so seductively, that I would have been jealous had I not seen Ben's spirits rise. We both knew at that moment. She *was* Annunziata. She would be wonderful. Her eyes begged. "I won't stand in your way," Ben said.

Through the dusty lounge's tall dirty windows, framed by ragged burgundy-velvet drapes, we could see a huge once-elegant Aston-Martin chug up High Street and park directly in front of the hotel. Rod Geiger came bouncing into the hotel foyer, jolly as Santa Claus and about as truthful. "Everything," he assured us, "is being taken care of." He asked me to summon my mother, who was still in the dining room trying to persuade Luli and Johnny to drink the chalky substance. Rod embraced Mother, told her that the greatest specialists in the world were right here in London on Harley Street. His apparently genuine concern won her over. He then seduced the children, each with a gift he'd picked up in Czechoslovakia, a nest of painted wood peasant women for Luli, and, for Johnny, ingenious wooden chickens set in a row pulled by a string that made the chicks peck their way along. As if that weren't sufficient, he won them over for life by telling them that if they crossed the road with their granny to Kensington Gardens, they would see the king's sheep grazing in the park. "It's much smarter," he confided, "to have a shepherd bring in sheep than to run a lawn mower. The sheep nibble the grass, do caca that makes the new grass grow better."

Alone with us, Geiger had to face the "money" situation. Before either of us could utter a word, he said with deep compassion, "Most important now is for Ben and you to come with me to Denham Studios, I want you to meet the cast and crew! You won't see a finer lot!"

Geiger was no dope. I began to feel he was including me not because I was also a screenwriter, but so that I would urge Ben to sign. We found ourselves seated in the Aston-Martin, getting our first real glimpse of well-preserved London—Parliament, Westminster Abbey, London Bridge, The Strand—then miles and miles of suburbs so ravaged, it was hard to look.

Unexpectedly, Denham Studios appeared. Rod made a proud, proprietary gesture, giving a subtle impression that he was, in his own way, responsible for its beauty. Set in an expanse of emerald green lawn, Denham's stately and undamaged Georgian central building was surrounded by soundstages.

When Geiger left for a moment, I said, "Ben, you've really got to tell him in no uncertain terms that you won't sign the clearance until you're paid."

A Bit Soupy, eh Guv'ner?

At that moment, England's foremost literary agent, Cecil Tennant, the representative of William Morris in London, materialized. A tall aristocratic man in his forties, Tennant made one feel that the work he did and even life itself was a kind of hobby, which he enjoyed and was rather good at.

"I've been informed," he said, focusing his piercing blue eyes on Ben and me, "that William Morris, Beverly Hills, was horrified to discover you'd gone off to England with neither a down payment nor a signed, valid guarantee of money in escrow." He paused for effect. "Furthermore, they have ascertained that Mr. Geiger is not *sueable*." This was the first time I'd heard the word. It meant that Rod had no known assets he could be said to own.

"Mr. Geiger has assured us that we will be paid out of the first monies—"

Tennant interrupted, "The Bank of England refuses to release any monies to cast or crew unless you, Ben, sign a declaration you've been paid." Rod listened like an interested bystander. Staring directly at Ben, Tennant said, "Should you succumb to the enormous and grossly unfair pressure you're being subjected to, I'm afraid William Morris cannot continue to represent you." He then shook hands warmly with us, nodded curtly to Rod, and left.

Pleased that such a stalwart figure had formally borne me out, I told Ben when Rod disappeared again that he *must* insist Rod get the money for us immediately. "Lay off!" Ben said.

The man slated to be production manager ambled over. "I am to have the pleasure of showing you around," he said, looking and sounding like what he was, an ex–English army captain who'd survived malaria, the war in Burma, and internment by the Japanese but still had a ready smile. Proudly, he took us through the constructions of Manhattan's Lower East Side, making us verify that the replicas of New York brownstones, even their stoops, on which he made us sit, were authentic. He then conducted us to one wing of the main building that housed the dressing rooms and rapped on the door marked "Mr. Wanamaker."

Sam was being fitted to his costumes. He was happy to see us, smiled hugely, dimpled deeply. "Ben, I love your script. I'm honored to play Geremio."

We'd never seen him on the stage in New York, where he'd just played opposite Ingrid Bergman in *Joan of Lorraine.* He was a surprise to us. Beautiful, he'd let his curly hair and sideburns grow for the part, and, in a striped shirt with an old-fashioned rounded starched white collar, he was already Geremio. With a fencer's grace, he darted about the furniture piled high with tailor's bolts of cloth, leapt over them, put out his hand to me, "You're 'Nawm.' We have to get together with Char. The four of us. Sunday morning. We'll take you to our favorite pub."

As we left the main building, we saw Eddie Dmytryk. "Eddie," Ben demanded, "don't you want to talk about revisions?"

"No, I think we're in agreement about everything. The only changes will be what the censor demands." He waved and was gone.

When we finally found Geiger, I raised my eyebrows meaningfully at Ben. "Rod," Ben began, "I just want to remind you—"

Rod interrupted. "Oh, I'm so glad I remembered. Katya's going to whip up a fantastic Swedish meal tonight. Can you two come to dinner?"

We never did find out if the sweet middle-aged German-Jewish refugee who drove us back to the De Vere in the tin contraption we'd driven from Southampton to London was Geiger's flunky or his moneyman. It turned out to be his car, and when it grumbled, he sang to it.

Rod had managed to acquire a baronial mansion. His wife, Katya, a tall, slim, attractive flaxen-haired woman who dressed in her own designer clothes, had put forth a mouthwatering smorgasbord. There was no appropriate moment for Ben to pull Rod aside and talk tough.

Later that night in our chill suite at the De Vere, Ben and I had one of those bleak reality-facing discussions, which were to become a periodic feature of our lives.

"You got downright tough, even violent with that pathetic Phil Brown," I said, "but don't you see? Rod Geiger is an entrepreneur. He got you to work for nothing, to sweat it out late at night, weekends, while you were tearing your heart out on another project. He's gotten you to give up your home, your job, your country so that now there's no turning back—and you hesitate to demand the money he owes you?"

"He doesn't stand still long enough."

"Ben. He's just trying to put you in a position so he'll *never* have to pay you. What are you frightened of?"

Ben sank into a plush armchair, leaned his head on the filthy antimacassar. "Everything!" he cried hoarsely. "That we'll never be paid, there'll be no picture, and we'll float all over Europe without money. I can see Mumma with all those kids, scrounging around." His voice hardened. "But you—! Somewhere in the back of your head, you figure your mother won't let us starve."

I began to sob convulsively.

"What is it?" he demanded, bewildered. "The children? Are you worried about the children?" I shook my head. "You're worried about the new baby. Where you'll have it?" Again, I shook my head. "Your mother? Her health?"

"No, no."

"Then what?" I said nothing. "Suppose Geiger's telling the truth?" he said. "There is no money. Do we pack it up? After all this?"

"That's the difference between you and me. I don't believe in Murphy's Law. Things aren't always the worst possible. It isn't the best of all possible worlds—but it isn't the worst!"

He started screaming at me. "It's easy for you with your goddamn silver spoon!"

Luli and Johnny were asleep in the next room, if we hadn't awakened them. Mother was in the room next to them. Ben stopped shouting when he realized I was anxious about the children. I tiptoed in. Luli was fast asleep, a frown puckering her perfect features; Johnny, almost asleep, was nibbling his fuzzy Blinky-Blanket.

When I returned, Ben whispered, "Don't you see that if I don't sign now, the Bank of England will pressure Rank to abandon the project?"

"This isn't about that."

"What is it about?"

I wished I hadn't started it because I couldn't tell him that in the filthy, moldy Hotel De Vere I'd realized that our fantastically beautiful life together had disappeared. At this moment with Ben, I felt we'd never get it back again, that I'd never feel the glorious glow that all was right with the world and that we would help make it so. "I think I'm just very tired," I said.

He got up, put his arms around me tenderly, drew me to the bed, where he made love to me as if he were trying to cure me of a disease.

12

For King and Country

On our first Sunday morning in London, a mini "Austin shooting break," British for station wagon, rolled up to the De Vere. Charlotte Wanamaker was at the wheel. Lean, lithe Sam Wanamaker, wearing tweed knickers and a striped cricket shirt, leapt gracefully out of the car. Sam and Ben hopped into the backseat. I sat in front next to Charlotte. She exuded warmth, her elfin face bewitched me, but her English accent came as a surprise. For a while I thought she was uppity. She'd only been in England a few weeks. "How come you have an English accent?" I asked.

Sam answered for her. "Char always spoke like that, even before she knew there was an England. We went to drama school together in Chicago. I fell in love with that throaty British voice when I met her." I hadn't realized he always dimpled when he smiled. "Did you ever hear her?" he asked. "Her name was Charlotte Holland. Her speaking voice was reputed to be the most sonorous of any on radio."

In the front seat, Charlotte and I compared notes. She and Sam also had two children. "The first," she said crisply, "is Abby, the second and last, Zoe. From A to Z. No more." (But there would be a third daughter, Jessie.) I thought: Here is an American blacklisted family taking their exile comparatively well.

The Wanamakers drove us to an industrial area of London, Southwark, farther down the Thames. We parked between two rat-infested warehouses. When Charlotte stepped out of the car, I saw she was small, wide-hipped, and not well proportioned, but I'd already been won over by the voice, the copper hair, and the wit and whimsy with which she delivered her own lines.[1]

"Shakespeare's London," Sam said, waving his arms and breathing in the sooty air.

"The Globe Theatre burned down in 1613," Char volunteered. "We're walking just about where it was."

Not even a sign marked the spot, but the site of the Old Courage Brewery was clearly advertised.

Sam pointed. "Over there, see that small tumbledown building? That was a prison called The Clink. It's why we say 'He's in the clink.' "

"Oh, *Sam!*" she said, pronouncing "Sam" to rhyme with "bomb." "Why don't you tell them?" Sam looked sheepish. Char went on, "It's Sam's dream to rebuild Shakespeare's Globe."

"People laugh at me," he said. "There have been so many attempts but nobody could get the rights to the land or the money. I will. I'm glad *Christ* brought us to England."

Sam said that in 1949. His passionate advocacy, his years of devotion, energy, and determination rebuilt Shakespeare's Globe Theatre. He made it his life's work, and eventually moved to Southwark to oversee the restoration progress. According to Oxford scholars, "Completion of the project came after his death, but it remains his achievement."[2] Sam convinced Prince Philip to play exhibition polo to raise funds for its restoration and prevailed upon the Prince and Queen Elizabeth to gift the theater with the Royal Oaks, the trees of Windsor Park. The queen bestowed on Sam the title of Commander of the British Empire (CBE). In 1994, the year after Sam died, Queen Elizabeth dedicated the Globe.

That morning in Southwark, I couldn't have foreseen Sam's distinguished career: his agile, devilish Iago at Stratford; his production of *The Rose Tattoo* with himself and Léa Padovani at his Liverpool art-gallery-theatre-complex; directing opera in Australia; his television and movie roles including *Guilty by Suspicion* in which he played lawyer Martin Gang, who tried to get McCarthy victims to stool on their friends before they testified at the House UnAmerican Activities Committee.

Sam led us out of the grimy air into a venerable pub, The Anchor. I had a Pimm's Cup—pineapple, orange, mint leaves, maraschino cherries, a stalk of fresh celery—and lifted my drink high. "To Shakespeare's Globe."

Christ in Concrete seemed to be at a standstill. We couldn't find Rod, and when we went to the studio, the cast and crew looked at us accusingly as though we were holding up the works. I visited the Tate while Ben hunted for the graves of his favorite British authors in the Abbey or Saint Anne's. Mother took Luli and Johnny to the zoo in Regents Park and to Buckingham Palace to watch the changing of the guard. Johnny loved the guards' tall furry hats, kept repeating "busbies" and giggling.

Ben and I decided Mother needed time off from the kids. We asked a sweet young Norwegian maid at the hotel to take over in the evenings so Mother could go to the theater with us—Bernard Shaw, Ibsen, Molnar. Her lips moved soundlessly in the darkened theatres—she had never read novels, only plays, and these were the playwrights she knew by heart.

After three weeks of Geiger's disappearing act, we began to lose hope. That was the moment Adrian and Annie arrived with her daughter Julie Payne and their adopted son, Michael, the war orphan. We were horrified to discover that Anne Shirley, a former child star whom Adrian had helped to sanity, did not comprehend his politics or why he had taken his position. Bewildered and frightened, Annie refused to listen whenever he tried to explain to her.

Adrian's hair had turned prematurely silver, his face lined with worry. Gentle and soft-spoken, he now considered it a real possibility that he and the others of the Hollywood Ten would be sentenced to a year in the federal penitentiary. He, Eddie Dmytryk, and the rest of the Hollywood Ten who had defied the Committee by refusing to testify about their political beliefs, had been cited with contempt of Congress. Hollywood Ten members John Howard Lawson and Dalton Trumbo, who had been found guilty at their separate trials, were appealing. The rest of the Hollywood Ten had stipulated they would let their fates rise or fall on the outcome of Lawson's and Trumbo's appeals. So far, they had lost. Only the judgment of the U.S. Circuit Court and the Supreme Court remained.

Adrian told us the political situation back home was lethal. As I listened to him describe it, I wondered what had become of the bold, brilliant, talented producer who had saved RKO with his films *Crossfire, Murder, My Sweet,* and *Cornered.*

He now doubted that they would win in the courts as all of us had once thought. "Not in today's atmosphere," he said. "Everyone's terrified. HUAC has found a new ploy. They're in Hollywood, subpoenaing their victims secretly, interviewing them behind closed doors in hotel rooms so they think it isn't official." In his soft voice, Adrian mimicked the victim. " 'I thought it was understood. You promised it would be secret. You promised I wouldn't have to rat on my friends!' "

" 'No sirree!' " Adrian hollered back as if he were the HUAC inquisitor. I jumped. I'd never heard Adrian shout. " 'National security is involved. This *is* official. If you don't tell us about your friends, you'll be held in contempt!' "

Some of the victims, he said, had been threatened with perjury. The Committee claimed it had information that proved they'd lied. Perjury. Five years in jail. An illegal bluff, but the victims didn't know it then. "Panic!" Adrian went on. "No one knows who stood firm or who informed but it's certain many cracked."

Ben and I felt even more pressured to sign Geiger's clearance. If a film of ours was actually made, it would help us all get work with the Europeans. "That's our only hope," Adrian said.

The other hope was to finish the original script I'd started just before we left America, which Ben and I had agreed to work on together. It was based on my sister's experiences as a lawyer—*Young Woman with Ideas.*

• • •

For King and Country

A month passed. No one on *Christ in Concrete* had been paid. One morning we picked up a puzzling message at the hotel desk. Would we meet for luncheon at the Denham commissary at half past noon? A car would pick us up. When he arrived, singing to his car, Geiger's flunky said he had no idea who had instigated the lunch. At Denham, we found Sam, Phil Brown, the production manager, and the pretty, competent young woman who was to be production secretary. As we walked in, all faces turned to us hopefully, but when Ben said nothing, everyone slipped back into an uneasy chill.

Sam turned to Ben. "Was there some reason you wanted us to meet?" he asked.

"Who? Me? No," Ben replied, "not me."

Long silence.

"You don't happen to know why this lunch was called?" Sam demanded.

"No," Ben said. "I don't."

Sam looked questioningly at me for a moment. "Nawm?"

I shook my head.

Another long silence.

Ben glanced furtively at the others, who were glancing furtively at him. I watched. When their eyes met, they looked away hastily. It seemed painfully obvious that Rod didn't have the money. We sat suspended, indecisive, trapped, awkward. Finally, Sam shrugged, picked up a food-stained menu, glanced at it. "What the hell," he said, "we might as well order."

Bangers (a sausage patty that could have been invented only by the English) and potatoes. I'd never seen potatoes offered in so many different forms, some with a thin sprinkling of something reminiscent of cheese.

The production manager shifted nervously, then smiled brightly. "Not a bad menu today, comparatively."

"Compared to what?" I asked.

Phil said, "I imagine compared to what he got as a prisoner of the Japanese."

"Especially when I was with the English civilian prisoners."

Ben said, "I thought you were an officer. How is it you were interned as a civilian?"

"Well," he said, cheerfully, "there was this lovely pond in a Burmese jungle. I thought I'd have a bathe. Hung my uniform up on the bushes, went in starkers. A Nip scouting party came up at that moment. I tried to flee—without my uniform of course. When they caught me, they insisted on interning me as a civvie."

"Were you interned long?" I asked.

"Long enough. Put on a good show, those civilians," he reminisced with a sigh. "Gave dinner parties."

"In a Japanese camp?" I asked.

"The International Red Cross had sent us magazines. Photographs of food galore. In color. People cut them out and traded them around. A man would offer a Cornish Hen for a Trifle Pudding. We'd dress as best we could, sit together as each course of cutout photos was passed around. The Nip commander occasionally supplied candles."

"What did you actually eat?" I asked.

"Why, a handful of rice." He seemed surprised we didn't know. "Interned there for three months. Many died. Odd thing was, we got so we knew who would die—the man or woman who wouldn't wolf down their ration of rice but put it aside and saved it. We called them 'rice happy.' " He was lost in thought. "Heard most of them died, rice happy or not."

I caught Ben's eye. Ashamed, we looked down at the Denham menu.

"It seems apparent no one here knows why we were called to this lunch," someone said.

"I think I know why," Ben fumed.

"You think Rod could be that Machiavellian?" Sam asked. "Would he bring us together to pressure you? I heard he sold his interest in *Open City* for a few thousand dollars. To be fair, nobody expected it to create the sensation it did. Rod acquired a reputation out of it, but not much else. Listen, Ben, if I were you, I'd be goddamned if I'd sign that clearance. Hold out. We're behind you."

There was an immediate chorus of approval, even a "Hear! Hear!" It was heartwarming, but that lunch made me shed my delusions: Rod obviously didn't have the money, nor did he have access to important sums of money.

Outside, we ran into Rod. Again, this surprising man surprised us. When Ben lit into him, Rod angrily cut him off.

"Goddamit, my first obligation is to get this film made!" He shucked off his confident swagger. "I was sure that with money from Rank and a distribution guarantee, I'd get the money. But the situation with Dmytryk makes money uneasy. They think right-wing groups in America will stop the picture's distribution. Between you and me, they may be right. But we've got to have a film first! And I'm going to find other money—before yours," he said, amazingly frank, "money that will guarantee the film is finished. Now you know! No other money will come in until I find end money. Give me a chance. I'll get you your money one way or another."

"Oh, come on, Rod," I said wearily.

When Rod was gone, I turned to Ben, "Y'know, he's not really sure the film will shoot."

"Why do you say that?"

"You're the one who told me the film can't shoot unless it has official English censor's approval, and Rod hasn't even tried to get it yet."

I guess when Ben actually called for the meeting with the censor, a Mr. Trevelyan, Rod saw it as Ben's capitulation. An appointment was made. Ben invited me to come along. "You'll be amused," he said. "Just keep your mouth shut."

I had never dealt with Hollywood Hayes Code censors. Ben had. "I'll tell you what they used to say: 'Had a good day, cut out six asses, eighteen pair of tits.' Producers knew they'd never get away with the shots, but they had fun shooting them, the censors had fun looking, and—" Ben made snipping gestures. "That's the way those guys imitated cutting."

It was a mistake to associate Mr. Trevelyan even remotely with "those guys." He was cultivated, knowledgeable, sensitive, and intelligent.

Nonetheless, both of us and Eddie were completely taken aback by his objections to a scene in which the new bride, Annunziata, bathes nude in the copper washtub in the kitchen, her husband, Geremio, comes home from work, walks in, sees her, makes what Ben described in the script as "an Italian gesture of delight."

"You object to the 'Italian' gesture?" Eddie asked hopefully. "We'll tone it down."

"No," he said stiffly. "It's more basic than that. A man in the presence of a nude woman is unacceptable."

"But the audience doesn't see her nude," Ben protested. "And they're married! He doesn't do anything erotic. He's fully dressed. And she's his wife!"

"A fully dressed man in the presence of a nude woman is not acceptable," Trevelyan repeated icily.

"*Pas de Déjeuner Sur L'Herbe*," I said. It just popped out. Manet's painting, the nonchalant grouping of two fully clothed men and a nude woman in a park, shocked Parisians as flagrant immorality.

The men frowned at me. A compromise was reached. Geremio would have his back to her. At least Annunziata's nudity, Ben felt, was suggested and it would be something of an intimate glimpse of their lives. But what the audience would think of a newly married man, an Italian to boot, who kept his back turned to his beautiful nude wife, I shuddered to think.

That was not all. Trevelyan insisted that if the newlyweds were shown in bed, they would have to be in twin beds.

"An Italian mason!" Ben howled. "During the Depression—with twin beds? It's lugubrious!"

"Indeed it is," Trevelyan said, "but it's *your* American Hayes Code which demands *that* one. I'm here to protect our people's investment. The Rank Organization is counting on American distribution to amortize their investment. If your film violates the Hayes Code, distribution will surely be stopped."

From the way he delivered the last line, we realized he was fully aware that Americans could grab at that as a reason for not distributing instead of the true reason—because the film had a blacklisted director.

"Okay!" Ben said. "We simply won't show any scenes in the bedroom."

Eddie and I looked at Ben, surprised. How could there be a real feeling of Italian-American life without the bedroom?

Trevelyan made a cool gesture. "That is your decision." He paused. "Now this is an English objection: The scene in which your Geremio is so-to-speak crucified," he began, cautiously. "When the construction they're working on collapses? When he's caught in a casing, the liquid concrete pours in over him, he feels himself being crushed and knows he will die."

"The scene of his death?" Eddie asked, incredulous. "The *climactic* scene of the picture? His crucifixion in concrete? The scene from which the title comes?"

"By the by, Mr. Dmytryk, the title, *Christ in Concrete,* is not permissible. We cannot, in England, use the word 'Christ' in a title."[3]

I gasped.

Ben said, "If we can't, we can't. Mr. Trevelyan, what's wrong with the death scene?"

I was frightened. Ben's blood pressure was rising.

"He calls the names of the saints to help him," Trevelyan said.

"He just calls the names of the saints," Ben said. "He's being crushed to death. He doesn't have time to ask them to help him."

"A man knowing death is imminent calls the saints for only one reason," Trevelyan stated. "And he is not helped. He dies."

Eddie looked bewildered. I didn't get it either.

"So?" Ben asked.

"It's a prayer unanswered." Trevelyan enunciated each word clearly. "We cannot have prayers unanswered."

I could see Ben trying to pull himself together. Finally, he said, "You're kidding."

"I seldom have time or energy to, as you Americans put it—kid," he answered dryly.

"We're only a few years past a terrible war," Ben said. "Night after night pilots went out on missions, never returned. There've been millions of unanswered prayers."

"I'm sorry." Trevelyan was Gibraltar. "We cannot show a prayer unanswered in a film."

Ben had to cut out Geremio's call to the saints. All that is heard, as he knows he's about to die, is Geremio calling the names of his wife and children. No saints. No unanswered prayer. Just a last desperate grasp at a life slipping away. Perhaps it's even more effective this way. I know I weep at that point every time I see the film.

After the meeting, Ben and I took Mother's advice and went to Wheeler's for fish. After all, the English still had lovely Dover sole.

"Let's have expensive white wine," Ben said, "and face it all."

"At lunch?"

"It's not even going to be called *Christ in Concrete*."

"*Give Us This Day* isn't bad."

"Maybe one day, it'll go back to its real title."[4] We ordered a fine French Chablis.

"Ben," I said, "maybe it's time you signed?"

When Ben wanted to be charming, he was irresistible. He put down his knife and fork, wiped his mouth with his napkin, rose ceremoniously, came around and kissed me. Ben was not given to displays of affection. In his lexicon, along with being happy, loving might attract the evil eye. Ben had told me that when he asked Mumma "Do you love me?" she had replied, "When you're a good boy." Wheeler's was the first time Ben admitted he loved me.

Later that day, March 23, 1949, Ben signed. Shooting began the next day. Of course, we were never paid for the screenplay.

Except for the demands of the British censor, Ben didn't have to touch the second draft of the *Christ in Concrete* screenplay he'd completed in California and had given to Rod and Eddie to show Rank. I hadn't expected to go to the meeting with the censor and thought it might be a way to encourage me to prevail upon Ben to sign the clearance. However, after Ben signed, it was still taken for granted that I would accompany him everywhere, as if Geiger and Dmytryk, too, regarded *Christ in Concrete* as our project. In any case, I was really surprised when

Geiger specifically invited me to the set for the first day of shooting. Certainly Eddie as director would not want me there but I found out that he assumed I would be, perhaps because to be actually shooting was a triumph for the blacklisted, and for us all, a holiday.

The first day of shooting is always important. The air was thick with tension. We were still worried that someone, somehow, might get the film canceled. Maybe our embassy would bring pressure.

None of that happened. Shooting began.

Sam Wanamaker—Geremio—carries his new bride, Annunziata—Léa—over the threshold of the house she thinks is theirs, the house he promised her. In truth, he's only borrowed it for a few "honeymoon" days, and we are anxious about the moment she'll find out they have no house.

Geremio and Annunziata can't wait to be in each other's arms. But she must do something before they make love. She has brought salt to sprinkle in the corners of the house to keep away evil (very Ben!), which is why one of the titles of the picture was *Salt to the Devil.*

For hours, Dmytryk, the camera crew, technicians, and cast struggled to get the right lighting and makeup, to get exactly the feeling he wanted. Eddie had Sam carry Léa over the threshold a dozen times until he was satisfied. Then, just as the cameras were ready to roll, we heard a rumbling clatter at the soundstage entrance. All non-British looked on in utter disbelief. Tea wagons busily bumped through the stage doors. One of the crew explained, much surprised at our surprise, that it was the "elevensees," the tea break at 11 A.M. that after the war the British unions had fought for and won.

The lunch break came soon after, and then it took time to set things up again. Moviemaking was, as I remembered it from Hollywood, mostly waiting. Then Eddie got that first shot. Excitement was high. Léa and Sam were both beautiful. It was going to be a beautiful film.

All at once, in the middle of a scene with the two of them, when there was that deep, hushed absorption in the actors' reading their lines (Léa had learned them all), a sudden whisper surged across the soundstage, sweeping technicians, crew, extras with it. My God! I thought, it's all going to go down the drain. A mad rush toward the soundstage door left Eddie following it in his viewfinder. It was like a scene from one of those early German Expressionist films where huge mobs unexpectedly flee across the screen as the end of the world is announced.

The production manager restrained himself long enough to explain. "The princesses have come! They were scheduled to visit the set on the soundstage next door—you know?" Princesses Elizabeth and Margaret were curious about the American film people. "Haven't had Yank film people that often," he said, running off with the others.

"Hey, Phil!" Eddie called out to Phil Brown, his assistant, who also had a small role in the film. "Jesus Christ! Princesses! What are we supposed to do? Isn't there a kind of protocol or something?"

"Hell." Phil shrugged. "It's got to be like in the army. Stand at ease and try to look like you didn't do it."

That's pretty much what we did. The stage doors burst open, two lovely excited young Englishwomen hurried in, flushed and bubbling along with their entourage of girlfriends.

Padovani and Wanamaker were presented to the princesses. Sam bowed to them. The princesses seemed impressed by Sam and asked him a few questions.

Later, Sam told us that Princess Margaret had been the more inquisitive. "What, may I ask, is the subject of the film?" she'd demanded.

"I play an Italo-American mason," Sam told her. "My wife and I have deprived ourselves for years, saved up for a house. It's the middle of the Depression in New York. There are no jobs; we and our kids are literally eating the money we saved for our house. Finally, I take a job as a foreman on a construction job I know isn't safe, and risk the lives of my friends, the construction crew. I'm killed when the building caves in."

"Oh, dear!" she exclaimed. "It's sad. Why is it being made in England?"

"The blacklist," Sam said. "The director, the writer, and I can't work in the U.S. They think we're subversive."

"Are you?" Princess Margaret asked, stifling a giggle.

"Not very." He dimpled.

Princess Elizabeth listened intently to every word. She turned to Margaret. "We should wish them well."

"Isn't there some sort of superstition about not saying good luck to theater and film folk?" Margaret asked.

"You're absolutely right, Your Highness."

"What does one say?"

"In New York," Sam replied, "we say, 'Break a leg.' "

Margaret smiled mischievously. "Of course the French have a naughty word they use."

"And what is that?" Elizabeth asked.

Margaret whispered to her sister. The young women giggled.

Elizabeth said, "Consider it said," and swept off, followed by their entourage.

13

April in Paris

Eddie wanted Ben on the set every day just as he had during *Back to Bataan*. A break came for the few days Rod took Ben and Adrian to Germany to discuss making a film of *The Devil's General*, a play by Carl Zuckmayer about a German flying ace who turns against the Nazis and is assassinated.

Ben returned from Germany with two gigantic hamburgers for Mother and me, a liter of rich chocolate milk for Luli and Johnny, and a grim bitterness. He and Adrian had been through an ordeal but they would only say, "An unexpected death made it necessary to postpone the project indefinitely." I pestered Ben until he told me what had happened.

Rod Geiger's German colleagues and Bernhardt Wicki, slated to direct *The Devil's General*, had driven Rod, Ben, and Adrian to a tavern in the Black Forest. Wicki told them in good English that it had "the atmosphere and stench of Hitler's Munich *Bierhalle*."

Wicki was like a huge bear but very gentle for such a big man. He had black hair, a neatly trimmed dark beard, and striking blue eyes. In 1964, during our Zanuck period, when Wicki would direct *The Visit*, starring Ingrid Bergman, he still had the gaze of a man who'd seen unforgettable events. As a teenager, he'd thought of becoming an actor. His actress-mother got him into Frau Goering's School of Drama. He hated everything about Germany, called Mady Goering "Mrs. Shit," and one day said her face was as big as her ass. A half hour later this sixteen-year-old brought up in a refined Swiss family was in a death camp, witnessing the execution of a man slowly strangling to death at the end of a rope. Through the efforts of his mother's powerful friends, and because he was a Swiss citizen, Wicki was released after several weeks.

When Rod, Adrian, Ben, Wicki, and the producers entered the tavern, only one table for six was free but on it stood a half-full stein of beer.

"How many at this larger table?" Wicki asked the beer maid, a buxom woman in Bavarian costume.

"One," she replied, a shadow of apprehension on her face.

"Would it be all right," Wicki asked, "if I moved the stein to a table for two? We are six."

"Why not?" the beer maid said after a moment's hesitation.

Wicki moved the mug to the smaller table and they all sat down at the big one.

"We have the money," one of the German producers said, "and the perfect actor, Curt Jurgens—"

"But there are other problems," Adrian interrupted.

"If you're worried about, how do you say, that you are on the blacklist," the producer said, "forget it. It's no problem for us. We can make back the cost just in Germany. If you have the rights, we can make a deal."

At that moment, a man of about forty-five lurched out of the men's room in the back of the hall. He saw his beer on the table for two, picked it up, and made straight for the large table, leaning forward between Adrian and Ben.

"Which one of you Jew Communist bastards," he said in German, sweeping the table with a look as sharp as an ice pick, "dared touch my beer?"

The producer moved slowly toward him. "Now, go sit down," he said quietly in German. "We don't need trouble."

Before anyone could move, the man swung at Adrian who, though startled, ducked away. "American bastard," the drunk snapped at Adrian. "Fighting on the side of the Communists."

Wicki was on his feet, trembling. He held off the drunk, a big man but shorter than Wicki, snatched the mug from his hand, hurled it against the wall, and lifted the guy with one hand. The drunk kicked and swung wildly, one blow catching Wicki on the mouth, cutting his lip.

The producer punched the drunk in the belly, doubling him over, but he was an accomplished street fighter. The Nazi brought up his right elbow and jammed it into the producer's teeth. Wicki flew at the drunken man, lifting him off the floor. The crazy drunk kicked his heavy boots at Wicki's groin. Wicki lowered him. The man kneed Wicki in the testicles. Wicki shrieked, the most frightening sound Ben said he'd ever heard. Wicki's arm shot out, connected to the man's jaw. He dropped to the floor like a puppet, strings cut.

The terrified innkeeper kneeled beside the crumpled figure. "*Tot*," he said, "dead. That man was a diabetic."

Wicki shouted to the beer maid to get an ambulance. "You, Rod, Adrian, Ben," he added, "you better go."

"We'll stay and testify for you," Rod said.

Wicki insisted they go. "I'll call you. Remember, you weren't here."[1]

Wicki received the lightest possible punishment, a suspended sentence of a year in prison, but the publicity prevented them from making the film. When it was filmed and released in 1956, it was a big hit and made Curt Jurgens a star.

When Ben got back from Germany, *Christ in Concrete* was nearing the end of shooting. Rod discovered that April 30 was Annie's thirtieth birthday. He suggested the Barzmans, Scotts, and Wanamakers charter a plane and take with them his wife, Katya, and Léa Padovani for a long Paris weekend. A French producer was willing to foot the bill to bring Ben and Adrian from London. To Ben, his first visit to Paris was a Geiger perk because he hadn't been paid for the script. To me, it was going home. I'd spent happy childhood years in France. In fact, I'd run away to Paris at the end of my sophomore year at college. In June 1939, when I tried to get a job on the *Paris Herald Tribune,* I hadn't come for the summer—I'd come to stay. On August 31, the editor of the *Herald* had offered me a job as a reporter. The free work I'd done in June and July, "Arrivals and Departures," had paid off for me. The next day, September 1, World War II broke out. My parents, rightly, brought me back against my will. The Germans were about to overrun France.

I had hoped these four days would seduce Ben and that he'd want to live in France, not in England where his life as a screenwriter would have been easier.

For Adrian, Paris was one last fling before going to jail, which now seemed almost certain. In June 1949, the Circuit Court of Appeals did rule against Trumbo and Lawson, and, in effect, against the rest of the Ten. Adrian, Eddie, and all of us were waiting for the last hope—the U.S. Supreme Court.[2] In Paris, if only for a few days, Adrian had a chance to try to find the work he badly needed to support his family should he have to spend a year in prison. He quickly found an inexpensive plane service that taxied us to Paris and back.

In spring 1949, Paris was beautifully unspoiled as it never would be again. The air was clear, fresh, fragrant (not like grimy London fog); the Seine was wide and clean; the boulevards, almost devoid of traffic, were bordered by opulent green shade trees exploding with chestnut blossoms. Ben drank it all in and sighed, "They say Paris is the only city in the world you can have nostalgia for when you're in it."

Our two taxis swung by the Ile de la Cité, one of the two boat-shaped islands in the Seine, home to soaring Gothic, gargoyled Notre Dame and to the Conciergerie, the prison where aristocrats waited to be guillotined. We drove along the river where *péniches,* barges, their bright-colored laundry fluttering like pennants in the breeze, cruised up and down; passed the quay of *bouquinistes,* outdoor bookstalls festooned with old prints; the Louvre, the Tuileries Gardens, and the Place de la Concorde.

"Look! Look! There it is! The Eiffel Tower!" Ben shouted, as if no one else could see it. "It looks exactly like the Eiffel Tower!" I knew what he meant. There it was. Not on postcards or in newsreels. Paris really did exist. "Even I," he went on, "know the Eiffel Tower is on the Left Bank.

Our hotel's on the Right Bank." He squinted at the taximeter. "The driver took us the scenic route and I don't even mind."

"I mind," Char said. "I'm starved."

We hadn't eaten since breakfast. "Goodness!" I exclaimed. "Everything closes."

"I have faith in Nawm," Sam cut in. "She'll know where we can get the best goddamn meal in Paris at four in the afternoon."

I bit off a nail. This was not just a challenge. It was a test. I could not fail. Paris could not fail! "Le Cabaret," I said. "Rond Point des Champs Elysées." My parents had taken my sister and me there in 1929 when the crash made them seek out "more reasonable" restaurants.

Char and Sam and Ben and I were in the first taxi. Our driver, a man with a few words of English, grumbled, "We have had a war. Many restaurants are—dead—like our young men!"

"You're passing it right now!" I shrieked. "*Voilà!*"

"*Fermé*," he cried delightedly. "Closed!"

A big *Fermé* sign stood in the window. "Norma," Ben reassured Adrian, Annie, Katya, and Léa, who had descended from the other taxi, "is from a long line of women who don't let '*fermé*' faze them." Among other exploits, my mother had picked up the *Fermé* sign in front of the Compagnie Générale Transatlantique, the French Line, at Le Havre on September 1, 1939, the day World War II was declared, and used it to batter down their front door. A man had poked his head out, announced there were already 1,500 passengers scheduled to sail the next day on the Champlain that held only 500. Mother lay down on the floor of the ship line's offices. This was, at last, a moment of triumph for the woman who had, at sixteen, run away to go on the stage. She wept, she stormed, she cajoled. She played her scene à la Sarah Bernhardt: we were only three extra passengers, her husband was ill, he'd have a heart attack if separated from his only child (Father was quite well and I was not his only child). The ship licensed to hold 500 passengers sailed the following day with 1,503, zigzagged safely home, passing the British *Athenia,* which was sunk by a Nazi U-boat.

I pounded on the Cabaret's glass door. When the *propriétaire* opened,

April in Paris

I recognized him, ten years older, grayed and corpulent. I spread my arms wide to embrace him, reminded him of 1929 and 1939. He didn't recall. "In 1939," I said, "I was a young girl of eighteen. Now I am a pregnant woman of twenty-eight."

As soon as he heard the word *enceinte*—pregnant—he hurried away and returned with the chef, a mountain of a man, in his tweed jacket ready to go home for his afternoon nap.

"*Pauvre petite Madame! Dans son état*—in her state—has been eating English food for more than two months!" the proprietor lamented.

"Say no more!" the chef replied. He leaned sympathetically toward me. "I shall make a meal to remember. *Laissez-moi faire.* Leave it to me."

We were served *pâté de foie gras truffé au porto,* and a beautiful Margaux that did what wines are supposed to do, help you enjoy the food. After thick, tender, rare tournedos crowned with *moëlle*—marrow—accompanied by the lightest, airiest soufflée potatoes, fresh spring peas, and *haricots verts panachés,* we were romanced by dessert: tingling exotic fruits in a ring of flakey patisserie, a caress of ice cream, titillating Grand Marnier, and hot chocolate sauce. The chef came out and bowed. We applauded and I kissed him on both cheeks.

In 1949 it was still possible to see the Impressionists in the Jeu de Paume, an eighteenth-century handball court on the Place de la Concorde where aristocrats played a game similar to ours. As we emerged, properly thrilled with the Monets, Renoirs, and Cézannes, we suddenly realized we had to change money. An American from Texas told us not to go to a bank but to a café called "Le Sporteef."

"Isn't that black market?" Annie queried innocently.

The man looked straight at her. "Ma'am, if it weren't for the black market, we'd all be dead. Even our American G.I.'s go there."

In the taxi, Ben sat next to the driver; Adrian, Annie, Sam, and I were in back. Ben was telling the driver he was afraid he could never drive in Paris. "How do you get around a place like the Etoile where eight wide avenues radiate in and out?" he asked.

"Why in the name of God would you want to drive in Paris?" the driver asked.

"I think it's a good idea since my wife," Ben said, "is pregnant and delivers quickly. That way I can get her to the hospital in time."

Again, we saw a complete transformation at the word *enceinte*, just as there had been at the Cabaret. The chauffeur considered, then enunciated each syllable. Ben, Canadian, understood French pretty well but couldn't speak it.

"The greatest danger for a driver in Paris is indecision," the driver said. "He who hesitates behind the wheel in Paris is a dead man. For example, you see a pedestrian crossing where there is no light. Head for him at full speed. *Foncez!* Aim! Go at him." He demonstrated on the first convenient pedestrian, who, seeing a cab heading full speed for him, jumped as fast and as far as he could, hurling epithets at the driver. "You see, *foncez!* Go for him! This he understands. He knows in which direction he can take refuge. Otherwise, if he's undecided, he will most certainly be hit. If you aim for them and accelerate, you will miss them."

Le Sportif was a small *café-tabac* with a zinc bar and a few tables at the back. At one of them sat a thin, distinguished-looking, white-haired gentleman in a winter overcoat three sizes too large, nursing his coffee and sizing us up. We were wondering what to do when the white-haired gentleman sprang to his feet and held out his hand to Sam. "I am Pop."

Pop Landau turned out to be a Jew who had fled Germany at the last minute. His non-Jewish wife promised she would follow with their son. She didn't. Mother and child were picked up by the Russians and sent to a camp in Siberia.[3] Pop had been hidden, fed, and kept alive in rat-infested cellars by non-Jewish French during three and a half years of the Nazi Occupation of Paris. When he told his story to the G.I.'s, they brought him to the Joint Distribution Committee, a refugee agency that searched for displaced persons. Young American Jews like Milton Gilbert, later chief of the Bank for International Settlements at Basel; Sohne Zelter, Chicago music critic; and Pulitzer winner Stanley Karnow[4] found jobs in Paris with "the Joint."

"Come next door, folks," Pop said. "Chez Goldenberg. It's more *hamish*—homey, comfortable." Pop spoke good English with a German accent, peppered with French, German, and Yiddish words. "You'll eat some *foie haché,* chopped liver, maybe a little herring—"

Sam seemed nervous. "We just want to change dollars," he whispered.

"Don't be in such a hurry. *La vie* is for enjoying," said the man who had just spent three years in a cellar with rats. "What brings you to Gay Paree. Not the sights?"

Pointing to Ben, Sam replied, "He's a blacklisted screenwriter. I'm an actor—"

Pop put up his hands. "Your American Nazis, McCarthy and his anti-Semites!"

Ben clasped Adrian's hand in his two. "Adrian here," said Ben softly, "isn't Jewish. They're probably putting him in jail for a year."

Pop was bewildered, not because Adrian wasn't Jewish, but because Adrian was going to return to the States and almost certain prison. "Don't go back!" he shouted. "I beg of you. Don't be stupid. They're Nazis! Stay here! You'll have a good life!"

Adrian shook his head sadly. Annie's eyes filled with tears.

"So what's the rate?" Sam demanded, anxious to leave sentiment. "I hear it's about six—"

"Six. Yes. For you, six-fifty. No. Six-sixty. No, no. Victims of McCarthy—six-ninety!"

Pop looked over at me tenderly. "When is it—we expect?"

"End September, beginning of October."

"Your first?" he asked. Ben pulled out a photo of Luli and Johnny from his wallet, showed it to Pop. "Beautiful," Pop said softly. "I have no more my son. I'll be your grandpops."

The city of Paris had commissioned Rodin to create a tribute to Balzac. Among the clay studies he presented was one of Balzac, nude, arms akimbo, deep-set eyes beneath heavy brows, his potbelly and genitalia proudly displayed. Rodin preferred the nude sculpture but the grateful citizens of Paris had draped a huge cloak over him, covering his splendid genitalia.

On our second day in Paris, Ben wanted to see the original at the

Rodin Museum but I was tired and needed to sit down. We settled on the Coupole.

I saw them when they walked in—he, short, slumped, froglike; she, taller, dowdy, turbaned. They sat at a table in the back, put on their spectacles, and immersed themselves in their separate copies of *Le Monde,* talking with each other excitedly about something they'd read.

I got my courage up and went over to them. "*Bonjour Madame de Beauvoir. Bonjour Monsieur Sartre.*" They shook hands with me. "I thought you were habitués of the Flore—"

"We keep that rumor going to have some peace," she said in perfect English.

"I am a great admirer of both of you," I said, realizing I hadn't yet read a word either of them had written.

"*The Second Sex,* my new book, is just being published here, in French, of course." She looked me up and down. "It would interest you, I think."

When I got back to our table, Ben asked, "What did you say to them?"

"I wished them *Bon appétit.*"

"You're reviving," Ben said, "let's go to the Rodin Museum."

"Ben, we ought to look up Volodya and Ida."

"C'mon, Norma, we only have four days in Paris. You didn't try to see them in Hollywood when they lived around the corner."

"Volodya—Vladimir Pozner," I said, drawing myself up, "is one of the leading French intellectuals of the Left." The Pozners and their children had been exiles in the U.S. during the Nazi Occupation of France. "I was crazy about his book *Conversations with Gorky*—"

"You loved *Gorky,* not Volodya—"

"Ben! I want to see Volodya! You go to the Rodin Museum."

I found a new kind of strength, just being in France, a place that was mine. Ben chose to come with me. We didn't have the Pozners' phone number so we climbed five flights of stairs and were lucky. That Saturday afternoon, Volodya was working on a film script, which reminded me of another reason I wanted to look him up. He could help Ben and Adrian get movie jobs. It never occurred to me to ask him for help on my own work.

April in Paris

Volodya's deep Russian-black eyes were full of emotion. "Come with me!" he said. He drove us in a battered Citroën to the Right Bank behind the Louvre, parked where the sign said *Pas de stationnement*—No Parking—and opened the double doors to the *Maison de la Pensée,* the House of Thought. It was filled with flowers and people, many of whom seemed vaguely familiar.

Volodya threw back his head, ran his fingers through his thick jet-black mane. "It is because these are world-famous faces!" I felt as I had the night I arrived at the projection of *Chapayev* when my cousin Henry waved his hand to introduce the audience of three hundred or so as "the Hollywood progressive community." This time I was even more awed. I saw the handsome features of white-haired author Louis Aragon, head of the cultural section of the French Communist Party, and his lovely wife, poet Elsa Triolet, and near them Simone Signoret and Yves Montand.

Picasso stood, short and sturdy, in the center of an excited group. Volodya barged in and presented us as though it were an honor for Picasso. To my surprise, he embraced me with a hug, gave Ben the Spanish embrace (you've seen it, two Spaniards throw their arms around each other and pound each other's backs), and immediately took us around to his friends as if he'd known us for years, presenting us as fellow exiles, he from Franco Spain, we from McCarthy America. Ben mumbled that we didn't consider ourselves exiles, having been away only two months.

"We are the same," Picasso said, squeezing my arm. His wild, playful, intense brown eyes scanned me. "Exiles." He continued taking us around to his friends as "exiles who don't yet know they're exiles."

I was more excited meeting Picasso than I was in Princeton in 1940 when my then husband, Claude Shannon, introduced me to Einstein. Picasso was an artist. Picasso was a Communist. Picasso was us.

He presented us to Fernand Léger, a burly man in workman's clothes and cap. In his presence, Picasso told us that Léger had suffered an "interesting injury" as a youth. At the age of fifteen, while working on a farm in Normandy, Léger had been kicked in the groin by a horse. The blow had not interfered with his activities except that it left him sterile, a state of affairs which Léger, being no fool, refused to accept and spent a good part of his adult life trying to disprove. "A most agreeable pursuit," Picasso added. "It gave Léger the excuse for jumping on every attractive young woman he could to prove the doctors wrong. I," Picasso added cheerfully, "have the opposite problem."

Léger let out a boisterous laugh and told us he'd enjoyed America very much and had gone there to escape the Nazis. He asked Picasso why he had not taken the time to visit America.

Picasso made a sound between a chuckle and a snort. "I'm not welcome," he said. "Like our friends here," indicating Ben and me, "I am considered a Communist. The Americans will grant me a visa, but first they wish me to answer a lengthy questionnaire, especially about my private political opinions. I have refused to tell them. Instead, I tell them I express my opinions in my work that is there for the entire world to see. What I believe in, what I feel, is all there, plain and clear." He turned to me, "Did you attend the Peace Congress last week? Here in Paris? At the Salle Pleyel?"

I shook my head. "We were in London."

Picasso mumbled something to a young man passing by who returned quickly with a poster. Picasso unrolled it. "My Dove," he said, "for the Congrès Mondiale de la Paix. Last week, April twentieth through the twenty-third. You just missed it!"

The young man offered him a pencil. Picasso spread the poster on a table, signed it, and handed it to me. I kissed him on both cheeks fervently. I still have it.

Volodya introduced us to the Joliot-Curies. Irène Joliot-Curie was one of the two daughters of the Curies who had discovered radium. The tips of Irène's ears, I saw, were worn away by radioactivity. Frédéric Joliot, a handsome man in his early fifties, an ardent film buff, headed the French Atomic Energy Commission. As was frequently the custom in France and Spain, he had hyphenated his wife's name onto his, even though he was already a renowned physicist in his own right.

Joliot began to tell Ben a story. "When we knew Paris would fall to the Nazis," he said, "I gathered all the heavy water produced in Paris laboratories in drums, and fled with them to Norway, where I thought they would be safe. At that time, heavy water was a vital first step in making the atomic bomb. I managed to get the Norsk Hydro-Electric installation to produce heavy water, but the Nazis arrived and occupied Norway."

After a lengthy pause, Ben said, "What a wonderful movie that would make!"

Joliot burst into laughter. "Either I'm a bad storyteller," he said, "or it takes you a long time—like the English—to catch on." The story did, in fact, become the basis for the film *The Heroes of Telemark* (1965), which Ben wrote, Anthony Mann directed, Kirk Douglas starred.

"I'm happy things are better for you," said a painter we recognized as Arbit Blatas, whom we'd met in New York.

"Is that a joke?" Ben asked. "We're floating around Europe, exiles, jobless, scared—"

"No," Arbit replied, his voice still flavored by a strong Lithuanian accent. "You *must* have made some money. I heard you bought a painting of mine at the *Masses* auction before you left."

Volodya started touring us again, presenting us to the "painter's painter," Albert Marquet, who told a story about himself and Matisse that Ben treasured and told over and over.

"We once painted each other painting each other," Marquet began. "You understand? He was painting me painting him and we would then trade canvasses. We were great friends but Matisse was always concerned, not exactly with money, but what we should do with our money to make more money. One day, right after the American economic crash, Matisse came running up to my studio, all sweaty and excited and said, 'I have it! I know what we should do with our money. Gold! We should invest in gold!' I told him I had a better idea.

"'Better than gold?' Matisse asked.

"'Yes. Invest in Matisse!'"

That night in the hotel room, Ben smiled wistfully. "If Padovani can fall in love with a role, I guess I can fall in love with a city."

"You see," I said, "it's not going to be a complete tragedy, meeting the people we did and having such friends?"

"No," Ben agreed, "it wouldn't be all bad if we could find some way of living in Paris." He sat down at the desk, pulled a photo of Luli and Johnny from his wallet, stuffed it into an envelope. "She's quite right."

"Who?"

"Mumma," he replied, addressing the envelope and reading aloud as he wrote. " 'Yes, there are people everywhere. People with hearts and minds. And Paris is maybe the place where we could make a life and raise a family. There are no Cossacks here . . . ' "

14

Dépaysés—Uncountried

In May, when *Christ in Concrete* finished shooting in London, Ben and I decided to live in Paris. Feeling we needed a transition for the summer between hotel living in London and permanent living in Paris, we chose Cannes in the South of France, a town with a Communist municipal government and the beginnings of a film festival.

Adrian Scott and Anne Shirley were to follow. He'd stopped off in Paris to meet André Sarrut, the French producer of many popular French films. Annie was back in California, closing their home on Beverly Drive. When school was over, she would bring their children back to Cannes for the summer. Mother and I found apartments for the Scotts and for us near each other in residences built around 1917 when émigrés, Russian exiles, had been fleeing the revolution. Ours was called Palais Alexandre III in honor of the czar.

Our apartment was suffocating. Mother had always said she wouldn't be caught dead in Cannes in the summer. Perhaps that not only came from snobbishness—it was a chic winter resort—but also because the Riviera is murderously torrid from May on. However, much of the heat we were experiencing was emotional. The first few days in a hotel seemed temporary. This felt permanent.

Ben was suffering his first pangs of exile. England hadn't seemed foreign. After all, he'd been brought up in British Canada. In London, in the midst of moviemaking, he'd been far too busy. He'd had a job, even if he never got paid. The project itself had been inspiring, and because it had turned out so well, he had hopes for more work. Now, he felt cut off from everything. His old fears came home to roost.

He took refuge in the dining room, typewriter on the table, left the glass doors ajar so we could hear his mutterings, " . . . fucking woman lawyer . . . shit-ass deadline . . . " He feared the moment the studios would stop buying anything from blacklisted writers. Yes, *Young Woman with Ideas* had been my idea. Yes, I did want to collaborate with him, but I was more pregnant each day, too occupied, too weary. Housekeeping for a family of five was arduous, nerve-wracking work. I was beginning to feel that *this* was what my life was going to be and I'd better get used to it.

Madame Remor, *patronne* of the café-restaurant we came to know well, handed me a card: "Taxi Ribotti" with a phone number. "Call for Ton Ton and make him wait for you."

"Ton Ton," the nickname for uncle, drove up and helped Mother and me into his taxi. Wonder of wonders, he knew Ben and I were blacklisted American screenwriters! "Forgive me," I exclaimed. "But how do you know?"

"As a Communist member of the *Conseil Municipale,* the Town Council of Cannes," he said, bowing, "it is my business to know such things. We are aware of *le McCarthyisme.* We thought we put an end to *le Fascisme.* You Americans are now importing it."

"But how do you know about us?"

"The concierge of the Hotel Martinez is a *camarade.* We were in the Maquis together, the French Resistance."

"Ton Ton," Monsieur Artur Ribotti, waited while Mother and I bought a small low square Provençal table with two children's chairs to match. The owner of the store, noticing that I was exhausted, said she would send someone English-speaking to help with the children.

Johnny saw through the new mademoiselle immediately. "I don't want to sit in that chair," he said. She said, "Because—?" "Because I don't like it," Johnny replied, refusing the French cereal—like cornflakes but not cornflakes. "Because . . . ?" she said. "Because I hate it!" he shouted. "Because . . . ?" "Because it tastes terrible! Do *you* like that cereal?" he demanded. "Because . . . " she answered. "Because what?" He was livid. "Don't you have any other words?"

She paled. About to cry, she said very low, "Because . . . "

Johnny began to scream. "I don't want her!"

Luli and Johnny were *dépaysés* (day-pay-ease-zay), a word the hotel maids had taught us, which meant literally "uncountried," taken away from their normal environment and routine. Ben insisted he was *dépaysé* too; that's why he was so irritable. Luli didn't know why she was irritable. Johnny knew. Here, in this dreadful country, he enunciated clearly what he wanted and people not only didn't understand, they rattled nonsense at him. Johnny howled. He wept. He understood why he was *dépaysé*.

That night, chez Remor, I was tired, Mother wasn't feeling well, Ben and the children were out of sorts. Madame Remor apologized for intruding. "You need a young lady to help out."

Ben said, "No, no. We don't want anyone around. But thanks." I recounted the story of "Mademoiselle Because."

"Our Dédée has just now her *baccalauréat*. She speaks fluent English."

Dédée, Delphine Barbéris, was the niece of Ton Ton, Communist councilman of Cannes, taxi driver in his spare time, champion of *boules*. Dédée spoke perfect English and she was one of the best things that had happened to us in a long time. Luli and Johnny loved her, still do. She came to Paris with us, and stayed five years. She was pretty in a wholesome way with a sensuous dusting of down over her upper lip. I can see Luli and Johnny opposite each other at the little table; between them, Dédée sitting on the floor, their three heads at the same level, all cutting out, coloring, modeling clay, eating, drinking amid shrieks of rapture as they squirted each other with *le Coca-Cola*.

I knew Mother missed gambling and theater, her two entertainments, and asked her whether she'd like to go one afternoon to the casino.

"They only play roulette in the afternoon," she replied. "As you know, baccarat is my game, *Chemin de fer*."

One evening Mother took longer than usual to dress. When she appeared, her hair had been done and she was all gussied up in a beaded black evening gown from Bullock's Wilshire.

"That's not just for supper with us and the kids?"

"No," she answered, her rosebud mouth curled in a naughty smile. "Monsieur Ribotti—Ton Ton—is coming in the taxi to take me to the casino."

Mother returned about midnight, looked delighted with herself. "Although," she said, "it wasn't much fun without your father." Her small black evening bag was bulging. She opened it and took out two packages of new large bills. "I won," she said. "Two thousand francs."

"Wow! Five hundred dollars. What luck!"

"Oh, no," she said, "technique."

Our only friends in the south were Abe and Sylvia Polonsky. When Abe returned from the war, where he'd been in the O.S.S., the information spy organization that became the CIA, he'd scripted the outstanding *Body and Soul* starring John Garfield, which Robert Rossen directed. Abe then demonstrated his virtuosity by writing and directing *Force of Evil,* one of the best film noirs. The Polonskys had taken a house in the "Californie" section of Cannes so that he could work on his novel *The World Above.*

Abe and Sylvia invited us to dinner with an old progressive friend of theirs from New York, an advertising executive fired for her political opinions. Her new husband, Bill Pepper, who'd been an Army journalist during the war, accompanied Beverly. I liked her so much that when my picture *Finishing School* was shooting at Cinecittà in 1951, I got her a job doing the costumes and even lent them money. Eventually, Bill landed a job on the *Rome Daily American.* Beverly Pepper became a distinguished sculptor and close friend of our ambassador to Italy, Clare Booth Luce. Married to *Time's* founder, Henry Luce, known for his extreme right-wing political beliefs, Clare Luce was eager to rid Italy of Hollywood blacklisted film people. She was responsible for forcing Jules Dassin, Joe Losey, and Bernard Vorhaus to leave Italy on the run.

We never figured out where the Peppers fit in. Lillian Hellman, suspicious of them, wrote in her book *Scoundreltime* about a similar young couple, working for the CIA or the State Department, who had spied on American "Reds" in Italy. That clandestine activity was common in Europe from 1949 well into the sixties. In Paris, some people without funds hung around the Coupole and other cafés, listened, reported, and were rewarded with small fees by a CIA guy at the American embassy named Mr. Gray. He had suggested to several of us exiles that we "keep our ears open."

Annie arrived in Cannes with eighteen trunks, four suitcases, her daughter, Julie Payne, her adopted son, Michael Scott, and bad news. Back home, the Cold War was at gale force. Hollywood studios, the guilds, even some liberals were supporting the blacklist.

Annie seemed remote and odd to me, almost too bright-eyed. I felt she was holding something back. Not long after her arrival, Adrian showed up at our front door with little Michael, the inspiration for *The Boy with Green Hair*. Adrian had a sepulchral pallor and an air of bewilderment. He held out a short handwritten note. Annie had written, "I can't leave Beverly Drive. It's my life. If I don't go now, I will later. That would be worse. I'm taking Julie and leaving you Michael. I'll always love you. Annie."

We were appalled. How could she leave her adopted son, who had already lost his parents? How could she leave Adrian at such a dreadful time? How *could* she? "Come on in, you guys," I said. "Have breakfast with us."

A few days later, we heard from the French husband of Annie's best friend, operatic-voiced child star Deanna Durbin. Her nickname was Jeanne and she lived by choice as a French wife in a Paris suburb and sang only for herself. "Before Annie left for Europe," Durbin's husband reported, "she met Charlie Lederer, Marion Davies' nephew, a well-heeled writer with no McCarthy problems. Everyone knows he's alcoholic, worse, a *drogué*, but to Annie, whose world's being torn apart, he's a haven."

I never forgave Annie for leaving Adrian. He was a brilliant talent, the kindest of men, and should have, by rights, become a great producer, for he had worked with integrity, not with tough, *What-Makes-Sammy-Run* aggression or corruption. Annie, after years of being a mother-driven child actress, found in Adrian a loving person who helped her find herself. Her daughter, Julie, who'd suffered through her parents' divorce, was now deprived of her new father, Adrian, and subjected to the Lederers' unhealthy, drugged environment. Poor Michael once again lost both mother and father, for in a year, Adrian and all of the Hollywood Ten were in jail and Annie was in another marriage. Madeleine Dmytryk, Eddie's first wife, took care of the two Michaels, hers and Adrian's. The blacklist ruptured families.

I vowed that what had happened to many blacklist families must not happen to Ben and me. We must stick together and face the common enemy. Although we had few marital troubles then, I was becoming concerned about Ben's newly acquired chronic depression. I guess the pessimistic side of his personality had always been there, but our six years together in Hollywood had been so filled with his exciting success as a screenwriter, starting a family, and our involvement in the progressive community, that signs of depression were faint. Our relationship had been fulfilling, enhanced by work and politics, and by the romantic glow of "making the world better." Being pitched into an exile he took as rejection exacerbated the negative, depressive part of his character. Our relationship was being transformed into an alliance against a hostile world.

At the end of August 1949, it was time to leave for Paris. The baby would be born in about a month. I hadn't yet consulted a doctor. We heard we could rent, instead of a Paris hotel suite, an impoverished marquis's house in Passy for a short stay while we searched for a permanent home. I'm glad I said yes because the Marquis' Bretonne cook-housekeeper, Madame Josette, thirty-six, never married but with a son *en pension,* defected to the Barzmans. Like Dédée, she remained five years with us until she became a concierge with a *loge* so she could keep her son with her. For the next five years, 1949–54, Dédée and Josette made it possible for me to have a family and to write.

Joe and Ruth Hirsch, already in Paris, knew from friends that a French dentist, Dr. Pierre Robbes, had a big house in Boulogne, a nearby suburb, which he didn't use and might rent. He'd moved his residence and offices to the middle of town. It sounded plausible enough, but how could a dentist afford to leave a huge modern house vacant? Didn't he need the rental income? The house seemed perfect for us—a quiet suburban home, a postage-stamp garden, ten minutes from the heart of Paris, and only twelve minutes—we timed it—across the Bois to the American Hospital in Neuilly.

A good-sized kitchen, two bedrooms, and a bathroom occupied the garden floor of the house. Let's face it, Mother was living in one of the two maids' rooms, Madame Josette in the other. One floor up was the immense, ballroom-sized, marble-floored living room with a raised dais, the dining area that held a long marble-topped table seating twelve. A dumbwaiter delivered the food. The floor above the living room consisted of our bedroom and bath and what was destined to be the baby's room, in which the infant nurse was already installed. The top floor was one enormous room, the playroom, where Luli, Johnny, and Dédée slept. They had a bathroom and a roof garden. There was also a room that was locked.

Dr. Pierre Robbes, the affluent dentist who looked like a corrupt cherub, stipulated two conditions: rent payments be made in dollars, for which he'd give us signed receipts, and the locked room on the top floor would under no circumstances be opened or entered. French friends corroborated that it was the custom in France for landlords to ask their tenants to leave one room locked. The landlord could then claim the tenants were simply dear friends whom he'd graciously invited to stay, which meant the landlord, alas, had no income to report and no income tax to pay. Dr. Robbes made one other tiny condition: he would like to visit that room occasionally and would call in advance to let us know when he was coming. He said he had hunting and fishing gear there. Why didn't he keep his gear at his spacious Boulevard Haussmann apartment? We had questions but were desperate to move in before the baby arrived.

Shortly after we moved in, Lillian, Pierre's American wife, invited us to a cocktail party at their luxurious overfurnished apartment. The priceless antiques made us wonder how a dentist like Pierre could have amassed such wealth. Among the guests that evening were the Hirsches, their fellow Philadelphians the Gilberts, and their friends the Torems.

Milton Gilbert, a PhD in economics from the University of Pennsylvania, spent his first two years in Paris "overhauling" the Joint Distribution Committee, to whom Pop Landau had appealed to find his son. "Overhauling" meant what my old boss, city editor Jim Richardson, called "getting rid of deadwood." Milton was known to have fired one of his best friends, Sohne Zelter, for being a *luftmensche,* a man with his head in the clouds—who had been fired years before from the *Chicago Tribune* for turning in a review of a concert that was canceled.

Ruth Gilbert, Milton's wife, a beautiful, elegantly dressed woman, had worked as an artist's model, was the daughter of a painter, and had taught art. In Paris, she took classes at the Sorbonne and the Cordon Bleu, learned to buy the best couture at discount prices, and held soirées where the top musicians in the world played. At sixty-five, she picked up Milton's camera. "Put that down," he'd snapped, "that's a Hasselblad." Ruth bought herself a Nikon, studied with a top photographer. Her work now hangs in the photography museums of Tokyo, Paris, and Washington.[1]

Charlie Torem was with Coudert Frères, the international law firm. He was reserved, sharp, and seemed nine feet tall. He certainly was well over six feet. His wife, Irma, petite, bubbly, an irrepressible redhead, didn't quite come up to his shoulder.

With a ceaseless supply of champagne, the atmosphere became lighter, headier. Lillian casually showed us Pierre's prized objets d'art, cunningly worked pieces of extravagant erotica. She paraded one ivory figurine after another, each more explicit than the last. Irma took a close look and let out a cry. Slightly tipsy and glowing at the sensation made by her husband's collection, Lillian let us in on a little secret: "If you think these are something, you should see the others."

"What others?" Joe Hirsch asked, suddenly very interested.

Lillian looked over at Pierre on the other side of the room and made a slightly teasing sealed-lips gesture. *She* would never tell.

I let out a yelp. "So that's what's in the locked room!"

Lillian reacted in apparent wonder but she leaned closer. "For God's sake, don't let Pierre know I told you—"

"You haven't," I said.

"He'd kill me," she said, shooting a look at the far side of the immense salon.

I felt a peculiar, alien fear. Yes, Pierre could kill her.

"Whatever you do," she went on, "don't open that room. Even I have never been in it!"

Why, I wondered, wouldn't a man let his wife see his collection of erotica?

"Some of the pieces are priceless," Lillian hissed, "and have to be handled with care. Mustn't touch. Promise! Promise?"

Before the evening was over, I discovered that Ben had invited the Gilberts and the Torems to the dinner party we were going to have for his birthday. I had already asked the Hirsches, Arbit Blatas, and blacklisted harmonica virtuoso Larry Adler. With Ben and me, that made twelve to fit nicely around our marble-topped dining table.

Larry Adler, who had performed concerts of Bach, Vivaldi, and Gershwin, was on a tour in England when HUAC subpoenaed him. His agent said that unless he was willing to name Communists, he ought not return home. Larry was never in the Party but belonged to many front organizations. He felt that naming names was a sin. (Informers are denied burial in a Jewish cemetery.) Like us, Larry remained in England in exile with his family for thirty years. After that, he only visited the States on concert tours.[2]

Most of our guests arrived early. Joe Hirsch had hinted to them that something interesting was afoot. Larry Adler and Arbit Blatas trickled in late. Arbit had already had a few vodkas. After one or two more, he was toasting Ben and smashing the glasses in the huge ornate fireplace. Several others followed suit. I heaved a sigh of relief when Madame Josette announced dinner.

Since it was our first entertainment in our splendid house, Madame Josette and the infant nurse waiting for our unborn baby out-Escoffiered Escoffier—or so they believed. The first dish was Coquilles Saint-Jacques Mornay, a gem of French haute cuisine, particularly good in late September or early October when scallops come into season. Each of our twelve large scallop shells was filled with shrimps, scallops, and mushrooms in a creamy béchamel and white-wine sauce, sprinkled with a little Parmesan and browned lightly in a hot oven. When Madame Josette came for our empty plates, the guests clapped.

Then she and the nurse marched in triumphantly with dozens of the tiniest birds I'd ever seen. She served them with a flourish. The birds' heads were intact, attached to necks drooping limply over Dr. Robbes's ornate silver platter. The height of French culinary elegance made our guests pale. Irma let out a little shriek when she saw a minuscule glazed head stare directly up at her. The others pretended they weren't bothered but kept their eyes averted. Mortified, Madame Josette took the creatures back to the kitchen. Crêpes Suzette obliterated distressing memories of the birds, and the marvelous wines and liqueurs we'd been drinking caused a happy alcoholic haze to fall over us.

Impulsive, redheaded, uninhibited Irma Torem made the following pronouncement: "Charlie has a passion for locks and keys. It's his hobby." She waited until someone mumbled, "Freudian," then went on. "Charlie and I discussed it. French houses built in the twenties like this one have a set of keys for all rooms made from the same basic cut. Invariably, one is a passkey. Usually the one to the master bedroom fits all the other locks. Isn't that right, dear?"

"Yes," said Torem tightly.

Joe Hirsch rolled his eyes. "Then what are we waiting for?" His expression suddenly became boyishly mischievous.

In seconds, Joe and Irma were scurrying up the stairs to our bedroom. Ruth Gilbert rushed after them. The rest of us straggled behind or feigned indifference. The key to our bedroom was in its lock. Joe yanked it out, Irma snatched it from his hands and went jiggling up the stairs to the top floor. We followed. With an extravagant gesture, she shoved in the key, turned it, and triumphantly pushed open the forbidden door.

Silent, we crowded the doorway. Irma turned on a light. The first thing I saw was a stack of machine guns nesting in rounds of ammunition, a few grenades, a collection of small arms, and a mysterious pile of bricks I couldn't identify.

Milton Gilbert, the economist, pointed to the dusty bricks that gleamed dimly. "Those," he whispered, "are solid gold bullion." He counted the pile. "Two hundred thousand dollars' worth of gold here. No wonder Pierre Robbes didn't want us in that room."

In the last months before the Liberation, when it was certain the Nazis would be driven out of France, French collaborators still working for the Nazis refused to accept Nazi currency in payment. They continued only if they were paid in gold. After the Liberation, the resistance had immediately executed anyone caught with gold bars. Collaborators who'd escaped the first postwar raids kept the gold carefully hidden. It was said that millions of dollars' worth of Nazi gold was vaulted all over Paris.

Pierre *was* a dangerous man. As an ex-collaborator, he could still be executed if discovered. I wanted us all out of that room; I wanted it locked again. But Irma was high. She scooped up an armful of erotic books, drawings, and other promising objects, whooped and tripped down the stairs. Ruth Gilbert, floating on champagne, grabbed a sheaf of prints and followed her.

"What are you worried about?" Irma shouted at me. "You'll put everything back. You'll lock the goddamn door and that'll be the end of it."

"She's right," Ruth Gilbert said. "We'll look, then put it all back."

The two lovely ladies carried their hauls to the dining room table, where the light from a crystal chandelier was especially good. We all clustered round. Larry had his harmonica in his pocket but never had a chance to play. Even Arbit and Larry, who pretended sophisticated indifference, studied drawings of daisy chains, meticulously drawn acts of fellatio, anal intercourse, cunnilingus. Pierre's wife had been right. Some of the drawings were by eminent artists, one, Arbit said, was by Picasso when he was very young. Joe found several he thought were by a seventeenth-century artist, perhaps Caravaggio, beautifully drawn sketches of a nude woman attempting to make love to a hanged man dangling at the end of a rope and sprouting an enormous erection.

Charlie Torem, who seemed to have a store of strange knowledge, remarked, "There's a myth that hanged criminals die with great erections. I don't know if that's true. When the hanged man's spinal cord snaps, all sorts of involuntary reflexes occur."

The irrepressible Irma squealed with delight and obvious arousal. Her husband was clearly embarrassed. (They were divorced a year later.)

By two-thirty in the morning, everyone had seen everything. "I'm scared," I said.

"Norma has a right to be scared," Torem said. "Just make sure you put the erotica back carefully. Be sure nothing looks disturbed."

If Pierre ever heard about our getting into that room, we would be in danger.

Ben and I, exhausted and frightened, carried the stuff back up with great care, tried to put it all away in the spaces of the floor's dust pattern where the cache had been secretly lodged for years. We stood in the doorway a long moment, studying the room carefully. Everything seemed in order. We stumbled off to bed.

"We've got to get the hell out of this house," Ben said, his face pale and drawn.

"I know," I replied. "But we can't right now."

15

Pardon My French

The next day, Sunday, October 11, Ben went over to Milly's to work. Milly was Lewis Milestone, distinguished director of *The Front Page* (1931) and *All Quiet on the Western Front*. A liberal, Milestone, born in Russia, came to Hollywood in the early 1930s. During the war, he made a film called *The North Star* (1943) that was nominated for several Oscars. Scripted by Lillian Hellman, it was about the Soviet Union's struggle against the German onslaught.

The House UnAmerican Activities Committee had set their sights on Milestone, not because he was a Communist but because he'd been active in many popular Front organizations. He was one of the original Hollywood Nineteen, called to Washington in October 1947. The first ten unfriendly witnesses became the Hollywood Ten; the remaining nine were not called to testify. Milly and his wife, Kendall, fled to Paris soon after.

Ben was collaborating with Milly on an adaptation of Dostoyevsky's *The Idiot,* hoping for a movie deal with Amati, the Italian producer of Fellini films who had shown interest. Unlike Ben, who often interrupted my work, I never broke into his, but this Sunday, I phoned him at Milly's. "I just got a call from Pierre. He's coming over this evening." I tried to keep the hysteria out of my voice. "The room. We forgot to lock the door."

"We what?"

"We didn't lock the door! With the key. The door's unlocked."

"That's impossible." Long pause. "No, I don't remember locking it. Are you sure?"

"I went upstairs and looked for myself. The room's unlocked and I can't find the key. I went through all your clothes. No key. I called because I'm hoping you took it by mistake."

"Look around some more."

"I looked everywhere!" I said. "We all did. It's nowhere. And the lock-smiths are all gone for the day."

I could hear Milly say, "Better go home . . . "

When Ben arrived, Madame Josette was having a *crise de peur,* an attack of fright. At eighteen, she'd been "requisitioned" to work as a cook for a high-ranking Gestapo officer. She'd begun her resistance by spitting in the soup, then gone on to more serious efforts, like blowing her nose in stews, and had once done worse. She'd been terrified the Nazis would detect a strong telltale odor, but no, the Gestapo colonel had tasted the soup as she stood there. It was a common ritual in Nazi-Occupied France when "requisitioned" personnel worked for the occupiers, in case one of them added cyanide and the taster dropped dead. It was also a courtesy to the guests who waited stolidly through the test before eating. Since urine is not fatally toxic, the colonel had not dropped dead. Instead, he'd complimented Madame Josette and asked, "What is the magic ingredient that gives the soup its special zest?" Frantic, Madame Josette had given the name of the first Breton herb that popped into her head. The Gestapo officer noted it down in his little notebook, a recipe to send home to his wife. Until the day of Liberation, Madame Josette lived in terror because she'd discovered the herb she'd blurted out under stress did exist and was deadly.

"Tonight I am frightened in the same way." She shook from head to toe.

After a long moment, Ben said, "Charlie Torem said all our keys were basically the same. Maybe another will fit."

Pardon My French

Ben and I and Madame Josette gathered all the keys, rushed up to the top floor, tried one after another on that maddening unlocked door. Not one would lock it. Frantically, Ben compared the keys. They were all from the same basic cut. There were only tiny differences between them. He tried them all over and over, finally held one up.

"This one," he said, "seems to slip in more easily than the others."

"So?"

"So," Ben replied, "there's an electric emery wheel in the garage. He once had his dental offices here. I'll work on this key until it fits."

"Does Monsieur know anything about keys?" Madame Josette asked.

"Monsieur knows nothing about keys," I replied.

"I'll make this key fit before Pierre gets here," Ben said defiantly.

Slowly, I descended the four flights, big belly and all, to see what he was doing. He set the circular emery wheel whirring, gingerly working the key on it. Sparks flew. I wondered if he really knew what he was doing. He filed a few seconds, then ran up the four flights. I waited. He returned, cursing. Again and again, he worked the key, ran up the four flights and tried it. I don't know how many trips he made. Night fell. The overhead garage light bulb blew. Ben threw open the garage door. A ghoulish yellow light flooded the garage and with it came the freezing night air. I shivered. Ben was sweating. If Pierre drove up now, he would see Ben from the street, pushing the key against the emery wheel hard until sparks made a dragon's tail in the darkness. I could see Ben was encouraged. The key was slimmer. He raced up the four flights as fast as he could.

I stayed and waited.

Back he came, switched on the emery stone, and filed gently and doggedly. A bright flash sputtered as the wheel short-circuited. He took the rough stationary wheel with one hand, filed the key against the stone frantically with the other. He rushed up the four flights. I ran up the stairs after him. At the top floor, he tried the key. It slipped in but still wouldn't turn.

Ben sat down. I thought he was going to cry. "Why don't we just give up?" he said. "We don't belong here. We never will."

I said softly, "It slipped in. Pretty soon it'll turn. After all, what will he do to us? Kill all eight of us? Or have us killed?"

"*Precisément!*" cried Madame Josette, who had reappeared. "Then he'll flee with the gold!"

"Let's take the kids and go to a hotel," I suggested.

"No! Not yet! We can't do that. I'm going to make this key fit."

"Monsieur has blood on his face," observed Madame Josette. "Monsieur's hands are bleeding."

Ben said, "Thank you."

She said, "*Il n'y a pas de quoi*—you're welcome."

I staggered down the four flights with him. He continued to ply that small piece of metal against the motionless wheel. When his right hand became too painful, he switched to the left. He had actually been left-handed, but as a child in Canada they'd tied his hand behind his back and forced him to write with his right. I thought he was making progress when I became aware of a metallic rapping, gently at first, at our iron barred gate a few yards outside the garage. Ben heard it too. He stopped, peered out.

"It's Pierre," I groaned.

In the darkness on the other side of the gate stood the grotesque silhouette of a man-sized bird with its wings spread wide, a vague circular shape protruding from its middle.

I hid in the shadowy darkness. Paralyzed, Ben sat on the cold floor. The rapping became less gentle, finally imperious.

Ben said in his stupor, "Nothing to be afraid of, only a man-eating prehistoric bird rubbing its beak over the bars."

A sudden powerful flashlight found Ben's face, his bleeding hands, the glittering key.

The bird spoke French. "Open!" it commanded.

Ben got up and opened the gate, the bird advanced toward us, taking form.

At that time, a section of the French police patrolled neighborhoods on bicycles. They wore huge capes, which spread like wings when they raised their arms or pedaled rapidly. They were popularly known as *Les hirondelles*—the Swallows. A Swallow stood inside the gate, a bicycle by his side, holding a flashlight on Ben.

"*Oui?*" Ben asked politely.

The Swallow asked what he was doing. With his bloody hands, Ben held up the shining key.

"That is a key?" asked the Swallow.

"I am transforming a key," Ben explained cheerfully.

"For what purpose is Monsieur transforming a key at this hour and in the bitter cold?"

"To open a door. We live here. An important door won't open."

"Ah, you live here," said the bird. As he became more skeptical, he became less formal. "And an important door refuses to open. Why?"

I felt clairvoyant. I could see it all. The Swallow would enter the house to make sure nothing illegal was happening. He would find the room, which was still open. He would then find the gold, the machine guns, the ammunition. We would be "American Reds about to overthrow the French government."

The Swallow went into the garage, focusing the light on Ben's hands, which had been wounded more severely than we had thought. Blood was oozing out like red dough. Ben brushed his face.

"I am not normally an inquisitive or impulsive man," the Swallow said, "but you will agree that the spectacle of a foreigner clad in a light shirt, working with bloody hands in a freezing dark garage at this hour of the night is not a usual one?"

"It is not," Ben agreed, still not having figured out a scenario that would satisfy him. "I am passionate about keys and locks like your own Louis XVI."

On the street behind us a car slowed down and stopped when its occupant saw the flashlight. Ben and I wondered desperately if the car outside was Pierre.

"If you turn your torch off," Ben suggested, "the man in the car outside may move on."

"You are right." The cop turned the flashlight off, but not before it brightened the dark area where I was standing. He could not fail to make out the form of a very pregnant lady.

Ben turned to me, "I was explaining to Monsieur le Gendarme that I am making a key for a door which unfortunately locked itself."

"That is exact," I said.

"What kind of a lock is it," the Swallow asked reflectively, "that locks itself and then needs a special key."

I gave the only reply that would ever have satisfied the Swallow. "It is an American lock," I said.

The Swallow reflected, then sighed, shrugged. "Ah, *bien sûr,* of course, American," he said, then saluted. "*Excusez-moi, Madame, excusez-moi, Monsieur,* but the spectacle of a man with blood on his hands making a key seemed peculiar to me. But of course you are Americans?"

We smiled. "Yes," I said.

With that he saluted again, wheeled his bike out, and silently pedaled off into the darkness.

We were never happier in our whole lives to see anyone go.

The second he was gone, Ben started stumbling up to the top floor, I was right behind him. Madame Josette, Dédée, and the nurse were all there, waiting in dead silence.

Ben inserted the key and turned it. I thought, *What do we do now if it doesn't work?* I heard a funny, tiny sound from the lock. Ben jiggled the key, which was now slim enough for such maneuvers and the tongue of the lock must have moved into its appointed place. Ben turned the handle and pulled. The door wouldn't move. To make sure, Madame Josette stepped forward and tried the door.

"This door," she proclaimed gravely, "is now locked."

"Locked," the nurse whispered confirmation, awed.

Dédée laughed in relief.

"I did it," Ben said. "I made a goddamn passkey." He leaned against the wall. "The principle of the passkey . . . " He stopped. "I don't know the principle. I don't know what I did."

"Never mind," I said. "We're ready for the bastard now."

Ben and I went to the living room, tried to calm down and look assured. We waited. Madame Josette came and offered us liqueurs. We waited some more.

"The hell with him!" I said. "Don't you realize what just happened?"

Ben looked around bewildered. "No. What?"

"You made a key!" I answered. "If you did that, you can do anything."

"You're right," he said after a moment when it really hit him. He looked at his hands in disbelief. "I made a key!"

"If times get bad," I put my hand over his, "we can always open a mom-and-pop key shop here. We'd get the American trade. And it wouldn't matter if a hundred former friends name us! Oh, my God! I married a man who can make a key!" I felt protected by him. At that moment, I loved him unconditionally.

By ten o'clock Pierre still hadn't arrived. A French person would never be so ill mannered as to visit that late. We waited some more anyway. Pierre never came.

Years later, when the subject came up, Joe Hirsch had an owlish look. We listened carefully when he spoke English with a French accent as he did sometimes for fun. We knew he was mischievous and loved playing pranks. He never admitted to it but we always wondered if he had taken the key, then phoned with a phony French accent, and announced, as Pierre would have, that he was coming over.

At eleven o'clock, Ben said, "He's not coming. He wouldn't come this late. We might as well go to bed."

I didn't move.

He said, "What's the matter? Aren't you tired after all that?" He looked at me. "What?"

"I don't know," I said. "It might be—"

"Oh, my God!" he exclaimed. "All that running up and down stairs!"

I reached into my bra for the doctor's number and grabbed the phone. "Holy mackerel! He's there! *Docteur!* This is Norma Barzman. I'm having contractions."

"When did you first start?" he asked.

"Twenty minutes ago."

"Be calm, Madame, when they start coming four minutes apart, call me again."

"But *Docteur,* I showed you the letter from my obstetrician back home. With me, it's very fast." Our first two babies had been delivered in record time, Luli in twenty-eight minutes from the first contraction,

Johnny in thirty-five. Dr. Melinkoff had been explicit. Our third might come faster. It could be dangerous. Pinned to me at all times during my ninth month was a letter from him: "To Whom It May Concern, this woman delivers faster than one would expect. There is only one danger. She must not be left alone once in labor."

"When they start coming four minutes apart, call me again," came the voice of steel.

"We're leaving for the hospital now! You must be there!"

"I will," he replied with icy assurance. "I thought Americans were not given to hysteria."

"This isn't hysteria. I've had two babies. I have them so quickly—"

He cut me off. "Madame, I am familiar with your dossier." He hung up.

"Drive carefully," Mother said to Ben as we got into our black Citroën. The motor started but Ben couldn't find the lights.

"Don't panic," I said to Ben. "You've got the gate key on your key ring." He fumbled, got the gate open, and swung the car around. "It's the other direction," I said.

The Bois de Boulogne. Acres and acres of beautiful woods. Several restaurants, two racetracks, a recreational center and tiny farm so that Parisian children will not grow up without ever seeing cows and chickens. Wide tree-lined avenues crisscrossing in every direction made it a lovely drive if you weren't wondering whether your baby would be born in a car. With all the careful planning for just such a moment, the one thing we'd neglected to do was rehearse in the dark. It was scary. Nothing was recognizable.

"Why do you keep looking around that way?" I asked Ben.

"Looking for a sign, 'Direction Neuilly.' "

"Oh, you're not sure of the direction?"

The streets were silent. Suddenly the road forked. Ben swung to the right.

"You think it's that way?"

No landmarks. I knew we were driving blind. I couldn't hold it in any longer. I made a sound, not a groan, but a sound.

All at once we were out of the Bois. Houses appeared but not like

Neuilly, not like anything we'd seen. "I'll knock on a door," Ben said. "We'll call for an ambulance."

"If they have a phone," I said. (Paris had a five-year wait for phone installation.)

Then we saw a happy scene, two drivers leaning against their cabs, parked up ahead, smoking and chatting. Ben braked to a stop, jumped out, and ran over to the cabbies. I could see him explaining and their dubious looks. Finally, after much arguing, one cabbie, elderly, moved to his elderly cab, but instead of getting in, slowly bent inside, then straightened, holding a strange slender pipelike object.

"It's a crank," Ben said. "He's got to crank his car."

I moaned. After a breathtaking few seconds of squeakings and creakings, the motor barked angrily and broke into a rhythmic series of sounds like someone clearing his throat. The cabbie walked to the passenger side of the car, carefully replaced the crank, then thoughtfully moved around to the driver's side, got in, revved his motor, a really gruff sound, as elderly gears clashed, and the cab took its position in front of us and led the way.

The taxi led us through black, slumbering, completely unfamiliar streets. Suddenly, his indicator was blinking to the left. High on an incline I saw the silhouette of the American Hospital.

Ben stopped at the entrance. I burst out of the car clutching my valise. An elderly nurse at admissions was asking me the place of birth of my mother, when I heard Ben say, "I'll give it to you. Has the doctor come?" I hastened to what I thought was the main elevator. It didn't look right but I got in. Ben pushed the button for the fourth floor. As the elevator took off, my water broke. Elevators don't stop between floors with women in them about to give birth. This one did.

The admissions nurse who was running up the stairs cried, "Don't panic. I'll call the elevator from the second floor." After a few moments, the elevator lurched and crept up to second. We got out and the admissions nurse put us in another elevator.

On the fourth floor, the head maternity nurse took over. I was rushed to the delivery room.

"Is the doctor here?" I asked.

"No, Madame. Our head midwife will prepare you."

But since I had a doctor, the midwife was only allowed to examine me, not assist in the delivery. She announced that I was "dilated fifty centimes." I discovered, when it was all over, the French fifty-centime piece, made of cheaper metal at that time, was actually twice as large in circumference as the one-franc piece that had a silver content. Those coins were popular measures French obstetricians used to convey the progress of the birthing. Fifty centimes was the extreme dilation before the baby's head starts to crown.

The nurse didn't have to tell me that. I was in excruciating agony. When I asked for the doctor, they said he was en route and when I asked someone to help me, the answer was, "We must wait for the doctor!" I began to scream. One after another, interns and nurses would lift the sheet, stare, register shock, and run out of the room. I was alone. The one thing I should not be.

A tall, aristocratic man appeared. "I am here," the doctor announced.

"Help!" I screamed at him. "Help!"

"The head has crowned," he said. "But you have the best couturier in Paris right here."

Couturier? The sonofabitch meant if I ripped to bits, he'd stitch me up again with finesse.

I could make out something dark and round. I grasped the ether mask greedily and pressed it over my face.

16

Paris in October

When I was coming out of the ether, I heard Ben ask, "Is he all right?"

That's how I learned it was a boy and that something was wrong.

The doctor replied callously: "We won't know for twenty-four hours. He suffered head injuries. The birth was extremely rapid."

Was there any point in killing that doctor? Yes. To save other women from him.

When I came to for the second time, Ben was saying, "I haven't let anyone know yet."

I would have gone under again if I could have, but I couldn't. I wept noiselessly, remembering my laughter after the other births when I'd said, "Hooray, let's do it again."

Later, the pediatrician, Dr. Alexandre Minkowski, one of the first *médecins sans frontières*—barefoot doctors—France's Doctor Spock, strode into the room, grabbed my hand, and said with an educated-in-England accent, "There is nothing wrong with your son. He's a splendid little chap!"

"That bruise?" Ben asked softly.

"Is superficial. It will go away."

His simple statement brought us such relief that it could have been a chorus singing Beethoven's Ninth.

"Do you have a name for him?" asked "Minko" as we'd soon call him affectionately.

"Aaron," I answered. "Two A's. A-aron. Like the Old Testament Aaron. My husband's father's name."

Ben added, "Not Harold or Arnold or Allen or any other Anglicized version. Aaron."

Minko's angular skier's body bent forward into a gale of laughter.

Though the crisis over Aaron was past, our domestic tribulations were to begin in earnest.

Since I had not had obstetrical help when needed, I had no control over my bladder for the next two months. Each time I coughed (and I was coughing a lot), a few drops of urine would escape. I thought my cough was asthmatic, the result of stress. But one night at a Jewish restaurant, I was seized by a barking cough that went into a breath-stopping, high-C wheeze. The other diners were standing or poised in a crouch, fixed. The owner decided gefilte fish was the culprit. I was choking to death on a fish bone, a restaurateur's nightmare. He shouted for water. Suddenly, I exhaled. The crouching or standing diners lowered their derrières into their seats. Ben asked for "*l'addition*" but the owner cried, "No, no!" No bill. He was glad to see us the hell out of there.

Madame Josette met us at the front door. "Aaron has *coqueluche*," she said, "whooping cough. Perhaps that is what is wrong with Madame. Luli and Johnny have the chicken pox." After examining me, our doctor, Minko, announced that I had both chicken pox and whooping cough. I'd spent my childhood traveling with my parents and had missed out on the normal exposure to childhood diseases.

I don't recall the moment when it all became too much for Ben. I believe his decision to leave the house came at our lowest ebb, perhaps when Minko explained that with infants, whooping cough was frequently fatal and that childhood diseases could be dangerous for adults.

"I can't take it," Ben said simply. "I can't write. I can't be helpful. I can't anything. I need to get the hell out."

In fairness to Ben, I agreed that since he felt that way, the best thing was to go to a hotel. I could have said, "I need you here," but as always, I didn't say what I felt. Mother refrained from criticizing Ben, but to her, I later learned, his departure was a sign of weakness and a lack of solidarity she never forgave. How did I feel? Betrayed? Abandoned? Yes, but I was too ill to collect all my emotions. I itched unmercifully. The pox on my back burst when I had a long bout of whooping. Sometimes, I couldn't breathe and was frightened. I was already debilitated from a difficult birth and didn't have a lot of stamina. It never occurred to me to give up. Aaron was too terrifyingly ill. I had to keep him alive.

Ben telephoned from Hotel l'Aiglon on Boulevard Raspail, around the corner from La Coupole. "I'll try to work on the original story. Maybe if I change it from a woman to a man?"

"Why don't you try it with a woman first?" I said, exasperated, and hung up.

After he moved out, I tried to get my wits about me. I'd heard a new miracle drug had just come out that cured almost everything, a newfangled antibiotic, penicillin. Minko thought it might have an effect on whooping cough. Unfortunately, it was not obtainable in France because they hadn't yet been able to synthesize it. The Americans had limited supplies but not even enough for the American Hospital. Getting it on the black market was out of the question—the drug was watered down and dangerous. "Of course," Minko wound up, "if you have any contacts with the American military or the American embassy, I'd come any hour of day or night to give the injection."

Milton Gilbert!

Milton wasn't embassy and he wasn't military, but he was a figure in the American community, not because of his job with the Joint Distribution Committee, but because his wife, Ruth, hosted musicales with world-famous musicians and alerted wives when Lanvin and Dior had their annual sales. Ruth knew the *vendeuses*—the saleswomen who would save the desired models.

The Gilberts were close to embassy people! But one problem remained: Milton wasn't speaking to Ben. Fortunately, their first heated discussion had been halted when Julius Katchen, one of the great living piano virtuosi, and our friend, violinist Miriam Soloviev, began playing Brahms as if they were making love to one another.

After that, Ben and I decided we wouldn't get into any more fights with Milton, no matter what. Nobody ever convinced anybody. What was the point? But the next time we went to the Gilberts', I. F. Stone, a fiery, independent journalist of the Left, whom we revered, was among the guests. Izzy Stone had had irreverent columns in *PM* and the *New York Post,* and later edited his own courageous paper, in the tradition of George Seldes's, *I. F. Stone's Weekly,* in which he told the world what was really going on in Washington. Pudgy, myopic, hard of hearing, lovable, Izzy—half-blind at eighty—would master the computer and Greek so that he could research the trial of Socrates for a book he eventually wrote.

When we arrived at the Gilberts', Izzy was already in an explosive political discussion. The battle raged but true to our agreement, neither Ben nor I participated. We let poor Izzy valiantly fight on alone. The battle: Even in the early 1950s, the thousands of stateless dispossessed people created by World War II were living in camps all over Europe waiting for someone to give them a place where they could try to make their lives. Nobody wanted them, except Israel, which would accept only Jews. Izzy was blasting Milton for not trying to ameliorate the conditions under which refugees were living.

In the hope that Milton would raise allotments, Ben and I had once described the appalling living conditions of three "displaced" teenage girls who were struggling to make it through a Paris art school. At the height of his argument with Izzy, Milton turned to us, "The three Displaced Person (D.P.) girls you met? How much exactly were they living on?"

Ben replied angrily, "You mean how much were they starving on?"

Milton interrupted impatiently, "All I want to know is how much do they have for a month's living?"

"They're undernourished, live in a damp cellar—" I said.

"How much?" persisted Milton.

"Shit," Ben said finally, "less than twenty dollars a month."

Milton turned to a colleague of his and said with an air of triumph,

"Hear that? Less then twenty dollars a month. I told you we could cut our allotments."

Ben shouted, "Those girls are like zombies. They don't get enough to eat!"

Milton cut Ben off sharply, "Are they walking around? Doing their work?"

"Well sure," Ben managed to say.

"They'll develop tuberculosis," I put in.

"They're mobile, alive?" Milton demanded. "We're responsible for people like that. So what we're talking about is reality. We have limited funds that we're trying to spread around to as many people as possible." Then to his colleague, "Tomorrow we'll arrange to cut those allotments by a third."

At that point, our solemn resolution flew away. I began yelling, "Why in hell aren't you guys fighting for more funds instead of forcing them to live under concentration-camp conditions?"

"You," said Milton, "just don't know what concentration camps were like."

The fight escalated. Milton wound up accusing Ben and me of being "bleeding hearts," the bane of his existence. "You two," he said, "don't have to *do* anything so you can be as sentimental as you like!"

Ben and I were boiling. We just couldn't stop ourselves. "You don't have any compassion," I said. Ben shouted, "You're a heartless bastard!"

"This," Milton said, "is the result of being doctrinaire."

Ben looked Milton right in the eye. "You, sir," Ben said, "are a reactionary prick!"

Izzy smiled, utterly satisfied, and turned off his hearing aid. We had done it for him.

After that, Milton didn't speak one word to Ben and pretended not to hear him when he spoke.

On the way home from the Izzy Stone evening, Ben, needing reassurance, had asked, "Well, isn't he a reactionary prick?"

"That's a vast oversimplification," I'd replied.

Milton Gilbert! Even if he hated Ben's guts, I had to try. I telephoned Ruth Gilbert.

Hours later, around midnight, my telephone rang. "Milton's on his way over," she said. "He worked on it all day, into the night, finally found someone who knew someone who knew someone, then had to drive miles to the country for it."

I called Minko. At half past midnight, two cars stopped in front of our house. I could see from the window Milton putting something into Minko's hands, and getting back into his car.

I opened the door. "What a fine man! That Monsieur Gilbert," Minko said. "So kind."

We cannot be certain the penicillin Milton brought at midnight saved Aaron's life, but from that moment on, Aaron got better, and folklore would have it that "the heartless bastard" proved to be, in some instances, moral and human.

Needless to say, over the years, we became fast friends with the Gilberts. We sent them a case of champagne. They invited us over to drink it with them. Two years after Milton saved Aaron's life, when my passport was taken away, we warned Milton that he ought to be careful about seeing us, that we might be bad for his career. "You think we're going to let *them* choose our friends?" Milton demanded. He became Aaron's hero and an extraordinary rapport grew between them. Years later, at our home in the South of France, Milton taught shy Aaron to build bookcases.

After six weeks, when our home was no longer a hospital, Ben returned from the hotel. My feelings for him were not the same. Four years earlier, I had felt betrayed when he had failed to fight for me and had gone to work with a male writer on the screenplay of *my* story. I had eventually forgiven him for that, feeling it was a consequence of a historically male-dominated industry—and male-dominated world. But this was personal betrayal, abandoning me, abandoning the children when we needed him because his own well-being was more important to him. This time, I couldn't forgive. I still loved him but saw his weaknesses clearly. Most of all, I worried about how we could face a hostile world together if we couldn't even deal with our own family crises.

In December, two months after Aaron's birth, we were all well. I was beginning to be my old self, felt I could even make love again, but had no desire. Ben and I embarked upon a rich social life spurred by a letter we received from the Rank Organization. *Christ in Concrete,* now *Give Us This Day,* was to be shown at the Czech film festival at Karlovy Vary in July 1950.

When the French Left heard that our picture had been chosen for Karlovy Vary, we were invited to the Vichy Film festival. (The Cannes festival was only just beginning again, having been closed during the war and the Occupation.) Now we were asked everywhere—to the homes of Ruta and Georges Sadoul, eminent film historian; Paule and Roger Boussinot, editor of a film journal, *l'Ecran Français (The Screen);*[1] Ida and Claude Bourdet, founder of the liberal weekly *l'Observateur;* and the Ségals, Polish Jewish doctors and dentists whose son-in-law ran the Communist ciné-club that showed Soviet classics. Intellectually and artistically, Paris was the place to be during this period. Dozens of ciné-clubs screened distinguished old films and new films that had not gained regular distribution.

At our first Ségal luncheon, we met the couple who would be very close to us, Zuka and Louis Mitelberg. Zuka, the daughter of White Russians, was a Los Angeles artist who came to France in 1948 to study painting, and remained. She married Louis Mitelberg, the political cartoonist of *l'Humanité* who became "TIM" of *l'Express.* A latter-day Daumier, Louis is known for his caricature of de Gaulle on the cover of *Time.* Not far from Rodin's *Balzac* on Boulevard Raspail, Louis's sculpture *Dreyfus* stands at attention. The Dreyfus case split France into two factions, prompted Zola to cry *"J'accuse!"* at those who, because of anti-Semitism, framed an innocent, patriotic army captain and sent him to Devil's Island for many years before he was pardoned. Mitelberg's parents, taken from the Warsaw Ghetto and killed by the Nazis while he was studying art in Paris, inspired his Holocaust sculpture, "Les Deportés," at Père Lachaise, the cemetery of French notables.

Louis died in January 2002. One month afterward, the French government bought his sculpture of Daumier and placed it in the entrance hall of L'Assemblée Nationale.

Zuka's first exhibition, characters from the American Revolution, in a Naïf style, was shown at the Galérie Darthéa Speyer, Paris. It was followed in 1989 by a series of pictures commemorating the two hundredth anniversary of the French Revolution. The exposition toured the United States from Washington, D.C., to Los Angeles. Since then, Hollywood people—Gregory Peck, Robert Altman, the late Billy Wilder—have bought her paintings, including the newer ones of cows bursting with Fauve purple, red, pink, blue, and orange.[2]

Paris was thrilling, Ben and I were part of its extremely rich cultural life, and yet *we* were not happy together. Something had gone awry and both of us knew it. Our marriage, our partnership, was dying.

By the beginning of 1950, we probably knew more people in Paris than in Hollywood. Every time we went out, we bumped into someone we knew. We were sitting at a café one night when in walked Hilda and George Marton, Hilda's son Peter Stone, fresh out of Bard College, who would later write films like *Charade* and musical comedies like *1776,* and his pal, Art Buchwald, who had the "Coca-Cola beat," a *Paris Herald Tribune* column on nightclubs and restaurants.

George Marton, as brilliant and witty as Hungarians are supposed to be, headed the Fox story department in Europe and also an international literary agency, Martonplay. For years, he'd lived in Hollywood with his first wife and two daughters, as had Hilda, with her producer-husband and two sons. George and Hilda had fallen in love. Hilda and her husband had broken up.

"Not on account of me," George explained. "I just happened to be around when a beautiful woman's marriage was cracking. Pure coincidence," George said innocently. "Ben, how're you doing? It takes a long while to get used to French culture."

Chic Hilda, who had short white curly hair and blue harlequin eyeglasses, smiled contentedly. "A wonderful while."

George loved to be provocative. "For example," he said, "you'll never be invited to a French home."

"How wrong you are, George," I said, "we've been to dinner at the Boussinots—"

"That doesn't count," he replied. "They're Communists."

"And the Bourdets. *They're* not Communists," Ben said.

"That doesn't count," remonstrated George. "She's Jewish."

"But we're invited to the Sarruts," I said. "They're not Communists and they're not Jewish."

"Film people don't count," said George smugly. "I'm talking about French-French."

We took it as a challenge, got ourselves invited by the French-French family up the street whose three-year-old daughter played with Luli. They entertained once a year, hired waiters in white coats and gloves to serve a ten-course dinner with a different wine with each dish. We were supposed to have good conversation at the ready and to know what the hosts were interested in. If we had no comments on hunting and fishing, we could tell jokes. Our jokes were fresh for them. Their jokes were at least five years old.

"How in God's name did you find the dullest people in all France?" George exclaimed. "They're like movie dress extras in a restaurant who're told to keep saying 'bread and butter' over and over to each other to give the illusion of animated chatter."

In sharp contrast, an evening with Peter Stone, Art Buchwald, and the Martons had been lively. Art insisted on making us try a new restaurant on the Left Bank, Nuits Saint Georges. We rode in George's Mercedes, which seated six comfortably. He saw a parking place almost in front of the restaurant, maneuvered the car carefully into position. Wham! A French driver with gloves, at the wheel of a new Peugeot, quickly squeezed into George's spot. George leapt out, ran to the other car, inserted his hand through the partially opened front window, grabbed the driver's nose, and turned it round and round. The driver howled, tried to shut the window, but couldn't, then sped away. I'd never seen "tweaking" before. Instantly, I adored George.

The evening was off to a fine start. We all felt righteous, the dinner was superb, and George, a "Chevalier de Tastevin," could tell us without looking not only the kind of wine and the year, but the vineyard it came from.

"You better get your fill of this place," Buchwald said. "You'll never have another chance."

"It can't be going out of business," Ben said, "it's one of the best restaurants I've been to."

Art chuckled. "Of course not. But tomorrow, I will write about it and you'll never be able to get a table here again!"

No matter how jolly our social life, no matter how much wine I drank, I had no desire. I pretended to Ben there was still something temporarily physically wrong with me. Mother recommended that Ben and I take a holiday alone together, a romantic notion but also sensible, for it would take me away from the house of illness that constantly reminded me of Ben's dereliction.

I was about to suggest a trip to Ben when he said that Milly—director Lewis Milestone—had prevailed upon the Italian producer Amati to bring him and Ben to Rome for conferences on *The Idiot* project.

"Hooray!" I cried. "It'll hardly cost anything for me to go along."

"I'd like to take you but I can't. Next time."

"I won't be any problem. I love to wander around on my own."

"You don't understand. Milly wants my constant attention."

"Oh, that's all right," I reassured him. "I'll visit ruins, museums, the Vatican. I won't get in your hair."

Ben shook his head. "He wants me at his disposition day and night. That's why he's taking me along."

"Ben, I've been sick for months. We've been apart. This is perfect."

"Milly wouldn't stand for it. Don't you see?"

Later, I discussed it with Milly's wife, Kendall Milestone. She wasn't going either. "You know directors," she said, "but it's a bit disconcerting. Amati, the producer, reserved the Excelsior's bridal suite for them." She had a well-bred laugh like the whinny of a horse. "It's a good thing we both know how incontrovertibly masculine the two of them are."

Kendall reached for the Chivas, didn't ask if I wanted any, poured two large tumblers.

17

Shalom

I didn't forgive easily Ben's trip to Italy, especially since he was idiotic enough to recount "the incredible time" he'd had in Rome including "a date" with Anna Magnani. He said the producer, Amati, wanted him to charm the star into playing a supporting role. He'd met her at her apartment. After a long wait, she appeared, disheveled, dirty, and unappetizing. They'd had a drink, and then she suggested they go out for dinner. According to Ben, he'd said, "I don't care if you are La Magnani, I don't want to be seen with you looking like that."

She laughed, disappeared for a few seconds, returned wearing a long mink coat with next to nothing underneath, her hair still uncombed, her face dirty. "Is that better?" she demanded.

I thought he told the story to keep me from being jealous. I wasn't jealous of *her*, only of his trip. As usual, Ben looked for a way to make it up to me. The opportunity presented itself almost at once. That February 1950, an Israeli producer, Yonah Friedman, and his wife, Lilykin, had seen *Christ in Concrete* in London. Both were smitten. They wanted Ben to develop an original screenplay for a film to be shot in Israel. Friedman owned five Israeli cinemas and would put up half the money; the other half would come from the government agency, Keren Keyemeth Leisrael, the Jewish National Fund.

Instead of proposing that we find an idea together, Ben suggested to Friedman that I accompany them to Israel as "researcher." I don't think he ever told Yonah, or anyone else, that I had sold two original stories to the studios or that I'd been a Hearst feature writer. When was I going to be able to say to anyone that I was a writer? I felt tossed into the Israeli deal. Ben knew he needed someone to find and build a story with him. If I had been a man, he would have asked for me as collaborator. Besides, it was a flat deal and would not even have cost Friedman an additional penny. Instead, Ben included me as "researcher," presenting it as if he were giving me a trip to Israel to make up for not taking me along to Rome when he'd gone there with Milestone.

As usual, I acquiesced. I agreed to work on the Israeli film for expenses for one month even though it was clear to me that I'd find the story idea, start developing it, and when Ben took over, my heart would break. Israel was a new nation torn by fighting. On a smaller, more personal level, our experience there was to be a struggle between Ben and me.

With the Friedmans, we flew El Al to Israel. They were pleasant traveling companions, sophisticated as only ex-Budapest theater-goers can be. Yonah was a crafty, well-tailored Hungarian Jew without the charm of George Marton. Lilykin was tall, slim, elegant, and brainy, with a diamond as big as a kumquat on her finger.

The day before departure from Paris, Yonah had instructed me to wear long sleeves on the El Al flight. I couldn't think why, except that Orthodox Jews, for religious reasons, might consider a woman's bare arms offensive. The answer came just before landing. Yonah approached me and began strapping four watches on my left arm.

"I don't want to smuggle anything into Israel," I protested.

"Everyone does," Yonah said impatiently, strapping four more on my other arm.

We had already sent a refrigerator and other household appliances to them on our tickets. The import tax they did not have to pay could have paved roads, created nursery schools, and whatever else the new state needed.

Founded in May 1948, when the United Nations partitioned Palestine into two parts, Israel declared its independence as a state. Arabs whose home it had been for generations fled or were forced from their villages. Fighting ensued. Under a 1948 United Nations resolution, the Arab refugees were to be allowed to return home or be compensated for loss of property. The UN resolution was never implemented.

In the mid-1800s George Eliot wrote sympathetically in her novel *Daniel Deronda* about the Jewish dream of a homeland in Palestine. From the 1880s on, Jewish immigrants had been trickling into British-controlled Arab Palestine. Many Jews fleeing pogroms in Russia and Eastern Europe in the early 1900s were socialists who had abandoned the beliefs and practices of Judaism. They wanted to create a socialist state, to build a cooperative agricultural community where everyone would be equal and all would share in the work of "turning a desert into a garden."

An ancient chauffeur-driven Cadillac town car, with the young Friedman sons on the jump seats, ferried Yonah and Lilykin and their mountains of luggage piled high on the roof from the airport in Tel Aviv to their home in Jerusalem. We followed in a broken-down English taxicab, over the bumpy, dusty road, climbing up the hilly, stony Jerusalem terrain for a couple of hours until a panorama of the Old City came into view. The golden Dome of the Rock looked like the sun rising over a granite wall that circled the past. Breathless, we gazed at minaret prayer towers and church steeples punctuating the skyline, and at the shifting colors of Jerusalem limestone in the streaming light. The city, a clutter of pointed and rounded geometric forms, a tangle of walls snaking in and out, seemed like two thousand years of history exploding.

I never felt the exhilaration some Jews experience at being in "a free Jewish country." My parents had brought me up without religion, ignorant of the culture and traditions. I felt American. I felt socialist. Like most Communists of the time, I had been against the formation of the state of Israel, thought Jews should be assimilated in all the countries of the world and join the class struggle. Moreover, Ben and I were appalled by the expulsion of the Palestinians. Once Israel became an independent democratic nation, however, we ceased being anti-Israel, welcomed the idea of a haven for Jewish refugees, continued fighting for the Palestinians, and naively expected the fledgling country of Israel to be exemplary.

The morning after our arrival in Jerusalem, the chauffeur-driven Cadillac reappeared at the King David Hotel to fetch us. One passenger was already seated in the back. Joe Leytes, a hefty, red-faced Jewish refugee from Poland was wearing a trenchcoat on a sunny day. He had been hired to direct the picture even though his only experience was directing shorts for the Israeli government. He smiled, shook hands with us. I could feel Ben bristling and assumed it was a symptom of his animosity toward all directors—even those he liked. Ben sat on one of the jump seats. The three of us exchanged a few trite observations, but as the day progressed, Joe Leytes's repartee remained at the same mundane level. What's more, as far as we were concerned, he might as well have farted when he gestured at the dark-skinned driver, whispering, "I don't trust them. Knife-carrying Franks!" which was how the *Jerusalem Post* had been referring to North African Jews from the French-culture countries, Morocco, Algeria, and Tunisia, since a recent outbreak of burglaries in Tel Aviv.

The old Cadillac bounced slowly over Jerusalem cobblestones, stopping frequently—no traffic lights—for an old Jew in long black sheath and saucer hat, pious curls dangling; for an Arab in a brown robe with the black headband of his white and black checkered headdress; for a chic Sabra on her way to work; for a baby-faced soldier; for children on their way to school. Leytes's banal comments accompanied the ride across town. By the time we stopped in front of the Friedmans' large, newly built home, Ben was convinced we were stuck with a director who was "a dumb, untalented, racist bastard."

Yonah, now in Israeli attire: patched blue jeans and short-sleeved blue cotton sport shirt open at the neck, jumped into the car next to the driver, and we were under way again. At the door of the Jewish National Fund building, a "very British" JNF executive in a dark suit, sporting a pince-nez, showed us into a conference room where the long shiny table had been set with paper pads, pencils, tumblers, and small bottles of soda water. He and Colonel Michael Kaplan, an Israeli Army psychiatrist, seemed left over from colonial days.

Shalom

"We're here to help you plan your, shall we say, 'sightseeing.' I'm sure you have questions." The JNF guy rubbed his hands. "The colonel will answer them."

The colonel smiled, raising his meticulously trimmed English army mustache. "Fire away!"

Ben shot back, "Okay. Crime?"

"No less, no more than any other country," he proclaimed. "The same bell-shaped curve."

Angrily, Ben demanded, "Are you telling me that the shattering experience of concentration camps, families wiped out, being hunted down, had no effect?"

"That is correct, sir. Name it, we have it, and in the same degree. Prostitution, incest, petty burglary, murder—"

"People don't change," Leytes declared sententiously.

Ben shot him a look.

"Nevertheless," the colonel continued, "you can see, early on, which children will break the law, which will integrate into society. We have a school for boys, orphans brought to us from Germany, Poland, Morocco, the far corners. We're able to predict how they will fit in."

"Maybe we ought to visit them," I mumbled, thinking of all the film classics with school backgrounds from *0 for Conduct* (Jean Vigo) to *Maedchen in Uniform* and *Goodbye Mr. Chips,* in which an understanding, dedicated teacher changes the course of a child's life. "Ben, maybe that would make a film."

The JNF guy was drawing our attention away from the school. "The *kibbutzim*—that's the plural—the collective farms of the socialist movement, are of particular interest to us." I was excited by the kibbutzim. One of the attractions of socialism had been the liberation of women by communal child care, *kholhoz,* and city day nurseries. On the plane, Lilykin had told me how the *kibbutzim* started. In 1909, a small family-like group that lived and worked together in absolute equality hired themselves out as a work crew to learn farming, then acquired a 750-acre tract of land from the JNF on the western shore of the Sea of Galilee. When the socialist women who had come to Palestine to be pioneers and equals found themselves sewing, cooking, cleaning while the men worked in the fields, they fought and won. By 1917, child rearing, like everything else in their society, became a communal responsibility that freed the women for other tasks.

"The women's struggle for equality," I said, "is another good story."

The government guy cut in, "We'd like to see a film made about the *kibbutzim,* but we don't want to seem as if Israel is socialist. Only four percent of Israelis live on collective farms."

Yonah looked unhappy. "This picture," he said, "must at least make back its costs. You think audiences want to see a movie about farm life?"

"We can show kibbutzniks learning to handle a gun," Leytes said placatingly, "fighting off Arabs. The French kibbutz—"

I interrupted, "The school story is the best idea yet."

"I can give you an idea of the many problems this country faces," interjected the psychiatrist, "any one of which, to my mind, would make a suitable subject for a film."

"We don't have to know what we're looking for before we set off," Ben said, ending the discussion.

The next morning, Keren Keyemeth's Cadillac, with driver, was waiting for us. Leytes, who'd sensed Ben's antagonism, had left us to see Israel on our own. Instead, a government guide took us around. He tried to keep me from seeing the conditions of a "temporary" refugee camp and from talking to its inhabitants. When he trailed me through an Arab village, I turned on him. "I've heard they do this in the Soviet Union—but not in Israel." After that, he disappeared.

At one point, I asked our driver if we would pass the school for displaced children.

Ben snapped, "Never mind about that."

We followed the coast up to Haifa, a busy port, traversed Arab villages with dirty-faced tots playing in the middle of the road, and to Nahariyah, a town where the signs were in German and coffee was served with *schlag,* whipped cream. In the ultra-Orthodox city of Sfad where I wasn't allowed in the synagogue for the Hasidim's wild dancing because I was a woman, I sat outside speaking French with our driver, David, who told me more about the school.

We spent the night at Merhavia. Every kibbutz, besides its agriculture, had an "industry." Merhavia's "industry" was publishing—Marx, Engels, and "your Albert Maltz." After dinner, we sat with the kibbutzniks around a blazing fire while they told stories of their comrades killed in the recent hostilities.

Ben was not feeling well and wanted to get back to Jerusalem. As ashen as he had been in Mexico, he'd been asking to stop frequently. He turned to the driver. "We won't go anywhere tomorrow. I'll rest."

"Do you think I could use the car?" I asked.

The driver nodded. "*Bien sûr*—of course."

"What would you do with yourself?" Ben asked.

I gave the answer most men expect. "Shopping," I replied. "I'll spend the day in Tel Aviv."

"Buy gifts for the children," Ben instructed. I tried again to persuade him to visit the school but he seemed to think it pointless.

The next day, when I was alone, I asked David if the school was hard to get to.

"I'll take you," he said. "It's a difficult mountain road. When it was life or death, I did not think I would make it."

"You were running away?"

"No, not *my* life or death. The children's. They had no water," he said. "I was bringing them water in my truck. The Arabs were shooting at me. If the tires punctured, or if I got hit, the children would have died." He pointed to the sky. "Someone was watching."

"They had no other way of getting water?"

"The Arabs blew up the pipes."

"How many kids are there?"

"Forty, maybe fifty. Then there's the American, Sam. He's the teacher. And the trained nurse. The kids are always getting sick. There's the cook, a couple of cleaning people, the old man who tells stories while he shows them how to cultivate the soil."

"Without water?"

"*Eh bien,* the first thing we did after the shooting stopped was fix the pipes."

When we arrived, a bunch of eleven- to thirteen-year-old boys galloped out, whooping with joy as they closed in on David, whose grizzled gray head came barely up to their shoulders. They hugged and thumped him, gave him friendly smacks on the back, and cried in their boys' bass and soprano, changing voices, "David," "Dovid," and "Shalom!"

Running after them, brandishing a trowel, Sam, a blond American in his late twenties, shouted a stream of angry Hebrew at them. They didn't look worried. When he saw David, he grinned. Sam had fought in World War II, attended college on the G.I. Bill, hadn't known what to do with his life, volunteered in 1948 to fight for Israel when American Jews could fight in the Israeli Army and not lose their U.S. citizenship. The Israelis found out Sam had been a camp counselor in Vermont. They told him he was more valuable as a teacher than as a soldier.

"I've been up here for two years and I've seen some mighty big changes."

"Like?" I asked.

"The boys. You should have seen them. Little gangsters. Tough, nasty, suspicious." He pulled the window curtain back for me to see. "Those two. The blond, Kurt, and the dark one, Ibrahim. Spat at each other like wildcats. I couldn't keep them apart, always tearing each other to pieces. Kurt was picked up on a German street, selling cigarettes, selling himself—to stay alive. When he saw Ibrahim, he called him 'Arab!' Ibrahim beat him to a pulp, screaming 'Nazi!' They were like animals for a long time until they saw we were all together and that someone cared about them."

"You?"

"Yes. Me. When you arrived," Sam said, "we were building a dry wall, the way the Romans did, without anything between the stones, each one resting the right amount of weight on another, wedged in close together, fitting each other, giving each other balance and strength."

That night when I returned to Jerusalem, Ben was feeling better.

above: Norma at 17, on the roof of Cabot Hall, her dorm at Radcliffe, 1937. **below:** Claude Shannon, Norma's first husband, takes her for a ride in a Piper Cub when he gets his license, 1939.

left: In *L. A. Examiner* photography room, 1944. Norma blows her raise on a plaid gingham suit. **below:** Goodbye Party: [Left to Right] Adrian Scott, me, Jeannie Lees, Bobbie Lees, on the floor Annie Scott (actress Anne Shirley), 1949.

above: Ben, producer Rod Geiger, director Eddie Dmytryk discussing Ben's script of *Christ in Concrete*, 1949. below: Sam Wanamaker and Lea Padovani in *Christ in Concrete (Give Us This Day)*, 1949.

above: Adrian and me in Paris, 1949. Adrian tells me he's going back to the U.S. even if it means jail. **below:** Julie Dassin and Ben enjoying a joke as "Script" Lucie Lichtig (a Barzman) looks on, 1956.

above: Joe Losey, photographed by Norma, Cannes, 1956. **below:** Abe Polonsky, photographed by Norma, Cannes, 1958.

left: Ben, me, director Tony Mann at jai alai Madrid, 1961, while shooting *The Fall of the Roman Empire.* **below:** Sophia visits us in Paris. Ben, Sophia, and our son Aaron, 1961.

above: John, Luli, Ben carrying Marco, me, and Aaron holding the poodle Kafka; in the front row, Daniel and Paulo, 1962.
right: Suzo, the youngest, who looks just like my mother, 2000.

above: Mougins, house, pool, court, from the air Near Picasso's, 1963. **below:** Ben convinces Mohammed Lakhdar-Hamina, head of the Algerian film industry, to let *Z* be shot in Algiers, 1967.

Shalom

A distinguished professor from the School of Medicine had told him with a German accent, "You haf made an amoebic dysentery. You must eat only grilled meats. Here—I vill make you the prescription." It read: "This man must eat grilled meats at a Black Market restaurant."

Ben laughed, his first laugh since we'd arrived. Encouraged, I recounted everything about the school. Sam, Kurt, Ibrahim, as if it were a story starting in 1948 before the hostilities commenced and ending with David bringing the water to save them. Ben liked it. "When you're better," I wound up, "we must go there."

"No!" he said emphatically.

When Ben was well, we continued making trips around the country, but in my notebook I was inventing situations and scenes of the "school story," and when I could, I was combing newspaper files. More than three weeks passed before I brought up the subject again. I knew that once he saw it, he would realize its possibilities. I was right. Ben loved everything, thought Sam was a terrific character, talked Yiddish to German Kurt, who understood him, talked French to Ibrahim, considered it an ideal place to shoot.

"Love interest?" I asked Ben. "The nurse?"

Sam overheard. "Hard as nails," he said. "Engaged to a guy in the army. She thinks sex is hygienic. Nobody should be without it. Tried to jump me with no preliminaries."

Ben said, "Hey, Sam! This is not a documentary. We're inventing a story, using what we can of what really happened."

"Yeah," Sam replied, "but everyone's going to know this guy is me!"

"Everyone?" Ben said. "We're lucky if *anyone* sees this picture."

On the way back to Jerusalem, I asked Ben what he had meant. "You need a good director to direct kids," Ben said. "Leytes will make it seem amateurish."

"Why don't you get Yonah to dump Leytes? Sam Wanamaker could play Sam and direct it."

"The JNF would never go for it. Neither would Yonah. They've already paid Leytes."

"It'd be worth it to buy off Leytes," I enthused.

Ben called London. Sam Wanamaker was free and willing to come at once. Yonah's reaction to the idea of Sam directing and starring in the picture was not at all what Ben and I expected. We'd thought Yonah would say no, but never guessed the reason. "One blacklisted person is enough," he said. "If Sam Wanamaker plays in it and/or directs it, the film will never be shown in the United States."

We took Leytes to the school on my last day in Israel. David showed us where he'd been ambushed and how he had driven off the road, zig-zagged and avoided the Arabs. With Leytes, we discussed story, scenes, locations, and casting. All went well except for his one snide remark: "The boys need discipline." Ben, sullen, held his tongue.

On the way back to Jerusalem, Leytes asked David, "Aren't we going to pass the road to Neve Ilan?"

"Tonight is the beginning of Passover," David said.

My last night in Israel, the end of March 1950, just happened to be the first night of the holiday. I was twenty-nine and didn't know what Passover was.

"Neve Ilan?" Ben repeated suspiciously, sick of Leytes's ideas. "What's that?"

"The French kibbutz," Leytes answered. "Three hundred people who wish they were home in Paris." For the first time, we saw Leytes smile. "It's a good story," he said.

David swiveled around. "It is customary to be home by sundown for the Seder—the Passover dinner." It was the only time David, extraordinarily agreeable, objected to anything.

"David," I said, "if we don't have time, just say so. It doesn't matter."

"Norma," Ben interposed, "can't you see David's family are waiting for him?"

"I have no family," David said. "Friends invited me. Every Jew has a place to go for Passover."

"If we make you late," I asked, "will you join us?"

He laughed. "*Bien entendu.*" His third way of saying "of course."

"They're up here," Leytes explained, "high above the Syrian border for strategic reasons. The land is too poor to grow anything." The car climbed to the top of a craggy mountain. The desolation was total. Not a tree. A few pathetic chickens straggled about pecking at the rocks.

Maurice, secretary of the kibbutz, introduced himself, his wife, and his mother, a chic Parisienne with a fourteen-room apartment on Avenue Foche, who was visiting them. She was trying to convince her son and daughter-in-law to move back to Paris. The kibbutzniks were preparing for the fête, decorating long tables with flowers and wine, hanging out lanterns. "We're poor," Secretary Maurice said, "but we shall make the Seder like everyone else."

So my first Seder was at a kibbutz too poor to buy fish to make gefilte fish, but with a French chef who magically turned the fish heads they'd been given into delicious *pains de poisson,* fish cakes. He served the traditional beet horseradish he'd brought with him from France, along with his favorite herbs. These latter he'd used to stuff and dress the scrawny chickens, which, with eggplant, peppers, and onions, made an admirable main course.

French-speaking David was warmly welcomed. He thoroughly enjoyed the Seder so I felt no guilt. As I tasted the bitter herbs, "the bitterness of slavery," and a carrot and raisin confection, "the sweetness of freedom," I learned that Passover was the celebration of the Jews' flight out of Egypt.

Even at this late hour, Leytes was still trying to talk Ben out of the school. I realized that the story of self-sacrificing Parisians who had given up the good life for their ideals was the picture Leytes had wanted to do from the first. Leytes had promised these kibbutzniks that they would be in a film. Three weeks after our visit we heard they had packed up and returned to France.

When we arrived at our hotel that night, Ben wasn't speaking to me. "Okay, what is it?" I asked him.

"You're leaving tomorrow," he said. "I'm stuck with it!"

"It's not my fault the blacklist has forced you to take shit jobs."

"Everything is shit! In more ways than one!"

"Why can't you laugh?"

"I can't!" he said. "Everything *is* shit."

"How can you say that when you have a lovely wife, three lovely kids, you're not broke like the others—"

"Shit!" he broke in.

"You still have work, you live in Paris where life is exciting—"

"Shit!"

"—and you're surrounded by stimulating people!"

"Shit!" he said.

It wasn't a fight. It was worse than a fight.[1]

18

L'amour Toujours L'amour

"It's Bernard." I hadn't heard his voice since the night we'd switched houses to avoid subpoenas. Here he was, the night I got back to Paris from Israel, Bernard Vorhaus, director of low-budget, eight-day-wonder, B movies. "I'm cutting the picture I just shot in the South of France at Pathé Labs here in Montmartre," he said. "It's from a script by Adrian and Eddie Dmytryk's ex-wife."

"Is it the film Adrian was trying to set up before he went back to the States?"

"Yes. *Pardon My French*. Lousy screenplay, even if Adrian did write it. He was in bad shape after Annie left him."

"And Madeleine Dmytryk?"

"She's comforting Adrian and taking care of the two Michaels, his and hers. Why don't you two come out to dinner with me?"

"Ben's not here. He's in Israel making a picture."

"Then you come to dinner with me."

"Why don't we wait till Ben gets back?" I said.

"Why should we do that? Let's go have a really good dinner to celebrate our escape from the slim-jims." I felt guilty going out, leaving the children after a month's absence, almost a sixth of Baby Aaron's life.

When I returned from Israel and tried to pick him up, he reached out his arms to Mother, who cuddled him. "Just spend time with him every day," she advised.

Luli, four, and Johnny, three, both bigger than I remembered, pulled at me forcefully, *wanted* me desperately. In English-English, "want" means "need." With a pang I realized that in Israel I hadn't thought a great deal about them. Yet, all at once, with a great rush of feeling, I knew my children were immensely important to me.

Guilt or no guilt, I dressed carefully but hurriedly and in forty-five minutes was parking the Citroën on Montparnasse, a block from the Closerie des Lilas.

Bernard was already at a corner table. He jumped up and kissed me, not on each cheek in the French manner, but full on the lips, then laughed at my astonishment.

"Shalom," I said. "I just got back from Israel."

"Shalom," he said. "Was it great? Don't answer."

The leafy lushness of the Closerie and his exuberance made me feel better. I'd forgotten that Bernard, as anxious as he was, tics and all, was optimistic by nature, eager for solutions.

"Don't answer?" I repeated.

"No. Not before we make the important decisions. What are we going to eat?" He grinned sensually when he talked about food.

"There's a maxim I follow at restaurants," I said. "Never eat what you can have at home. What are you going to have?"

His eyes lit up. "I'm waiting to see what you want," he replied, "not because I'm going to take the same thing."

"Then why?"

"I like to share—like in a Chinese restaurant. If you get frogs' legs and I, turbot poché, and after that, one of us has blanquette de veau, the other lamb, we'd have four dishes to taste instead of only two."

"Ben doesn't like to share. If he wants something, he wants it all. He minds terribly when I taste his food."

"Probably a holdover from childhood," Bernard said. "If you're poor, you don't want to give up what you have."

"You weren't poor. Neither was I."

The waiter hovered.

"Go ahead," I whispered to Bernard. "The way you said."

After the waiter had gone, the sommelier presented himself. In those days we thought we had to have white wine with the fish course and red with the meat.

"Chablis first?" Bernard asked.

I nodded.

"Then a Brouilly? Not too serious? Right?"

I smiled. Life didn't have to take place on a battlefield.

"How's Ben's Israeli film going?"

"Not well."

"I can't be sympathetic. Ben and I are lucky to be working. You guys made the right decision to come here."

"Bernard, Ben's depressed. He always was, even before the blacklist. But this is worse. He takes exile as a personal rejection."

Bernard tasted the wine. I thought he was wondering whether to send it back. But he was thinking of Ben. "Therapy?" he suggested.

"He won't go. I tried to get him to go in Hollywood." I laughed. "He sent me."

"But I heard *Christ in Concrete* turned out well."

"Oh, yes, it's been selected for the festival at Karlovy Vary."

"A film made in England by all blacklisted people! Ben should be proud. Everyone else is going to jail or wondering how to make ends meet or where to live. Hugo and Jean Butler moved to Mexico. Trumbo and Lawson are going to a jail somewhere in Kentucky in June. Adrian is still ill so they aren't sentencing him now."

In April 1950, the worst had happened and when it hit us we still couldn't believe it. The U.S. Supreme Court refused to hear the cases of Lawson and Trumbo. Not hearing the case meant that the convictions for contempt of Congress stood. The Hollywood Ten were going to prison.

"I'm sorry about Ben," Bernard said. "Maybe what I'm going to tell you will help." All of a sudden, his voice grew energetic, businesslike. "We have to make a life in France now, we can't hope for anything from the

U.S. anymore. Johnny Weber and I are forming a company. Our families are investing in it. I'm going back to the States to get Hetty and the kids. Johnny will bring his family, too. If we have work, living in Paris is hardly the worst thing in the world. We thought you and Ben could be a part of the company. You two put up the scripts. We put up the money. Do you have a project you like? What are you working on?"

Ben and I had been struggling for a year on *Young Woman with Ideas*. It was far too American for production in Europe.

"Didn't you just direct a film about girls in a reform school?" I asked.

"*So Young So Bad*. Jean Butler wrote it. We made it for almost nothing. It's making money."

"What about a 'reform school' for wealthy girls, a finishing school, like the one my sister attended in Switzerland? Seventeen-year-olds discovering sex—"

"*Finishing School*," Bernard cut in. "You should write it alone. Without Ben."

"As an original story? In treatment form?"

"No. Go straight to screenplay." I must have looked dubious. "You can do it," he said.

"My experience has been mostly with original stories—"

He cut me off. "I read your screenplay *With This Ring*. It was good."

"Janet Stevenson collaborated with me."

"Do the screenplay alone. I'll help you. Let Ben write his own screenplay. Johnny and I would like to set up two pictures to shoot in Italy, one for me to direct. *Finishing School* is perfect." He reached into his briefcase and brought out a script. "I may have a deal on this in England. I could shoot it while you're writing *Finishing School*. Read it. Scribble all over it."

The Inspector of Missing Persons Is Missing was awful. Would Bernard be angry if I told him the truth? I called him the next day.

"Hi," he said, his voice warm and reassuring. "Did you read it?"

"Maybe it could be turned into a spoof. Make a joke of how unsuspenseful it is. Wind up with the missing inspector playing hooky—taking a holiday fishing on a quiet river?"

"You want to talk about it at dinner?" he asked. "I already invited Volodya and Ida."

"I'll pick you up at Pathé. We'll have time to talk before we meet them."

I fetched him from the lab at seven. "I know *The Inspector* is a piece of shit," he began, "but the producers have been good to me."

"It's not a project that will do you any good—"

"Unless it works as a comedy."

Volodya and Ida, who had spent the war years as refugees in Hollywood, were already seated at a table at Chez l'Ami Louis, an Art Deco bistro near the Marais. They kissed both of us on the cheek three times, for by now we were very dear friends.

Bernard asked me what I would like. I tried to think of dishes he'd want to taste, sole Normande and *lapin Chasseur*—rabbit with a thick red-wine sauce.

To the Pozners, our exchange of food must have seemed intimate. I didn't care because at that dinner, I became aware of how close I felt to this man who was warm and loving, who treated me as an equal and had appeared just when I needed him.

All through dinner we discussed the appalling Supreme Court decision and the certainty of jail for our friends. Eddie Dmytryk and Albert Maltz had been sentenced to Mill Point, West Virginia; Ring Lardner, Jr., to a prison in Connecticut. It seemed utterly incredible. The world as we'd known it was breaking apart and our friends were being crushed. Everyone had a lot of wine—except me because I was the driver.

As the evening ended, my thoughts about Bernard were undergoing radical change. I wanted to go to his hotel with him and make love. But I was the one taking everyone home and his hotel, the Lutétia, was the first stop. When we got there, Bernard gave me a quick hug, got out, said good night to Volodya and Ida, and was gone.

I let the Pozners off at their place, turned around, returned to Bernard's hotel, and rang him from downstairs. "I'll be right down," he said.

When he appeared, he seemed flustered, like a man who has been awakened out of a sound sleep, although it would have been impossible for him to have gone to sleep in the time I'd been gone. He led me into the bar. "Anything wrong?" he asked.

"Nothing."

"Why did you come back?"

"Because I wanted to make love." As I said that, I realized I wasn't afraid of Bernard.

He looked around as if seeking help.

"It's not as if I don't know you." I laughed. "I've known you longer than Ben. I met you my first night in Hollywood, my twenty-first birthday. We all went to the Trocadero."

Bernard stood there, said nothing.

"I don't make a habit of this," I said softly. "It's the first time in the seven years I'm married that I've wanted to sleep with someone other than my husband. Does the idea seem that terrible?"

"Ben is my friend."

"I'm alone," I said. "I feel so lonely. I—" I wanted to but could not say that I longed for affection.

"But . . ."

"*You've* had affairs."

"Yes. But Hetty and I have been seeing a shrink and trying to make our marriage work."

"Oh. I understand," I said. I leaned toward him, put my arms around him and kissed him. I was saying good night. He responded with such passion and hunger that a moment later we were in the elevator.

April in Paris. We did everything lovers do. We lost the little black Citroën in a tiny street around Les Halles. Everybody had a little black Citroën and all the tiny streets looked alike. We searched and searched in the damp, chill night air, sat down on the curb and cried, then giggled. At the Olympia, we held each other's hands tight while Yves Montand, in his brown shirt and brown pants, sang "*J'aime flâner sur le grand boulevard . . .*" In the Bois de Boulogne, Bernard rowed me around the picture-book lake, then took me on a ferry to the 1900 teahouse on the romantic island. We saw each other every day and every night for six weeks until he'd finished cutting his film. I knew that when he left I'd miss his combination of manliness with a woman's understanding, and his sharing nature that extended from food to words to love.

When I drove him to the Gare des Invalides, he kissed me good-bye and hopped on the bus to the airport, but as it was about to leave, he beat on the folding door until the driver let him out.

"I'll be back," he said, kissing me and holding me tight. Then sadly, "Shalom," as he broke out of the embrace.

"Shalom," I said, starting to laugh. He looked at me perplexed. "'Shalom'," I repeated, "is like a duckbilled platypus, the same coming or going."

He laughed, too, as he dashed for the bus that was starting to leave without him.

19

The New Man

Bernard had left and Ben had not yet returned.

Working independently on the screenplay, not as an appendage, restored my faith in myself and helped me get through the awful days of late spring–early summer 1950 as one by one each of the Hollywood Ten went off to serve a year in prison, except for Adrian, whose illness delayed incarceration until September.

I was typecast to write *Finishing School,* based on my sister's experiences in Switzerland and on mine as a Radcliffe freshman. Because Bernard respected my work and me, I felt freer and less inhibited as I wrote.[1] Ideas for characters and situations bombarded me. The script was "writing itself." Yet, I was scared. I felt a duty to Bernard's production company. That little company was a defiant gesture aimed straight at HUAC. In 1995, blacklisted director John Berry commented in an interview with Pat McGilligan in *Tender Comrades:* "Ben Barzman, Bernie Vorhaus and John Weber had a company and eventually they made two pictures. That's pretty goddamn extraordinary— a blacklisted director, writer, and agent from Hollywood making two movies in Italy. How? How did they manage to do it? I sometimes wonder."[2]

The New Man

My pleasure writing the script was tempered by my anxiety about Ben's return. I was afraid he'd still be shrouded in a black, self-pitying mood unless I could quickly put an end to it by telling him about our part in the new company. I worried, too, that Ben might see I was in love with someone else. I hoped his reunion with the children whom he hadn't seen in almost three months would divert him from noticing the difference in me.

I hadn't needed to worry. On arrival, he was mainly concerned with himself.

"I'm sick," he complained, "not the dysentery. Of Israel. I went to visit a professor who lives in the Mea Sharim district of Jerusalem, you know, the ultra-Orthodox quarter, I took a taxi. When it slowed down, we were stoned by zealots who believe you shouldn't ride on Saturday. I'm okay. But the driver was hit in the head by a rock!"

"Oh!"

"And the picture's a disaster. The boys speak as if they're trying to remember their lines."

When we were alone, I told him about the company, that Paris would be its headquarters and he and I would each write and invest a screenplay.

"It makes sense," he said after a moment. "What would be a good project for me?"

"You'll find one."

Ben went doggedly back to work on our original story, now titled *Young Man with Ideas*. I was happy to be on my own project. Bernard had once told me how much he loved skiing, and that he'd shot unbelievable snow footage for an English film. I remembered Milton Sperling's "Put it on a mountaintop" and "Give it more jeopardy." The ending for my film came to me in a flash: a moonlight search for the heroine on skis in the Italian Alps.

Ben chastised me for working before there was a deal.

"*You*," I countered, "have no deal. You're speculating, hoping to sell an original. I already have producers and a director who want to make my film."

The telephone rang. Once again, as in the movies, it was Bernard. He was in London, hoping I'd come for a few days to see the producer of *The Inspector of Missing Persons.*

"Does he have a deal?" Ben asked.

"Maybe we will if—"

"Why can't Bernie do it himself? Why does he need you?"

"I'm the one with the idea."

Ben seethed. He'd just returned from a long absence and here was I, intent on taking off. Nothing could dissuade me, neither loud nor soft words. I packed, made a reservation on the next plane for London, and was gone.

Like April and May in Paris, June in London reinforced everything I already felt, that I was truly in love. Bernard was not the most brilliant or scintillating of men, but he was not aggressive. Life with him was calm and cheerful.

When I returned to Paris, Ben asked me if I'd checked with the embassy about going to the film festival in Czechoslovakia. "Perhaps one should ask if it's all right to go?" he asked, "considering how things are in the Cold War world."

"We've been invited along with the film you wrote."

"We wouldn't want to look as if we were sneaking in, would we?"

"How can anyone sneak in? The world press will be there. Oh hell, if it'll make you feel any better, I'll call the embassy."

The personnel at the embassy kept passing me around. Each time, I had to repeat what I was calling about. Finally, one said, "Are you asking me if you should accept the invitation?"

"I'm asking if you know any reason we shouldn't go?" I said.

Long pause. Then he spelled it out syllable by syllable in careful bureaucratese. He sounded as though he were dictating a cable: "The United States has normal diplomatic relations with the Czechoslovak government. There is no reason an American citizen should not travel to Czechoslovakia."

Much later, I realized that a diplomat is a person who can say one thing very clearly and make you understand just as clearly that it means the exact opposite.

"Did you remember to get the thin needles for Eleanor Wheeler?" Ben demanded.

George and Eleanor Wheeler were the "bête noire" of the U.S. State Department. When Professor Wheeler was thrown out of an American university for not signing the loyalty oath, he accepted a job teaching economics at Charles University in Prague. This nice American WASP family with four children moved to Czechoslovakia by choice! The State Department was livid!

It so happened that George, his younger brother, and Eleanor had all gone to Ben's alma mater, Reed College, in Portland, Oregon, and Ben had been a classmate of the younger brother. Eleanor Wheeler had sent word to our friend David Leff, editor of the UNESCO magazine in Paris, that Eleanor, a diabetic, couldn't obtain thin enough needles in Prague for her insulin shots. The thick Czech ones hurt. Would we bring some? (That should have been the tip-off that Eastern socialism left something to be desired when a highly developed industrialized nation like Czechoslovakia was not manufacturing optimum medical supplies!)

"Yes, dear," I answered Ben. Since London, I answered all Ben's "question-orders" with "Yes, dear."

We left Paris for Prague in a snappy Air France Caravelle. (A weary-looking Aeroflot with tassels on the window shades would bring us back, since the two companies had a contract—Air France going, Aeroflot returning.) A Czech film historian, a tall, graying, undistinguished-looking man, who, despite the July heat, wore an undistinguished, fully buttoned, winter-weight suit, complete with white shirt and a woolen muffler, met us at the Prague Airport. He shook hands with us, leaned forward, and said in tones so low it was more like part of his breathing, "Be careful." We didn't have a chance to ask what he meant because as we entered the long official-looking black Zim, he put his fingers to his lips, eyeing the driver suspiciously. The professor, we learned many years later, was one of Stalin's hatchet men.

"In Karlovy Vary," he suggested, "be sure to see the crystal works, and drink the evil-smelling waters. They cure everything." His conversation was as mundane as his clothes. By the time we reached the Hotel Alcron, we weren't sure he'd uttered any warning at all. He handed us over to a wide, cheerful young woman who would be our guide until we left Prague. As soon as he left, she leaned close and said in the same mysterious low voice, "Be very careful." Her tone and his were similar to that used by our embassy people when I had telephoned.

"Of what?" we asked.

She seemed thrown by the question. With the slightest inclination of the head, she indicated a handsome white-haired man seated in the hotel lobby reading the *Paris Herald Tribune*. "He's an American," she whispered.

We waited for her to elaborate but she didn't. Finally, noticing our bewilderment, she added, "Anyone who publicly proclaims himself an American these days has to be wondered about."

That night, we enjoyed a very American dinner with the Wheeler family: baked ham, spinach, mashed potatoes, famous Pilsner Urquell beer for the adults, milk for the children. "The children have already made friends," Eleanor said, "and they've picked up a great deal of Czech." She sighed. "A miserable language to learn. Fortunately, George is permitted to teach in English. All the students speak and read it well."

"An American Marxist teaching Marxist economics to Czech Marxists?" Ben laughed.

"I'm not the first American to teach at Charles University," George answered in a serious tone. "Two years ago, in 1948, Professor Matthiessen of Harvard was here teaching American literature when the Communists took over. His friend Jan Masaryk, who was foreign minister, either fell, jumped, or was pushed out a window. Matthiessen went into a deep depression, returned to America, and himself jumped, from the window of a Boston hotel. He'd believed that Czechoslovakia, situated as it is, between European democracies and Eastern Communist countries, would be able to steer a middle course toward a democratic socialism."

For the next two days, the wide young woman toured us around

The New Man

Prague, one of the oldest, most beautiful cities of Europe. Less battle-scarred than London, Prague retained its medieval flavor. We saw the Opera House where Mozart had introduced *The Magic Flute,* the synagogue and Jewish cemetery as they had been in the Middle Ages. In the center of the city, hectic children were screaming on the rides of a popular fair. A hot dog was a *horky porky,* and, instead of candied apples, people walked around eating huge pickles. We could have been in any European city, not behind the Iron Curtain. Men and women were well dressed, well fed. Nothing was sinister except those "Be carefuls" in the beginning. We could roam about freely, and, as it turned out, the only persons who followed us were CIA informers.

I remembered Karlovy Vary when it was Carlsbad, a spa I visited with my parents, quiet, picturesque, serene. It was unchanged. Festival guests were lodged at Pupp's Hotel, which was still a romantic Old World destination similar to the one in Alain Resnais's *Last Year in Marienbad.* The old peasant women with kerchiefs over their heads were still selling big fat dark cherries on both sides of the promenade.

At other festivals, a feverish pitch dominates, the goals being hyper-sexual, hyper-gourmand, hyper-glamorous, hyper-agitated film selling. At Karlovy Vary, the emphasis was on the art and technology of film-making and on film content. Each morning an impressively accurate and detailed listing of the films to be shown that day was distributed to the guests in English, French, German, Czech, Russian, Polish, Italian, Arabic, Chinese, and Hindi, noting the time and place of each projection, a brief multilanguage synopsis of the film, and biographical notes on each filmmaker.

Give Us This Day was scheduled to be shown on the last day of the festival. Ben and I hadn't yet seen a finished print so we lived in a state of heart-lurching intensity until the last morning, when we finally saw it. We liked it. No one applauded. As we left the projection, a festival functionary, with great formality and in a perfunctory manner, officially congratulated Ben. When we filed into the press room immediately afterward, there was no applause. Press representatives were present from all the Eastern countries, Asia, Africa, Australia, Canada, and Western

229

Europe (with the conspicuous absence of Franco's Spain, Salazar's Portugal, and the colonels' Greece). *The Daily Worker* covered for the U.S. and Great Britain. The reporters were stony-faced; the questioning began on a muted, cautious level with an ominous query from a Polish journalist: "Why was the film made?"

Ben sat there stunned, wordless.

Finally, I asked, "Exactly what do you mean 'Why was the film made?' "

He replied he was certain he was speaking for a good many of his colleagues from the East. This seemed such an unusual film to come out of the West, so far from the standard American fare, particularly now, given recent events.

A Soviet journalist, seeing Ben's bewilderment, asked, "Did the producing company think this was a film which would have a wide audience? In short, will it make money?"

"Well, they hope it will," Ben answered shakily. "I can't imagine any producing company putting money into a film they didn't think would make money."

Another journalist expressed the question more clearly: "How could a Western nation permit a film so implicitly critical of its own economy to be made at all?"

"The kind of direct censorship you're suggesting doesn't exist in our country," Ben said.

Georges Sadoul, the French Communist film historian, cut in. "*Attention*, careful, Ben! It remains to be seen if *Give Us This Day* will get wide distribution in the United States."

No one had yet expressed any opinion about the quality of the film. But good or bad, it had upset them because they had to revise some of their opinions about the West.

"I think you should be aware," said Ben, "that in America, small independent film groups make controversial films if they can convince the money people that the film will make a profit."

"I'm hoping to hear some personal reactions," Ben said. This brought forth a few formal comments about its being judged as "cinematically important."

The New Man

That night at the awards presentation, Ben and I, seated smack in the center of an immensely long row of the jam-packed audience, felt strange and lost. We really needed an interpreter. The famous Czech bureaucracy had failed us utterly.

After interminable, what we guessed were minor awards, with young people stumbling all over themselves to reach the stage, where they were handed scrolls to big applause and thanked innumerable people—much like our own Oscar night—only after all this did we see the signs of heightening tension: people fell silent and leaned forward in their seats. Another obviously important personality took center stage, spoke with great solemnity, picked up a sheet of paper, and perused it carefully while it seemed as if the audience held its breath.

Ben whispered, "This feels like the big one."

A great hush. Again it was exactly like Oscar. Imagine waiting for the Oscar envelope to be opened when some starlet says, "And the winner is—" It was announced in Czech! If *Give Us This Day* had won, we thought we would have recognized some of the names he was reciting. Di Donato? Dmytryk? Geiger? No.

Thunderous applause erupted as the man on the stage, shielding his eyes, surveyed the audience. When no one appeared, heads swiveled. I tugged at Ben. "I think I heard him say 'Gorrywoodsky Persecutni.' "

A woman seated in our row leaned over two people as she tried to make herself heard above the thunderstorm of clapping: "I am thinking your film has winned. *Give Us This Day*—is you? No?"

"Ben." I pushed him. "Barzmanova! That's me in Czech!" The "ova" to make it female. "They mean us!" I started right and Ben stumbled left, then changed directions suddenly so he bumped me and I stepped on the same person's toes twice. Finally we were both going in the same direction, made it to the aisle, where hands reached out to steady us. We staggered to the stage amid rhythmic applause. The important personality waiting to hand Ben the silver cup was the minister of culture, who held on to us as if he were afraid we'd run away.

He glared at the audience with severity, daring them to contradict anything he was about to say, and then began in low, funereal tones.

Actually, he *was* talking about us because as his volume built, he pushed us forward into the central spotlight, handed Ben a large silver cup for Best Picture and a small silver cup for Best Screenplay, then handed me three small silver cups for Best Director, Best Actor, Best Actress. A clean sweep!

At that moment, a young man came running from the wings with a sheet of paper and yet another cup. He whispered in the minister's ear. The minister nodded. The young man took the microphone and announced in impeccable English, "A Special Award has been given to the documentary film *The Hollywood Ten,* produced by Paul Jarrico and directed by John Berry."

While he spoke, a second wild-eyed young man rushed out from the wings with another microphone and translated into Czech.

The first young man continued, "The Hollywood Ten play themselves: Alvah Bessie, Herbert Biberman, Lester Cole, Edward Dmytryk, Ring Lardner, Jr., John Howard Lawson, Albert Maltz, Adrian Scott, and Dalton Trumbo." Ben and I were stunned. Tears rolled down my cheeks as the audience rose, applauded, and cheered. We felt the applause was not for us but for the Ten, for the struggle, the sacrifice. Most of all, I was thinking of Adrian and how this moment, this clear honor to him and all of them, would make him well.

"We ask Ben Barzman and Barzmanova," the young man finally said, "to take this award with them and to present it to the Hollywood Ten with the thanks of the Czech people for continuing the fight against Fascism." He pushed the cup into my arms and the minister steered Ben over to the microphone. As I recall, Ben thanked his colleagues and the English crew, Geiger, Dmytryk, Padovani, Wanamaker, me, whom he called Barzmanova to cheers, his mother, the festival, and the Czech people. He wound up with the hope that we might all live in a world of peace and creativity, held up the large silver cup. "To Peace," he said— "*Za Mir*"—and brought down the house.

In Prague, the night before our return to Paris, we attended a reception at the Soviet embassy.

The New Man

Tosi and Casarighi, Italian film critics staying at the Alcron, were on their way to the party. We asked why they hadn't gone to the press showing of *Give Us This Day*. They replied that they had already seen it at an advance projection and had sent rave notices back to their newspapers. They guessed it would win; in Italy, where it was still called *Christ in Concrete* (*Cristoforo Muratori*), it was already enjoying a huge success.

Two couples at the hotel seemed to think they had a right to crash the party at the Soviet embassy—a tall, middle-aged, rangey British couple who proclaimed themselves members of the English Communist Party, and newly married, impoverished British aristocrats who had chosen Czechoslovakia for their honeymoon because they thought it was cheap.

We eight, bound for the embassy, took two cabs, put Tosi and Casarighi, both of whom had been invited, with the British Communists who hadn't. The newlyweds rode with us.

"Didn't you think there might be heavy security at the Soviet embassy?" I asked the young bride.

She seemed startled, then dismissed the problem with a girlish laugh. "I've always wanted to dance with one of those men with that lovely red sash across his chest."

I had visions of tanks and a platoon of large-hatted Soviet plainclothesmen lurking in the shadows.

"If they refuse us," her groom said cheerfully—I think he was an earl—"we shall simply stay in the cab and go back to Prague."

The taxis swung off the main highway and entered what seemed a deserted area with few houses. A private road took us uphill. Ahead on the crest of the rising terrain stood a moon-silhouetted figure in large hat and trenchcoat.

I gasped. Even from that distance the man looked like a movie stereotype of a Soviet plainclothesman. I couldn't decide whether he, like the other plainclothesmen we encountered in Prague, was trying to resemble characters in our movies or whether it was his normal attire.

The cabs slowed down. I stiffened. Were there tanks hidden in the deep shadows? The lone, wide-hatted guard ambled toward us, looked us over, exchanged a few grunts with the cabbie. As I flashed the invitation, which he examined, I pointed to the other taxi. "They also are guests of the film festival."

He shrugged as if giving up, handed back the invitation, and motioned both cars on.

The imposing, brightly lit mansion came into view. The heavy circle of security we had braced ourselves for never materialized. A footman suddenly sprung open our door and made a sweeping gesture of welcome.

We entered the large reception hall that bubbled with a babble of two hundred people speaking twenty different languages and queuing at a long buffet for what turned out to be *zakusky*, appetizers, more Czech than Russian. Many guests wore dark suits and dark ties. Tosi told us that dinner jackets, a symbol of the bourgeoisie, were never worn. He pointed to the other side of the room at a tall, distinguished man wearing a red sash diagonally across his chest—the president of Czechoslovakia. Our young bride came over to us. "What would happen," she asked in her very English English, "if I were to ask the president to dance with me?"

"He would be flattered," Tosi replied, "and if he's at all a man, he will be pleased."

We watched as she crossed the dance floor and headed directly for the president. The murmur of the crowd's conversation halted as they realized she was making a beeline for the top man himself. She waited respectfully for the president and the Soviet ambassador to notice her, then said something that the president, apparently not believing what he heard, asked her to repeat. As she did, he appeared astonished, pointed like a delighted boy to himself. She nodded. The president made a wide gesture of pleased surprise, and murmured to the ambassador, who walked over to the orchestra. After a few moments the orchestra began playing "Tea for Two." The president swept her on to the dance floor. A murmur of admiration rippled over the crowd. Other couples took to the dance floor and the evening lit up.

The Soviet ambassador came straight over to us, introduced himself to Ben and me. "I know who you are," he said. "Congratulations." Tosi and Casarighi announced their credentials. "Yes, yes. The press. You are most welcome." Then he asked us in his most jovial manner if we were enjoying ourselves.

It was obviously a question to which he did not expect an answer, for he was about to leave us when Tosi, being on his third drink, stopped him by saying, "Frankly, I am somewhat disappointed in this evening."

The ambassador turned with raised eyebrows to Tosi, who said calmly he had imagined a Russian reception quite differently, with caviar and vodka. Before the ambassador arrived, Ben had remarked about the absence of vodka and caviar. Tosi turned to Ben and asked blandly, "Don't you agree?" Ben nodded in embarrassment.

We were taken aback by Tosi's brashness, but the ambassador did not seem in the least disturbed by it, which is why I suppose he was an ambassador. Tosi flashed a happy grin at us as the ambassador gestured to follow him into an inner room of the embassy and carefully shut the door behind us. From a refrigerator he brought out a huge tin of Beluga Imperial (golden) caviar and a bottle of chilled Polish vodka, the color of whiskey. He placed the vodka and caviar on a table and then laid out lemon and pepper and a box of French *biscottes*— toasts. He spread generous helpings of the caviar on the toasts and poured us little glasses of vodka.

It was what caviar is supposed to be! As for the vodka, the ambassador explained that this kind was not sold commercially but was prepared and aged in five-century-old vats in Poland, which accounted for the fine color, and I suppose the mellow aged-liqueur taste. Because the glasses were so small, our drinks had to be tossed off in one swallow.

After about the third or fourth drink, the ambassador, now glowing, startled us by asking if we'd brought any new anti-Soviet or anti-Stalin jokes. Naturally, we all hesitated. "Have you heard the one about the contest," he asked us, "held in the Soviet Union to select an appropriate sculpture commemorating the anniversary of the great poet Pushkin?" We said we hadn't. The ambassador plunged into the story with gusto. After a nationwide competition, the official commission tried to make up its mind between the many submissions. Pushkin seated, deep in thought; Pushkin standing, declaiming a poem; Pushkin fighting the duel that cost him his life. And what do you think won? *Stalin reading a poem by Pushkin!*

The ambassador laughed heartily. I wasn't so sure we should laugh. The ambassador was pouring vodka again. Ben picked up his little glass and held it high. "I propose a toast," he said. "To Peace! *Za Mir!*"

The ambassador raised his glass a trifle higher than Ben's. "*Za Mir!* To Peace!" he said. "And to the New Man and a Better Mankind!"

20

Finishing School

Walking down the Champs Elysées a week after we returned, we ran into Art Buchwald, whose *Paris Herald Tribune* restaurant column was growing ever more popular.

Less chubby than the way we think of him now, he wore a sporty, small-brimmed brown hat tilted over his horn-rimmed glasses. "Didja know your little foray behind the Iron Curtain made all the big wire services?" he said.

"Is that good or bad?" Ben, acquainted with the Talmud, often replied to a question with a question.

"A little foolhardy," Art replied.

I stuck out my chin defensively. "We were the only ones who could pick up the awards."

Art shrugged. "I just wanted you guys to know you're no longer low profile," he said with his wide grin. His warning deflated some of the elation Ben and I were feeling from the triumph of seeing *Christ in Concrete* recognized politically and cinematically.

On a personal level, and secretly, I was worried. I'd just missed a *second* period but let Ben think it was the first as if it were the result of our stay in Pupp's romantic hotel. I had no doubt I had conceived in London. It was Bernard's child, the only accident I'd ever had and the first time I did not want a baby. For my own health, it was wrong for me to have a child. Also, I wanted to be free to work. I asked one of our French doctor friends where to go for an abortion. "London," he insisted, "where it's done properly."

I told Ben I was pregnant but that it was too soon after the bad delivery I'd had. He accepted that and accompanied me to London.

On the strength of my new writing assignment, I had bought myself a small featherweight Hermés portable. I wanted to take it with me to London so that I'd be able to work on the screenplay of *Finishing School.*

"What's the use lugging that along?" Ben demanded, eyeing the typewriter.

"I'll have to rest for a couple of days."

"I know you. You'll never work. I'm the one who has to do the schlepping." He shoved it in the corner to be left behind. I almost grabbed it myself but I felt so much guilt that I went without it. I told myself it was my punishment.

Like everything that cuts off life, the abortion, though painless, hurt emotionally. In the final analysis, I cared more for my children than for anything else, and to end the beginning of life was traumatic. The surgery did not leave me with any physical problems because six years later, when Ben and I were ready, I had the other four children we desired.

Bernard, Hetty, and their children, David and Gwynny, arrived in Paris that fall with Johnny Weber and his family. We'd made reservations for them at the friendly little Derby Hotel on the Left Bank near UNESCO.

Their first night in Paris, Ben and I took them all to eat *nem*—Vietnamese restaurants were just beginning to spring up all over the city. Ben and I loved the egg rolls wrapped in lettuce and mint leaves that one dipped in *nuoc mam,* a dried-fish sauce. As soon as the children were settled, eating *nem* with their fingers, Johnny Weber broke out: "Do you know the latest?"

"What?" Ben asked.

"Your friend Dmytryk!" Johnny exclaimed. "It looks like he's going to stool."

"Don't be silly," I said. "He's serving his term where Albert is—Mill Point Prison Camp in West Virginia, isn't it?"

Apparently, after Eddie's wife visited him, Bernard went on, he swore out a statement in front of the warden to the effect that he was not now nor had he been a Communist during his deposition, and got his lawyer, Bartley Crum, and his agent to try to negotiate a deal with Columbia Pictures. the *Hollywood Reporter* and *Variety* had run stories saying Eddie asked for parole for the other eight of the Ten. That blew his deal with Harry Cohn sky-high. Eddie became so furious he began talking about naming names.

"That's impossible!" Ben cried. "How do you know this?"

"Albert is in the same prison. He sensed it was coming and he's kept everyone informed," Johnny said.

His wife, Ripsy Weber, shuddered. "I never thought after what they went through that any one of the Ten would . . . crumble."

I looked at Ben. "As you know, I never liked Eddie but this is hard to believe."

"Do you realize what this means?" Bernard asked. "He'll name directors. He's liable to name me even though he's never seen me at a meeting. Jack Berry and—oh, my God! You guys." He turned to Ben and me. "He'll name you two!"

Johnny Weber laughed mirthlessly. "We're forming a company of people who are going to be named!"

"Maybe he won't name us," I said, ever hopeful, "not after what Ben did for him, writing *Christ in Concrete* on spec, moving to England without being paid."

Hetty pursed her lips. "These are strange and terrible times. Who can say what anyone will do?"

I looked at her and realized this was the first time since my liaison with Bernard that I had to face Hetty. I'd always thought of her as a Welsh sprite. She was elfin, had the thin face of a bird, and darted about like a swallow. I had also thought of her as a leprechaun, but when she appeared before me at that dinner, a real live woman with whom I could identify, I felt guilty. I watched Bernard's nervous tics with growing anxiety. Eddie might name both of us in the upcoming spring HUAC hearings, but on a much more narrow and personal level, if Bernard and I continued our relationship, I realized we would have to learn duplicity. How could we possibly go on keeping Ben and Hetty from knowing? The answer was *Finishing School,* a real reason for Bernard and me to see each other frequently.

I don't like to think about some aspects of this period—Eddie's betrayal of all of us, and Bernard and I sneaking into out-of-the-way hotels, getting home late, being away from our children too long. I wrote scenes, which we discussed thoroughly when we met late morning or at lunch. Once we drove to a poetic auberge on the banks of a river outside Paris that reminded me of Seurat's *Dimanche à la Grande Jatte.* We ran into Volodya and Ida, who, seeing us, disappeared, showing no signs of recognition.

Neither the duplicity nor the often shabby surroundings marred my personal happiness. I loved working on a story of my own that I was suited to write; I loved being with Bernard, who was not competitive but gentle and comradely. One of our greatest pleasures was the long talks in bed when we shared problems, spoke openly about our marriages, our children, our work, and the script. This frankness between us led me to believe I could say anything. Although instinctively I'd hidden the abortion, eventually, I told him.

He shot out of bed, horrified. I thought his reaction was so sharp because the abortion dramatized the dishonesty of our lives. Not at all. "How could you?" he demanded. "Our child?"

"It wasn't a child—"

"It *was* a child and you didn't ask me. You didn't give me a choice."

"There was no choice. You have two children. I have three!"

"Who says we can't start a new family? In a proper world, one would be able to live with the person one loved."

"Proper world!" I laughed hysterically. "Bernard, I did the only thing I could do. You weren't here. I couldn't tell you. But it would have made no difference. Too many are involved. I was afraid!"

He came to the edge of the bed and sank to his knees. "It must have been god-awful for you!" He spoke so low I could barely make out the words. "What have I gotten you into, you whom I love . . . ?" He didn't finish, took my hands, kissed them, then placed them over his eyes.

Johnny Weber and Bernard had had a series of conferences with Ben about the creation of the new company. I christened it "Riviera Films" and, since I spoke French the best, was delegated to ask a young lawyer to draw up the papers for a *société* that he would then set up with a French citizen as "gerund," as required by French law.

Our company's plan was to have two Italo-American coproductions shooting simultaneously. Ben, on the lookout for a project for himself, found an unpublished story, *Bottle of Milk*, by someone named Nissem Calef. Riviera bought it. As Johnny Weber put it in *Tender Comrades,* the story "was cribbed partly from *Crime and Punishment,* partly from *The Bicycle Thief,* partly from who knows what else." By January 1951, Ben and I were hard at work, each writing our own movie, while Johnny and Bernard were deal-making, casting and preparing them for production.

Meanwhile, in Washington, D.C., the House UnAmerican Activities Committee was gearing up to hold hearings in April and May, in which scores of people would be named.

By mid-April, Ben and I had finished writing the scripts. We believed that Riviera had Italian money to make the two films. On the basis of my screenplay, Bernard had arranged a distribution deal with United Artists for both. For Ben's script, Johnny had signed the distinguished Paul Muni for the leading role. Bernard, who'd contracted to shoot *Finishing School* at Cinecittà, rounded up a bevy of lovely young European actresses, led by Bovo, of *Miracle in Milan,* and Marina Vlady, who'd played in his *Pardon My French* and would later become a French star.

Johnny and Bernard were already in Italy negotiating with Andrea Forzano to shoot *Bottle of Milk,* or *Stranger on the Prowl,* as it is now called, at his rickety studio, Produttori Cinematografici Tirrenia, near Pisa. They wired us to join them. Then Forzano ran out of money but they found a second producer to finance the two films—Albert Salvatore, an American of Italian origin who'd recently returned to Rome. (We didn't know until much later that both producers had had ties with Mussolini.)

The telegram from Bernard said we should rent a house in Viareggio for August and September to be nearby while the pictures were in production. The wire finished: COME AT ONCE STOP BEN YOU'RE JUST THE GUY TO DO A JOB ON SALVATORE WHO IS HESITATING.

Ben and I took the overnight train from Paris to Pisa, where Bernard was waiting in the railroad station with an absurdly large bouquet and an idiotic grin on his face.

Smothered in spring flowers, I sat in the backseat of his mouselike Fiat Topolino, probably the tiniest car ever made. Ben and Bernard, in front, discussed how to keep the news of HUAC from Salvatore, who certainly would not come in with the money if any of us were named.

The next day, Sunday, I found and agreed to rent the *casa grise,* a gray house, because the kitchen was near the garden. That evening we were tense. We were to sign the deal with Salvatore the next day. But in America, Dmytryk was to testify, and Ben might be named at any minute, in which case Salvatore would back out. Eddie's potentially explosive testimony was wrecking all the hard-won production plans blacklisted people were trying to patch together in Europe.

Johnny Weber stopped by. He was on his way to Rome. "Who do you think should direct *Bottle of Milk?*" he asked.

"Joe Losey," I suggested.

"He'll be named," Johnny said with his mirthless laugh.

"I don't think so," I argued. "Nobody in Hollywood knows he's in the Party."

"She may be right," said Ben. "In New York, he's known, but he hasn't been active in Hollywood. Still, it's a big risk."

"You said it!" Johnny cut in. "Two blacklisted directors. Two blacklisted films."

"He's a big talent," I said. "We ought to get him out of the States."

Bernard frowned. "If we get the contract signed tomorrow, we're okay. United Artists promised they'd hold to their deal with us. If need be, they'd change the titles and use Italian names on the credits."

"*D'accordo,*" said Johnny, with a sick smile.

No sooner was he gone than Salvatore, who hated to be alone, knocked on the door. He was sipping a huge glass of milk.

"For your ulcers?" I inquired.

"Appropriate, no?" he joked, making himself comfortable, "for the producer of *Bottle of Milk?*"

We couldn't get rid of him. Near midnight he was still telling bad jokes, although I could see he was censoring them because of my presence.

The phone rang. New York. For Bernard. Although he was a competent director, Bernard was a lousy actor. His voice was uncertain, his hands trembled, his complexion turned chartreuse. He said things like "How nice of you to tell me" and "So good of you to call." Salvatore listened and watched with a fishy stare. Bernard explained to Salvatore, in what he thought was a casual tone, that it was only an insurance company calling him about an accident he'd had with his car.

"That must have been one hell of an accident," Salvatore remarked dryly, "either that or one hell of an insurance company to phone all the way from New York to Viareggio."

We finally wore Salvatore out. As soon as he left, Bernard burst out with the news: Eddie Dmytryk had named him, Ben and me, Jack Berry, and many other former comrades—six directors, seventeen writers, and three others.[1] The news had already made most of the American press. Bernard and Ben and I stayed up until three in the morning trying to figure out what Lenin had once titled a pamphlet: *What Is to Be Done?* Since the United Artists people in Paris were ready and eager to hold to their bargain, a guaranteed worldwide distribution of the two coproductions even if Bernard were named, we decided that what was to be done was to push on with the deal. The signing was just ten hours away.

At seven that morning, Bernard appeared at the door, haggard and unshaven. The *Rome Daily American,* which was sold at a kiosk across the street from the hotel, had picked up the story and mentioned Bernard by name. "C'mon, Norma," he said. "We've got to buy up all the *Rome Daily Americans* around so Salvatore doesn't see. Ben, you stay here and wait for him."

Bernard and I bought and quickly stuffed the twenty-five newspapers from across the street in the back of his Topolino. He began to speculate that there was another kiosk a few hundred meters up the road, and that Salvatore was exactly the kind of pain in the ass who might walk that far for his paper. "We can't possibly buy up all the *Daily Americans* in Viareggio!" I said.

But that's what he wanted to do. Every half kilometer, he said, "What the hell, we've gone this far, we're in the car, we might as well go on to the next kiosk." When we came to the outskirts of Viareggio, he wanted to go forty kilometers to Pisa, a good-sized city. I couldn't restrain him. We did the whole city of Pisa. His Topolino wouldn't hold any more newspapers. He drove into the driveway of a big Agip Motel and screeched to a stop. "We can't leave them here," I protested. "They'd be suspicious."

"They'd be right," he replied, kissing me passionately.

Meanwhile, Salvatore turned up for breakfast, Ben told us later, but couldn't enjoy it without his paper, so the two of them had crossed to the news vendor opposite who said some son of a bitch had bought up all his *Daily Americans*. Kiosk after kiosk—the same story. Ben couldn't stop Salvatore from getting back in his car to find yet another kiosk. When they reached the outskirts of Viareggio, like Bernard, he wanted to go on to Pisa, but Ben had screamed at him and threatened to get out of the car and hitchhike back to the hotel if necessary. Only then did Salvatore give up.

We signed the deal later that day.

What did the deal mean? Two blacklist films were made. *Stranger on the Prowl*, directed by Joseph Losey. Instead of Ben's and Joe's names, Italian names appeared on the credits until 1999, when the Writers Guild of America (WGA) corrected them. A limited distribution was agreed upon at the time by UA and Roy Brewer, the fanatical anti-Communist IATSE labor leader who was one of the functionaries who cleared people and films. Paul Muni, the star, had cancer. The film was shot in a broken-down studio without the necessary equipment. Joe Losey was repeatedly threatened with expulsion from Italy on the demand of U.S. ambassador to Italy Clare Booth Luce, who prevailed on the Italian government to chase him and Bernard from Italy before they completed the two pictures. That was only one result of Eddie's testimony.

Finishing School, a tender study of adolescence, became *Luxury Girls,* directed by Bernard Vorhaus, original screenplay by Norma Barzman.[2] United Artists booked it into a 42nd Street movie house known to have the jerk-off trade. The engagement was for only two weeks until UA recouped their distribution costs. Outside the theater, photos of nude young girls, having nothing whatever to do with the film, were displayed as a come-on. In France, Italy, and England, the film fared well and was eventually shown at the Edinburgh Film Festival in 1989.

March 17, 2001.

This afternoon I telephoned Johnny Weber in New York. I needed his excellent memory, undiminished despite his ninety years.[3] He had been a trade union organizer, a Marxist teacher, a Party functionary, a story analyst, and head of the literary department at the William Morris Agency between 1945 and 1950. Johnny was one of the few Communist men I knew in Hollywood whose high intelligence and complete integrity I trusted.

"Johnny," I asked, "did I have a contract with Riviera Films?"

"No. We three admirable 'high-minded' Communist men exploited you."

"You mean I wrote that original screenplay and there was no provision for paying me?"

"Ben didn't have a contract for his screenplay either, but he was the third member of the company, he was a producer like Bernard and me. As such, legally, he would have been remunerated had there ever been any money."

"I was neither part of the company nor employed as a screenwriter?"

"That's right. You were conned by your friend Bernard Vorhaus. We were all good friends. You were treated as a good friend but not an equal. You were a woman."

"It's sort of laughable, isn't it?" I said.

"It's hilarious," Johnny said, "because it shows how sexist three guys who thought they were decent and moral could be!"

"And if the film had made money, what would have been my share?"

He laughed. "Oh, we might have voted to pay you but it would have been less than what Ben would have received, although you should have been paid more than he. *Finishing School* was based on your own original material. Ben adapted someone else's story for which the someone else—a man—was paid." Johnny stopped to laugh again. "In other words, if we had made money, you would have been conned again—because you were a woman!"

When Ben and I had finished the two screenplays for Riviera Films, we took time off and made a concerted effort to finish the original script about a woman lawyer that I'd started in 1948 before we left Hollywood. We were afraid that since we'd been named we wouldn't be able to sell it but felt we had to try. Ben had turned it into the story of a young man studying for the bar with a brilliant female law student. He has problems with his needlessly jealous wife. I did what I could, fixed and retyped two or three scenes, and felt guilty about not having helped earlier.

Ben said, "Think of a pseudonym."

"It should sound like a real person," I replied, "not one of those lovely WASP names like James Thompson."

"Right. How about your father's first name, Sam?"

"Fine. And my mother's maiden name, Levinson. Sam Levinson."

"Okay. Type up the title page."

We walked ceremoniously to the post office and airmailed it to Sammy Weisbord at the William Morris Agency.

The damage of Eddie's testimony and that of others at the hearings that spring continued to wreak havoc in the U.S. and in Europe.[4] In July 1951, on the eve of our departure for Viareggio for the filming of the two movies, I received a strange letter from the U.S. embassy in Paris. Would I come in at my convenience so they could rectify a detail in my passport?

It sounded peculiar but would the U.S. embassy use a ruse to get me to come in? Could it be to serve a subpoena on me? Was the embassy American soil? I talked it over with Ben and Bernard (Johnny had already left for Italy) and with the other friends who'd recently arrived in Paris. Didn't one have to stay *en règle,* i.e., comply with rules and regulations?

I was born in New York City. What did I have to fear? For Ben, it was different. He was born in Canada. Anxious about his vulnerable status as a naturalized American, Ben thought he ought not to be in Paris if the State Department came to our apartment looking for him. He went to Saint-Malô in Brittany. Bernard drove me to the embassy and waited outside. I walked to the desk marked "Passports" and showed the letter to the young woman behind the counter. Her brow furrowed. "Did you bring your passport?"

I took it out of my purse. She snatched it out of my hands. "Sit over there!" she commanded, pointing to a bench on the far side of the room. It was not the tone of someone whose salary was being paid out of my taxes.

After about three-quarters of an hour, an older, purple-haired woman, Vice Consul Agnes Schneider, with a face to match her nickname, "Schneider the Spider," called out "Barzman!" loud and clear.

"Mrs. Barzman," she said, acidly, "we have canceled your passport. We are keeping it. It will be returned to you when you are on an American ship bound for the United States. The passport will be marked 'for this voyage only.'"[5]

"There must be some mistake!"

"You, Mrs. Barzman, may not stay in Europe."

"How is that possible? What are you telling me?"

"Mrs. Barzman," she said, "your travel abroad is not in the best interest of the United States government."

I wondered if I should scream. I looked around. No one was paying any attention.

"What's the problem?" I asked. "Is it that we went to Karlovy Vary? I checked with this embassy. The man said it was all right to go to Czechoslovakia. Is it that?"

"You went to Czechoslovakia and you didn't come back here and report."

"You mean I didn't spy? Is *that* it?"

She glanced at her notes. "You visited the Wheelers. Your husband accepted a prize from the Czech government—"

"Is that it?"

She was still looking at the file. "Your husband's film shows the United States in a bad light—the Depression, no jobs—"

"Good Lord! Are you saying that this is happening to me because of the content of my husband's film? I'll give this story to the papers. It's important for people to know what you're doing! This is unconstitutional!"

"I'm not saying *why* we're keeping your passport," she snapped. "All these actions are not in the best interest of the United States."

She was treating me like an international spy. "You can't do this! I'm an American in a foreign country with three small children—"

"If you know what's good for you," said Schneider the Spider, "you'll take your children and go home. You'll have your passport back, I repeat, when you are on an American ship bound for the United States. It will be marked 'for this voyage only' and will be taken from you when you land."

"This just can't be!"

She cut in, "And don't think because your husband still has his passport that he can travel on it. It will be seized at whatever border he tries to cross."

Once more, I scanned the room for help. If I screamed, would anyone there help me? I felt raped. I turned away from her and fled.

Outside, Bernard was gnawing his nails. I fell into his arms, blurted it all out between hysterical sobs. He took me home to Hetty, who gave me a tumbler of cognac. Funny, I remember thinking how cozy their apartment was. When I downed the cognac, she refilled the glass. "There, there," she said, patting me affectionately.

Being without a passport, without papers, in a foreign country and subject to expulsion at any moment, had truly shaken me in ways I could not have foreseen. Bernard was leaving shortly for Italy, where *Finishing School* would soon start shooting, but I couldn't go there or anywhere. I wouldn't see him for months. Because we didn't vacate our apartment as planned, the owners, afraid we might overstay our lease, rushed back from America and encamped in our living room like watchdogs. They took turns, day and night, one of them was always there. We had to move.

Mother was becoming more ill each day. Months before, Dr. Myers, of the American Hospital, had informed us that her diabetes could no longer be controlled by diet. He prescribed insulin shots. We had just moved out of the house of "*le gangster-dentiste* Robbes" into an apartment in Auteuil in the 16th arrondissement. From the convent around the corner, Soeur Thérèse came every day to give Mother a shot. We'd inherited the apartment from the Robert Rossens. Bob, who had become a director, had been shooting in Europe, and the Rossens were on their way back to America, the only progressive Americans going in that direction. They left us with a $1,760 telephone bill that they never paid even after repeated requests. Perhaps he assumed that he didn't need to pay us, since he soon would become an informer.

Despite the shots, Mother's health was deteriorating. Sister Thérèse told us she was horrified at the enormous amount of insulin, prescribed by Dr. Myers, that she'd been injecting every day for several months. We accompanied her to the pharmacy, where the pharmacist called Dr. Myers. An egregious mistake had been made! Dr. Myers had prescribed the insulin in American units. The pharmacy had filled the prescription in French units. Mother had been receiving twice the amount of insulin she should have.

I was horrified. What had this done? At first, Mother improved on the reduced dose. But after some time, she began to suffer from abdominal pain, which Dr. Myers called "gallbladder trouble," hinting that she might be dying of something else.

When I developed a frightful case of bleeding hives, the physician who cured them suggested that I was under great stress. "Have you thought of making your *psychanalyse?*" He handed me a piece of paper with a name and a phone number. Dr. Kestenberg, Zif's opposite number, received me at his home in Neuilly. He suggested we begin on

September 2 at 9 A.M.

"But today is July thirtieth—"

"All year I wait for this moment." His eyes were far away. "*Les vacances, Madame.*"

"But my mother is dying," I protested, "and I'm a prisoner. I can't leave the country, can't go to Italy where my picture is shooting—"

"Madame," he said sternly. "In France, the month of August is sacred. *Vous allez vous débrouiller.* You will manage until the second of September at 9 A.M."

I did *débrouiller*. I spent much of the time with Mother, which may have led her to suspect she was terminally ill. As if they sensed something, Luli and Johnny, more than ever before, wanted her to tell her stories.

One day, an envelope with no return address arrived in the mail. Inside, the handwriting was Sammy Weisbord's: "You can't use 'Sam Levinson.' He's a comic who stooled (23 names). You'll be contacted by the Bank of the Holy Spirit. They'll inform you they are holding $40,000 in your names." It was unsigned. Scribbled in one corner, in tiny letters, we thought we could make out three initials—an "m," a "g," and an "m."

"We sold it! We sold it!" Ben shouted. "Even if it was pretty bad."

"Holy smoke!" I cried. "MGM. Sammy means MGM bought it. Maybe Dore Schary guessed it was us and bought it because he's feeling guilty! Wow! We've got to celebrate!"

We hugged and Ben said, "Let's take your mother out."

That was the last time Mother went out, September 14, the eve of my birthday. She wore her new fall hat. On October 17, Mother was taken by ambulance to the American Hospital. I assured her that her pain was the result of gallstones, that her gallbladder might have to be removed surgically, but that it was a banal operation, nothing to fear. She seemed glad to believe that.

Dr. Myers confirmed it was as he thought, cancer of the pancreas, inoperable. I couldn't and wouldn't believe that she was dying. I'd spent thirty-one years keeping her from joining the daughter who died nine months before I was born, with my smiles and giggles and silly faces and funny stories. But here she was in a white-walled hospital room with the shades drawn, as I somehow expected it would be.

I thought she was asleep but suddenly she said one of those truly lovely things. "Sorry I was so old-fashioned. I would love to have been a young mother today."

She was wrong. She wasn't old-fashioned. She was ahead of her time.

The nurse had just given her a shot, and her words were slurred: "I really loved the theater. Gertrude Lawrence. Ina Claire. Lynn Fontanne . . . I only saw *The Guardsman* once, but I remember Fontanne's lines." Then she delivered the last line of Molnar's play, "Of course, Dahling, I knew all along," and sank into a drugged slumber.

I'd always been too busy feeling sorry for Mother to recognize her extraordinary capacity for life.

Toward the end, when I entered the hospital room quietly, barely breathing, Mother said softly, "Norma, you don't have to tiptoe."

"Oh, you're awake? How do you feel?"

"Wonderful," she replied, barely audible. "I'm having a new experience."

"A new experience?" I repeated, supposing the morphine was making her mind wander.

"Yes, I'm dying," she said, as if it really were an interesting new experience.

She died peacefully several hours later. I sat by her side for a long, long time. Finally, I got up, kissed her on the forehead, and left.

Outside her room, in the hospital corridor, I found John Berry sitting on the floor, leaning back against the wall. He was weeping, too.

"But Jack," I said, choked. "You didn't know her that well."

Jack lifted his rugged, tear-stained face, looked hard into my eyes. "I was crying for all of us," he said.

21

The Herring Barrel

Ben christened the Hollywood exiles in Paris "The Herring Barrel." He likened all of us, working together, incestuously sharing our personal, psychological, political, and financial problems, to a barrel of herrings packed close together in brine. When Larry Ceplair interviewed me for *Tender Comrades,* he said, "Yes, but Ben was *fond* of pickled herring." True, but Ben liked it with sour cream and onions. *Our* herring in Paris was marinated in fear. From 1951 through 1956, we were frightened most of the time, felt our own country was spying on us, and never knew if our next job was our last.

We must have communicated our fears to our children. In 1955, when Ben's nephew, Alan, a G.I. stationed in France, turned up at our front door in uniform, Johnny, age eight, ran out the back door and fled. He hid on the block until Alan was gone.

The U.S. embassy had taken away my passport in July 1951. To be without one in a foreign country meant much more than not being able to travel. Our short residence permits expired in October. Without passports, we wouldn't be able to get new permits to remain in the country. We all knew that the French authorities were expelling Asian and Latin American émigrés with less than twenty-four-hours' notice. We were scared and we were not the only ones. That summer, in the wake of the HUAC hearings, a mini-colony of new American exiles arrived in Paris. The unthinkable was happening. For the first time in history, Americans were fleeing the United States with their families, seeking political haven in Mexico, England, Canada, and France.

When my passport was confiscated two months after the hearings closed, I warned our new fellow exiles to stay away from the embassy and to hang on to their passports as long as they were valid. We began meeting with them at the Coupole to discuss what to do. We all needed ways to make a living as much as we needed security. In many ways, being with each other gave us the assurance that somehow we would survive the blacklist.

My immediate challenge was to know that our family would not be thrown out of France tomorrow or the next day. Ben and I consulted a French Communist lawyer who was internationally known for his fight for liberty. Volodya recommended him.

"With luck," the attorney told us, "perhaps I could arrange for you and your family to stay in France for another three or four weeks. France needs American Marshall Plan money to build up its postwar economy. It does not need Americans without passports who are being pursued by a committee of the United States Congress."

Outside, the day was as beautiful as only an October day in Paris can be, but we couldn't appreciate it when we emerged from the lawyer's office. We were beaten, ready to give up. We walked across the bridge to the Ile Saint-Louis, the smaller island in the Seine that is shaped like a ship's prow. We flopped down on the one bench, squinted at the sequined, shimmering river, stared hard at a *péniche*, barge, passing under a bridge, and tried not to weep. Ben came up with a joke that was apropos: "A little old Jew goes to a travel agency. He and his wife want to go somewhere new. 'Try to decide where you want to go,' says the busy travel agent, handing the little Jew a globe. He spins it around. 'Do you have another world?' he asks."

"Little old Jew" made me think of Pop Landau. Ever hopeful, I said, "Ben, let's go see Pop. He'll know what to do."

And, of course, he did. The next day, on Pop's advice, Ben and I accompanied a small, shuffling, elderly man to the forbidding Préfecture de Police, across from the Conciergerie. Pop had assured us that though the "shuffler" might look like a poor slob, he was a "hero of the resistance," a personal friend of General de Gaulle, and could fix anything.

Not only did the fixer shuffle as he walked, he actually shuffle-talked both of us past ten or so grim-faced bureaucrats in flagrant violation of the three-or-four-hour ritual wait. He got us about twenty meters into the heart of the killing zone. We were brought to an abrupt halt by a bark from a dark-haired woman carved out of granite. The fixer-shuffler mumbled something unintelligible. Granite Lady kept barking, "What? Who? Where? What are you doing there?" He scratched his armpit and uttered vague wordlike sounds. The words "Americans . . . No passport . . . " activated her radar. She pointed an iron finger at a row of seats halfway across France where terrified supplicants for extension of residence permits waited. That's where the shuffler was to sit. We were to sit in the two chairs about ten inches from her.

Briskly, she asked our names, put her lips deep into the telephone mouthpiece, the stand-up kind they had in those days. Forty seconds later, a file was on her desk. She held it up so there'd be no doubt in our minds that it was *our* file, and immediately lost herself in a fascinated perusal of it. We hadn't been in France that long but our file was thick. She read every line of every document. Finally, a real live expression cracked Granite Face, sort of bureaucratic glee. She confided demurely that the file contained a letter about us from the American embassy. "They would like us to throw you and your family out of France," she said sweetly.

We looked at the fixer but he was carefully examining his shoes. We could have told him they were badly scuffed and worn down at the heels. I had mental images of Luli, five, carrying baby brother Aaron, now two, and Johnny, four, dragging a little suitcase, all of them knowing something awful had happened.

Slowly, I realized that Granite Lady was saying the French equivalent of "Who the hell do they think they are telling *us* whom we should or should not keep?" Was I hearing her correctly? I glanced at Ben. He seemed bewildered. Only when we saw her shredding the letter from our embassy and several other documents did we grasp what was really happening. "Furthermore," she announced crisply, "I shall, of course, give you the longest possible residence permits."

They were for ten years. Lovely pale blue. With lots of pink stamps.

Was it blind luck our stumbling on that particular woman, or did she reflect official policy? We never knew.

Later that day, we ran into another charming Hungarian, Bob Capa, who was with David Seymour (Shim)—two great Magnum war photographers. Capa had become famous during the Spanish Civil War when his photo of a Loyalist child searching for his dead mother in the ruins of Madrid had been the cover of *Life*. Cynics used to say, "Nowadays, no one starts a war unless Capa's free to photograph it."

Ben and I had met Capa two years before when I was pregnant with Aaron. Capa had been on his way to the races. Could he pat my big distended belly for luck?

We told Capa and Shim how we'd just gotten our French papers. Now we were safe in France. "But," complained Ben, "we don't have passports. If I had one, I could probably get a job in England," which prompted Capa to launch into a story of his own passport-less days. Years before, in Budapest, when he was barred from travel, he went to see an old pharmacist friend. The man pulled out a parchment and engraved on it: "To whom it may concern, Please let this valiant man, Robert Capa, pass unharmed. He has done numerous services for humanity."

"I traveled on it for years," Capa said, laughing.

At La Coupole, we often heard our exiled friends whispering about the need to make plans to flee to other countries in case France deported them. Ben was lucky. Born in Canada, he had put out feelers about living there. The Canadian government replied with an offer of citizenship for the whole family if we would reside for a year as "new immigrants." But for Americans, the choice was Israel or Czechoslovakia. Most wanted to go to Israel.

"I know the cultural attaché," Ben said one day. "She arranged our trip to Israel last year for *Faithful City*."

"Why don't we apply as a group who, once there, will form a film kibbutz?" another person suggested.

"Great idea!" somebody cried. "It's to their advantage. 'Hollywood know-how' for their new film industry. Teachers for their young filmmakers—"

I whooped, elated. Ben was dispatched to ask the cultural attaché to forward our request formally. She thought it a splendid idea.

Several weeks later, she made an appointment to meet us all at the Coupole. We were sitting at two small tables joined together outside on the terrace, Jack Berry and his wife, Gladys, Jules Dassin, Bea Dassin, Mischa Altman, Lee and Tammy Gold, Ben and me.

When she appeared, her expression was dour. "The Israeli government," she recited, "would have wished to welcome you with open arms. We are saddened that we must refuse. Many American Jews who give large sums of money to Israel would be offended if we were to give sanctuary to those they consider 'Hollywood Reds.' "

It is almost impossible now to communicate how scared many people were at this time—and for good reason. The long arm of the U.S. State Department was reaching into Europe, even into international organizations. One example of their interference was *L'affaire Leff*. Lee Leff and her husband, David, editor of the UNESCO magazine, were among our closest friends. David had asked us to bring "thin needles" to Prague for Eleanor Wheeler. The State Department pressured UNESCO to force David to testify before HUAC. Their power play failed only because, in the nick of time, the United Nations issued UN passports to the Leffs and their three small children. The Leff family left immediately for Czechoslovakia. Some years later, David and Lee divorced; he returned to the States. Lee remarried. She and her Czech husband were part of the Prague Spring movement for "socialism with a human face," and suffered accordingly when the Soviet tanks ground through Prague.

Dr. Michael Sacks was another friend who was being hounded by the State Department. Sacks was an old China hand who'd been part of a

The Herring Barrel

United Nations relief organization (UNRRA) with the Eighth Route Army and had known Mao and Chou En-lai.[1] How did we meet Mike and his breathtakingly beautiful English wife, Barbara, who closely resembled Princess Grace? Progressive Americans traveling to Paris were often told to look up Les Barzmans. When art historians Professors Milton and Blanche Brown arrived, they made an appointment to meet us at the Closerie des Lilas. Another young couple was with them. We couldn't take our eyes off them, paid no attention to the Browns, were positively rude, we were so captivated by Barbara's beauty and Mike's exuberant, good-natured wit. They became close friends. We saw them through the years except for the five years the World Health Organization protected the Sackses from the State Department by sending them to India and keeping them there.

Our friends Ira and Edita Morris were high on the State Department's list of "subversives." Ira was the scion of the Chicago Morris meatpacking family. He had traveled around the world writing pleasant novels set in unusual locations and had given large sums to progressive causes. His wife, Edita, a Swedish activist, wrote a memorable book, *Flowers of Hiroshima*. The Morrises' chateau, Nesles, just outside Paris, hosted wonderful gatherings of the world's literati and great scientists, among them Haakon Chevalier, a nuclear physicist whom HUAC was trying to force to return and testify.

One day in the spring of 1952, Ben and I were sitting with John Paxton (*Crossfire*) at Fouquet's, a sidewalk café. I had the distinct feeling we were being surveyed. Johnny had just arrived in Paris and was very upset. His agents had cabled him, strongly advising him to deny "everything." His problem was that he did not know what to deny. He'd searched his soul, he wrote them, but all he'd come up with was stealing a yo-yo from Woolworth's at the age of ten. His agents were not amused. Unless he took out an ad, denying being a Communist, they threatened he would never—repeat, never—work again as a Hollywood screenwriter. After an almost unbelievable tangle of misunderstandings, Johnny finally discovered what it was all about. In his testimony before HUAC, Eddie Dmytryk had complained that the Communist Party tried to foist a Communist screenwriter on him but that he, Eddie, had obstinately refused. Instead, he'd insisted on hiring a non-Communist screenwriter, John Paxton.

The *Los Angeles Examiner* followed the hearings avidly. Its front page carried a special box captioned: NAMED TODAY IN THE WASHINGTON HEARINGS, which listed anyone mentioned in the hearings. Paxton's name had appeared in the front-page box. The *Examiner* had neither space nor inclination to note such details as that Paxton had been referred to as a *non-*Communist writer. Johnny told us that he'd found himself in that strange limbo—the gray list, as it came to be called. A number of years passed before his agents were able to find work for him. He then wrote some memorable films, including *On the Beach.*

It must have confused the State Department and the CIA that we also had friends from America who were *not* wanted by HUAC. One was James Beard. Ben had met Jimmy at the Portland Civic Theatre, where Beard's build and talent suited him to play Falstaff. When Jimmy Beard saw Ben and me at the Deux Magots, he dragged us to a cocktail party for the world's great chefs. There, they stood poised, bright-eyed, having maneuvered themselves into the most strategic positions to pounce on the hors d'oeuvres. When all the canapés were gone, I, high on champagne like many there, invited the great chefs to our place, where I promised to fix them my specialty, "*Hachis d'agneau*—lamb hash." Behind me, I heard Ben uninvite them. "For Chrissake, Norma!" he hissed.

"We've got a half a leg of lamb left," I replied.

Almost all of them turned up. One said, "We have often wondered what went into the mysterious American 'pot luck.' "

"Just make sure there are plenty of mushrooms," Jimmy Beard advised, giving me an affectionate pat.

Some of the chefs actually took notes as I added garlic and herbs to the mixture.

NORMA'S LAMB HASH
(Credit goes to screenwriter Johnny Paxton, a great cook who

gave this recipe to me, and to Jacqueline Renaudin, our young lady, who had learned to make a similar dish from her previous employer, Madame Zinc.)

Sauté lightly 2 tbsps chopped onion in 1 tbsp butter, adding 1 tbsp flour until mixture is golden. Add 1 ½ cups water and 3 tbsps ketchup. Cook slowly for 20 minutes. Stir from time to time. Add 1 lb. diced leftover lamb, ½ cup sliced mushrooms, 1 tbsp chopped parsley. Dust with thyme, rosemary, and garlic powder. While making the above, boil 3 or 4 potatoes. Dice. Cover the meat mixture with the potatoes. Sprinkle with grated Parmesan, ½ tbsp bread crumbs, and a little melted butter. Brown in hot oven.

Ben used to like it with a poached egg on top but many of the chefs wanted the hash "pure," without the egg, to better appreciate the real taste.

A year later, Jimmy Beard confided to Ben that he'd received a note from the FBI, inviting him to tell anything of importance that he might have overheard from his meeting with Ben and Norma Barzman. Being watched and reported on became part of living, a condition of the times. We feared the worst and lived with it every day.

Ben and I didn't have to worry about our finances as most exiles did. We had $40,000 from the sale of the original script to MGM, which we felt more and more certain had been Dore Schary's mild gesture of defiance to the Committee. Mother had left everything to my sister, Muriel, and me, but the estate would not be settled for years because she had died abroad. Nevertheless, Ben worried about money, a combination of his childhood anxiety that his parents wouldn't be able to pay the bills, and a new, real apprehension about being a writer in a foreign land. Since we did have enough to live comfortably, perhaps his money fears were just part of his growing discomfort at "having had everything taken away from him."

Television saved many exiled blacklisted Americans. In America, the new medium was just beginning but it was Hannah Weinstein who heralded its arrival for us. This remarkable woman, a former advertising executive, had been responsible for putting on the gargantuan Madison Square Garden mass meetings for vice-presidential candidate Henry Wallace, and for courageously protesting HUAC. She arrived in Paris with her three daughters, Dina, Lisa, and Paula, a lovely black nanny, and enough progressive money to start a television studio in England. Johnny Weber, an old friend of hers, installed them in the Hotel Derby, where he and Bernard were staying.

Blond, small, and slim, she looked determined, had a businesslike manner, was a powerhouse of enthusiastic energy. Her aim in coming to Paris first, before London, was to learn moviemaking. This she did by initiating a pilot for a TV series about the French Resistance, prevailing on Ben and Volodya to write it and Jack Berry to direct. Though it turned into a beautiful half-hour dramatic show, starring France's top stage actress, Suzanne Flon, it was never bought. But Hannah learned to make shows for TV.[2]

She left us with an order to write a half-dozen scripts for a series she was to produce in London, *Adventures of Robin Hood*. She farmed out more assignments to Ring Lardner, Jr., Ian Hunter, and others in England or still hanging on in New York. I wrote three of those with the musician Mischa Altman.

Phone calls came from people we'd never heard of, giving us assignments on other series, mainly half-hour dramatic shows like *Orient Express* and *Foreign Intrigue*. A fever of under-the-table writing began. Tammy Gold and I rewrote the unproduced screenplay I'd written with Janet Stevenson, *With This Ring,* changing the characters, setting, and title (*Disaster*); Jack Berry and I rewrote *He Ran All the Way;* Lee Gold and I wrote a one-hour pilot for a series called *International Airport,* starring Herbert Lom and Mai Zetterling. One of the most rabid "Commie-haters," Adolphe Menjou, bought it for the dramatic TV series he introduced!

We wrote these teleplays under false names for far less than the going rate, pooled everything we earned, and divided it according to need. When Ben wrote or rewrote a picture, his fee, much more than what we earned from TV, was added to the general fund.[3] After a while, Ben was not happy about that. Nor was he pleased about the group encouraging me to write by farming out teleplays to me.

One night, when we were dispersing the funds, I said to the group, "I don't think it's fair. Jack has a wife and two kids, but receives twice as much as Tammy and Lee, who don't have kids but want to. I think they should get more so they can have a baby." We did vote them a larger stipend and soon Tammy was pregnant with André.

John (Jack) Berry ached to direct, but unlike writers during the black-list, directors and actors could not work anonymously. Even though Jack yelled when he talked and was a hard man not to notice, Ben hoped that somehow in Paris, bigger-than-life Jack would pass unnoticed on a fea-ture film based on Ben's old short stories. They set up a two-language sketch picture, a 1930s classic format of six half-hour dramatized stories. Gérard Philipe agreed to play in a sketch about a con man who meets and falls in love with an heiress (Evelyn Keyes). They marry. Suddenly, the con man has all the money he needs and the woman he loves, who loves him. There's no reason to con anymore. But he can't stop, he can't play it straight, and, of course, loses everything.

The producer, unable to find the money to make four or five sketches, asked Ben to turn the con man episode into a full-length pic-ture (*It Happened in Paris*). Ben did, but Gérard Philipe had to bow out. His schedule permitted him only a few days' shooting. An obscure actor substituted. He was no Gérard Philipe.

Needing someone to handle publicity, Jack hired a Hollywood starlet he knew, Julie Gibson, the girlfriend of the man putting up the money for the film. Given the twisted nature of the times, the choice of a press agent was crucial because her job was to keep publicity *away* from the film. Ben and Jack tried to explain the critical need for *no* publicity. Julie under-stood about the blacklist, being blacklisted herself, but she thought they were exaggerating the danger of it becoming known that Jack was directing and Ben writing the film. Exasperated, Jack bellowed at her, "Maybe it'll be more helpful if you think of yourself as a non–press agent press agent but you'll be paid as if you are a press agent-press agent."

That was only part of the lunacy of making a two-language film with non-English-speaking French actors and non-French-speaking American actors, each group learning the other's language phonetically. Even more difficult was getting a top French screenwriter to turn over the French version in time for the American actors to mouth the words. His wife was having a baby, he was having numerous affairs, he was writing two other films and a column for a satirical French weekly. He wasn't focusing on our film. Finally, desperate for the pages, Jack and Ben lured him to the producer's villa outside Paris and locked him in the toilet with paper and pencils. After an hour of furious banging, pages of French dialogue came slithering out.[4]

We learned that the best way to get publicity is to let it be known that you don't want any. The set of *It Happened in Paris* was besieged by well-intentioned French critics, photographers, columnists, who discovered blacklisted Americans valiantly trying to make a film in Paris sub rosa. One day, Julie Gibson swept onto the set with a huge American news camera crew. She was exultant. *Life* wanted to do a spread on the secret blacklist picture!

Jack vanished. Ben found him in a back office howling at Julie Gibson. "I'll kill you dead if you don't get them off the set in the next twenty seconds!"

It Happened in Paris was one of our most notable achievements. Ben and Jack made a dreadful film. Happily, their names were not on it and it never had real distribution!

Around this time, it didn't go unnoticed that Eddie Dmytryk got a four-picture deal with the Stanley Kramer unit at Columbia Pictures.

Artists always speak about "Paris light," but the truth is Paris has a long dark winter. After Mother's death, I found a small apartment around the corner from Montparnasse. Before the *propriétaire* fixed it up for us, she graciously asked what color scheme would please us. "The walls all sunshine yellow," I told her, "and a grass-green carpet." For three and a half years, that apartment felt a little like California, especially when the floors and walls trembled as the *métro* passed underneath.

Concierges were supposed to be police spies. Our Madame Lina had a boyfriend, a policeman named Monsieur Jean. Ben and I were particularly careful with our scrap baskets.

From 1950 to 1952, "Les Rosenbergs" rocked France. The trial, sentencing, and coming execution of Ethel and Julius Rosenberg for espionage in the U.S. was the talk of Paris. Public walls were plastered with Louis Mitelberg's striking poster of Eisenhower's gruesome grin, each tooth an electric chair. People stood in little groups, muttering about the dreadful Americans. We were astounded that even Madame Lina was tearful. "*Ces deux petits garçons*—those two little boys!" she wailed, referring to the Rosenbergs' sons. At first, we thought she was trying to trap us into agreeing with her that "*Les Amerloques,*" a pejorative for Americans, "*n'étaient pas civilizés*—were not civilized." Then we began to realize that Madame Lina and Monsieur Jean couldn't conceive of a nation that would execute a father and mother who probably didn't know how to read atomic plans, much less transmit them. They were baffled *and* horrified.

"*Voyez-vous, Madame,*" Madame Lina said to me one day, "even the stony-assed Queen of England has sent a message through the Pope to your *président,* begging for clemency." Monsieur Jean, who drove a police car just like our little black Citroën, picked up Madame Lina and drove her across Paris to the Right Bank to place a wreath at the corner of the Place de la Concorde, near the American embassy, a massive bed of flowers already stretching for blocks.

"*Pauvre Monsieur! Pauvre Madame!*" cried Madame Lina. She felt sorry for us because we were Americans. To make it up to us for what we must be suffering, Monsieur Jean invited us to go fishing with them on the following Sunday. He had discovered an unknown pond on the outskirts of Paris where there were *brochets,* large delicate fish used in making *quenelles de brochet,* a culinary delight, a sort of creamy fish sausage. We went with them, and, with our children cheering him on, Ben, his clothes sipping-sopping wet, caught a big fish.

By June 1953, Ben and I estimated that we could rent a house on the Côte Basque for the second summer in a row. Artist Joe Hirsch and his wife, Ruth, decided to vacation with their children near us. I drove Ruth down in our Citroën. We stopped at Lascaux, the last year the prehistoric caves were open to the public.[5] In the caves, Ruth and I, atheists, were profoundly shaken by a sense of entering a timeless cathedral, a feeling of being one with all humanity. We proceeded to Hendaye-Plage, on the Spanish border, where we found houses near the beach. On the way back to Paris, Ruth and I stopped at Chateauroux, a city in the middle of France. After midnight, we realized we were in a whorehouse frequented by American G.I.'s from a nearby camp. The groaning, creaking, banging, and slamming lasted the rest of the night. In the morning, we emerged from our rooms, looked at each other, and burst out laughing. "The thing to do," said Ruth, "is think of Lascaux."

Ben and the children drove down to the rental house on the Côte Basque while I stayed in Paris working with Jack Berry against a tight deadline for an *Orient Express* episode. We were sitting in the sunny yellow-walled, green-carpeted living room on Avenue de l'Observatoire, pushing for an idea, having discarded many. Nothing came. Jack began to yell at me, "Why didn't you take up violin instead?"

"What about you?" I countered. That gave me an idea. "How about using *He Ran All the Way* on a *péniche* in the Seine? A gangster on the lam hides out on a barge, falls in love with the captain's daughter. As he gets to know them, he changes, is ready to go straight, when the cops pick him up—"

Jack laughed. "Okay. We've done a good morning's work," he said. "Now we can go to lunch."

We were walking down Montparnasse on the way to the Coupole when I noticed Jack was still in a foul mood, even though he agreed with me that we had a good idea to work on.

"What's the problem?" I asked.

He turned on me with such ferocity that I shivered. "I don't mind your having an affair," he said, "I just mind it's with a B director."

"How dare you stick up your nose at Bernard?" I snapped.

"He's not just a B director. He's a B person."

"What? Because he's not a screaming, aggressive, macho—" I broke off, wondering if he had told Ben. I felt I was drowning. Ben was down at the rented villa on the Basque Coast with the children. He'd made it clear he wanted me down there, too, instead of working on the script with Jack, and Jack, ornery and outrageous, was hell to work with. Then there was Bernard, still in Paris, but his passport was expiring and I was afraid he wouldn't be able to get French papers, which meant, since his wife was British, that he'd be forced to leave for England, where he would be safe.

Two weeks later, I showed up on schedule at the beautiful vacation house to spend the summer with Ben and the children. Ben told me he'd been brooding about why he didn't have his wife with him full-time, why he'd let the group encourage me to write, and why he shared his hard-earned money with them. He was angry about the money but equally angry that my writing jobs took me away from him and the children. By winter, with no writing assignments for himself, Ben was deeply depressed.

Paris winters are damp-cold and marrow-chilling but the winter of 1953–54 was the coldest in recorded history. For a week in early February, the severe weather caused the deaths of one hundred people, especially infants and the aged. The morgue filled with the frozen bodies of *clochards,* the homeless who lived under the Seine's bridges.[6] The authorities seemed unable to cope until a remarkable Jesuit priest named Abbé Pierre appeared.

A short, slight man with a craggy face and unkempt beard, Abbé Pierre wore a threadbare soutane, a beret, and thonged sandals, and carried a gnarled cane like a medieval monk. Son of a wealthy Lyons silk manufacturer, he'd always been concerned with the plight of the poor. This was his chance. He organized Paris's response to the emergency; he floated a loan to buy a huge army barracks, which he turned into a shelter for three thousand; convinced the authorities to convert three *métro* stations into shelters; collected money, clothes, blankets, food; interrupted movies to ask for help; inspired schoolchildren to contribute their pocket money; and founded a successful junk business, which still exists. All its profits go to the poor.

Ben said the freezing bitter winter had made him homesick for California and had convinced him it was time to get out of Paris, go south and write a novel. He had an idea. Science fiction was comparatively new. He would use a sci-fi premise, that another world exactly like ours existed but one that hadn't experienced World War II. He set the story in "our" Paris.

I couldn't marshal any arguments against leaving. I knew Ben wanted to get me away from the other writers in the "herring barrel" who saw to it that I had constant TV writing assignments. Moreover, because Madame Josette had found a job as concierge and Dédée was about to marry the man who had waited for her, I would not have the help at home that I'd had for five years.

"We need sunshine," Ben announced. "Norma, find a house in the Midi for six months—not expensive. I won't take a job even if one comes up. If you leave now, we can be there for Easter and the children can start the new school term down there."

I found an inexpensive villa high above Nice—*Lou Paradou,* Provençal for "Paradise," with a spectacular garden overlooking the Mediterranean. I didn't know that the *propriétaire* (owner), Monsieur Guérin, who lived beneath us in the garden basement, had been a collaborator. It was good material for a screenplay, *A Walk in the Night,* which Ben and I eventually wrote,[7] but in real life, it became a five-month nightmare. The villa's owner tended his garden meticulously and screamed at our children, "Hitler should have burned the three of you—along with the others."

Luli, Johnny, and Aaron learned early about the Holocaust. Unlike our younger children, our three eldest remember well the early years of exile when we lived in fear. At *Lou Paradou*—no paradise—we were out of the herring barrel, into a can of worms.

22

Home Sweet Home

"The phone's not ringing." Though the stay in the south suggested what living in the French California might be like, Ben couldn't stand a silent phone and, after only four months, was ready to return to Paris. Mother's estate had finally been settled. Ben dispatched me to buy an apartment.

In Paris, at a corner café in the 16th arrondissement where the schools were reputed to be good, I scanned the ads in *Le Figaro*. A sympathetic woman asked, "Are you looking for a job, my dear?"

"No," I answered, "A house or apartment."

"I shall take the liberty of telephoning Mr. High." She rose. "An American real estate agent who is *très correcte*." Soon after, Mr. High rolled up in his Peugeot. He described a house nearby on the tiny rue des Perchamps. "These houses are like brownstones."

"Oh!" I exclaimed. "We've been there often, at number 30, the Gilberts.'"

"Renters," he mumbled. "They moved away."

"Yes," I agreed, "to a duke's apartment on Francois Ier."

"It's number 30 that's for sale," said Mr. High.

"How much do they want?"

"Squabbling heirs. You can have it for nine and a half million francs—"

That was a surprisingly small sum for a four-story town house in the nicest part of town.

"There's only one condition," I said. "School begins September fifteenth. They must give me immediate possession so I can get it ready." I paused. "I'll take it for nine."

"Trust me," said Mr. High.

By the time Ben, the children, Jacqueline (who'd replaced Madame Josette *and* Dédée), Grisette the cat, Rikiki the kitten, and the two turtles arrived, I had furnished the house and convinced stony-assed bureaucrats to enroll Luli, Johnny, and Aaron in neighborhood public schools.

It almost didn't matter that I had no passport and couldn't go anywhere. This house was ours. Paris was home. I went out and had fancy stationery printed. What made it seem more like home was that the part of Paris we lived in, Auteuil, had recently been a village and still had its village ways. The *pharmacien* and other *commerçants* quickly knew us by name, and our children by their first names. It was our *quartier,* our *marché,* our *Prisunic* (five and ten), our *boucher,* our *boulanger,* our Russian deli, where Ben took the children Sunday mornings to buy lox and dark bread; and our neighborhood restaurant, the Mouton d'Or, where Molière had read his plays aloud to his friends.

Jacqueline was one of thirteen children on a Norman farm who had gone to work at an early age in a glove factory. She soon saw a way of eliminating one whole operation in the manufacture of a pair of gloves. Rewarded with a bonus but not a better job, she left for Paris where her first employer taught her to make gastronomical delights.[1] She called us to table with a giggled warning, "*Vite! Le soufflé va se gâcher!*" "Quick! The soufflé will fall!"

After three bubbly years, when Jacqueline was about to leave us to marry an opera singer, her jolly parents arrived for the weekend. Even after bringing up thirteen children, impeccably, in a three-room farm without plumbing, Madame Renaudin still had Jacqueline's tinkly, infectious laugh. Their farm was only fifty miles away, yet this was their first visit to Paris.

A few weeks after moving into our house, John Berry asked us to take a look at *Oasis,* a French picture he was dubbing into English. Jack had directed the dubbing of numerous films, frequently assigning dubbing jobs to himself and his wife, Gladys.

Ben watched the film. "It doesn't make sense. How can you dub it?"

Jack grinned crazily. "We'll be paid—even if it's unreleasable."

"Can everything be dubbed?" Ben demanded. "Every line?"

"Sure."

"So," Ben persisted, "you mean you don't have to stick with that cockamamy story? Dialogue can tell any story you want to tell."

Jack looked skeptical. "You could do that?"

"Of course."

The expensive film, shot in the Sahara with four major stars including Michèle Morgan, would be a catastrophe for Fox if it were unreleasable. Jack went to Spyros Skouras. "Okay," Skouras said, "and while you're at it, take out the camel stampede. We just found out camels don't stampede."

Ben wrote what was actually a new script in less than a month. The actors were dubbed, the film reedited. *Oasis* got distribution, did okay at the box office. Ben received a bonus and the undying gratitude of Darryl Zanuck, who, it turned out, had a good memory.

The big house was an invitation. We were playing with the idea of having two children close together so they'd have each other and not feel distanced from their older siblings. In some ways, this was an act of defiance; we would thumb our noses at HUAC and continue to create healthy, bright, progressive children. *My* part of this decision came from my unhappy certainty that 1955 was the end of television assignments and screenplays for me, the end of my writing. I had been out of the loop of the TV assignments and I knew how uncomfortable Ben was with writing that took me away from him and the children. I had always been brave, I felt: I had had a job as an economist with the League of Nations before I'd ever met Ben; without any experience, I'd landed a job as a reporter; I had always come up with commercial film ideas rapidly and easily, but for reasons I have never fully understood, during this period I lost the courage to write.

Suddenly, energetic Hungarian Marta András, who ran George Marton's international literary agency, Martonplay, asked me to be her assistant. Actually, it wasn't so suddenly. Even if they hadn't materialized, I had put together deals without realizing it. For years, I had recommended books to Marta as possible films, and suggested directors whom I thought were right for them. Marta knew I was a good story analyst and had a lot of contacts. She specified that it was a demanding full-time job. I wanted to do it, knew I'd be good at it and would enjoy it. Moreover, the timing was perfect: our youngest child, Aaron, was six years old and in school all day; Jacqueline could handle the household.

Thrilled to death, I came home and excitedly told Ben. He worked himself into a frenzy. "Agenting is twenty-four hours a day!" he shouted. "*You cannot do it!*"

"Ben," I pleaded, "I want very much to do this. It'll lead to wonderful things."

"No!"

"But Ben, can't you see? I need to! I'm going to do it even if you don't approve!"

He was livid. "I told you, you can't! I'll tell George Marton not to let Marta hire you!"

I had no way to fight back. I didn't want to embarrass Marta or cause her difficulties with George. In agony, I told her I couldn't take the job. I had reached a major crossroads in my life, and it was unforgettably painful and frustrating. Sick with frustration, my eyes and nose ran. I wheezed and coughed. Ben's response: "Why don't you go back to your shrink?"

My psychoanalyst was a man and not only a man but a French man. He saw my role as that of helpmate.

Underneath, I seethed. But I did nothing. Instead, I spun the web more tightly and thickly around me. Some women escape into drink. I had more children—and affairs.

• • •

Daniel, the first child I had *accouchement sans douleur,* painless child-birth, without anesthetic, was born in the Clinique du Belvédère, Napoleon III's hunting lodge in Boulogne-sur-Seine, now a Paris suburb on the Bois.[2] I had a corner room on the ground floor. Ben brought Luli, Johnny, and Aaron (who were not allowed inside the maternity hospital) to my window, where he held each one up to see the newborn pink blond infant.

The night I gave birth to Daniel, Bea Dassin managed to penetrate the hospital at two in the morning and find my room. She entered screaming, "He did it again!"

In my groggy state, she seemed a frightening apparition, like one of the Furies, disheveled, howling. "Julie's gone off with Melina!" I put my fingers to my lips, pointed to the sleeping infant in the bassinet beside me. "I don't care," she cried. "It's your fault. You and Ben! If you hadn't accepted her, Julie would never have done this"

Bea had been a promising young concert violinist. She had turned down a Juilliard fellowship to study in Paris, and had taken a job playing fiddle with Phil Spitalny's all-girl orchestra to support a struggling young actor, Jules Dassin. He acted, and eventually was signed to direct films. During the shooting of one of his last Hollywood pictures, around 1950, he announced to Bea that he was leaving her and their three children to go off with the leading lady, Valentina Cortese.

Bea had gone to pieces, finally hied herself to Prades on the Spanish-French border, to play for Pablo Casals, the great cello virtuoso. Casals listened. He told her it was not too late. If she devoted all her time to the violin, she could still become one of the world's greats. She had run through the streets of Prades at night, screaming, "Fuck Julie! Fuck Julie!"

She put the three children in school in Switzerland, devoted herself twelve hours a day to her violin, prepared for a concert, cut records. Isaac Stern fell in love with her. She worshipped him but, according to Bea, she wanted to retain her newfound independence.

Suddenly, Cortese sent Jules away, telling him she was pregnant with Richard Basehart's child. Julie came back to Bea, imploring forgiveness, insisted on taking the children out of boarding school so they could become a family again. Between the children and making cheesecake for Julie, Bea did not have enough hours for the violin.

Four or five years passed. Ben and I had become close friends of the Dassins in '54–'55. After five years of unemployment, Julie was at last making a French gangster movie. One night, he called us to watch him shoot across from the Ritz. The rue de la Paix and the Place Vendôme and environs were cordoned off from traffic. Julie was directing the burglary of one of Paris's most reputed jewelers as if he were conducting a symphony orchestra. He invited us to see a rough cut. The film was exciting.

"It would be breathtaking," Ben said, "if the heist were soundless. You should be able to hear a pin drop. You're on the edge of your seat. You want the thieves to get away with it."

Julie replied, "We hired the best film composer in France, Georges Auric. He gets paid for the number of minutes of music he writes. It would be impossible not to use the music he already wrote for that scene—"

"Julie," said Ben. "Show *him* the rough cut."

After seeing it, Auric, a real pro, admitted that the seventeen minutes of the robbery would be more suspenseful without music.

The silence during the heist was declared "a masterful stroke" by film critics and helped make *Rififi* an enormous hit in France.

We had no film in the Cannes festival of 1955, no real reason to attend, but our friend Betsy Blair had prevailed upon her then husband, Gene Kelly, to stand up to Louis B. Mayer and demand the blacklist be lifted long enough for her to play the female lead in *Marty*, for which she was later nominated for an Oscar. So, at this festival, not only was a blacklisted actress starring in a film representing the United States but a film by Dassin, a blacklisted American director, was representing France. The moment was too good not to savor. Ben and I stayed at a little hotel on the unfashionable part of the Croisette and applauded Betsy when she won the Palme d'Or for Best Actress.

It was at this festival that Jules Dassin met and fell in love with Melina Mercouri. She had starred in a Greek film at the festival, *Stella*, directed by Michael Cacoyannis. Julie introduced Melina to us as "the toast of the Athens stage." Striking, angular, exuding strength, she spoke in a half-laughing raucous voice, "I play S. N. Behrman." Sam Behrman's scintillating, sophisticated drawing-room comedies were the toast of Broadway. Afterward, when we had drinks with Melina and Julie, we found her quiet, subdued. She confided huskily that she lived in fear. Many of her family had died of cancer and she knew she smoked too much. "That is the way I will die," she whispered, as she and Julie puffed away at their cigarettes.

The festival over, we returned to Paris, where Ben, sick with a sore throat and high fever, took to his bed. Our progressive American friends Joe Bellfort, then RKO manager of distribution for Europe and the Middle East, and his wife, Rhoda, came in from a suburb to give us a book that she described as "nice and thick and will keep Ben in bed."

"*Christ Recrucified*," Joe Bellfort explained, "or *The Greek Passion*, its British title, is by a great writer who's been in exile since the colonels took over Greece—Nikos Kazantzakis."

Ben and I took turns reading it, and agreed with the Bellforts that it would make a superb movie. From the moment Julie met Melina, he'd talked of nothing but Greece. Since he'd suggested that he'd like to do his next project with Ben, we sent the book over to him. He read it quickly, wanted to direct it. Henri Bérard, producer of *Rififi*, could get the financing. "And," Julie added, "Melina can play the Magdalene."

"No, no!" shouted Ben. "That's a role for an eighteen-year-old—more like a Brigitte Bardot!"

Julie cut in, "Melina will be sensational."

"Julie," I remonstrated, "it won't be credible. The whole point is a sexy teenager is forced to marry a very old man. In Greece at that time, a widow couldn't remarry. It's the end of her life at eighteen. She becomes a whore. That's all that's left for her."

"Melina will do it beautifully," cried Julie.

Ben and I hoped he would see reason but of course he didn't. Julie came to our house every morning, flared his nostrils, read aloud from the New Testament. After a while, Ben retreated. "You see, Ben," Julie called after him. "I inspire you."[3]

The Kazantzakis novel takes place during the Turkish Occupation of Greece. Greek villagers, locked in a tradition of presenting an annual Passion Play, resist the Turks. The young shepherd who plays the role of the Christ becomes their leader and heads the resistance.

By the winter of 1955, Ben had finished the screenplay, which Julie then revised. Melina induced her father, a deputy in the Greek Parliament, to procure for Julie, who had no passport, some sort of special paper to enter Greece. Julie shot *He Who Must Die* on the island of Crete, the home of Kazantzakis, and returned to Paris to finish editing it in time for Cannes. That's when he told Bea it was over—he was leaving her for Melina.

For the second year, the U.S. embassy had to deal with needling from the French press. Were blacklisted Americans Ben Barzman and Jules Dassin to be invited to the U.S. embassy reception? At last, Julie received an invitation but when asked if he planned to attend, Julie, to his credit, replied, "No, I can't come because you haven't invited my collaborator, Ben Barzman."

Finally, Ben was invited and they both attended.[4] "But as they proceeded down the receiving line, full of Hollywood actors and actresses and functionaries, backs were turned to them, and stars held up champagne glasses to cover their faces."[5]

The best moment for me at the festival was when Ben and I descended the wide Palais steps. Kazantzakis came over to us, grabbed Ben's hand in his two.

"Thank you," he said. "Most novelists cannot bear to see the films adapted from their books. I, on the other hand, congratulate you. The end of the film is powerful, and though not in my book, is my meaning." Kazantzakis was referring to the picture's last moment, when it is apparent what faces the Greek villagers—a Turkish enemy allied with and backed up by the more well-to-do Greek landowners. Ben has the Christ figure, in a revolutionary gesture, pass the ammunition to fight the enemy. "The film," he said, smiling at Ben, "is an extension of my thought."

On Le Train Bleu on our way back from Cannes, we had a delightful dinner with Marcel Pagnol (*Marius, Fanny, The Baker's*

Wife). He reminisced about Raimu and Fernandel, and we learned that, as president of the jury, Pagnol had wanted to give *He Who Must Die* the first prize. The reason they had had to give it the "Special Prize of the Jury" was, he said, because the Americans had threatened not to return the following year if it won the Palme d'Or!

He Who Must Die, prevented from having a regular release in the United States. because of the blacklist, was successful in Europe. As a result, Henri Bérard asked Ben if he would like to write and direct a picture. Bérard had the backing for it. "But since it's your first directorial effort, the money people want you to ask your friend Dassin to give his assurance that if something goes wrong, which it won't, that he'll be there for you."

Ben asked Julie to agree to provide whatever assistance might be necessary.

Julie turned purple. "What makes you think you can direct?"

"You mean you won't help?"

Julie replied, "Of course not. That is what *I* do. *I* direct."

Ben had picked up a chair to clobber Julie when Bérard, who'd heard it all, came in just in time and made peace. Ben never really forgave Julie, who went on as if nothing had happened.

After I related the incident in *Tender Comrades,* Julie notified me that he would never speak to me again. He hasn't.

Two years before, in 1953, Joe Losey, based in London, telephoned Ben in Paris. "I need your help," he said. Joe had directed two screenplays of Ben's, *The Boy with Green Hair* and *Stranger on the Prowl.* "I have a play by Emlyn Williams, *Someone Waiting.* Not much money. Not enough time to get a screenplay written. If you could get yourself here—"

"You know I have no passport," Ben replied.

"I've heard that the French issue stateless passports if you can prove you're no longer a citizen of any country."

"I have a letter from the American embassy advising me I'm no longer a U.S. citizen," Ben said. "They say I've been out of the country for five years. We left in February 1949. They can't count. That's not five years."

Ben made inquiries and found that on Avenue Kléber the wife of a former minister and a hero of the resistance headed an organization for *"apatrides,"* stateless persons. He ran over there with his birth certificate, his French *permis de séjour,* and the letter from the American embassy that informed him he was no longer a citizen. Without any bureaucratic shenanigans, he was instantly handed his travel paper, a pleated document with many folds for visas—*l'accordéon,* as it was nicknamed. When he showed it to me, I felt it was unfair that I, born in the United States, could not travel while Ben, a denaturalized American, could.

With his *accordéon,* Ben proceeded to the British embassy, where they scolded him for having given up his British citizenship, but were sympathetic. In no time, he had a British visa stamped on the first fold of his new document, a British Airways flight to London, and dinner at Simpson's with Joe Losey.

Ben had read the Emlyn Williams play on the plane. He saw in it the chance to do something against capital punishment, which, after the Rosenbergs, was on all our minds. A father, drunk all the time, could not get himself to England to save his son who had been convicted of a murder he did not commit. That was the play. The film, *Time Without Pity,* explores justice in a class society. The audience knows immediately who killed the girl—a big industrialist, drunk with power, who is utterly contemptuous of the girl he murders and of the innocent young man to be hanged for the crime.

At last, in spring 1955, Joe Losey found the money for *Time Without Pity.* He sent Leon Clore, John Arnold, and Tony Simmons, producers of British Harlequin Films, to Paris to talk to Ben about doing the screenplay. All three became our good friends. Joe later described the project as "a straight thriller which Barzman and I and the producers, notably Leon Clore, turned on its head by revealing the identity of the murderer before the titles." I distinctly remember the night Ben suggested to the three that if the audience knew from the beginning, the suspense would be unbearable. We were having dinner at La Grenouille because Tony Simmons had complained we'd been taking them where the food "wasn't French enough."

"Frogs' legs taste like chicken," John Arnold observed.

Ben was annoyed. "You're not listening."

John said, "Indeed I am. To know from the start who the killer is and to see an innocent young man go to the gallows—is unbearable."

The following January, Joe phoned Ben from London. The picture now had backing from Phil and Sid Hyams, American brothers controlling Eros Films. Moreover, they were prepared to "front" for Joe and Ben to protect them from the blacklist. Ben was to be paid close to £10,000, twice as much as Joe's fee for directing. The pound was worth ten times its present value. British producers were hungry for the American market.

Time Without Pity was to start shooting in a few months. Joe urged Ben to begin work immediately. With Joe, it was always an emergency.

During the Cannes festival, May 1956, when Ben's film *He Who Must Die* won the "Special Jury Prize," our phone at the Hotel Martinez rang incessantly—Joe, in London, nervous before beginning shooting—how should certain scenes be done? What did Ben mean by various notations on the script? In those days, Ben wrote very full screenplays with minute stage directions.

Time Without Pity was shot from June through August 1956 at Elstree Studio, London, and on location. Joe was always extremely nervous during shooting. When the Hyams brothers visited the set, Joe blew up and ordered them out. He so infuriated them that they vowed they'd have nothing further to do with the film, which, consequently, opened without a press show or promotion, and therefore attracted little notice in London.

Three years later, however, it caused a storm of excitement with French cinephiles led by Pierre Rissient. Bertrand Tavernier, one of France's top directors, said it inspired him to make his distinguished *Horloger de Saint-Paul,* also against capital punishment.

After the last shot, at the end of August, Joe Losey, having repaired his passport trouble, turned up at the Grasse villa we'd rented for the summer. Joe was weary but in good spirits, convinced he'd done a good job of bringing in production designer Richard MacDonald, "who gave the film a look." Joe said he loved working with Michael Redgrave "even if he was always drunk." I thought that line was amusing, coming from Joe Losey, who drank constantly.

Joe always wanted attention. He was miffed that Ben would not break away from work and spend the day with him. Our place was far from the Cannes beach and Joe didn't have a car. Every day, I drove Joe to the Plage Sportive (Picasso's beach) and stayed there with him, rather than having to return to pick him up a few hours later.

I found myself spending days with Joe, who wanted to see the Léger Museum in Biot, the Picasso Museum in Antibes, the Renoir house in Nice, and to visit the Montands at the Colombe d'Or in Saint Paul. In the beginning, I was irritated at being Joe's chauffeur. Daniel was only six months old, and while we had a nurse and housekeeper, I didn't like being away so much. Also, I'd heard stories about how terrible Joe was to women and I had a lasting and vivid image of Joe humiliating his second wife, Louise, in front of Ben, me, Dan, and Lilith James back in Hollywood in the forties.

I hadn't realized how condescending Ben had been to me until that night when Lilith marched Louise Losey and me upstairs. "The two of you," she lectured us, "have got to defend yourselves. Leave those shits for a few days, come to Catalina—"

I'd protested that I couldn't leave Ben with the babies. Even though we had a housekeeper and a nurse, Ben would not have stood for it.

Louise dried her eyes. "It'll do me good to get away from that—" She sampled the word, "shit!"

Joe's first wife, Elizabeth Hawes, a top American fashion designer, author of a best-seller, *Fashion Is Spinach,* had been everyone's model for the "Independent Woman" of the thirties. She became a hopeless alcoholic but there was no way of knowing if Joe had been in any way responsible. It was common knowledge that he had treated his many ex-mistresses shabbily. Hannah Weinstein had been his lover right up to his marriage in June 1956 to a very young actress, Dorothy Bromiley, whom he called his "child bride."

At the beach at Cannes, I was aware that when Joe gave me the olives from his vodka martinis or smoothed suntan oil on my back, this groom of less than three months was flirting with me. I was attracted. Bernard had fled to England just before his American passport expired. He would not be able to travel for some time. I could not travel. Without his love and companionship, I felt abandoned and alone. I hadn't seen him in three years and our passionate letter writing had ebbed.

Joe had a huge laugh, a great smile, incredible energy. (See photo insert). Normally, he wouldn't have appealed to me because, like Ben, he was chronically depressed, but during those days he was in devilishly good humor, having finished shooting what he judged to be a fine film. He was drinking to relax, not drinking too much—for him. He never stopped talking. But I didn't want to hear him complain about his women: "Hannah was too rigid politically," Ruth "too possessive," and Dorothy, his new bride, "too babyish." I asked him to talk about Brecht, the difficulties of metamorphosing from stage to screen director, the problems he'd had shooting *Time Without Pity*. What he said was fresh, exciting, often brilliant.

He knew I was responsible for getting him out of the States, that I'd prevailed upon Johnny Weber to bring him to Italy the very week a subpoena went out for him, but he didn't seem at all grateful. He seemed to think it natural. He liked being able to talk to me as one Communist to another. He was still in his "we're all in this together" phase.

The only fight I had with him was over *The Boy with Green Hair*. I said, "I know you hate what you call the sentimentality of the war orphan posters coming to life—"

He cut me off. "I'm not ashamed of any picture I made but I'm ashamed of parts of that one."

"But, Joe, you were the director. All you needed to say was no." His face contorted with fury. We were somewhere between Juan-les-Pins and Cannes.

"Let me out!" he shouted as he tried to get to his feet in the moving car.

I apologized. We never fought again for the week he was there. On one of our first sallies into the countryside, I think it was to Vallauris because he wanted to bring back "a pot for Dorothy," I noticed him eyeing the inns. "It's hot!" he said. "What about a drink?" He pointed to a café with parasols on one side of a small hotel-auberge.

I parked, followed Joe inside, and saw that he was negotiating for a room for the afternoon. I could have objected. I don't think he would have put up much opposition. He simply believed I was dessert to complement the excellent luncheon.

That was the way it began. From then on, he assumed it would be like that every day. I entered into it similarly. It was part of enjoying life. It didn't get in the way of anything—least of all my marriage, which jogged along as usual, busyness with Ben's projects; joy with our babies; a whirl of interesting people around us; and no troublesome "what-you-really-care-about" intimacy.

Daniel was born in 1956, the year of Kruschev's Report to Russia's Twentieth Communist Party Congress, detailing the hideous excesses of the Stalin years. Many friends, realizing the accusations against Stalin and Stalinism were true, became bitter about the period they'd been Communists or sympathizers. Ben and I thought it wonderful that a country could own up to having committed such horrible acts. For me, it meant the Russians were going to turn over a new leaf. Not even the Soviet tanks invading Hungary that fall changed our opinion. In fact, we believed the USSR would now try to become what it had set out to, return to its ideals and begin afresh.

Later, we found out that many who visited the Soviet Union over the years had concealed what they'd seen. French novelist Nathalie Sarraute admits she traveled to Russia, saw that everything she'd been told were lies, but was too afraid to speak up when she came back to Paris. Our friends Louis and Zuka Mitelberg returned from the East with hints of the horror to which we paid no attention.

One night, while waiting to get into a new Chaplin picture around the corner from the Champs Elysées, Simone Signoret came running over to us. "Ben—Norma. We've saved you a place in the line. Yves wants you to listen to us. We've just come back from Moscow. It's unbelievable!" The two of them recited all the ways they'd been disappointed in the Soviet Union. We shrugged it off. There had always been attacks on the Soviet Union. There always would be.

In 1957, Ben was again working with French director Yves Allégret, whose 1949 film *Dédée d'Anvers* had made a star of his wife, Simone Signoret.[6] Yves felt he owed Ben for having saved *Oasis*. This time, the picture was called *Méfiez-vous, Fillettes (Be Careful, Little Girls)*, about the white slave trade. Allégret had taken Ben on a tour of Paris whorehouses to do research. On the plus side, Yves saw to it that Ben had Mary Ann, the same wonderful secretary he'd had on *Oasis*. She was progressive and bilingual! Ben wrote in English. She would almost simultaneously translate while typing. Yves installed Ben and Mary Ann in an office just off the Champs Elysées. One day, feeling sorry for himself that he had to work on "shit," Ben wended his way down to one of Paris's most elegant restaurants, Fouquet's, and sat down at a table for one. When he looked at the menu, he had second thoughts; he didn't feel like eating expensive gourmet dishes all alone. He rose, threw down his napkin, and looking neither right nor left, walked out with dignity.

Half an hour later, back in the office, Mary Ann came skipping in. She threw her arms around him. "My hero!" she said.

"What did I do?"

"The most wonderful thing in the world! When you saw Eddie Dmytryk sitting there with the *Young Lions* people at Fouquet's, you got up and left. You stuck your nose up like you didn't want to breathe the same air and stalked out as if Dmytryk had stunk up Fouquet's. Everyone's talking about it!"

That was the last time Ben "saw" Eddie.

July 3, 1999.

I walked down the driveway this morning and picked up my *Los Angeles Times*. Even without my glasses, I could see low down on page one: DIRECTOR EDWARD DMYTRYK DIES; TESTIFIED IN BLACKLIST ERA.

The *Times* obituary of Eddie Dmytryk surprised me because it made no mention of *Christ in Concrete*, the award-winning film Eddie was so proud of. The cover of his book, *On Screenwriting*, shows a photograph of himself with Ben, who wrote the screenplay, and Rod Geiger, who produced it. (See photo insert).

Just after I arrived in Hollywood, before I knew Eddie, I became friends with his first wife, Madeleine Dmytryk. She and I attended a class in story analysis at the School for Writers taught by Al Levitt, then a reader at Paramount. After class, she and I used to have drinks. She was tall, thin, angular. Her short-short platinum hair crowned a cold, expressionless face.

Therefore, it came as a shock to me one night when her hard mask came off. "I am married to a brute." Her voice broke with emotion. "I don't mind so much for myself but he's cruel to our son, Michael." Her face crumpled and her eyes filled.

"Why do you stay with him?" I asked, horrified.

"You have to understand that Eddie himself was mistreated as a child."

"What about therapy?"

"He won't go. He sent me."

In London in March 1949, when Eddie was directing *Christ in Concrete,* Jeannie Porter, Eddie's second wife, asked me to lunch and told me through sobs that Eddie was cruel to her. "I really think I should leave him," she said.

"Why don't you?"

"Because I'm afraid what people would think. Eddie's been cited for contempt by the Committee. Who knows what they'll do to him when he goes back to the States? I don't want to look as if I'm deserting him when he's in trouble."

"Jeannie, it depends on you. If you can't stand living with him, I think you should leave."

Jeannie told Eddie I'd recommended that she leave him. I later learned that she must have been pregnant at the time because she bore their son in July 1949. She remained with Eddie for fifty years until his death.

I'd always thought Eddie cold but I'd seen only one example of his cruelty. Around the Christmas holidays in 1948, Eddie, Jeannie, Ben, and I went to hear Sarah Vaughan at the Pantages. Eddie was driving recklessly. Ben said, "Take it easy. You know Norma's pregnant."

"You've already got two children," Eddie said. "That should be enough." He went on driving like a maniac.

All informers are not alike. Neither Eddie Dmytryk nor Elia Kazan ever said he was sorry, but Kazan was in a position to defy HUAC. In 1951 he was at the peak of his career as a New York stage director (*A Streetcar Named Desire* and *Death of a Salesman*). He could keep working because the theater had virtually no blacklist. And he could write, did in fact write the book *The Arrangement.* But as Eddie told Ring Lardner, Jr., "You guys are all writers and can write under other names. I've never directed on the stage. I only did film editing and direction in Hollywood, and there's nothing else I can do."[7]

Paulo[8] was born prematurely in May 1957 after a cocktail party hosted by the Japanese at the Cannes Film Festival. I stayed with him for a month until he was big enough to travel, then returned to Paris with him and found Johnny, ten, and Aaron, eight, beginning to ask questions about how things worked. Here was something I could do with pleasure, children's books. I had an idea for a series about a family named Learnmore. As each book told a story, it would explain how a machine worked. Zuka, who also had two little boys asking questions, had just illustrated a book. She would do the drawings. We started with the automobile.

The Learnmores are driving to the country to visit Grandma. Their little girl is carsick. They stop until she feels better. When they get back in, the car won't start. Daddy Learnmore checks it with the three children. There's gas, oil, water, and the battery is charged but the motor stalls. Dad explains the principle of the combustion engine. He tinkers. The car won't go. The mystery is solved when the youngest Learnmore says, "A squirrel put a nut up the exhaust pipe." He was, of course, correct. When carbon monoxide can't escape, the motor doesn't turn over. In the fifties and sixties, few children's books of that kind existed.

However, our work was interrupted when Ben decided that with five children, we needed a country place for vacations. We'd finally realized we weren't going back to America and had sold our home on Sunset Plaza Drive. I left for Cannes in early November. By the week before Christmas, I had seen eighty-four houses. I phoned Ben to fly down.

"Buy the best of them," he said.

"No, not without you seeing it."

"Okay. I'll look at the two best."

We wore boots to see the first. In the *entrée,* the water was up to our knees. That did not put him off. "I don't need to see the second," Ben said. "This is fine."

And it was. The Mas du Pont de Campane may have needed a new roof but it was a hundred-year-old Provençal farmhouse with apparent beams and a lot of charm in the midst of acres of olive trees surrounded by towering cypresses. An English family had added on three wings, including four bathrooms, a separate studio for the sculptor husband, a three-room caretaker's cottage, and a rose garden.

No sooner had we handed the real estate agent the check than the antiquated wall phone rang. The voice at the other end announced, "This is King Zog."

"Whoever it is, come off it," Ben snapped.

"I am King Zog of Albania," said the voice, very formal. "Your real estate agent promised to await my decision. He had no right to sell to you. But I shall give you a million-franc profit. I must have it," King Zog proclaimed. "There's no other place large enough for me and my entourage."

Ben was beginning to get into the spirit of it. "I, too, have an entourage," he said. "Sorry, King," and hung up.

In the late fifties, an eighteen-year-old, Pierre Rissient, came to see Ben and me. He was an earnest young fellow who vowed he was going to see to it that the films of the blacklisted be shown in Paris. He started by convincing the manager of the Cinéma MacMahon to run old American film classics, John Ford and Raoul Walsh. That, said Pierre, would pave the way.

The interest of young French people in cinema and therefore in

McCarthyism and the blacklist was high. When *Salt of the Earth,* made independently in New Mexico, produced by Paul Jarrico when Adrian became too ill, written by Michael Wilson, and directed by one of the Hollywood Ten, Herbert Biberman, opened in the Student Quarter, double lines clogged the block around the theater for months.[9] Therefore, it was not surprising when Pierre Rissient achieved his goal. He arranged with Joe Losey to open *Time Without Pity* for the first time in France at the MacMahon and followed it up shortly afterward with the French premiere of *The Boy with Green Hair,* for which Pierre did a prodigious press campaign. One of our dearest friends, Pierre was responsible for starting the French Joe Losey cult. *Variety* called him "the least-known man of tremendous influence in the entire cinema world."[10]

Occasionally the U.S. Supreme Court makes rulings that restore faith in our system of checks and balances. In 1958, the Court declared it unconstitutional for the State Department to deprive citizens of their right to travel. In July of that year, during our first summer in our new Mougins vacation house, where we were camping without furniture, a cable arrived from our New York attorney, Leonard Boudin: NORMA GO IMMEDIATELY TO U.S. CONSULATE AT NICE AND DEMAND YOUR PASSPORT STOP THEY WILL GIVE IT TO YOU.

I hadn't been near a U.S. embassy or consulate since that fateful day in July 1951 when they snatched my passport and kept it. I trembled as I walked into the consulate. But, right from the start, this was different. Politely, I was shown into the office of the consul, an attractive, exuberant young black woman, a far cry from purple-haired Schneider the Spider.

The consul's first words were: "I'm so happy it's *me* who's going to give it back to you!" She took my hand and with hugs, kisses, and tears, added, "This never should have happened. I'm glad I was stationed in the Orient and didn't have to deal with—that stuff!"

I emerged from the consulate clutching my "Greenie," my U.S. passport, as if it were the pass to the crown jewels. Ben was waiting for me. I waved it gaily. Now I could accompany him to England, to which he was about to travel on his "stateless *accordéon*." He was to see Harry

Saltzman, who had just produced the film *Look Back in Anger* and would be known for launching the 007's, the James Bond series. Ben and I flew to Paris. I gave Ben my passport so he could pick up our London tickets at British Airways. (In those days, you needed to show your passport before they'd issue you tickets to a foreign country.)

After an hour or so, Ben came home shattered. "I lost your passport." He was hoarse with emotion. "The moment the taxi pulled away, I realized my wallet that I'd put it in fell out of my raincoat pocket and onto the seat. I ran after the taxi but the driver had too big a head start—"

I could see Ben was desolate. I tried to be a good sport, but was heartbroken. Even if they'd eventually issue another passport, it would be some time before I'd receive it. I wouldn't be able to go on this trip. We called the police and the cab companies. We learned there were 12,000 cabs in Paris. "There'll be other times," I said, choked up.

The telephone rang and a young girl's voice said she'd found Ben's wallet. Her name was Michelle and she'd wait at Bar des Amis on the rue Blondel. "For God's sake, no matter what, wait!" Ben screamed into the phone and was off.

He didn't see the look I gave him. He wouldn't have known what I meant anyway because he was probably the only male adult in Paris who didn't know rue Blondel was the street of the whorehouses. Its most famous establishment was known as "Aux Belles Poules."

Ben's account of his trip to rue Blondel became one of the funnier anecdotes of his repertoire: "Here I am, worried sick the girl might leave the wallet with the barman and God knows what might happen. I'm in a panic. There are lots of cabs but the drivers are having lunch. Finally, I see a decrepit taxi with a real live driver. By the time I get to him, I'm out of breath. I pant, 'Rue Blondel. Fast.'

"He takes the trouble to turn around and look at me and ask, as if not believing his ears, 'Rue Blondel? Fast?'

"I say, 'Yes. Bar des Amis. And please. It's urgent.' He stops whatever motion he started, thinks about that a long time, then repeats mostly to himself, but philosophically, 'Rue Blondel. Fast and urgent.'

"I keep panting. 'I'm in a hurry. You don't seem to understand.'

"'Ah, well,' he says calmly and reassuringly, 'I understand perfectly.'

"There's practically no traffic but he manages to hit every red light. I keep repeating that he must try to go faster. He's not impressed, replies with his mellow reflective serenity, 'It is far better to arrive at rue Blondel in a state of tranquillity.'

"By now, I realize something's eluding me. I say as earnestly as I can, 'There's a girl waiting for me and I'm afraid she won't wait.' He adds to my confusion by replying with even greater conviction that she'll wait. I'm so baffled that I calm down for a while, which he takes as tacit acceptance on my part that the measured leisurely approach is the best after all. He drives slower and just as I'm about to explode, he makes a sweeping gesture in the old grand manner.

"'*Voilà, Monsieur*' he says, 'there is your rue Blondel.'

"The street is lined, and there can be no mistaking it, with whores, one to about every three feet. At the Bar des Amis, a crippled barmaid is polishing glasses behind the bar. Two girls watch me with professional, friendly scrutiny. But the crippled barmaid, who's been studying me, says, 'Ah, you are the Monsieur for the wife's lost passport? You can reassure yourself. All will be well.'

"Two or three minutes later, Michelle, a pale blond girl in her late teens, comes in and hands me the wallet with the passport, my driver's license, and all documents intact. She apologizes for having had to look in the wallet to find my name. I tell her how deeply grateful I am, the documents are of enormous importance to me, that we're going to England, and that I'll get her anything she asks for in return for her kindness.

"Michelle says, 'I don't want anything.'

"The three women scream at her. Does she realize what she's saying?

"Michelle replies that it's her birthday. She's twenty-one years old today and that's her birthday gift to me."[11]

In London, Ben made his deal with Harry Saltzman. We leased an apartment on Regents Park for the coming winter—Harry wanted Ben there for at least six months. We secured places for the children at the Lycée Français de Londres, then bought a cashmere twinset for Michelle.

Two weeks later we returned to Paris and immediately went to the Bar des Amis. I wanted to thank Michelle personally. The crippled barmaid greeted Ben with a special smile. We showed her the package with the cashmere sweaters.

"Michelle's gone," the barmaid said.

When we looked at her in consternation, she went on to say she had no idea where Michelle was nor where she lived. "She's simply disappeared." The barmaid added with a touch of grievance, "You know how these girls are . . . unreliable."

23

Be Your Sylph

Who could have imagined that *Look Back in Anger* would pay our way to England? Harry Saltzman, who had just produced the film, borrowed from it to finance all our expenses for six months including transportation to London for the whole family plus the deposit and rent for a luxurious apartment facing Regents Park.

He had signed Ben to write a screenplay against capital punishment—Ben's second on the subject. *The Ceremony,* from a mediocre French novel, was intended as a starring vehicle for Laurence Harvey, who'd just hit in *Room at the Top.*

Like Ben, Harry Saltzman was Canadian Jewish. For that reason and, I suppose, because they enjoyed each other's humor, they became friends. Harry had come often to Paris to visit us. He was a small, jovial, pug-nosed, prematurely gray, curly-haired man who thought he was very attractive. He bragged about his friendship with the Maharanee of Baroda. For business reasons, the Maharajah had placed his immense fortune in her name. She immediately got a divorce and kept the money, according to Harry, who twinkled when he recounted it.

Upon our arrival, Harry gave us a whopping welcome party at his elegant Prince's Gate house in Kensington. All the "Angry Young Men" were there—John Osbourne, Tony Richardson, Lindsay Anderson. In 1949, when I had first arrived in England, I had been included in everything. I wasn't treated as a "wife" but as a partner on the production of *Christ in Concrete,* partly because I had loved the book, had seen the importance of the film project, and had insisted Ben do the screenplay at a moment when it was well-nigh impossible.

But in 1958, at Harry's party, more than ever before I was "just the wife." The only people at the party who seemed as overlooked and uncomfortable as I were young Alan Sillitoe and his wife. His best-seller, *Saturday Night and Sunday Morning,* had just been bought for Karel Reisz to direct. Nevertheless, they were so neglected by the other guests that Ben and I made a deliberate attempt to speak to them, and eventually we became good friends. Delighted to have someone to talk to, Sillitoe told us about his idea for his next book, *The Loneliness of the Long-Distance Runner.*

Ben, always a success at parties, and introduced around as "Harry's protégé," had no trouble charming everybody. I was overwhelmed and feeling sorry for myself, until Lindsay Anderson, kind and unassuming, although he had won an Oscar for directing *Thursday's Children,* came over to me and put me at ease by asking what I did. Astonishing! He actually asked what I did.

When I met Bernard in London for the first time in five years, I saw he expected me to pick up our affair where we'd left off. "It's over," I said, softly. "Years have gone by—"

He put his arms around me and tried to kiss me. I pushed him away gently. "I'm not in love with you."

"I've never stopped loving you for a moment."

"It's different now. I'm trying to make my marriage work." My method of making the marriage work could be questioned, but it was effective—compliance. Submission resulted in fewer arguments but I was unaware of the mountains of frustration piling up in me.

He took my hands in his. "I know you love me," he said. "You need time." He searched my eyes. "I understand."

"What I'd like is for us to be friends. And, right now, I really need

Be Your Sylph

you. You've been redoing Victorian houses, and you know where to find furnishings."

He greeted this enthusiastically, probably expecting that if we'd be seeing each other, I'd succumb to his charm. We went to auctions, he helped me acquire a Steinway concert grand, which went for one pound because no other buyer had a living room large enough; he saw to it I always came away with distinguished bargains, like a red-and-gold leather-topped mahogany library table, and an inlaid mother-of-pearl wig table with side chairs.

December 5, 2000.

Recently, I've been fileting my newspaper before my morning coffee, pulling out the section with the obits. So many of the people I've written about have died during these past two years—Abe Polonsky, Ruth Hirsch Bocour, Ring Lardner, Jr., Dr. Michael Sacks, Jack Berry, Bess Taffel. This morning, I opened the paper to see: BERNARD FELL VICTIM TO BLACKLISTING

Bernard was fifteen years older than I. He would have been ninety-five on Christmas Day. The obit called him "a prolific B-movie director whose quickie British films of the 30's have recently achieved a renewed following."

Jack Berry had been furious at me because I was having "an affair with a B director." The obit vindicated Bernard as a B director. In his last years, New York's Museum of Modern Art, Los Angeles's American Cinemathèque, and the UCLA Film Archives' Festival of Preservation had celebrated Bernard's work, citing his early films "for their documentary style, short scenes, clipped dialogue and action that moves steadily toward a conclusion," also for his "stamp of unexpected sophistication and inspiration on low budget fare." He confided that he liked making films "on a shoestring" because it forced him to use all his ingenuity to find "new means of expression."[1]

Bernard's one-pound concert grand turned our Regents Park apartment into an after-the-show hangout. One evening, Zero Mostel of *Fiddler on the Roof,* in London to play *Ulysses in Nighttown,* dropped in after the performance. Zero was the comedian known for having said: "I am a man of a thousand faces, all of them blacklisted."[2]

When our block-flat neighbors complained of our late-night laughter, Zero went out on the balcony and serenaded them. Unlike the French, who tended to look upon *les Amerloques* as primitive and uncivilized, the British were amused at our "Yankee ways."

We found that we could cross the roof of our apartment house to our sympathetic English neighbors, Monty and Lila Burkeman, who appeared to have a perpetual party of American exiles.

At one, blacklisted director Cy Endfield murmured in my ear, "I may have to go to Washington and do the unmentionable. I can't get work here."

"Oh, Cy!" I cried out. "Don't do that!" Later that night, I begged our old Actors Lab friend Phil Brown, then directing BBC television, to get him a job in a hurry. Phil did. Cy complained bitterly about being forced to direct TV.

We didn't believe Cy would actually try to testify before HUAC. The fifties were almost gone and with them, much of the virulence directed at us. At the Cannes festival, people we'd known in Hollywood who'd developed peripheral blindness had been regaining normal vision. Not only were they beginning to see us but they exclaimed our names in delighted surprise as if they hadn't seen us the year before and the year before and the year before that.

It came as a real shock when our neighbors announced that Cy had gone to Washington.

Cy Endfield's Calvary began when he discovered there were no longer clearly defined channels for clearance as there had been a decade before. Ward Bond had died and the old hard-line defenders of the true faith like John Wayne and Adolphe Menjou had lost a lot of ground. Cy was a heretic burning to confess heresy, only no one really knew where the Inquisitors had gone. He had to pay his own way. Years before, he would have been gifted with first-class transportation. In Washington, the new breed of crew-cut, clear-eyed, bright young men at the FBI had only vaguely heard of the Communist conspiracy in Hollywood. Cy dragged himself from office to office, begging someone to please let him name the organizations he'd belonged to, how much money he'd contributed, and who else had engaged in similar activities. Finally, he found someone who took careful notes, but at the second session, he was told politely that the files already carried the names he'd mentioned (by that time we'd all been named at least a dozen times), and, in general, he had no startling new data to offer. The ritual of confession had lost its magic cleansing power. He made the hegira to New York and Hollywood to bear the tidings that he'd spilled his guts. But a new breed was taking charge in the film world. According to our neighbors, he encountered open contempt. He returned to London, worn and harried, tail between his legs, with the dread realization that it had all been for naught. Work on multimillion-dollar films would not suddenly and miraculously open up for him.

When Cy did eventually find work, it was around the time others of us were being hired. He directed *Zulu* with some success, but we heard he wasn't able to enjoy it.

In Paris, we exiles were a small, tightly knit community. In London, the many expatriates were never as anxious about their safety or livelihood as we had been, and not as vulnerable because of the language and culture. This permitted bickerings and crosscurrents. Before we called anyone, we prudently asked a few questions from someone reliable: Who was and who was not talking to Carl Foreman? Joe Losey? Hannah Weinstein? Frank and Lee Tarloff?

When Ben and I moved to London, many of our friends had stopped speaking to each other. Ella Winter and Don Stewart, the recognized social leaders of the colony, had naturally expected to be the ones to give "the big do" honoring Paul Robeson,[3] about to arrive for his Stratford opening of *Othello*. Bernard's wife, Hetty, a British citizen, born in the Welsh *How Green Was My Valley* mining district, was able to be openly political as no exile residing in London could be (we kept a very low profile). As one of the heads of the English "Ban the Bomb" ladies who were constantly being thrown in jail, Hetty had invited Robeson to a party sponsored by her organization. The tug-of-war over who should give the party was finally resolved by holding the event on "neutral ground," the home of British screenwriter Roger MacDougall and his charming art-gallery-owner wife, Renée.

At that party, we renewed our friendship with the Stewarts, who lived in Hampstead at 103 Frognal, the residence of former Prime Minister Ramsay MacDonald, where, in the garden, Ella managed to have a second reception for Robeson the following day. We again became close to Char and Sam Wanamaker, who was to play Iago to Robeson's Othello; and to Phil and Ginny Brown, who now lived on a houseboat on the Thames. Ginny Brown, wardrobe mistress, bootmaker, jewelry designer, had written a sweet book about life on the houseboat, published as *Swans at My Window.*

Book? Published? Of course! We were in England. Ben must finish his novel. I harassed him so that when he was not engaged in writing *The Ceremony* or *Chance Meeting,* he was finishing his sci-fi novel, *Out of This World.*[4]

Ben's novel posited another world exactly like this one except that for some reason or other they never had World War II. Millions of people hadn't been killed and there had been no Cold War. Nations cooperated with each other. As a result, their world had marvelous scientific advances—a cure for cancer, unlimited energy, no famine, no pollution, no poverty, no homeless. Ben said, "Rather than show how terrible it would be if everything were destroyed, I wanted to show how wonderful this world *could* be."

Ben did not know that I sent his completed first draft to Ella's friend, pacifist-philosopher-mathematician Bertrand Russell, asking for comment. I received the following note: "Barzman has a rare gift—he manages to treat serious themes amusingly," which I then used to pester someone at Collins until he promised to publish Ben's novel the following year.

Not counting the one he would later do with me, he wrote only that one novel. It had good reviews and moderate success in England and the States, where Putnam published it. Ben didn't have much joy in it. His films brought him renown and lots of money, which was what he wanted.

Out of This World, or *Twinkle, Twinkle Little Star,* as it was called in America, became a collector's item. An old copy, even a paperback, fetches over one hundred dollars. Ben would have loved that.

I organized the book party at The Cheshire Cheese, which was filled with Canadian, American, and South African expatriates from Mordecai Richler to Doris Lessing, as well as the usual London literary crowd. One very British lady with a "lorgnette" voice inquired of Ben, "And who might you be?"

"I'm a Brooklyn dentist," Ben replied pleasantly.

To have a passport and be free to travel after seven years was heady. On top of that, to be in London on the verge of the sixties, where all hell was breaking loose in film, fashion, music, food, and mores, transformed my headiness into happy frenzy. My Paris haircut seemed pitiful. At the brand-new Vidal Sassoon Salon on Regent Street, Mr. Vidal refused to "trim" my hair and sharpened his scissors gleefully. He didn't let me escape until I was light-headed in a brand-new way.

It all began with the haircut and the MacDougalls' party, New Year's Eve, 1958. MacDougall, a charming and witty screenwriter, and director Alexander (Sandy) Mackendrick were responsible for those great comedies made at the Ealing Studios with Alec Guinness, *Man in the White Suit, Lavender Hill Mob, Arsenic and Old Lace,* to name a few. At the party, Mackendrick, whom I so admired, sidled up behind me and delivered a sloshed whisper, "You'd be smashing—with about thirty pounds off." I didn't get angry. I made a New Year's resolution to take off thirty pounds by bathing-suit time. I paid no attention to funny, attractive Ted Allan, who was mumbling, "No, not that much!"[5]

From January 1 to May 20, I took off the thirty pounds, went down to 103, and in Cannes, bought for the festival a strapless white dream of a gown, appliquéd with delicate white organdy flowers. It had a built-in bra, my first off-the-shoulder experience.

Losing that much weight in a short time, doctors will tell you, is ill advised. I became permanently manic, in and out of love, drunk with myself, and utterly frustrated with the lack of meaningful work in my life. I succumbed to a succession of Teds, Sams, and Joes, all with wives *and* mistresses. I was a comfortable, sexy pal they could confide in and talk shop to.

One Sunday afternoon when Donald Ogden Stewart and his wife, Ella, were entertaining Nkrumah, the president of Ghana, she put her hands on my shoulders. "What's up?" she asked crisply, her accent still Australian even after so many years. "You look different."

"I lost weight."

"Ah," she said. "I've tried everything. I can't lose. Which diet are you on?"

"I'm trying to find what's right for me." I was reading diet books of the period: no fats, no carbohydrates, high protein, low calorie. They were not helpful. How could a plump schoolgirl go on the same diet as an obese businessman?

"Why don't we both diet and write what we find out?" she suggested.

"A diet book adapted to the kind of life you live?"

Ella thought about that. "What do you do if you're a movie star and have to go to a lot of cocktail parties?"

"You accept the drinks," I replied, "and toss them into the potted plants."

"Oh," she said, "a funny book."

I'd known the Stewarts only slightly in Hollywood. Don and my cousin Henry, both great wits, had been pals in New York in the twenties when Don was a struggling young actor who wrote for *Vanity Fair* and the *New Yorker*, and Henry, a Broadway press agent, was trying to get his own plays on. In the thirties and forties in Hollywood, they were in every anti-Fascist association that later became known as "subversive." Both helped organize the Screen Writers Guild.

Don was a patrician product of Exeter and Yale, eminently qualified to write the screenplay of *The Philadelphia Story*, the play by his Yale classmate Philip Barry. Don said of his own politics, "I didn't want to stop dancing or enjoying the fun and play in life. I wanted to do something about the problem of seeing to it that a great many more people were allowed into the amusement park. My new-found philosophy was an affirmation of the good life, not a rejection of it."[6]

Ella Winter, author and widow of turn-of-the-century muckraking journalist Lincoln Steffens, an activist in her own right, was proud of Don. "People said that when President Roosevelt awoke in the morning," she related, "he rang for his orange juice, his coffee and the first eleven telegrams from Donald Ogden Stewart."

When the Stewarts had first come to London, they'd been offered a dilapidated house gnarled by dry rot, suffering from a leaky roof, and framed by a garden decomposing into a jungle. Its condition was so wretched the owners, the former prime minister's family, felt they couldn't ask for rent. Katharine Hepburn, the Stewarts' bosom friend for years, took one look at the house, said it was beautiful, came over every day for six weeks with a packed lunch from the Connaught Hotel, and helped Ella fix it up.[7] Hepburn took a scythe, hacked away at the six-foot-high grass. She and Ella fixed and painted until Hepburn demanded, "Are you going to buy this house or not? If you don't buy it, I will pour creosote over it."[8] That convinced the Stewarts. They bought the house and every year thereafter Kate Hepburn came to inspect it and see if they were happy. They were.

Ella and I worked in the living room, which was floor-to-ceiling with Klees. The Edward Weston photographs hung in the bathroom and kitchen. Their pet monkey came swinging through, back and forth to the garden, knocking over a vase or lamp on its way. Ella ran after him, bringing him back, reasoning with him.

The phone rang. She hurried to catch it. "It's Chew again—" Chew turned out to be Chou En-lai, China's minister of foreign affairs.

"I don't mind Chew," Don said. "It's Nkrumah I can't take. He calls Miss Winter at five in the morning, wanting to know how to make a compost heap." Don continued to pad through in his pajamas, hoping Ella wouldn't see him spike his orange juice.

"Did *you*—?" she started to ask.

Don had a "Who me?" guilty gesture I adored. He used it often, extended his left arm toward an unseen audience, then bent it inward, until the cupped hand touched his chest.

As Larry Ceplair wrote, "Stewart's guilt, like that of many of his left-wing colleagues, colored his radicalism with a certain romantic tinge. . . . From his perspective, change was more a question of sharing the spoils than destroying the system."9

Ella's periods of concentration were short. Her worries intruded—Don's health, her own; the health of her son Pete by Lincoln Steffens, and Pete's wife, Young Ella; Don, Jr., who wrote for the *New Yorker;* and Ames, Don's other son, who wandered about looking lost.

Our book was not progressing. Then, one morning, Don, balder and lankier, or so it seemed, shuffled by in his pajamas, his eyes glittering more mischievously than usual. He listened to us for several moments, sipped his orange juice thoughtfully.

"Why don't you call it *Be Your Sylph?*"10 Don was one of the wittiest people I've ever known but that was not what was extraordinary about him. Ring Lardner, Jr., put his finger on it when he said: "Before Don Stewart, there was a tradition associating wit with detachment from human struggle. Now we know the same person can be wonderfully funny and wonderfully concerned with his fellow man."

One evening in January 1959 when Ben was writing the screenplay of *The Ceremony* for Harry, Joe Losey telephoned. He insisted Ben drop everything and "help him out." Joe had a commitment with two companies to direct a film from an Eric Ambler screenplay that had been adapted from a Leigh Howard novel. It had to be ready to shoot in a couple of months. "Come over," Joe said. "Now!"

We were familiar with the Ambler script. Ben told Joe we were on our way to dinner but we'd stop by.

Dorothy Bromiley, Joe's third wife, the "baby," let us in. She had a peasant-girl rosy Renoir softness and roundness, a striking contrast to Joe's decor—lean, hard, masculine Conran furniture.

Joe was greatly relieved that Ben had come. He handed us each a drink. I took mine to Joe's study, adjacent to the living room, and sat down at the typewriter. I don't recall exactly what I wrote. Joe hated the Eric Ambler hero, "Bob," with his "very masculine self-assured manner" and his red sports car; he wanted to change the character into "Jan," a Dutch artist living in London, for a darling young German actor, Hardy Kruger, whom Ben and I were crazy about. Interested in the problems of a contemporary artist, which Joe Hirsch had just exposed in a letter from New York,[11] and eager to suggest a way of developing the Kruger character, I typed:

> While Jan defends abstract art, he himself is a Social Realist, obsessed with the conditions of coal miners and factory workers. He is far from alone in his discomfort with the developing mainstream, in his hunger for the full range and complexity of human experience, with his belief that it could still be expressed in painting. At some point, Jan could shout, "I'm weary of their mad desire to preserve the status quo, as if the only valid expression of our time is art with the New York Look!" Jan's work itself might be an idiosyncratic blend of figuration with abstraction, of fantasy with myth, of the cool observer's eye with the guilty passion of the subjective participant. . . . The social themes inherent in the Ambler plot could be mirrored within the character of the artist.

At noon the following day, Joe Losey called. "Ben's not here," I said automatically.

"I didn't remember how well you wrote." Joe was warm, amused. "You left the paper in the typewriter on purpose!" I laughed. "You want to talk about it?" he asked. "The pub at the corner of Montpelier. Twelve-thirty."

As soon as Joe appeared, I could tell what he wanted. More than a roll in the hay. Less than a relationship. He said, "I liked what you wrote. But Hardy is naive, fey—"

"Artists often have that fey quality. It doesn't prevent them from being serious about their work."

In bed later, Joe turned to me, rested his head on his hand, and looked at me piercingly. "If you want to write," he said, "write! Work at it till you have no more juice for anything else."

I wanted to but I no longer felt I had the "juice."

While Ben was working on *Blind Date*,[12] he'd complained that Joe was very hard to get along with. Then a letter from Joe arrived in the mail. "As you know, I'm an asthmatic and ought not to contain my feelings. My mother and my analyst died last week. I have to tell you you're an arrogant bastard. You've always given me the feeling of bestowing a gift when you condescend to work with me. You've treated me with scorn."

The phone rang. "Did the mail come?" Joe asked. "If there's a letter from me, tear it up. Don't read it."

Ben said, "I already have but I'll disregard it."[13]

Afraid the screenplay of *Blind Date* might not be done in time to shoot in March, Joe asked Ben if he'd like some help from Millard Lampell, who happened to be in town.[14] Ben liked Millard and gave him the love scenes to finish off. Ben was deeply involved in the "suspense" part of the story, making it into a critique of British society. It later won an Edgar, the British Screenwriters Award for best mystery of the year.

In February 1960, the American Legion picked up news of the impending American distribution of *Blind Date,* now retitled *Chance Meeting,* and accused Paramount of violating the Waldorf Declaration of 1947, when studio heads agreed not to produce films made by "subversives," not to employ anyone known to be a Communist or Fellow Traveler.

Variety obligingly ran a piece, "Alleged REDS, in partnership with ex-Nazi, sell *Blind Date* to Paramount."[15] Barney Balaban, president of Paramount, canceled both Hardy Kruger's projected tour of the U.S. and the film itself, but then struck a deal with the Legion and in October 1960 released the film in New York as the second feature on the Loew's circuit. The *New York Times* recommended "the absorbing new murder mystery that crept quietly into neighborhood theaters yesterday." Joseph Losey—by name!—was "a strikingly adept technician with an alert and caustic personal style. . . ."[16]

In May, Ben was back at work on *The Ceremony*. Considerably less worried about money since the advent of Saltzman, Ben asked me to go down to our new Mougins house and supervise the building of a swimming pool and tennis court. He said the children didn't need me, that our young ladies, Arancha, Basque, and Augustine, Marseillaise, had things well in hand. I, in my light-headed, dieting mode, agreed. I was irritated that our three eldest had learned to take the 72 bus from our door in St. John's Wood to the Lycée Français de Londres in Kensington without speaking a word of English, but my heart burst with pride when Daniel, three, who attended a neighborhood nursery school, recited in English with a strong French accent: "Please put a penny in the old man's hat. If you haven't got a penny, a haepenny will do. If you haven't got a haepenny, a farthing will do. If you haven't got a farthing, God bless you!"

For the first time in five years, Ben missed the Cannes festival. I was alone in the *mas,* that immense empty country house. When it became insufferable, I drove to the Carlton Terrace, ten minutes away, for a breath of liveliness. The festival was about to begin. The press always came early and many of my *copains*—buddies—were already there. The Cannes festival, conceived in 1939 as a response to Mussolini's Venice festival, only got under way in 1947 when the war was over. In 1949, a starlet took off her bikini top and embraced Robert Mitchum for the photographers on the beach. The festival took off. By 1959, Cannes was a wheeling-dealing live-wire annual trade fair, serviced by three daily festival newspapers, which published lists of prominent industry figures with the names of the hotels they were staying at under headings of either: "Buying" or "Selling."

Gene Moscowitz, *Variety,* saw me sitting alone. "Hey! Where's Ben? How's *Blind Date* turning out? Joe Losey as ornery as people say?" and table-hopped away.

Lo and behold! Abe! Abe Polonsky! "Whatcha doin' here?" he queried.

"Getting a pool and court built at Mougins."

"Jeeesus! Where's Ben?"

"In London. What are *you* doing here, Abe?"

"I got my passport. Thought I might as well use it. Litvak—a coupla producers—want to talk to me about a job." He stared at me from behind his thick lenses. "You look like they just let you out of Auschwitz."

"You mean I'm thin. I thought I was prettier."

"You are! You are! Holy Christ! You don't have cancer or anything?"

"Abe! You know I look beautiful. I took off the thirty pounds on purpose—"

"I always thought those pounds were great!" He made a sound that might have been an appreciative chuckle. "Anyway, what difference does it make? You're always pregnant."

"I'm not now!"

After we'd had a couple of drinks, Abe said, "I'd like to see how the rich live."

"C'mon. It's gorgeous. Of course, there's no furniture yet."

"Is there a bed?" Abe asked.

"King-size!"

Abe had long since gone when the English pool engineer and his colleague arrived and moved into our little gatehouse. In the early Midi mornings, the engineer, bare-chested, muscles flowing, drove up the cypress-lined driveway to my door in his Rover truck, and picked me up to go on a purchasing expedition. He needed me to speak French. When the *matériel* had been bought and a bulldozer and several other machines had made a gargantuan hole, he hired half a dozen Algerian day laborers. Construction began in earnest.

"D'ya go down to that bloody festival every night?" he demanded.

"Sure, but—"

"Why am I obliged to 'ave me evenin' meal with me bloody borin' mate." He paused, then spat out, "Wha' about 'avin' dinner wi' me?"

I'd spent my life fighting for workers' rights but had never mingled socially with a worker. I took him to a restaurant where I was sure I wouldn't meet anyone I knew. After I'd been to bed with him, I grew more relaxed, more careless. Since he didn't like "French food," we ate at La Pizza on the Port, where I never failed to see someone I knew.

Be Your Sylph

One afternoon a flashy Maserati breezed up the driveway. Out popped Simone Signoret and Yves Montand in cream-colored outfits and big round sunglasses. "I hope we don't disturb you," said Simone after making me the *bise.*

"Not at all," I replied, introducing my muscled friend, who was in his usual topless attire.

"We heard you were going into the swimming pool business," she explained.

Yves advanced a step. "We have the intention of building a pool at our house outside Paris."

Simone smiled at her husband, with complicity. "We also heard you know how to do it—inexpensively."

I laughed.

" 'oo told you we was startin' a business?" The pool engineer obviously didn't know who they were. "It's just a thought we're bouncin' around."

"You were overheard," Simone said, embarrassed. "You can't keep anything a secret around here."

"To answer your question," I said, trying to be businesslike, "this pool cost very little. It's a do-it-yourself pool. The only expenses are hourly wages and the *matériel* at wholesale prices."

Yves scratched his ear. "Would you think of making one for us? An inside-outside one? The climate up there is—"

Simone chimed in, "Think about it and let us know." She proffered a card with about five telephone numbers. "I hope we didn't disturb you."

"Not at all," I replied, kissing them on both cheeks.

Our three winters in London, 1958 to 1961, showed us, or rather showed me, that exile in England would not necessarily have been better for us than France. At least my career would not have been any different unless I'd found a way to fight Ben's resistance to my working. I've often wondered why I didn't go to Hannah, Joe, the Harlequin producers, or others with a project of my own.

There is something in the adage "Use it or lose it." If you stop working, paralysis sets in. There was no apparent reason why I was not writing. For a while, I thought I was lazy. But that was not it. I no longer believed in myself as a writer. Where was the person who had lied about her newspaper experience, walked into the city room of the *Los Angeles Examiner* to become their first "girl" reporter? Where was the young woman who sat herself down and wrote an original screenplay, *Luxury Girls,* that became a popular European film?

Answer? My creativity had gone into making babies, having affairs (with creative men), being a *chatelaine* (lady of the castle) presiding over a salon of film folk.

I asked myself how other women I knew were faring.

In London, Charlotte Wanamaker, once a successful radio actress, was housekeeping and taking care of children while Sam worked and had another life. Ella Winter wrote several books while Don wrote his memoir. Lee Tarloff, former singer and entertainer, kept an elegant house while Frank (*The Andy Griffith Show, The Dick Van Dyke Show, Father Goose, A Guide for the Married Man*) wrote under and over the table.

In Paris, Zelma Wilson, an architect, fired from her Los Angeles project when her husband, Michael Wilson, was named in the HUAC hearings, couldn't work as an architect in France. Mike, however, never lacked for work (*The Bridge on the River Kwai, Friendly Persuasion, Lawrence of Arabia*). Bea Dassin played the violin for herself and kept house for the children. Julie had married Melina, lived and worked in Athens. Gladys Berry, actress, did a little dubbing, kept house while Jack directed Eddie Constantine films, and had another family. Tammy's husband, screenwriter Lee Gold, shared house and children chores with her and encouraged her to write. From 1955 on, however, Tammy's output was negligible (one collaboration on a film with Lee and Jack Berry, *Tamango,* until 1972, when she published her first novel, *Among the Survivors*). From time to time, the announcement of another baby from Jean and Hugo Butler in Mexico City made us wonder if we were competing for "biggest family." Unlike many women during these years, Jean, under her own name, Jean Rouverol, sold *Autumn Leaves,* a novella, which was made into a film, and *Shadows Under the Mexican*

Sun, a magazine serial. She still received money from her screenplay *So Young, So Bad,* directed by Bernard Vorhaus (1950) before the blacklist was in full force.

Then I looked at our life, Ben's and mine. I don't know how Ben felt but I was disappointed that we had grown apart. Occasionally, when Ben was charming, witty, and exuberant, a wave of my old love for him would sweep over me and I knew I didn't want to be with anyone else. But his work was his life. I no longer shared it or had work of my own. I reveled in my slimness and thirty-something radiance, but was well aware that the way I was living was not the solution to anything.

In August 1960, Ben and I agreed to go to the Olympic Games in Rome and stay at my sister's for the first time. For three years I hadn't spoken to her when I had reason to believe she'd gone along with her Italian husband's denunciation of Bernard Vorhaus and Johnny Weber to the authorities.[17]

We had many friends in Rome, but Italian men are always on the prowl, even when their wives are with them, even when the women they are pursuing are accompanied by their husbands. Their overt comments and Rome's oppressive heat stifled me. Somehow, the days there seemed like the culmination of my year and a half of illogical, mindless sexual activity. I had a sudden revulsion to maleness that extended from Olympic events like the Roman wrestling in the Baths of Caracalla to my brother-in-law Edoardo's pinching my derrière.

My way of escaping from that aggressive *droit du seigneur* male world, and from myself, was to get pregnant. I knew I was pregnant by the time we returned to London in September. It was the first time I hadn't talked it over with Ben first. He was surprised but had no objections.

24

La Mamma

One of the stories Ben enjoyed telling most was "The Making of a Prince." Ben would explain that he'd known Anthony Mann at RKO back in the forties, that they'd met again at Harry Saltzman's in London. Because of Tony's interest in *The Ceremony,* we assumed he would direct it, and Harry let us believe that. Tony read Ben's script, called to say he was in love with it. Quite unexpectedly, Harry told us that Laurence Harvey, scheduled to play the lead, would direct. Harry Cohn's widow, Joan Cohn, Columbia Pictures' Statue of Liberty, who was having an affair with Laurence Harvey, said the discussion was closed.

"The Making of a Prince" is a complicated story. Tony celebrated his misery by taking Ben and me and his new flame, Anna Kuzko, to London's poshest restaurant. When we arrived at the Mirabelle, we were astonished to be shown to a table for fourteen. Tony had invited a friend, Mike Wachs, production manager for Sam Bronston, Spain's new epic-maker who had two multimillion-dollar flops on his hands. Tony whispered to us that he'd wanted to entertain some of Bronston's entourage, hoping to make a deal with Bronston. Tony had asked Mike, who had a Polish accent, to make a reservation for fourteen. Mike had used his haughtiest tone. The Mirabelle's even haughtier maitre d' informed him that he should have known the Mirabelle was booked at least four days in advance. No table was available.

Tony was so irritated that he'd yelled, "Gimme the goddamn phone!" He called the Mirabelle again, announced to the maitre d' that he was the aide of His Highness Prince Michael Waszynski of Poland, that His Highness would require a table in a quiet area of the restaurant for fourteen of his retinue, and in twenty minutes. To his complete astonishment, the maitre d' told him the Mirabelle would be honored.

Mike, an overly elegant dresser who carried himself with unassailable self-assurance, looked every inch a prince. The Mirabelle staff fell all over themselves to please His Highness and his guests—the film people Tony and Mike wanted to butter up.

Mike played it, nose high. Everything displeased him. The sommelier brought a burgundy for His Highness to approve. Mike tasted it, curtly sent it back. The wine waiter bowed humbly and brought a better bottle, which Mike finally approved. When we'd eaten, Mike, with a princely gesture, indicated the bill was to go to his aide, Tony, who paid.

From then on, Mike was *Prince* Michael Waszynski. Franco Spain recognized his title. Later, when Sam Bronston gave Mike a Rolls-Royce, Mike zipped through Madrid flying the little flag of monarchist Poland on the radiator.

"By God!" Tony shouted, eyeing the long table at the Mirabelle, and turning to Ben. "I swear, not by the inconstant moon, you and I will work together!" Tony's speech was always well seasoned with Shakespeare.

And then, one Friday in November, Tony Mann called. "Be ready in an hour, Ben. I'm picking you up and taking you to Rome with me." Ben protested. "You're a blacklisted writer with five kids—"

"—and one on the way," Ben added.

"You don't have any choice!" Tony barked. "Be ready!"

From then on, I only know what Ben told me.

On the plane, Tony shoved a script at him and smoked a pack of cigarettes while Ben read. "It's such a piece of shit," Ben said when he'd finished it.

"I'm offering you a rewrite on a twelve-million-dollar picture[1] and with two of the hottest stars around—Chuck Heston and Sophia Loren. Bronston's willing to pay you a hundred thousand dollars."

"Sam Bronston? That small-time Hollywood producer who couldn't get a job?"

"Your small-time Hollywood producer," Tony said with that straight, dry manner he loved to use, "discovered two things. One. Spain is a 'dry' country, which means it has no oil. Two, the Du Ponts want to sell Spain oil but don't want to be paid in pesetas, which you can only spend in Spain. Bronston tells the Du Ponts, 'You sell your oil to Spain. You give me the pesetas. I'll build a modern motion picture studio in Madrid. I'll make super-spectacles in English which'll go out on the world market and bring back the currencies we all love—dollars—yen—marks.'

"The Du Ponts took him up on it and Sam built Estudios Bronston. Unfortunately, the first two spectacles bombed. Unreleasable. Bronston is in deep shit. Then he gets this great idea. *El Cid,* after Spain's eleventh-century hero. Me to direct because I can handle crowds. Phil Yordan, Bronston's story consultant, hires a coupla screenwriters. Sophia turns down their third rewrite, says she won't do the picture."

The plane landed.

"You'll have to work fast," said Tony. "Today, Friday, you convince Sophia. Tomorrow, Saturday, we all fly to Madrid. You work on the plane. By tomorrow night you have to have the first scene ready for Heston and Loren—he's already there—so they can learn their lines and we can rehearse on Sunday—and start shooting Monday."

Tony disappeared as Ben became aware that parked smack on the airfield next to the plane was a brand-new, chauffeured Rolls-Royce. Ben wondered what head of state it was destined for, but a middle-aged man with black hair took Ben's briefcase and ushered him solemnly into the Rolls. For Ben, there were no customs formalities.

The man turned out to be Hajaj, who stood to make $3 million if Sophia would sign. Hajaj had been married to Bronston's wife, Dorothea; he was a successful distributor in Rome. When Bronston fell in love with Dorothea, the agreement that she would divorce Hajaj to marry Bronston included an amicable and lucrative settlement—that Hajaj would become the sole distributor of Bronston product in Italy.

"You read the script?" Hajaj asked in a Middle Eastern accent.

"There's no point in asking me what I think of it."

Hajaj misunderstood completely, sighed in relief. "Then it's not so bad. Something can be done with it?"

"We can keep the title," Ben replied acidly, "although in England, CID means Criminal Investigation Department, so even the title could cause confusion."

Suddenly, Hajaj asked, "You like the Rolls?"

"What's not to like?" Ben asked sourly.

"If you persuade Sophia to sign," he said in low tones, "it's yours."

"Stop the car!" Ben cried. "I'm going back. I can still catch the plane I came on."

At Sophia's apartment on Ara Coeli—Altar of Heaven Street—facing the Forum, Sophia and Carlo Ponti and Basilio Franchina were waiting to receive Ben.

Sophia was then twenty-six. She dazzled Ben, her wasp waist, curvaceous hips, enormous, eloquent eyes, the enchanting grace with which she moved, and the way she was constantly in motion.

Carlo and Basilio were older, both good-looking, intelligent. Carlo, a successful producer, had been a Milanese businessman. He gave off an aura of strength and bold assurance. Basilio was a writer, dark, Sicilian, intense, and he had a delightful wit. Carlo had met Sophia at a beauty contest he had been judging. He'd given her a good role in *Woman of the River* (1955), scripted by Basilio. Sophia was a teenager when both men fell in love with her. She chose to marry Ponti. Already a power in the film industry, he was the father figure she had never had and badly needed. Her real father had not only not married her mother but had deserted them, leaving Sophia's mother to care for two very young daughters, Sophia and Maria, during World War II.

Sophia needed Carlo. But she also needed Basilio. She loved and treasured him. He was her schooling. He was also full of a special kind of fun. Who else played Scrabble with Sophia in three different languages simultaneously? An unspoken understanding existed, which Carlo accepted. She would never give up Basilio. Sophia's friendship for Basilio freed Carlo to travel all over the world making deals, which he loved to do.

Ben, still breathless from meeting Sophia for the first time, looked at the three of them and waited. Sophia twinkled. "Don't you want to know why we brought you here?"

"I thought Tony—"

She interrupted. "No. I mean why particularly *you*?" She laughed mischievously. "Carlo and Basilio and I have just seen your *Christ in Concrete*. It's a beautiful screenplay. I would have loved to play Annunziata. So that is why you are here. What do you think of the screenplay of *El Cid*?"

"It's silly."

Sophia laughed delightedly and mimicked a line of dialogue from the script, " 'I want you to kill him, but so it shouldn't hurt.' "

"It *is* silly," Basilio said, turning to Ben. "Do you think you can make something of it?"

Ben didn't answer immediately. At last he said, "It'll certainly be better."

"Anyone," observed Carlo sardonically, "could improve *that* script."

"What we want to know is," Basilio asked Ben, "can you make a valid script out of it?"

"No," Ben answered flatly. "I would have to write a new screenplay starting from scratch. Only you give me no time."

"I am just at the beginning of my career." Sophia's bantering tone was gone. She faced Ben squarely. "I am putting my fate in your hands."

Ben jumped to his feet excitedly. "No. No. I won't accept that."

"What will you accept?" she asked.

"We're all taking a chance together. I don't know whether I can write straight for the camera. I'm willing to try. All I can guarantee is what I said, I'll do my best."

That night, Friday night, Ben telephoned me in London. Sophia had signed to do the film. Tony had already left for Madrid. The next day, Saturday, Sophia, Basilio, and Ben would follow.

Ben sounded frightened. "I don't know how I'm going to do it."

"There's something I don't understand," I said, and I guess that's what wives are for, "Didn't we see Gérard Philipe on the stage in Paris in the great classic tragedy by Corneille, *Le Cid*?"

"Yes. We loved it."

"So what was wrong with it?"

There was a long pause. "It's Friday night. We leave early tomorrow morning, Saturday. The next day is Sunday. How in hell am I going to get a copy of Corneille's *Cid* in French in Madrid?"

And this, too, is what wives are for. "*Somebody*," I said, "must have the phone number of the French ambassador to Spain."

When I arrived in Madrid on Tuesday evening, Ben was following Corneille's story line and batting out pages that were sent by messenger on a motorcycle to the studio, where Sophia, Heston, the other actors, and Tony awaited them. But Ben took the time to come to the airport to fetch me. I was laden with what I had been instructed to bring, three kosher salamis (unobtainable in Madrid), one for Phil Yordan, one for Bronston, one for Ben.

"Sophia's fixing something special for you for dinner," Ben said. "But first we have to deliver a salami to Phil Yordan. It's urgent."

At the Castellana Hilton, Ben had barely rung the bell of Yordan's suite when the door flew open, Phil pounced on me, grabbed the long salami out of my hands, and ran with it. Yordan's swarthy clean-shaven face, his dark-framed, thick-lensed eyeglasses and thin black hair brushed slickly back made him look like a Chicago gangster, which he was rumored to have been. He'd had a sizable chunk of money when he'd fled to California under dubious circumstances. In Hollywood, he was known as a shrewd and highly calculating "operator." He wrote and/or produced some fifty or sixty scripts, which gave him the reputation of having "a script factory," which later became close to the truth—he had a number of blacklisted writers working for him.

Phil ran to his desk, where he began to slash away at the salami with a letter opener. "Why don't you ask the floor waiter to bring a knife and maybe some bread?" Ben suggested.

"Nah," said Yordan. "They're a *vilde* folk—uncivilized people. Yuh follow? They don't understand," and he continued hacking away at the salami as though fighting a bull. The last time I'd heard "*vilde* folk" was from the Jewish restaurant owner in Mexico City who had been referring to Mexicans.

Ben and I taxied to the Torre de Madrid, Franco's pride, a swaying steel skyscraper, where Ben, Sophia, and Basilio had been installed. Ben insisted we take the elevator right up to Sophia's penthouse, the floor above his apartment. I tried to get him to let me change but he wouldn't. "Don't worry," he said. "Wait till you see *her*."

And there she was, the most beautiful, the sexiest woman in the world, towering over me in a big rough man's sweater that hung over the longest, lithest stockinged legs I'd ever seen. No makeup. A towel turbaned about her freshly washed hair. When we arrived, she was twirling around, dancing with a large skillet as partner and singing, "I'm pretty. I'm pretty. I feel so pretty . . . " from *West Side Story*. Instead of music, the very British voice of John Gielgud was delivering the "Alas, poor Yorick" soliloquy on a phonograph record.

"She's in love," explained Basilio, "with Gielgud's voice."

"That's how she learned English," Ben said, "listening to the great British actors."

Sophia rhumbaed over to me and kissed me. She stared at my slightly swelling belly and caressed it gently. Then she pinched my cheek. "La Mamma!" she teased. "What month?"

"Only the beginning of the fourth."

"Aren't you awfully big?" she asked.

Burning with humiliation because Sophia had called me "La Mamma!," I could hear nothing, see nothing, barely realized that Basilio had kissed me, that Carlo, stocky, jolly, and businesslike, had put down *La Stampa,* Milan's biggest newspaper, to greet me.

La Mamma

Carlo seemed about to leave but Sophia drew him over to the couch and sat down on his lap. When he was around, she became babyish, often curling a wisp of his hair around her finger. He was affectionate but had to leave. He always seemed to be on the point of leaving.

When he was gone, Sophia sat us down and served her spaghetti with the four cheeses and Basilio poured the Chianti. They were so warm and loving that the momentary chagrin I'd felt vanished and I felt completely at home.

PART THREE

EUROPE IN THE '60S

25

Cold Pasta

A teenage boy sat twiddling his thumbs in the entry to Ben's apartment on the thirty-sixth floor of the swaying Torre de Madrid. Ben, glued to his desk, furiously batted out the pages. A charming young secretary, Renilde Matute, typed them in quadruplicate. As soon as she had a scene or two, the boy pounced on them, rushed to his motorcycle, and careened to the studio where Sophia Loren, Charlton Heston, and Tony Mann waited.

During this madness, as Ben demonically churned out the new script, he naturally had no time to spend with me. Basilio took me to the studio, introduced me to Heston, who was striding back and forth anxiously, dressed in woolen pantaloons and coat of mail, brandishing his sword. He bowed deeply to me, in his character as an eleventh-century nobleman.

Charlton Heston was twice the size of anyone I'd ever met. "Impressive" is not an adequate description. He *was* Moses, Ben-Hur, Michelangelo—and God, all rolled into one. When I stopped to think about it, he was also just an oversize, overgrown, good-looking midwestern farm lad.

Tony Mann greeted me warmly although anyone could see he was having trouble with Heston. Basilio installed me in a chair near his own, close to where they were about to shoot the first scene.

Although filming *El Cid* officially began Monday, November 14, 1960, this was November 16 and they were just starting to shoot the first scene in earnest. Ben's pages had arrived in time, since he and Renilde had worked Saturday and Sunday, but Monday morning, Sophia's costume hadn't arrived.

No rule of filmmaking dictates a film be shot in sequence. Sometimes, for various production reasons, the last scene is shot first, the first scene later, and so on. To shoot in sequence is a luxury with many advantages. For one thing, as they work, the director, actors, and editors have a better sense of the story unfolding. Under the circumstances, *El Cid* was shot in sequence as Ben supplied the scenes. Otherwise, it would have been too confusing and he wouldn't have been able to develop the story line. But there was another complication. Carlo Ponti had negotiated a contract for Sophia that spared her from spending a half year away from home. All of the scenes in which she appeared, regardless of where they were in the script, had to be shot first, in a maximum of twelve weeks. While Bronston might have seemed crazy to accept such a condition, he was getting financial backing from Italy and needed an Italian leading lady to qualify for government subsidies.

Suspense hung over the set as everyone wondered how the first scene would turn out. Ben had remained faithful to the first scene of Corneille's *Le Cid*, which was beautiful and dramatic, but he was not sure if it would work. Just as crucial was the question of that mysterious element in filmmaking called "chemistry," a magic quality that either occurs or doesn't when actors are put together in a film. It does not apply only to members of the opposite sex. For example, when Redford and Newman teamed in *Butch Cassidy and the Sundance Kid,* additional fireworks and unexpected tensions leaped off the screen whenever they were together, and nobody knew why.

Bronston, Yordan, Waszynski, and Mann all hoped fervently for this chemistry when Heston and Loren were put together. If that did not happen, all chances of an exciting film were gone.

Basilio had been present when Heston and Sophia met for the first time. I asked him about their chemistry.

"Chemistry?" He scowled. "It was like cold pasta."

When the first scene was about to shoot, everyone on the set was anxious, especially Tony, the director.

"Chuck," Tony was saying, "when you speak, you should look right at her, right into her eyes."

They did the take over but again it wasn't right.

"Your face is too far from hers, Chuck, and you seem to be talking to someone over her shoulder."

More takes. Finally, unsatisfied, Tony called it a day.

Sophia told us later that Tony had visited her that night. "Listen," Tony had said, "I have a theory. It's just an idea. Forgive me, Sophia, but maybe it's the garlic?" She seemed baffled. "Maybe the reason Chuck doesn't come close to you is the garlic?"

"What garlic?" she cried. "I love garlic but I have been ass-sid-u-ous-ly avoiding it for that very reason. No, Tony, it is not the garlic. He just cannot stand *me*."

When I came back that evening to the Torre, Ben said Bronston wanted us to come over.

The Bronstons were living in a gorgeous apartment on Via Eduardo Dato, 19, while they were building their palatial house. I know the address well because the following year, when they moved into their new home, they generously let us live in their apartment on Eduardo Dato while Ben wrote *The Fall of the Roman Empire*.

A Spanish *chica* opened the door and ushered us into Bronston's study. He rose from his desk with great dignity. Carefully tailored, he was a short man with broad shoulders, built rather like Ben. His soft, pale, round face was crowned with impeccably trimmed thinning gray hair. Blue eyes are often cold but his were warm and welcoming.

I found myself contemplating this man. Hardheaded and pragmatic, he had created a motion-picture fairy tale world with an opulence that rivaled and surpassed Hollywood at its height. Yet Bronston hadn't been able to make it in Hollywood. Perhaps he was too continental in manner for Hollywood, a cultivated, intelligent, widely traveled gentleman of the old school.

He had produced several distinguished films in Hollywood (*Martin Eden, A Walk in the Sun*), and because he'd been a friend of Jack London's widow, he had had at his disposal London's literary estate. Still, he had not been able to stay afloat, perhaps for the same reason that caused the failure of his first two super-epics in Spain, *John Paul Jones* and *King of Kings*. He had concentrated on production, not enough on script. Now, with Phil Yordan, he was paying attention to script. You can't make a great film without a great screenplay. But inside the Bronston-Yordan deal curled a conflict of interest, a fatal flaw. Bronston's vital goal was to have the best possible subject and screenplay for his super-spectacles. Yordan's desire was to get a screenplay written as cheaply as possible.

At one time, Yordan confided to Ben that he'd figured out what was wrong with the movie business. "Filmmakers *try* to make good films. That's their big mistake." It was his serious and considered opinion that anyone had as much chance of ending up with a good film when they didn't try but just pushed ahead and made it. That way you didn't waste time and money on revisions, alterations, and changes of concept. If you made a film and that was that, you were just as likely to come out with a good piece of work as not. The result? Phil got rich, but often the scripts he developed were awful. Once again, Bronston may have put himself in a position that in the end would not ultimately work out even though this time he was lucky—with Ben and Corneille.

Sam Bronston smiled at me, nodded, then shook Ben's hand and held it almost tenderly. "I understand what terrific pressure you're under," he said, "and I want to say two things to you. I have a deep conviction you will write a beautiful script for me. Second, we are all here to help you, Benny. Anything you need or want, we'll bring you."

Sam Bronston was the only person in the world who ever called Ben "Benny." As he talked, I became aware of his slightly Russian-Jewish accent, and remembered that Ben had told me Bronston was Trotsky's nephew. From time to time, he mentioned affectionately his uncle Lev, Lev Bronstein, or Leon Trotsky. Trotsky's name had originally been Bronstein, as Sam's had been.

Cold Pasta

Twenty years had gone by since I had joined the CPUSA, where Trotsky's name was anathema. My comrades told me that Trotsky had betrayed the Revolution. They hated him. They taught me that "Trotskyites," a pejorative word, were those who did not fight for social justice but tried to worsen existing conditions under capitalism in order to hasten the Revolution.

But we are interrupting ourselves. Now, Sam Bronston was saying, "I want also to tell you, Benny, you have nothing to fear here." He looked around quickly. There was no mistaking he referred to the Franco government. "A high-ranking official who is in *my* pay has been assigned to protect us from any disturbing influence. Everything has been arranged for you."

"Thank you," said Ben. "I'm mindful that my arrival in Spain was made easy and agreeable." Ben had been shitting in his pants at the very thought of entering Spain. He'd been active in the Joint Anti-Fascist Refugee Committee, which had saved poets and writers from Franco's killers, and had given money to the Loyalists during the Spanish Civil War, which must have put him high on Franco's hit list.

Bronston was smooth. I began to understand how it had been possible for him to arrange the fabulous deal with the Du Ponts that had created this fairyland kingdom, this Bronstonia. Ben had told me that Pierre Du Pont, head of the international chemical company, had signed blank completion bonds that permitted Bronston to borrow money, almost without limit, for production because the Du Ponts would be paid for the oil they were sending to Spain in dollars and hard currencies that Bronston films would make.[1]

Bronston had become an international broker of complex deals involving three or four countries short of hard currency. The pesetas that Spain paid Du Pont were used for below-the-line film costs. Bronston only had to come up with dollars for the above-the-line costs: cast, director, writers, composer, film, and lab work. He had learned to make international deals in advance for territories all over the world that could be discounted at the bank and provide up-front funds for production.

"Now, Benny," he said, "let us proceed to what is important." He looked into Ben's eyes. "This you will do for me."

Ben nodded encouragingly.

"Heston," Bronston said and paused. "Heston," he repeated, "is upset. He's heard Sophia has brought in *her* writers to rewrite the script for her. You understand, Benny, it is urgent. Tomorrow you must speak to him and reassure him."

"Sam," Ben asked, thinking of the scene waiting for him to write, "how much will it cost you if we lose a day's shooting?"

Bronston replied promptly, "One hundred thousand dollars or so. But listen, I don't mind losing that because you *must* take time off and reassure Heston. If you don't, we won't have any film at all." He turned and called out, "Dorothea." A beautiful, middle-aged, exquisitely dressed All-American girl pushed in a tea trolley that had no tea, just liquids like Chivas Regal, Stolichnaya, and Veuve Clicquot.

I barely saw my favorite drinks, was barely able to select a preference. My mind was still on Trotsky. He'd always seemed like the incarnation of the devil, yet here was Sam Bronston, painting a picture of his lovable uncle Lev, who brought toys *he* enjoyed playing with as much as the children he bought them for. None of that coincided with my image of Trotsky. What I heard that afternoon with Bronston began to sow some of my first true political doubts.

Not until eight years later, in May 1968 in Paris, did I learn the truth from my sons, members of the JCR, Jeunesse Communiste Revolutionnaire, a Trotskyist group tendency that led the student uprising. Only then did I see, with my own eyes, the treachery perpetrated by the French Communist Party. Only then did I regurgitate the lies I'd swallowed. Only then did I admit that Communist agents had murdered Trotsky in Mexico. Only then, did I permit myself to understand the terrible truth of Stalinism and to face the millions of dead.

The next morning Basilio brought me back to the set, where Tony was going to have another go at the first scene. *El Cid* traces the story of a minor Spanish nobleman of Castile who fought the Moors and came by his exploits to embody the golden age of medieval chivalry. King Alphonso VI distrusted him despite all these victories and banished him from Castile in 1081. Cid, which means lord, entered the service of the Moorish king, Saragossa, who ruled Valencia. Cid fought both Moors and Christians, a common practice at the time, then conquered Valencia in 1094, which he ruled until his death in 1099.

That morning, Sophia had to change costumes at the last minute. She, the consummate pro, who took pride in never being late on the set, was late. Heston took it as a personal affront.

Trying to get Heston in the mood, Tony recited a long speech of Romeo's. "Now, Chuck," he said, "look lovingly into her eyes when you speak. Tenderly, with feeling. Okay? Okay. Roll 'em!"

Chuck whispered the words of love tenderly, with feeling, only he seemed to be saying them to someone in back of Sophia.

"Cut!" Tony was mad. "Okay, Chuck. Spit it out. What's eating you?"

Heston thought a moment, took a deep breath. "Like Spencer Tracy once said, 'I come to work on time, I know my lines, and I don't bump into the furniture.' I simply don't like people who come late."

"But Chuck," Tony cut in, "it wasn't her fault. *I* ordered her to change costumes at the last moment."

"Yesterday," Sophia said quietly, "when I was not late, he didn't look at me or speak directly to me."

By the time they shot El Cid's death scene, Chuck, more furious than ever at Sophia, played the entire scene without looking at her. He was proud he got away with it. In his journal, he wrote, "The Cid is mortally wounded. He really can't think of his love. He looks off at the future, at the beyond."[2]

At home, in his apartment, Charlton Heston was dressed in his coat of mail when Ben arrived. "I wear my costume at all times," he said, nervously flourishing his sword. "Makes me feel the character. Frankly, I'm worried about my character."

"You needn't be, Mr. Heston."

"Call me Chuck," he said. Ben observed later that he'd never in his whole life seen anyone who looked less like a Chuck than Heston.

"Okay, Chuck. Bronston told me you were concerned that I was Sophia's writer. Look. We're trying to get a great love story here. Every great love story is between two people. If I write a great role for her and she's supposed to be madly in love with you and you come out a jerk, the audience won't believe the love story. You must have stature and character and color. If you want a real love story, it's got to be between two great people."

"Heston rose," Ben told me. "It was, his rising, a movement equaled only by the sense of dimension you get when a flag is hoisted to the top of the flagpole."

Chuck stuck out his hand and said: "I'm with you all the way."

That Sophia had "her" writers was not the sole reason Heston was angry. He had a long list of grievances. He'd discovered that her contract called for her to be on the picture only twelve weeks while he had to be there six months. Actually, that was perfectly reasonable. He played the main role, the legendary hero the film was about. His part extended from beginning to end as he fought battles, jousts, duels, and played scenes with his followers, with the king, with others of the court, with the Moors—all without her. But her twelve-week limit made him feel pushed. Her scenes had to be shot first so they'd be on film before her time was up.

He became particularly uptight as it came time for the Big Love Scene in the hay in the stable. The scene literally, as tradition would have it, took place in the hay in the barn of a wayside inn. It began playfully, Heston pretending to be asleep, Sophia tickling his face with a straw. It was so simple. What could be bothering him?

"What do I wear?" Heston finally asked.

"What you've got on," Ben replied. "You're worried the audience is going to wonder how you get out of the coat of mail to make love? Listen, Chuck, the masculine part of the audience will be focusing on Sophia and envying you. The feminine part of the audience will be wishing they were there with you instead of Sophia. They'll both get a huge bang out of the scene. They'll let their imaginations run riot."

Cold Pasta

Chuck said okay and then finally got down to what was really bothering him. "What happens to my horse, Babieca? She was carrying the two of us and then we never see if she's being taken care of. There are things you do for a horse."

"I'll tell you what, Chuck. We'll show a stable boy taking care of Babieca. I'll write a scene where we see the stable boy rub her down with warm water and then dry her." That seemed to satisfy him.

Ben said that in some ways he thought Chuck was right. Babieca was no ordinary horse. To the Spanish-speaking world he was a mythical animal. Members of the audience knew about horses and would have worried about her, too. "Besides," said Ben, "it gave me something to cut away to." "Something to cut away to" in film parlance is the *sine qua non* of any film—you can't stay on the principals every minute of screen time; you have to have something else to look at while the story moves forward.

Tony began to get used to the enmity of his two big stars, shrugged it off and tried some of the more difficult scenes. Besides, in the Wedding Night scene, Sophia could glare at Heston as much as she liked. El Cid has just killed her father and the king had forced her against her will to marry El Cid. Instead of love, she vows undying hatred.

In most of the film, Sophia's hair is concealed by a wimple, the eleventh-century headdress, but in this scene, her long lustrous black hair falls loosely over her white nightdress embroidered in gold and over the golden lamé robe that covers it, the robe whose velvet motifs took five women fifteen days to weave. Exquisite in her fury, so very desirable, Sophia sails majestically across the bridal bedchamber.

Verna Fields, the sound editor on *El Cid*, later a picture editor (*American Graffiti, Jaws*), and then a vice president of Universal Studios, cried out when she saw the scene. Everyone turned to her. "I can hear the metallic clank of the robe," she said. "Too much gold! The audience will laugh."

Shooting on that scene ceased until as sumptuous a golden robe could be confectioned—but soundless!

"The golden robe," explained Veniero Colasanti,[3] one of the two production designers who also directed the art, set, and costume design on

El Cid, "was one of seven hundred regal costumes made by a Florentine fashion house."

"Two thousand more costumes were farmed out here in Spain," John Moore added, "to be worked on by the whole feminine population of three villages near Madrid." Moore was the other half of the Italian-American team, recipients of Europe's top awards for art direction. "The costumes are all authentic. For example, the king's belt. It bears the emblems of every province in his kingdom. Museums permitted us to examine fabrics preserved from the eleventh century. We had silk brocades hand-loomed of the same texture."

I enjoyed my time with Colasanti and Moore more than anything during that week in Madrid. They let me see not only the prodigious enterprise of art and set design that they'd accomplished but how they'd worked it out. Like curators of an exhibition, they had captured the spectacular pageantry and ambiance of the early Middle Ages, an era never before portrayed on the screen in color, and about whose culture comparatively little was known.

"It's been a tremendous research project for us," Moore continued. "Come and see." They escorted me on a tour of the twenty-nine studio interiors they had built.

First, the palace. Everything had been researched. Every detail from the throne room's alternating round and pointed archway to the fireplace in the great hall had been planned with stone-by-stone fidelity. Colasanti whipped out sketches. Every mosaic, every banner had been designed with infinite care.

As we passed the studio-built exterior of the cathedral, Moore said, "Look carefully at the rose window. We got an accomplished artisan, very skilled in painting on glass, to copy it from a Romanesque church. The cathedral at Burgos is still standing but it's sixteenth-century Gothic. It would have shocked. They built it over the eleventh-century Romanesque one in which El Cid and Chimene were actually married. We *had* to build this."

"We didn't spare anything," Colasanti said. "We knew the money was there."

Cold Pasta

The three of us entered the awesome cathedral interior. I saw what they meant. They had ordered thousands of replicas of medieval objects, ancient candelabras, altar cloths, mural panels of saints and angels, sculpture, tapestries, canopies.

"We only had two illuminated manuscripts from the twelfth century to work from," Moore explained. "But we managed to get artisans to make scepters, crowns, trumpets, tents, shields, the horses' trappings, heraldic banners, pennants, Moorish flags, Saracen bracelets, earrings. The knights' armor, well, imagine! Six hundred and fifty suits of chain mail. We had them woven of hemp rope coated with metal varnish to give the appearance of true armor. The steelworkers of Toledo made the swords—real swords, even though they have dulled edges."

"You guys must be very happy," I said.

John Moore answered for both of them. "We are," he said. "It's been the most exciting experience of our life to re-create a century that's almost forgotten."

Colasanti said, "We couldn't be happier—"

"The only thing we don't have," Moore confided, looking discreetly at my belly—I was slightly pregnant with our sixth child, "is a baby. Veniero wants one very badly."

Tony made a big fuss the one time Ben was a trifle late with pages. Ben discovered that the delay in shooting was caused by the costumes, which were being made in Rome, the only way to allow Prince Michael Waszynski to get a cut of the costume budget.

A day later, when Prince Michael questioned a couple of lines of dialogue, Ben furiously asked him why he was having the costumes made in Rome.

Mike, or Mischa as some called him, was fast on his feet.

"Did you ever have a suit tailored in Madrid?"

"No, I haven't," Ben replied.

"Well, don't," Mike said with unassailable self-assurance. "The Spanish thread is so lousy, your suit will fall apart. You have to bring your own thread." He walked out.

Around this time Bronston gave a Rolls to Prince Michael, his trusted right hand, whose role in film production no one ever truly discovered. When Michael ordered the escutcheon for the door of his car, Rolls refused because the shield he'd designed, a five-pointed coronet, was one point more than the queen's!

Ben, Basilio, and I were on the second floor at the studio waiting for Tony when two Rolls-Royces arrived—one for Prince Michael, one for Sam Bronston. Sam's was identical except it had the Bentley radiator grille. A Bentley, also made by Rolls and just as expensive, gave one the dubious luxury of not being forced to own up to owning a Rolls.

"I'm giving you the Rolls," Sam had said to Mike, "and I'm keeping the Bentley for myself. Just, please, see that no one else on the lot has a Bentley."

The two midnight blue cars had been driven all the way from London, ferried to France, crossed France and Spain in terrible weather, and had finally arrived. It was winter, the roadway in front of the studio was icy, and from our second floor window we saw the two cars start to skid over the ice, gently at first, then more dramatically. They crashed into each other.

The fender on Mike's was badly crumpled. The two British drivers who'd traveled across Europe and were just meters from their destination were near tears, inconsolable. Prince Michael had to wait another month until a new fender could be fitted on his Rolls.

"We're supposed to go now and see the rushes," Ben said to me, turning away from the window.

"End of the first week of shooting and you haven't seen the rushes?"

"Not only that," he said, "but Tony's scared shitless. He won't let Sophia or Chuck or anybody see. He expects the worst. Chuck and Sophia don't seem right for each other. He just isn't her kind of guy. And they're not crazy about each other."

"Chemistry?" I asked.

"Yeah."

The lights dimmed in the tiny projection room. Nervous uncertainty descended. Images jumped on the screen, a few takes of that first scene. Even with Chuck looking as though he had weak eyes he couldn't focus, there was no mistake. Despite all the animosity, the chemistry leaped off the screen full force. Not just chemistry, but CHEMISTRY! The excitement was palpable. I felt it had something to do with Sophia and Heston being such fine specimens, she so feminine, he so masculine. Even from that first truncated piece of film, I knew audiences would find themselves in a romantic haze, fantasizing about the untamed thumping of the walls and the flailing of limbs that would go on when these two extraordinary creatures embraced. They'd become mythological—like the horse Babieca.

Tony smiled. "I knew it all the time," he said.

Back at the Torre, we walked toward a bank of elevators. From the moment of my arrival a week earlier, I hadn't liked the elevators. Not only was the Torre de Madrid a swaying steel-free skyscraper, but the elevator shafts were slightly off plumb. Ben had reassured me. An automatic device would stop the elevators if they dropped ten floors. We lived on the thirty-sixth floor. How could you be sure the device would work? "The elevators also sway," I said.

Just back from the first thrilling rushes, we were on our way to Sophia's penthouse. She was going to make us "something light" like spaghetti with meatballs. We were happy, we could tell her how great the rushes were and that she'd see for herself the next day.

The elevator behind us arrived. I turned. Two of Yakima Canutt's daughters-in-law came staggering out. Canutt, the greatest stunt man in Hollywood, had been working since 1922. He was part Native American, completely fearless but prudent. He'd invented the fabulous stunts and action sequences of *Spartacus* and the chariot races in *Ben-Hur*. His sons and their wives were professional stunt persons in the film, and like Yakima, fearless. Pale and deeply shaken, the two women stumbled out of the elevator, hysterical, followed by the frightened elevator boy. They leaned against the wall for balance. When they could speak, they said the elevator had just fallen a great distance.

A crowd had gathered, including the French-speaking manager, a worried-looking man who might have stepped out of a silent picture in which he played the role of "manager." He immediately tried to disperse the crowd, claiming there was no danger. "*Mais voyez-vous*—don't you see," he said, "after the cars fall ten floors, the device stops the falling. The *Señoras* have not been hurt in the least."

During the momentary silence, I asked, "What if the elevator starts falling at the ninth floor?"

He looked at me sourly. "That does not happen," he said in a superior tone. A storm of indignant doubts drowned him out.

At that moment, it hit me. I had been away from my five children for a week, and I had a sixth in my belly. What in hell was I doing here, calculating how many floors the elevator might fall? I packed my bag and flew to London the next day.

I didn't even wait for Hedda Hopper's visit. She was coming to Madrid to investigate a rumor that a blacklisted screenwriter was working on the new Bronston super-epic. Ben said Bronston called him and told him to lay low for the next five days. "Don't come to the studio." Hedda could have found Ben had she truly investigated, but she didn't. She talked with Bronston, with Sophia and others on the set, but everyone was quite careful about what they said to her. Ben stayed in his hotel room, working. "Hedda probably just wanted a free trip to Madrid," Ben commented.

26

The Fall

Four hours after her last shot, when Tony told her she could go home, Sophia fell downstairs and broke her shoulder. Apparently, it's well known in the film world that actors, after an intense shoot on a difficult picture, frequently have an accident the day it's all over.

Three or four times Tony had told her she was finished, she could go, but each time he'd called her back for an extra line of dialogue or another angle on a shot. Finally, on a Friday, Tony said, "Your work is definitely over. You can really go home." It was a tremendous relief. The film had been a strain. Not just because of the hostility between Sophia and Chuck throughout the shooting (she told me later), but also because of the role of Chimene. Sophia considered it a challenge to play a woman who loved passionately but gave up her love for a larger cause. Also, it had been a struggle to make herself into an eleventh-century woman, to learn to walk, to move, to eat, to speak like a medieval courtier's daughter. Colasanti and Moore had been helpful. She laughed when she remembered. "It was hard just to get used to sitting in an eleventh-century chair."

No one was surprised that on her last day Sophia slipped on a stair-case and broke her shoulder bone. She was flown back to Rome in a cast and she healed remarkably quickly.

"Meanwhile, back at the ranch," Ben continued to grind out pages. When he had more than Tony could shoot in three days, he took a weekend off to see us in London. Heston complained bitterly of his absence, so the next commute, I spent a week in Madrid. On January 12, when Ben managed to be thirty pages ahead, he flew to London for a couple of days. Charlton Heston noted in his journal: "To make matters worse, Ben Barzman's gone off to London for the weekend. With Ben gone, I don't know what the hell we can do, but we can try."[1]

Ben had come to see the family and to talk to Joe Losey about *The Damned*. It was a sci-fi story about radioactive children that he wanted Ben to write, as usual, in a hurry.

During this period Ben was working on *El Cid*'s battles, the court, the jousts, all the scenes that Sophia was not in. Ben traveled with Tony, Chuck, and the crew to locations—to Peniscola, where they shot the siege of Valencia, and to the castle where they staged the tournament of Calahorra. He enjoyed Spain, the Spanish people, and being part of the clamor and excitement of a major production. Everywhere they went, hundreds, sometimes thousands, came out to see El Cid, their national hero come to life. Ben put his heart into the character of the Cid. Like Ben, the Cid was an exile. "Maybe exile won't be so bad if I'm with you," the Cid says to his love, Chimene. Ben told me that he wrote that line for me.

He discovered from the ninety-three-year-old Spanish historian Pidal that the Cid had been a controversial figure. He'd earned that Arabic title meaning "merciful lord" by releasing Moorish captives. But he'd also been branded a traitor by his own people. Although famous for driving the Moors out of Spain, the Spanish hero remained on amicable terms with the Moors all his life, only fighting them when it seemed they were going to invade from Africa. Ben felt entitled to write the scene between Heston and Herbert Lom, the leader of the Moors, in which the two recognize they have no power against the forces that pit them against each other. Ben was thinking of the Arab-Israeli conflict.

With Sophia gone, Heston grumbled about Tony. Why did Tony insist on directing the big battle scenes himself instead of leaving the action to the second unit director, Yakima Canutt? Chuck confided to Ben, "If only Tony concentrated his creative energies on directing the actors and left all the action to Canutt, we'd have the greatest epic ever." In his journal, Chuck wrote: "If Wyler was willing to trust Yak with his chariot race, why can't Tony trust him to take Valencia? Tony was a gifted man and made some good films, but I don't think he was the right director for *El Cid*. The most relentless and painstaking control was needed to bring it off. It also had a great potential. The story and the characters are far more complex and subtle than in *Ben-Hur*. I've come to feel that if Willy Wyler and Tony had traded assignments on the two pictures, *Ben-Hur* would have been not much less than it is and *El Cid* might have been the greatest epic film ever made."[2]

Ben told me that long after Sophia had left for Rome, Chuck was still kvetching: "I wish we could have persuaded her to accept an aging makeup in the second half of the picture. The story covered twenty years, after all. It did look odd for me to appear in the second half as the graying, scarred veteran of the Cid's weary campaigns, while Sophia was still unchanged as the beautiful Chimene . . . "[3]

Peniscola was one of the last locations Ben visited. A walled town, it was founded twenty-five centuries earlier by the Phoenicians. Colasanti and Moore hid every vestige of modernization behind a masking wall matching the twelfth century fortress to make Peniscola look like Valencia in the eleventh. The crumbling sections of the original wall were repaired and an intricately carved Moorish arch installed in the gateway.

El Cid is mortally wounded in the battle for Valencia. He is taken through the gateway into the city but dies in the night. In the morning, in a stunning silence, the dead body of El Cid, mounted on his horse, rides down from the fortress. Dressed in white, with silver armor, he shines as if touched by the hand of God. The frightened Moors, who thought he was dead, fall back at the sight of him, abandon the battle. A burst of organ music swells up and the narrator says, "And thus the Cid rode out of the gates of history and into legend."

In London later, Ben and Tony, drinking and laughing, told me about that morning. Heston had complained that he couldn't sit immobile on his horse. "I'm not saying I won't do it. I'm just saying it's not easy to look completely lifeless without falling off the horse."

"But you're strapped on, Chuck," Ben had said. "You can't fall off."

"You two just don't realize. It's tricky. Sometime you guys try it. Sit on a horse without moving."

Tony had been lying on the sand looking up. A rider passed, not Heston, just an extra, but as he came out of the shadow into the light, his armor shone. Ben and Tony saw it at the same second.

"Tony!" Ben had cried.

Tony yelled at Bob Krasker, the brilliant Oscar-winning cinematographer. "Look! That's what we want. That's God! We've got to get the sun." He shouted to Chuck: "Come on! Now! Just do it! Just ride your white horse across the sands and across the ocean right across the scene."

The moment when the sunlight glints off El Cid's armor was one of those happy accidents of location filmmaking.

"In ten minutes we got it," Tony explained. "I'd never have done it except that I saw it. It was there and there was El Cid strapped to his white horse."

When I saw *El Cid* again recently, I thought that was one of the most powerful visual moments in any film.

While Ben and Basilio were still in Madrid, Sam Bronston signed them and Tony Mann to another picture, *The Fall of the Roman Empire,* a more lucrative deal for all of them than *El Cid* had been. Somehow, Sam already sensed that *El Cid* was going to be one of the biggest-grossers of all time and wanted to do another film with Heston and Loren. For various reasons, including his incompatibility with Sophia, Chuck refused.

Before returning to Rome to research *The Fall,* Basilio stopped in London. There began a permanent love story between him and our children. Basilio, who had only one true love, Sophia, never married, never had children, became uncle to ours and later to Sophia's.

It was February 1961. Joe Losey was to begin shooting *The Damned* in

The Fall

May. Ben worked incessantly. In April, when the children had Easter vacation and we flew to the South of France, he already had a rough-draft screenplay. Joe called from London to say he wanted to stay with us and work on the script. Ben tried to dissuade him because he expected Bronston and Yordan to come by to discuss *The Fall*, which Ben was supposed to be working on. Joe was aware of the situation but insisted on staying in our caretaker's cottage and keeping himself out of sight when Bronston and Yordan turned up. We didn't like the idea but said okay because Joe was always so quick to get peeved.

Joe flew down, read the rough draft, was very enthusiastic. *The Damned*, adapted from H. L. Lawrence's *The Children of Light*, edged science into science fiction with a myth that human organisms—in this case, radioactive children imprisoned underground by the state—can transmit radiation without being destroyed by it. Set in a bleak, wild, and ancient part of England, it was, I believe, near where the Ministry of Defence had a biological laboratory.

Right after Joe read the script, Sam Bronston called. He, Waszynski, Yordan, and Tony were all at the Carlton. Could they come over? Ben invited them to lunch and, very nicely, very carefully, told Joe that the moment had arrived when he should clear out for a few hours while the conference took place.

Joe walked down the driveway, not answering. I was a hulk, pregnant with Marco, who would be born in a few weeks. I dragged down after Joe to the little cottage. He was standing there as though the world had come to an end.

"I won't hide!" he sulked, as he tried to walk me back up to the main house. "They'll just have to face that Ben is doing *my* picture right now!"

I tried to get him to turn around and back down to the cottage. I didn't want him to have a fight with Ben just before Bronstonia arrived.

"They may take it amiss," I said. "After all, they've paid him a great deal of money. You knew Ben had already signed a contract with them."

His naturally florid complexion turned a shade of purplish red. He began to wheeze. "I see that now money talks for you, too."

"Joe," I reasoned with him, still trying to walk him back down the driveway, away from Ben, "we're a big family, you never pay him much—you can't and we understand, and Ben likes to work with you." I was getting winded. "He took this because he's fond of you."

He kept turning around, trying to walk uphill.

"Joe," I said, "he's worked on *The Damned* every minute since he agreed to do it."

Joe blocked my way, faced me. "Norma, there's nothing you can say that will change my mind. I should be at that luncheon with Bronston and Yordan—let them see Ben has another commitment."

He started walking uphill again.

"It's impossible," I cried, out of breath, following him up and down the long steep driveway. "Bronston's bringing Tony Mann. It's a work session. It's not appropriate for you to be there."

"You don't care about me either," he shouted. "You're just like Ben. You only care about money."

"Joe!" I shouted, unnerved. "You know that's not true! Please do this for me. Spend a few hours in Cannes. You love the beach. Have lunch on the beach. I'll call Alex North."[4]

North, the prolific film composer, also blacklisted, lived near us in Grasse. I phoned him, told him the situation. "Please, Alex. Come and get Joe. Take him away. And keep him away from here for a few hours."

"You don't have to beg, Norma. Of course I will. Tell Joe I'll be there in a half hour."

At five o'clock in the afternoon, long after Bronston, Yordan, Waszynski, and Tony had left, there was no sign of Joe. I was worried. Finally the phone rang. A boozy, self-pitying Joe. "Norma, come and get me."

He didn't have to tell me where he was. I drove down to the Carlton Bar.

I had to half-carry him and pour him into the car. All the way to Mougins, he raved and ranted. With bourgeois values how could you have an honest relationship between a man and a man, or between a man and a woman? His jibes went from the general to the particular. By the time we rolled under our Provençal archway, Joe was savagely attacking the beautiful stone entrance, the majestic cypress-lined driveway, then Ben, then me. "You've sold out for a swimming pool with a pump that doesn't work! I used to think *you* were different. But you're no better—in your doll's house with pool. You don't deserve to write. What would you write? It wouldn't be worth reading or seeing. Corrupt shit! You're both shits!" It came out "Schlitz" like the beer. "I'm through with you guys. I'm leaving."

I told Ben that Joe said he'd never forgive what Ben had done. However, Joe didn't leave for days, working with Ben on the script as if nothing had happened. Ben didn't think there was anything to worry about.

I drove Joe to the airport. In spite of my bulk, he managed to kiss me and hold me tight. He was crying. He'd already had a few, though it was early in the day. "Good-bye," he said, and I had a feeling it was going to be for a long, long time.

On Joe's return to London, while Ben was doing rewrites, Joe hired another writer, Evan Jones, who received sole screenplay credit. Ben had worked on the script for three months, Jones for only a few weeks. Joe wrote Ben another one of those terrible letters. "Your violence and unreasonableness I have known for as many years as I have known you and I can predict them to the day and the degree—and yet they never cease to astound me." He went on to say that Ben would still receive equal monies and percentages with himself, so what more did he want?

The Damned, later titled *These Are the Damned,* had both good and bad reviews: "A clumsy space fiction with noble pretensions that remain submerged in the heavy symbolism"[5] and "a disturbing work of real importance."[6] Film buffs now regard it as a minor classic.

Three events marked the 1961 Cannes Festival for us: Sophia won the Palme d'Or for Best Actress for her role in *La Ciociara (Two Women),* the work of Vittorio De Sica and Cesare Zavattini, who wrote *The Bicycle Thief* and *Umberto D.* Sophia also won the Oscar that year, a first for an actor or actress in a foreign film.

The second event was the birth of our son, Marco, on May 18, during the last days of the festival.[7] The third was Sophia's visit to me in the Clinique Beausoleil in Cannes. Right then, I was so happy with the new addition to our family that I didn't mind when she pinched my cheek and called me La Mamma. Besides, I had begun to realize she had a superstition that if she were close to fecundity, she would eventually bear children herself, her most devout wish.

When Sophia walked into anyplace "incognito," it was always a big joke. No matter what she wore, or did with her hair, or how big her sunglasses, she attracted attention. When she arrived in all her glory in her yellow dress and yellow coat, having just received the Palme d'Or, nurses and even doctors all but fainted.

In the summer of '61, Mougins seemed blissful. We quickly forgot what had happened with Joe. We were the closest to "happy" we'd been in a long time. At the deep end of the pool, Ben and Basilio, in a canopied sofa swing, talked out the story line of *The Fall of the Roman Empire*. Near the shallow end of the pool, where sand had been brought, we called the "*si jolie petite plage*," the pretty little beach. I made sandcastles and mud pies with the children. Basilio showed them his Vesuvius trick. Beneath a mountain of wet sand with a hole in the center, he built a tiny fire so that the volcano smoked. Ben loved cuddling the new baby, Marco.

Where the rose garden had been, we now had a *potager*, a vegetable garden. Monsieur Gorda planted early so we were eating our own salads and *haricots verts extra fins*, fine string beans. I had planted Golden Bantam. I discovered that I loved to work in the garden. The French friends we'd made in Nice in 1954 visited with their children on Sunday or we visited the Golds, who'd bought a house near us, or the Wilsons, who rented a villa on the beach.

In September, I was packing to go back to Paris. "Don't they have schools down here?" Ben demanded. He was right. We were scheduled to spend the winter in Madrid while Ben and Basilio wrote *The Fall*. Why go to Paris, then to Madrid, then back to Paris, then Mougins?

Once we made the decision to remain in the South of France and return to it in the spring after Madrid, our way of looking at Mougins changed. We were camping out in a vacation house. If it was to become

The Fall

a year-round place, we would have to make it *home*, instead of Paris, which didn't feel like home anymore after our three winters in London.

I can see Ben and me sitting outside Felix of Antibes one evening in late September, drinking Pastis, watching the sun go down, about to go inside for dinner, and talking logistics as we so often were obliged to do. How to make the move to Madrid without upsetting the children? Yes, the end of November we'd take the little ones, Daniel, five, Paulo, four, and Marco, six months, with us. The big ones, Luli, sixteen, John fifteen, and Aaron, twelve, would stay in Mougins with the *demoiselles* and join us for Christmas vacation.

"Barzman," a French voice called out. It belonged to Pierre Prévert, brother of Jacques Prévert (*Les Enfants du Paradis*) and sometime collaborator. His white hair, black mustache, healthy glow, his knowing, sophisticated smile made him what the French call *sympa*.

"Come," he said, "we're having a party." Pierre was proud of his English. "Marcel Duhamel has a house on the ramparts." Butressed by rocks, Antibes, once the Greek city Antipolis, sports an ancient revolving-eye lighthouse to stave off invasion.

At his door, Marcel Duhamel welcomed us. I almost laughed because he was so Jacques Tati–like, extremely tall and thin with a little mustache, a bow tie, and an obvious affinity for things English. Duhamel, one of the first Surrealists, editor of Gallimard's *Série Noire* detective-suspense novels, had translated into French the great American authors: Faulkner, Hemingway, Fitzgerald, O'Hara, Dos Passos.

Marcel took us upstairs to the second-story bedroom. "You must see the view."

We climbed the stairs, poked our heads in. Picasso was leaning over the balcony, taking in the view. He turned to us and said, "*Après tout,* for a painter, living here would be ideal: one blue line and the painting would be done."

Marcel and Pierre introduced us. Picasso was quick. He recognized us. "When *was* it," he asked, "1949? Maison de la Pensée?" He cocked his head and his eyes sent off mischievous sparks. "*Now* do you know you are exiles?"

During the course of the evening, it became apparent that Picasso was going to be eighty in a month and that he didn't want to be reminded of it. "You," said Marcel, "have nothing to say about it. It is a public event. You will be given the biggest birthday party ever."

Picasso protested angrily. Pierre laughed. "Marcel is right. You won't have anything to say. *Le Parti s'en chargera*—the Party will take the responsibility!"

Picasso was furious. The other two dropped it. All the same, in October, Ben and I received invitations to Picasso's birthday, the twenty-seventh and twenty-eighth, a two-day affair, with an exposition, a corrida, a cocktail, a dinner, and a theatrical soirée in which the great singers, dancers, and musicians of the world took part, from the Soviet pianist Sviatoslav Richter to the Cuban Ballet. Ben and I had to sneak off from time to time to have a nap, but Picasso attended every event in excellent form, and with gusto.

Picasso's birthday became the subject of a story I initiated, one that Ben and I wrote together. It just missed being a film when the producer, Frank O'Connor, died.

I often wondered whether the FBI or CIA noted that Ben and I had been seated in the Royal Box at the birthday corrida with Picasso and Marcel Cachin, the head of the French Communist Party.

27

Bronstonia

In November 1961, *The Fall of the Roman Empire* brought us back to Madrid, one of the few great cities of the world without a river, lake, ocean, or even a canal. Philip IV of Spain chose Madrid to be the capital because it was right smack in the center of the country. The city has no special beauty, suffers from blustery, freezing winters and hellishly hot, dusty summers. Its buildings seemed gray-green like the cloaks of Franco's Guarda Civil, who stalked the streets menacingly, and its depressing skies were the color of the guards' black patent-leather hats— a subjective evaluation, certainly. As a high school girl, I had become left-orientated partly because I'd seen the people of Madrid, who had voted for a democratic government, suffer the bombs of Hitler, Mussolini, and Franco. In the 1960s, Franco was still in power and Spain was a Fascist country.

Of course I adored the Prado, a national museum founded in 1810, spent much time studying the Goyas, Velasquezes, and El Grecos. Ben and I loved the Plaza Mayor and its restaurant Bottin, where the poor waiters ran up and down the narrow staircase to the Moorish cellars far below the street. They served *angulas,* tiny baby eels (already dead) jumping in the boiling oil.

I learned to market, found it odd that butter, which is *beurre* or *burro* or something like it in most languages, was *mantequilla,* and that carrots were *sanaoria,* a word I could remember because "sana" seemed healthy and "oria" golden. Excursions to Toledo and Segovia taught me about Spain, the people, the richly diverse history. From approximately the eighth century to the end of the fifteenth, Muslims, Jews, and Catholics had lived side by side in harmony and religious tolerance. Ferdinand and Isabella became rulers of all Spain in 1492. In their zeal to unite the country, they expelled Jews and finally Muslims.[1] But the influence of all three cultures on that country, particularly the Muslims, is beautifully visible.

I waited to do my antique-hunting expeditions until Carlo Ponti arrived. He turned up in Madrid more than once to visit Sophia. An amateur architect and decorator, he was refurbishing their new home in Marino, outside Rome. I sent what proved to be a freight-car-full of seventeenth-century furniture to Mougins. I was glad I had Carlo with me. The Spanish cabinetmakers were adept at fabricating "antiques," constructing them of pieces of old wood. I saw why Sophia appreciated the learned, powerful father figure.

One day, in an antique dealer's back garden, we came upon an immense sixteenth-century stone fountain that Carlo admired. It must have weighed several tons. With his usual assurance, he said to the antique dealer, "Just send it along with the other things."

The apartment the Bronstons lent us for the winter came with four *chicas.* We were told to pay each the equivalent of sixteen dollars a month in pesetas. When we raised their salaries, Dorothea Bronston was horrified. "Now everybody will want more."

The *chicas* seemed unhappy with us. One day I asked them why. They didn't like the food I was buying. At noon, they wanted *cocida,* a big soupy dish with meat and beans. The minute I told them to have that for themselves, they became jolly, and I often enjoyed it with them.

Eduardo Dato, 19, was situated in a beautiful neighborhood directly across from the most "fashionable" church in Madrid, San Fermin de los

Navarros. Sophia asked if we'd mind her visiting us early on a Sunday morning. She really meant early. She arrived at 6 A.M.—all her life she arose at 4 A.M. and retired as early as possible, sometimes at 8 or 9 P.M. She went immediately to our living room window and pointed to a curious spectacle that was unfolding below.

Marriage parties started at six because it was a source of pride to be able to say they'd been married at that church. The poorer you were, the earlier the hour set for the marriage. Moreover, one could estimate each couple's economic situation by their clothes, the number in their party, and by the quality and quantity of the flowers. At six, the couples were a trifle shabby, the photographer a member of the family with small camera, the groom often reluctant, the bride often pregnant. Ceremonies for the well-to-do middle class began around 9 A.M. Sophia breakfasted with us, instructed Ben to amuse her with stories of Hollywood to make the time between marriages pass more quickly. But she kept her eyes peeled across the street. She was waiting for the affluent couples. As the morning rolled on, we were struck by how well she'd predicted. She didn't stay till the end of the show, but by noon, when the last of these ceremonies was held, the flowers were costly and more abundant, the clergy dressed better, professional photographers were shooting away, the groom wore a cutaway, the bride was splendidly attired in what today would be called a designer gown preceded by a train of little flower girls. This cavalcade from low to high, poor to rich, all framed by the act of marriage, was what Sophia wanted to see. She loved weddings.

We had seen how enthralled Sophia had been by John Geilgud's voice on a record. She had learned her English listening to the voices of Leslie Howard, Ralph Richardson, Laurence Olivier, and Alec Guinness, adored the very British diction, its clarity and dramatic impact without overstatement. When alone, one of her secret pleasures was listening to their recordings as others listened to great music.

When Alec Guinness came to Madrid to play Emperor Marcus Aurelius (Sophia played his daughter) he took an apartment in our building. Guinness got cozy with Ben, came upstairs frequently to our apartment, obviously not to see me. I disappeared during his visits. He liked to gossip, Ben said, played out scenes that had actually happened. One was quite visual and involved Sophia. Before meeting him on the set, she bumped into him downstairs in our lobby. He spoke to her. To her, it was incredible that his real voice sounded even better than his recordings. From that moment on, "she felt 'so pretty,' as if she were in love."

She enjoyed believing she was in love. We all warned her that Lady Guinness would be arriving, but for her, romance was a kind of dreamy game.

One night, Guinness told Ben that the first evening he'd invited Sophia to dine out with him a windy rainstorm was raging across Madrid. He had called for her with a hired limo, she came to the lobby, breathtakingly beautiful in a gown worthy of Oscar night. He shielded her from the rain with an enormous umbrella but she slipped and fell smack into a deep puddle.

He helped her up. She seemed a trifle nonplussed for a second—outfit, hairdo, makeup ruined. Then, with perfect composure, she said, "Give me a few minutes."

Guinness was surprised when, only moments later, she reappeared in another glamorous getup, perfect from head to toe. "Do you not say, in English, 'She is . . .' " Sophia paused, " 'a quick-change artist?' "

Ben asked Guinness why he had converted to Catholicism. He answered without hesitation that when his only son was dying of infantile paralysis, the doctors said the crisis would come that night. He wandered the dark streets of London until he came upon the open door of a Catholic church. He entered. Candles were flickering. The Holy Virgin looked out and seemed to radiate comfort. He said out loud, "Save my child and I will convert." His son lived and Alec Guinness became a Catholic.

One day, Guinness, very disturbed, asked Ben for help. His chauffeur had taken him for some air in the nearby countryside. On a lonely country road, they'd hit and killed a cow that had broken out of her pasture. To Guinness's horror, a Guarda Civil had arrested the peasant owner of the cow, who had not only been crushed by the loss of his cow, but was sentenced to six months in jail for permitting a public nuisance.

Bronstonia

Ben called the Bronston-paid man in the Franco administration who'd been assigned to "protect" Ben and told him about the cow. The official was outraged. It was absolutely right to send the peasant to prison. It was his responsibility to see to it that his animals didn't break out and constitute a public danger. Ben said simply that *The Fall* would suffer if Guinness was upset. Reluctantly, the official got the peasant off. Guinness paid him for his cow.

Alec Guinness alerted us that Lady Guinness was flying in with a gift for us. I tried to guess. A fine English tea? Fortnum and Mason biscuits?

Lady Guinness, Merula Salomon, an artist in her own right, daughter of an English-Jewish country gentleman, arrived at our apartment one afternoon. She was a rather dowdy, very British woman who pushed into my arms what I thought at first was a bundle of soft wool. It was not a sweater. It wiggled. It was a Shih Tzu puppy that we named *Perrito,* Spanish for little dog. Lady Guinness raised Shih Tzus. She couldn't have made a worse choice for us. We would soon be returning to the hot Côte d'Azur, where the little dog was miserable. He lost all his beautiful hair. His skin became itchy and scabby. We took him to the best vets from Monte Carlo to Cannes. They all said the same. The Midi is not the climate for him. He needs cold. He needs snow.

We all loved him, but when our Geneva friends Mike and Barbara Sacks visited us, we gave them the puppy. As a doctor, Mike agreed, the only possible remedy was to send him to a proper habitat. Not long after, we received a letter with an enclosed photo of the little Shih Tzu, restored and revived, with all his lovely hair, disporting himself in the snow above Geneva. They took him often to the high Alps, where it was like his native Tibet.

One feature of Madrileno life, the *Serrano,* reminded us we lived in a Fascist regime. Official keeper of the keys, each Serrano was a quasi-cop whose domain consisted of four square blocks. To have a key of your own to your home, you registered with the police and paid a monthly tax. Obviously, it was a way of keeping tabs on people. We did not know this and had no key. When we came home late at night, usually in the wee hours, since dinner in Madrid began somewhere between ten and midnight, we simply stood outside our apartment house and clapped our hands and shouted "*Serrano!*" Silence. After many screams and more hand-clapping, he came flying, in ankle-length greatcoat with an ankle-length club-stick, opened the door, bowing and scraping, and unlocked the apartment. Then we gave him a few centavos.

One night when I couldn't sleep, I watched from our window as an unfortunate neighbor waited at least a half hour in the cold for the Serrano.

In my sleeplessness, and perhaps because I was seeing firsthand evidence of Fascism, I remembered the rumor that the French army based in Algeria was poised to fly into Paris and stage a coup. We'd even heard that General de Gaulle had urged citizens to arm themselves. The invasion didn't occur, but for several years afterward de Gaulle made it clear he was committed to leaving Algeria, and French terrorists targeted the French Left, which wanted Algeria to be free and independent. During those years, the early sixties, terrorists planted *plastique* bombs all over Paris. The lycée Luli had attended was *plastiquée* in the night. No one was hurt. But a bomb left in the apartment house of our dear Volodya (Vladimir Pozner) exploded, taking off half his face. He lived but was badly disfigured even after much plastic surgery. The explosion occurred just after he had written a piece for *l'Humanité,* "I AM ACOMMUNIST!"

That night, watching the shivering, hapless neighbor wait for the Serrano, I thought also of the United States, where it was beginning to look as if the end of the blacklist was not far off. We had been happy to see the personable young John F. Kennedy beat Nixon in the 1960 election, but witnessed with increasing anxiety how Kennedy was being drawn into a war in Vietnam.

Ironically, that was a good time to be in Fascist Spain. Their Civil War had been so devastating, the Spanish people would have done anything to avoid war.

El Cid premiered on December 6, 1961. Tony let Sophia off for a day and Sam Bronston, Mike Waszynski, Sophia, Ben, and I flew to London.

No sooner had Ben and I arrived at Brown's Hotel than the phone rang. Sam Wanamaker. Ben invited him to the opening. "Prince Philip will be there," said Ben. "The premiere is for one of his favorite charities."

Without missing a beat, Sam said, "For the Globe?"

"No," replied Ben, "but with you in there pitching, I'm sure it won't be long before there's a gala for the Globe."

Ben spent the afternoon at the Metropole Theatre, where the black-tie royal command performance was to be held. No super screens had been available in Madrid, so Bob Lawrence, the film's editor, a very *sympa* guy, projected the film for the first time on a big screen.

Bob and Ben stared in amazement at an early shot. Crawling across the top of the frame in one scene was a Spanish military jeep! This was supposed to be eleventh-century Spain. To provide field extras, the Franco government had turned over to Bronston its army and famous cavalry free of charge. Bob had not been able to see the jeep while editing on the tiny screen.

It took hours to find the little jeep again, and then hours more for Bob to cut it out of the finished film. He was worried about the music track because any cut in the film created a bump in the flow of the soundtrack—even the removal of just one frame. Two hours before the gala was to begin, Bob began to splice the film and adjust the track to avoid distortion in the music.

As the work went on, Bob and Tony were frantic, Prince Michael flounced around hysterically, his huge chin wattles quivering. Sam Bronston was calm even though there might not be a premiere. No one was sure the film could be repaired in time.

Wildly anxious, Tony noticed Ben looking lighthearted. "What are you so goddamn cheery about?" he asked sourly.

"I don't have my name on the credits," laughed Ben.[2]

Bob removed the jeep with time to spare. I put on my black Dior, and slung the new mink coat that Ben had insisted on giving me over my arm, lining-side out. Fur coats hadn't yet become the cause célèbre they are today but I had fought against that mink. To me, mink symbolized being "kept." I hated the idea of giving wives mink. Ben had just received a $50,000 bonus from Sam Bronston, and by God, whether I liked it or not, he was going to give me *El Cid* mink!

Shortly after we arrived we ran into Charlotte Wanamaker. She pointed to Sam, talking to Prince Philip. We guessed what he was saying. Then Sophia made a queenly entrance in white satin and diamond tiara. After the performance, Prince Philip made a point of shaking hands with Ben and me. He indicated discreetly that he knew perfectly well Ben was the blacklisted Hollywood screenwriter who had written *El Cid* and who did not have his name on it.

"I understand there were many problems," said Prince Philip, who always boned up for such occasions. "What would you say was the secret of the film's turning out so well?"

Prince Philip had a reputation for appreciating humor, so Ben replied playfully, "You have to have a lousy script three days before shooting and be obliged to write directly for the camera, and—oh yes! two stars who don't get along."

Sophia, who had been listening and who likes nothing better than to be mischievous, glided gracefully up to Prince Philip and said in a naughty whisper, "And you have to steal from a great writer like Corneille."

28

The Kiss of Death

El Cid had been such a roaring success that before *The Fall of the Roman Empire* was finished, Ben and Basilio signed to do two more projects for Bronston.

The first, *Paris 1900,* a sketch film, was to be directed by Vittorio De Sica, who had ushered in the era of Neo-Realism with *The Children Are Watching Us* (1942), *Shoeshine* (1946), and *The Bicycle Thief* (1949). He was soon to be hailed for the Loren-Mastroianni comedies (*Marriage Italian-Style; Yesterday, Today and Tomorrow*), and for *La Ciociara, Two Women,* which won Sophia the Oscar.

The prospect of doing a picture with De Sica considerably lightened the ever more worrisome winter of 1961–62 as it became evident that *The Fall of the Roman Empire* was a gigantic scheme to swindle millions, a project over which Prince Michael Waszynski had probably rubbed his hands, anticipating profits. When Ben asked Sam Bronston why he let Phil Yordan get away with siphoning off so much money, Sam replied, "Peanuts—next to what Mike takes!"

Mike, always flamboyant, was by this time behaving like a crowned prince, even entertaining the American ambassador to Spain in his lavish home. In *The Fall,* Mike saw a chance to make millions. Before the script was written, the Roman Forum was built in Madrid on the Bronston Studio back lot at a cost of a million dollars. The screenplay by Ben and Basilio had no need for it. They finally wrote a twenty-second scene to play in the Forum. Under Yordan's supervision, the action was shifted and twisted so that scenes they hadn't written for the Forum were played there. It was clearly an excuse for another million-dollar expenditure on which there would be payoffs, as Ben wrote in his journal. He told me Tony Mann was under many stresses. There was nothing the three of them could do about the production excesses.

Ben and Basilio watched that screenplay, like a sinking ship, take on more and more water. However, they felt that some of the script problems were their own fault. Ben said they'd done an enormous amount of research, perhaps too much, that research alone won't help create realistic characters; after too much research, you tend to shape the characters to fit fascinating bits of history that don't give the story color, drama, comedy.

In the script, Emperor Marcus Aurelius's son, Commodus, is demented and delinquent. The emperor chooses his adopted son, Livius, to be his heir. Commodus has his father killed before that shift in power can take place. Lucilla, played by Sophia, in love with Livius since childhood, urges him to take over, as her father, the emperor, wished. He refuses, remains a commander of the armed forces. Commodus proclaims himself emperor, personifying one of the decadent, licentious monsters to whom Rome owes its fall. He marries off Lucilla to a faraway barbarian, who eventually dies. When Commodus discovers that he is not really the son of Marcus Aurelius, that Lucilla is the only true heir, he is about to have her burnt at the stake when Livius rescues her. Reunited, the two lovers realize that Rome is beyond redemption and leave to find happiness elsewhere.

The *New Yorker,* in 2000[1] pointed out that *Gladiator,* one of the top films of the year and winner of twelve Oscars, distorts history in precisely the way Ben and Basilio did in *The Fall.* Though she was paid one million dollars, Sophia's part in *The Fall* is small and unsympathetic; Stephen Boyd is no Heston; Guinness is good but has only a cameo role. That picture was, indeed, cold pasta!

The Kiss of Death

Reportedly the most expensive film produced up to that time, 1961–62 (*Cleopatra* was released in 1963), the production budget for *The Fall* was $20 million. Financing had come from Du Pont as it had before, but this time most of the funding came from Paramount Pictures, Rank, and others who were to share fifty-fifty with Bronston in the profits.

On December 31, 1961, at a New Year's Eve party at the Castellana Hilton, the male lead, Stephen Boyd, dead drunk, dancing with me, falling all over me, confided that he thought Bronston was going down the drain. He'd heard that Du Pont wanted Bronston to give him back the bank completion guarantees he had signed. That act could bankrupt Bronston.

Stephen Boyd was one of those pretty, lightweight youths who thought he knew everything. He liked to tell a secret. "Never mind," he assured me, "I'm certain that creep Yordan has something up his sleeve. I don't see production closing down." He stopped dancing, looked quite blank, then toppled over, nearly dragging me to the floor with him.

Yordan did have something up his sleeve though it was a year or more before it was revealed. When Bronston, like the true gentleman he was, eventually returned the bank completion guarantees to Du Pont, Yordan convinced Du Pont to sign a "deficiency guarantee" for $5 million, that could be used to get $5 million more out of Paramount. Since it cost him nothing, and he was already in for so much, Du Pont signed the deficiency agreement. With it, Yordan obtained a check from Paramount for $5 million. He flew to Rome, where some last scenes of *The Fall* were shooting at Cinecittà to make it eligible for government subsidies. Yordan handed the check to Bronston, who promptly gave him $200,000 of the new funds. Seeing that, Prince Michael "took Yordan's hand, bowed low and declared they should erect a statue to Yordan."[2]

But back in 1962, Ben, Basilio, Tony, and the actors struggled on. The Roman Empire took a long time to fall. The Bronston empire disintegrated quickly. We escaped from crumbling Bronstonia to Mougins in March 1962 in time to receive our freight-car-full of exquisite seventeenth-century rich dark-wood furniture for the *mas*. I had kitchen cabinets made in the cloverleaf pattern of that period, found elegant country fabrics, and met with our children's friends and teachers to convince them that we were, at last, home.

Ben and Basilio were happy, too. They were about to work with one of the world's great filmmakers. We'd met De Sica in Madrid during *El Cid* when he visited Sophia. He and Basilio had been close for years. With Neapolitan warmth, De Sica accepted us as family.

A collaboration with De Sica was not just an intimate and complex relationship between writers and director. It was a way of life. At that time, Italian divorce laws were complicated and divorce practically unobtainable. Vittorio was required to spend one night a week with his estranged wife (he slept on the couch, he said), and put up a show of having his friends visit her home. Otherwise, he could have been legally prosecuted for adultery. All this, despite the fact that he'd been married to his Spanish wife, Maria, for over fifteen years and had two teenage sons with her. Sometimes Ben and Basilio flew to Rome to meet him and to dine at the estranged wife's home "for show."

Vittorio was an obsessive gambler. He was enchanted that we lived year-round so near to Monte Carlo and Cannes. He made his temporary home at the Hotel Negresco—equidistant from his two favorite casinos. Since he was also a superb actor and a good comedian, you could get him to play almost any piece of junk as long as you paid his price, which was then a rather modest five thousand dollars a day. This money he immediately gambled away on roulette, a game you can't beat. His wife, Maria, told us she knew he'd lost several million dollars. Vittorio loved to laugh and laughed a lot, but his sense of humor did not extend to his gambling.

Once, Ben, Basilio, and I accompanied him to the Palm Beach Casino in Cannes. Vittorio had a streak of amazing luck and won a considerable amount of money. He had won so much that his chips took up all the playing space in front of him. He asked Basilio to stuff the chips in his pockets. Basilio did, keeping twenty-five thousand dollars' worth of chips in a special pocket.

De Sica started to lose and Basilio fed him back all his chips, except the last twenty-five thousand dollars' worth. Vittorio ended up losing everything. It was awful. He was so depressed. We were all silent. Then, when we were miles away from the casino, Basilio handed De Sica the twenty-five thousand dollars he had saved him.

De Sica's reaction was unexpected and shocking. He howled. Ready to tear Basilio limb from limb, he yelled, "You swine!" and much more in Italian I didn't understand. "If you'd given it back to me at the casino, I would have gone on to win. I know it! I feel it! You're a first-class shit!" Vittorio wouldn't speak to Basilio for days.

Paris 1900 consisted of seventeen sketches, each one opening with an Impressionist masterpiece. The stories re-created the world of Renoir, Degas, Monet, Manet, and other great artists of the period. A collection of world stars was to play in it. The sketches, based on a series of short stories by Erskine Caldwell, who had written *God's Little Acre,* all set in small towns in the Deep South, Caldwell's favorite locale, adapted unbelievably well to being transposed to Paris at the turn of the century.

Once in a while Ben, Basilio, and I met Vittorio in Paris to scout for locations. Vittorio had an amazing eye. As we drove through the city, he let out a whoop as he spotted a row of buildings that looked untouched since 1900. The chauffeur braked. Vittorio pointed to an Art Nouveau glass arcade or a merry-go-round or a fountain. He and Basilio broke exuberantly into rapid Italian like a vaudeville team. But when Vittorio flew to Nice "to work," he headed directly for the casino. We'd have to find him and fish him out. If he was winning, he would not stop. If he was losing, he would not stop. The trick was to find him when the last of his money was gone.

Sketch after sketch had already been scripted when Vittorio became ill with gallbladder trouble and was rushed to the American Hospital in Paris, the only hospital he had any confidence in.

De Sica had worked with Carlo Ponti for years but seemed to forget that Carlo made all the money arrangements for him. They had just had a heated quarrel. Vittorio accused Carlo of dozens of imaginary injuries, including preventing him from expressing himself artistically. Carlo and Sophia stopped speaking to De Sica and Carlo cut off his money supply.

While De Sica was at the hospital, Ben told Sophia it was intolerable that she didn't call her great friend when he was so ill. She replied heatedly in true Neapolitan fashion (both she and De Sica were from Naples) that she wouldn't expose herself in such a way as to allow De Sica to hang up on her. It would be too humiliating and would probably become public. There had already been a great deal of publicity about the Ponti–De Sica rift. Ben, completely without basis, assured Sophia that Vittorio would never hang up on her, that he loved her, that it was not like her to refuse to call a dear friend.

A strange and funny thing happened. Ben and I, Basilio, and the Swiss producer Arthur Cohn were lunching at Fouquet's. Cohn would produce most of De Sica's films, such as *The Garden of the Finzi-Contini* in 1971.[3] When he won the Oscar for Best Foreign Film (1976, *Black and White and in Color*) he was so surprised, he said, "I feel like Harry Truman when he held up the newspaper saying Dewey had won the election."

That day, Cohn said he was going over to the American Hospital to visit De Sica. "You are his friends, you should all come with me. It would make him happy."

We all agreed to go. Arthur Cohn was Orthodox Jewish and it was Saturday. He was not going to take a cab to the hospital that was miles away in Neuilly. In fact, he was not going to get into a car. He was going to walk and expected us to walk. In those days, I wore beautiful shoes with four-inch heels. I said, "You can walk. I'll take a taxi."

Cohn said, "You'd get there alone way ahead of us. That would spoil the whole thing, that his friends have been thinking of him and surprise! Here they are!"

I walked—miles. I don't know why I didn't hail a cab and wait for them in a café by the hospital. We got there toward the end of the afternoon. I had blisters. But all four of us went up the elevator of the American Hospital to Vittorio's big corner room—and he *was* elated to see us.

He played the wan invalid for all it was worth, pointing to his side, indicating his pain. Ben had hardly mentioned Sophia's name when De Sica forgot his ailing gallbladder and started to complain about Carlo holding up the money he badly needed. At the height of his fury, the phone rang and, since it was nearest me, I picked it up. Sophia.

When I announced that it was Sophia, De Sica raved and ranted in such a loud voice I had to cover the mouthpiece. I handed the phone to him. Stella Adler is the only other person I knew who could change expression as quickly. Vittorio's voice became soft, tender.

"*Cara! Carissima Sophia!*"

There ensued the most Neapolitan scene you could imagine. Within seconds they were both weeping. Sometimes Vittorio held the phone away from his ear so we could hear Sophia commiserating, repeating over and over again, "*Povrito Vittorio.*" They both played it to the hilt, Vittorio telling Sophia that the pain was barely endurable and Sophia making cooing sounds of comfort. By the time they finished, De Sica was saying what a dear, soothing manner Sophia had, a true Neapolitan, it made him feel a thousand times better. When we met Sophia later, she said "What a lovely man! What a real part of my life he is!" You would never have believed that her previous words about him had been "that selfish, unfeeling, egotistical bastard!"

The sketches of *Paris 1900* had become human, funny, moving, colorful. French actress Jeanne Moreau agreed to play Degas's Absinthe Drinker, Jean Gabin the role of a Daumier magistrate, Jacques Tati a Cézanne card-player. Top Italian, German, and American stars wanted to work in the film. Unfortunately, it was never to be. For some reason, which no one understood, the Du Ponts no longer wanted to be associated with Bronston and plunged him into bankruptcy. Could they have discovered with shock that they'd had a close business relationship with a Jew? No. They had probably always known. More likely, they didn't want to be associated with a phony Polish prince who was lucratively skimming their investment. Their investigations revealed that Prince Michael had purchased a Roman country inn, the Villa Floria, for half a million dollars, for his "adopted son." How did a production manager accumulate $500,000 in such a short time? No one ever got an answer to that because in Madrid, flabby, flamboyant Prince Michael suddenly dropped dead.

Ben's writing deal was with Yordan, who had no intention of paying. What Yordan did was rudimentary and embarrassing. His own company applied for a federal bankruptcy petition for something like a million dollars for the amount he claimed he had paid Ben and Basilio for *Paris 1900*. At precisely the same moment, when Ben's attorney, Charlie Katz, sued for the payment due Ben, Yordan filed a counter-claim in which he swore that since he had never received the script, he didn't have to pay.

Charlie Katz was horrified. That was a flagrant contradiction. Yordan was committing perjury and was subject to a prison sentence. Katz presented Yordan and his lawyers with photocopies of his sworn statement in Washington, D.C., claiming he had paid a million dollars for the script and, alongside it, a copy of the California affidavit refusing to pay Ben the small fraction of the million dollars to which Ben had originally agreed, swearing he'd never received the script. There was no question that it was perjury. Yordan paid promptly.

Later, Ben wrote in his journal, when Vittorio tried to buy the script back from the Du Ponts, he was told he would have to pay the million dollars for which Yordan had put in the claim.

De Sica had first noticed our sixteen-year-old daughter Luli when he was visiting Sophia in Madrid and Luli was visiting us. He had made much of her beauty. Now, after the demise of *Paris 1900*, he came formally to Ben as if asking for a young girl's hand in marriage, but in fact he wanted her to play the lead in his next film, *Un Nouveau Monde,* which was about to shoot in Paris. He said it didn't matter that she had no acting experience. He would teach her. Like most girls that age, Luli wanted to be an actress, and of course was wild to play in his picture. Ben said, "Absolutely not! Behind the camera—not in front of it." Accordingly, De Sica gave Luli a job as second assistant director on the picture, which started her thinking of writing and directing.[4]

About the time that Ben and I decided to make Mougins our home, Picasso bought a place there, and Marcel Duhamel, the publisher, moved there from Antibes. Jacqueline Picasso had refused to live in Picasso's house in the Californie part of Cannes, which was beginning to be overbuilt and crowded. The house, she complained, was like a warehouse, every room crammed with paintings, sculpture, and pieces of iron and wood he'd picked up.

Picasso's estate, Notre-Dame-de-Vie—Our-Lady-of-Life—was close to ours at the base of the picturesque hillside village of Mougins, also had an olive grove, was surrounded by stately cypress, and inside had huge whitewashed rooms and ceilings with great exposed beams. Since we'd attended his eightieth birthday, he had gifted us with his series of signed Toros posters (1954–1959) which climbed the wall next to the wide oak stairway of our immense *entrée*.

Through Marcel, we sent thanks back to le Maître for his generosity. The result: Marcel called to invite us to dinner. Just us. And Picasso. Marcel's wife, Germaine, would make something simple. Picasso wanted to become acquainted with "*les voisins américains*," the American neighbors.

A Royal Command performance.

I had already had one. Soon after leaving Madrid, Sophia asked Basilio to have me come to lunch at her Paris apartment. Just the two of us. I couldn't think what it meant and I asked Basilio. He replied that she wanted to have some girl talk. There was no one she could really "talk to about sex and things." I shouldn't have been surprised at how unworldly in some ways she was. She'd been *entourée*—surrounded—by Carlo and Basilio since age fifteen. Ines, her secretary-companion, knew less than she.

Sophia and I exchanged all kinds of giggly silliness, reminding me of the happy times when my chums and I had compared notes about boys over ice cream sodas at Don Q's soda fountain on 68th Street in Manhattan.

The Royal Command performance at Marcel Duhamel's was quite different. Picasso, like Sophia, was curious. He, too, couldn't go out in the world normally to learn what he wanted to know. But the difference was that Picasso wasn't sure exactly what it was that he wanted to find out. He asked many questions, didn't give Ben or me time to answer. His questions had a wide range. "How does a film get started?" "What was the American Party like?" "I hear you planted corn. How is it doing?"

We had questions we wanted to ask, and since we saw that Picasso loved to talk and was not eager to listen, at least to us, we asked him about his work.

"The key to everything," he said, pointing to his forehead, "is here. But you know that. You are writers. Before it comes out of the pen or brush, it must be at one's fingertips," and he rubbed his fingertips, "entirely, without losing any of it."

He thought about that for a moment, and added, "And one has to be like myself. I can't do anything other than what I *am* doing."

I had heard that he'd said that often but he gave it an emphasis that struck me. Perhaps my problem was that the need to create wasn't powerful enough in me. I rejected that. My urge was strong, even overwhelming, but my self-doubt was stronger.

Eventually, I asked him, "When you painted so many *Déjeuner sur l'Herbe* after Manet, were you searching for something in particular?"

My question may have been dumb. His reply was: "My old pictures don't interest me anymore. I'm much more curious about the ones I haven't painted yet."

We had many dinners at the Duhamels, once every week or two. Jacqueline never accompanied him, always pleaded ill health. Picasso enjoyed himself inordinately. He loved Marcel and Marcel loved him. Picasso always brought a thoughtful gift, once a fantastically beautiful barbecue he designed himself and had his *ferronier d'art*—artist blacksmith—execute. For Marcel's birthday, Picasso gave him a small sketchbook filled with his drawings and doodles. Marcel was overcome, almost to tears.

"*Ecoute, mon ami,* listen, my friend," Picasso admonished him. "I know your financial situation is not brilliant. One day you may be obliged to sell this, which will be worth—" Picasso made an enormous, sweeping gesture. "I give you permission. If you are really in need, sell the book. Only I tell you, never, never, under any circumstance break up the book or sell individual drawings from it. *Jamais!* Never! The book must stay intact."

Years later, we heard that Marcel had done just what Picasso had told him not to. Marcel found that by selling the drawings individually, he could realize a great deal more money than by selling the book, and so he cut it up. Picasso found out, and, of course, never spoke to Marcel again.

But that was much later. In this period, we basked in our friendship with Picasso.

In October 1963, suddenly, at dinner, he spoke about the itch he had to go back to engraving. He mentioned two wonderful Belgian brothers, the Crommelincks, great technicians, who had an engraving workshop in Paris and came down to Cannes whenever he called them. For a few weeks we heard no more about it. Then Picasso must have confided to Marcel that he didn't have space at his place to cut lithographs and was obliged to go all the way to Vallauris.

"*Mais les Barzmans!*" Marcel must have offered. "They have a big studio on their property. They love and admire you. They will be happy for the opportunity to be of service."

One day, our telephone rang. Picasso! "Barzman? You are too kind. *Mille remerciements*—a thousand thanks!"

"Not at all," said Ben, puzzled.

At that time, at least in France, the telephone had an additional listening device, an *écouteur,* a small round gadget on a cord. I picked it up from its cradle and put it to my ear so that I could hear what Picasso was saying to Ben, who held the telephone receiver.

"My equipment will be installed Monday," Picasso said. "I shall not be at your studio every day, of course. Only when my lithographer calls me to come over."

Ben was dancing from foot to foot, delirious with joy.

I was dying because I knew I could not let it happen. At that time, we had six children; three were small and running around free. That was the reason we had moved to the country.

"Tell him we're sorry, but he can't have it," I said to Ben. "The children—"

Ben shushed me.

I whispered hoarsely, "Picasso! People! Tourists! In droves! In their cars. All the time. Never any peace. If you want him here, we'll have him to dinner. *This* we cannot do."

Ben began to listen to me. "But imagine what that would be for a writer," he pleaded, his hand over the mouthpiece, "to have constant contact with a great artist!"

"It's not possible. The children would be run over. Give me the phone. If *you* can't say it, I will."

He saw I meant it, crumpled, mumbled an apology into the phone. Ben never forgave me.

We had been enjoying new baby Marco and our life in Mougins. It always seemed that when we were getting along pretty well, something happened that altered everything—in this case, his fearful anger. His fury at me was monumental. He acted as if I had ruined his life. There weren't many times when I defied Ben, but when I did, life was so unbearable that I committed no act of defiance for a long, long time. This time, a cloud of rage hung in every room of our home, and though we returned to a semblance of normalcy, in some ways, his anger at my decision was always with us.

29

Heavy Water

The Fall of the Roman Empire opened the Cannes festival of 1963. It was not a joyous event. We cringed. Ben in his tux, I in the black Dior (I hadn't been able to remain thin enough for the white off-the-shoulder) showed up with our three eldest children—Luli, in a pink and gold sari, Johnny and Aaron in black blazers, white shirts, and black bow ties.

After the three-hour ordeal, Ben and I came out of the Palais drenched in sweat but we descended the wide steps slowly and smiled broadly as if we'd just seen a surefire smash hit. A French enemy-friend shook Ben's hand and offered the oft-used, ambiguous comment, "You've done it again!"

Across from the Palais, on the corner of the Croisette, our old friend Paul Jarrico hailed us from a table at the Café des Festivals. I was crazy about Paul; Ben had reservations, used to call him "the Boy Marxist," but we were close and both of us loved Paul's ex-wife, Sylvia.

One thing Ben had against him was that he opted for being witty rather than sensitive, as he did that night.

Paul beamed with childish enthusiasm, embraced us, kissed the kids, and said, "Best thing about that picture is your Daddy's name on it!" The children, who may have been the only ones in the audience who liked the picture, barely understood English and thought Paul's quip was a compliment. Ben didn't live long enough to see Paul become a hero or prove himself a dear, loyal friend to me.

At the French reception after the premiere of *The Fall*, we were introduced to the then minister of culture, Monsieur Alain Peyrefitte. Ben pointed to the newsreel and TV cameras, as if to say, "Are you sure you want to greet *us* in front of the world?"

The minister saw the look, laughed delicately. "For years," he said, "Hollywood has been stealing talent from us. Maurice Chevalier, Charles Boyer, Yves Montand, many, many others. Now at last, through McCarthyism, America has found a way to return the compliment—rather roundabout, but a way. Welcome to France!" It was an elegant way of telling us how they felt about us.

I thanked him and told him his words had moved me.

"We've never known how we were regarded, officially, by the French," said Ben.

The eyes of Monsieur le Ministre twinkled. "Are you uncomfortable?"

Ben said "No." I shook my head.

"Are you being harassed?" the minister demanded.

"No," we both answered.

"*Et alors,* so . . . " Monsieur Peyrefitte made a wide gesture signifying "What more do you need?"

Tony Mann had flown in for the premiere of *The Fall* although he hadn't wanted to. His health was not good and he was having "woman trouble." His wife, Spanish actress Sara Montiel, was blocking the divorce he wanted in order to marry Lido nightclub dancer Bluebell Anna Kuzko. He couldn't face people who disliked or criticized his work. Now that Bronston was probably going bankrupt, Tony wanted to get another project under way. He'd come to Cannes to see Ben, who'd been telling him about an idea he had. It was more an approach to a war story than an idea: The camera would never get closer to the enemy (the Nazis, in this case) than the range of a sniper's fire. When the camera was close to the enemy, it would signal the kind of danger characters would be subjected to in a real war.

Frequently, in war films, the director shows the enemy close up to give a sense of melodramatic suspense. Ben wanted to use the sense of danger sparingly. He'd explained his theory to me over and over. "You see a Nazi close only when you're in real danger of being killed by him."

We'd argued about it. I thought it innovative but was afraid that not seeing the enemy, the audience wouldn't be sufficiently involved.

In essence, Ben was suggesting to a director a way to direct before a script was even written. He was envisioning how he himself would shoot the picture. To enhance suspense, the music would be sparse. Instead, real sound would be used for dramatic effect. For instance, when the commandos make a night raid, only the crunch of their footsteps in the snow, the wind in the trees, or other sounds in the silent night would be heard (as in the *Rififi* heist scene). Tony, enthusiastic, seemed to understand that unique quality of suspense.

The project Ben had in mind was based on what Nobel-winning physicist Frédéric Joliot-Curie had recounted to us in April 1949 on that long Paris weekend that convinced Ben we should live in France, not England. Monsieur Joliot had told the story of a Norwegian village in the far north, a kilometer or so from one of the main hydroelectric stations of Europe.

Nazi scientists were trying to develop an atomic bomb early in the war. One of the first steps was to produce enough heavy water, then believed vital to the production of the atom bomb. The Germans had occupied Norway and the hydroelectric plant in the village that produced heavy water. The Nazis producing the first atomic bomb was unthinkable. They could have won the war!

The Allied High Command in London was aware of the threat and wanted to eliminate any possible danger immediately. Their strategy was the classic military solution—aerial bombardment of the hydroelectric power station. That strategy was extremely dangerous. A huge ammonia-storage tank was stationed near the power station. With the acceptable margin of error in aerial bombing, it was certain stray bombs would strike the ammonia dump. Toxic gas would be released, smother the village, and kill its eight thousand inhabitants and every living thing in it. The Nazis believed the storage tank guaranteed that the power station would not be bombed by the Allies, who would surely not endanger the Norwegian population.

But this is exactly what the Allied Command decided to do. They did not inform the Norwegian government-in-exile that they had made up their minds to go through with the plan, for fear the Norwegians would try to evacuate the villagers. That would in turn arouse the suspicion of the Nazi High Command, who would immediately move the heavy water to someplace less vulnerable.

However, a group of young Norwegian commandos had been able to make their way through highly patrolled, dangerous waters all the way to England to reach the Allied High Command. They pleaded for the right to use their own plan of operation. Instead of aerial bombardment and the certain death of the nearby villagers, the commandos wanted to stage a guerrilla raid on the hydroelectric heavy-water power station and destroy it without danger to their countrymen. The Allied High Command agreed to take a chance. They allowed the commandos to try it their way first.

The Nazis decided independently that it was too dangerous to keep the hidden supplies of heavy water in the region. They planned to move it to a safe place in Germany. They hit on the idea of transporting it on a Sunday ferryboat loaded with Norwegian civilians off for a weekend excursion. The Germans were convinced the Allies would not bomb the ferry.

In 1963, Tony Mann took Ben with him to the Norwegian village to research the project.[1] They met with the Norwegian colonel who, during the war, had made the heartbreaking decision to plant a bomb on the Sunday ferry, timed to go off when the ferry would be over the deepest part of the lake. It was a desperate decision but in view of the enormous stakes—the outcome of World War II depended on it—it was considered unavoidable. The bomb went off, the ferry's terrified cargo, over one hundred twenty men, women, and children, were drowned.

The colonel showed Ben more than a dozen postcards he'd received, one each St. Valentine's Day, the day the ferry had been sunk. They were all from the same sender, a man whose wife and two daughters, eight and ten, had been drowned. The card read: "Just so you won't forget what I suffered."

Ben returned to Mougins with a collection of trolls, amusingly sculpted Norwegian elves, quite small in size; a story; and a conviction that the future lay in electricity. The village was so clean, the air so pure, he'd never had to change his shirt. Electricity was so cheap and plentiful there that the villagers had floral displays between their windows and their storm windows, which they kept illuminated, like everything else in the village, night and day.

In the film that emerged from all this, *Heroes of Telemark,* Kirk Douglas played the colonel. Around 1958, Kirk Douglas had initiated *Spartacus*[2] (released in 1960), to be directed by Tony Mann. Kirk and Tony disagreed and fought violently. The underlying truism of filmmaking is that on most films, especially expensive films, the star is always right. Tony was fired. Kirk admitted he'd had that on his conscience. When he heard that Tony was to direct *The Heroes of Telemark,* he asked for a copy of the script and volunteered to play the lead, the colonel.

On the next trip to Norway, Ben planned to buy more trolls. Everyone loved them. But there never was another trip. He had too many projects and couldn't be in Norway when Tony was shooting *Heroes of Telemark.* They had long telephone script conferences. Tony had completely accepted the concepts of raw sound and keeping the camera at a distance from the Nazis, which Ben continually reminded him of.

Nevertheless, when we flew to London for the gala premiere in 1965, once again for one of Prince Philip's favorite charities, Ben and I were shocked at the opening shot of the film, a close-up of Eric Porter, a fine British actor, in full Gestapo regalia, arriving on the screen in a Mercedes. Moreover, a heavy musical score coated the commando action so that any real sounds were drowned out. We were appalled to discover that men in rowboats were placed in the film near where the ferry was to sink and that the explosion was timed to sink the ferry close to where the guardian angels in rowboats were waiting.

This action was surely something the Norwegian Resistance and the colonel would *never* have seriously considered. There was too much danger the Gestapo would have noticed them and uncovered the whole plot. Tony later defended himself: he'd been overwhelmed by Kirk Douglas and the producer, Benny Fisz, who insisted the audience would never stomach the cruel reality of Norwegians letting their own people drown. Fisz decided the concept of keeping the camera a distance from the enemy and the use of raw sound with little music was "much too intellectual" for a large audience.[3]

Ben and I felt *Heroes of Telemark,* though well received, would have been a distinguished film had Tony stuck to the original concept.

Prince Philip once again shook our hands. "Congratulations," he said. "It's a fine film." He looked as though he meant it. Then he smiled and added, "I'm glad to see your name on this one."

Ben had a habit of picking up people and bringing them back like trophies. He went down to Cannes to buy a part for his razor, couldn't find it, returned to Mougins with Monsieur Dani, the blacksmith, who made the part for him. Once Ben came home with an elegant lady, a countess, leading an equally elegant dog. He'd admired her black standard poodle, informed her we had a pedigreed female whom we wanted to mate. The countess, enthused, wanted to make sure we were the proper sort of people for such intimate relations. Ben had brought her home to look us over. We passed the test. A date was made for when our poodle, Kafka, would be in heat. The countess arrived at the appointed hour with her elegant male, but Kafka would have none of him, and bit him when he approached until finally the countess withdrew herself and her dog.

Ben started talking to Harold Robbins in the barbershop. He had no idea who Harold was. They discovered they were both American writers living in France, not far from each other. Ben, of course, brought him home.

I'd heard about Harold Robbins. In his way, he was as famous as Picasso and as wealthy. His books had been translated into more languages than the Bible, and he was rumored to live a life that resembled his stories—full of sex, drugs, money, and violence, but especially steamy sex. His second novel, *A Stone for Danny Fisher,* had shown promise of his developing into a fine writer but he seemed to have made a pact with the Devil. From then on, he wrote trash that sold 750 million copies worldwide. He always had a good story and told it well, but was more interested in the twists and turns of plot and never tried for deep characterization.

I was annoyed when Ben brought Harold Robbins home. "This is Harold." A white captain's hat topped Harold's plain tanned features. I was in muddy overalls and smelled of fertilizer.

"Hi, babe," he said, "nice place you got here. I wantcha to see mine. We're neighbors. Mougins and Le Cannet are practically next door. Grace will call you. How about you come tomorrow, Sunday, for brunch? We had bagels and lox and sturgeon flown in from Barney Greengrass."

We appeared on Sunday and after brunch Harold said to me, "I'll show you around." Grace took Ben to see the garden. Harold ran ahead of me through a laboratory-like room, its long tables covered with stacks of papers and books. Hurriedly, he climbed a scrimpy, unsteady flight of stairs to the pigeon coop. I followed.

"This is where I work. No windows. Nothing to distract me."

The minuscule, unadorned, closet-like room had a desk and chair but barely space for the two of us to stand. We descended the narrow stairs, he in back of me. Just as I reached the bottom step, a gigantic violent thrust ripped into me, tearing my dress and panties, almost toppling me.

"Don't be disappointed," he said, chuckling and holding up the huge dildo with which he'd goosed me. "Even *my* penis isn't *that* big."

I took this in stride; that's the way he was. We invited Grace and Harold to dinner on the terrace. We did what we thought we did best, steak barbecue, Golden Bantam from our garden (at that time unobtainable in France). The Robbinses were in good form, enjoyed the food, the wine, the talk.

At the door, saying goodnight, Harold took me aside. "Fabulous dinner, babe, but if you're gonna serve steak, you hafta have the perfect cut. I'll introduce you to my butcher. Meetcha tomorrow morning at nine o'clock at Marché Forville. The boucherie on the southwest corner."

Command performance again. I was there at five minutes of nine in the gray Citroën *Déesse,*[4] circling the *Marché.* I saw several butchers in their white aprons and white caps. I parked. As I got closer, I did a take. One of the butchers was Harold. When he saw me, he turned to the butcher boy. "Bring out the beast," he ordered.

The boy and the butcher carried out half an animal, placed it on the marble slab of the counter in front of Harold. I was trying to collect my thoughts. Harold had told us he'd knocked around during the Depression from job to job—cashier, bookmaker, mechanic, cook.

"Harold," I started to ask. "What—?"

"Watch. Listen. Learn."

Harold carved the side of beef professionally, carefully cutting each of the parts and naming the various cuts. When he had finished, he wiped his hands on his bloodstained apron. "Ask us again to a steak barbecue."

"But Harold . . . ?" I asked in a whirl of perplexity.

"I toldja. There's nothing I haven't done. I mean it, babe. *Nothing.*"

Before I was up to having them again for dinner, an invitation came to a party on the *Graziella,* his eighty-five-foot oceangoing yacht with king-size beds.

Harold gathered hundreds of guests from different backgrounds: Hollywood producers, French literati, champion cyclists, an Asian diplomat, whores and bums from the port—a rowdy and preposterous gang. The noise onboard was deafening. All at once, loud Arabian music drowned out the drunken buzz and the shrieks of laughter. In a haze of soft, breezy, multicolored chiffon veils covering her black hair, Grace Robbins appeared in transparent bra and harem pants sparkling with sequins. She danced an authentic North African belly dance and she danced it well. Harold had sent her to Morocco to learn it.

30

Zanuckia, Oasis for a Lost Bronstonian

"Hey, Norma! Zanuck's a nice guy!" Ben came running in breathless. "He wants us to come to his daughter's birthday party!"

"Darrylin?" I'd heard the Zanucks were past masters at making up names: "Darvi," a combination of Darryl and his wife's name, Virginia, for Zanuck's mistress Bella Darvi; "Ric-Su-Dar," a mélange of their children's names, for their Palm Springs estate.

"The party is for Susan," said Ben, "the one married to André Hakim, the producer. I bumped into Art Buchwald. He was with Zanuck. They were talking about the birthday party, black-tie affair. Zanuck included us. What do you think?"

"I think . . . it isn't surprising. *Oasis.* You saved Fox about twenty million dollars—"

Ben cut me off. "Maybe four. Now it would be eight. Son of a bitch doesn't forget!"

"You saved his life! He was having trouble with the studio. It would have been the end of him. Maybe he wants to talk to you."

Susan Zanuck Hakim was drunk and sulky. I didn't know anyone at the party but I enjoyed meeting Zanuck's pal actor Gregory Ratoff, a big amiable bear of a man who was terribly funny in mangling the English language.

Darryl Zanuck, standing there enjoying Ratoff even when he wasn't funny, wore huge dark sunglasses with his tux and perky black bow tie. His white hair receded far from his large, wide, rounded forehead, his now white toothbrush mustache slightly obscured by his big, fat, trademark cigar. I'd read that he'd adopted the mustache, glasses, and cigar in order to look older when, at twenty-three, he'd become head of production at Warner Brothers.

Zanuck acknowledged me respectfully. He smacked "tarts" on their bottoms, was respectful to wives.

"Aren't you worried about smoking, Darryl?" Ben asked. Ben, Canadian, had quit in 1952 when his king, George VI, announced to his British subjects that he was dying of lung cancer and that tobacco was the culprit.

"I'd rather die with a cigar in my mouth than with my boots on," Zanuck replied. "I'm worried about a script."

"I never worry," said Ratoff. "My friend Dayril can *feex* anything."

"This time, I'm going to let Ben here *feex* it."

That night, I was most surprised that Zanuck called attention to our presence. At dinner, he had Ben and me stand up and introduced us as "my friends the Barzmans, the blacklisted writer and his wife."

All the hurrah about Susan Zanuck's birthday made me realize that Ben and I were entitled to a party for our twentieth wedding anniversary. Fourteen of the twenty years since 1943 had been spent in France. We were in Paris readying the house for new renters. We celebrated at home on two consecutive Saturday nights: the first with dear friends, the blacklisted: Lee and Tammy Gold, Jack and Gladys Berry, Mischa, Altman, Bea Dassin, Mike and Zelma Wilson, Ellie Pine, Actors Lab actress, and her French husband, Jean-Mathieu Boris, Betsy Blair and her French actor husband, Roger Pigaud (whom I had adored since seeing *Antoine et Antoinette,* in which he played the winner of the French lottery), and Zuka and Louis Mitelberg. The second Saturday night's guests were George and Hilda Marton; her son Peter Stone, who wrote *Charade, Arabesque,* and the musical *1776;* his girlfriend, movie star Martine Carol; Art and Annie Buchwald; Dorothy and David Schoenbrun, Paris head of CBS; the Gilberts; and others.

Our two parties also fêted the beginning of the end of the blacklist: Dalton Trumbo's name was on *Spartacus* (1960) and *Exodus* (1960), Ben's name on *The Fall of the Roman Empire* (1964). With Bronston's opulent Byzantine empire falling, Ben was in demand. His name may not have been on it, but everyone in the industry knew Ben had saved *El Cid*. Not only Tony Mann wanted to work with Ben again. Carlo Ponti counted on Ben "for Sophia's sake" to do something with the known-to-be-awful script of *Judith,* a project that Carlo had sandwiched between her other commitments, one that would certainly never meet its June shooting date. Zanuck, who now had his own European production company, DFZ, releasing through Fox, was in a similar predicament. *The Visit,* starring Ingrid Bergman, was scheduled to shoot in Rome in the summer. The screenplay was far from ready.

In 1960, Fox had bought the rights to Friedrich Durrenmatt's play *The Visit,* which Alfred Lunt and Lynn Fontanne had played successfully on Broadway in 1958. When Zanuck went off to Europe to start his own company, the head of Fox production didn't have the remotest idea how to handle this grim fable, which Ingrid Bergman had begged him to buy. It was, she said, so different from the usual gentlewomen roles she played.

I'd read the play. Don't ask me how or why. I guess, like my mother, I read plays. But *The Visit?* How could it possibly be a film? And with Ingrid Bergman?

The Visit was the story of the world's richest woman, who hatches a diabolical plan to avenge herself on her former lover and on the mean, straitlaced, self-righteous villagers who persecuted her when she was a poor young girl full of life.

Anyone could see how this theme might appeal to Ingrid Bergman, who felt that she herself had been persecuted for daring to love Italian director Roberto Rossellini. Incredible as it seems now, leaving her first husband, Dr. Peter Lindstrom, for Rossellini created a firestorm throughout the world; she was barred from making any American films for seven years. But she made some fine ones in Italy, one being *Stromboli* (1950). She returned to the American screen in 1956 in *Anastasia,* and won a second Oscar for it.

Production of *The Visit* was delayed for three years. When the first screenplay reached Ingrid Bergman, it had serious problems. The producers didn't want the story to present Ingrid as a vindictive woman who would bribe the townsfolk to kill her ex-lover.

William Holden was ready to defer his salary in order to work with Ingrid. Out of the blue, Anthony Quinn picked up the expired film rights, became coproducer, and substituted himself for Holden's role. As part of the deal, Tony agreed to the backers' demands for a distinctly less grim ending than in the play.

"You'll have to talk it over with Ingrid," Zanuck said to Ben, "before you write even one word."

"Gladly," Ben answered, smiling.

"She wants you to come out to the country and lunch with her."

"Norma's a great fan of hers."

"Say no more. I'm sure Ingrid will be delighted."

I was touched that Ben had thought of me and wanted me with him. Once, when we were in Geneva and he was invited to Audrey Hepburn and Mel Ferrer's chalet in the Swiss Alps for lunch, he'd gone alone. He reported later that I hadn't missed anything. He'd had what he called the lightest lunch of all time. In the middle of his plate was an extremely small tomato stuffed with a teaspoon of chicken salad. That was it. For a man who'd come all the way up there in the freezing cold, who was used to big French midday meals, which he ate with his family, it was not adequate. Ben remembered that lunch by the pattern of the china because so much of the dish had been visible.

I was thrilled when a long black American studio car with driver picked us up and drove us into the heavenly countryside an hour south of Paris, the Valley of the Chevreuse. I recall the name of the little village, Choisel, because my high school French teacher, Monsieur Schwerzel, an Alsatian, insisted on us calling him Monsieur Choisel, which sounded so much more French.

Outside the village, through poplars, chestnuts, and pines, a venerable quarried-stone manor house nestled in thick woods. Apart from summer, which Bergman spent in Sweden with her children, she lived here with her theatrical-producer husband, Lars Schmidt, when she wasn't making a picture. Schmidt seemed to be away much of the time.

Ingrid Bergman, her very own self, as beautiful as ever, in a rough tweed skirt and turtleneck sweater, was at the door to welcome us. She breathed warmth and graciousness. Her eyes twinkled with fun. I think one of the first things she said was: "Tony [Quinn] told me you have a lot of children."

"Six," I said.

Ben added, with a twinkle to match hers, "*Du même lit*—from the same bed, as the French say."

She focused her expressive eyes on me. "Six," she repeated. "I would have liked to have had six, but I didn't do so well with four." She laughed. "I don't relish being at home and being a mother all the time. Don't you find that when you are yourself, you have more to give them?"

Before I could speak, Ben both agreed and disagreed, "Theoretically yes, practically no."

"If you become your real self, you can bring them something irreplaceable," her eyes shone, "a radiant joy in work—in life."

"There's no question children suffer from a mother's absence," Ben replied stubbornly.

She turned again to me. "Don't you think being a mother is more a question of quality than quantity? I mean, that it's about the kind of time you spend with your children rather than how much time? I don't see my children often," she said wistfully, "but when I do, I'm totally theirs."

Ben bestowed on her his most engaging smile. "You are an actress, a great actress. There is no question—"

"Well," she said, "I wanted success as an actress and a home and children. I have them all, so I am happy. If the price I paid was too high, I only wish I had paid it alone. I feel guilty all the time because my children paid for it, too." She paused. "I suppose I am more interested in having 'actress' written on my tombstone than 'wife' or 'mother.' "

"I'm a writer," I said, wishing Ben were not there. "I'm lucky. It's something I can do at home. But for the time being, I'm not writing. I don't know why."

"For seven years with Roberto," she said, intuitively, "I didn't work. That is, I don't count the pictures I did with him because they weren't what I needed for myself. But it wasn't just that. I couldn't speak in his presence. I felt inferior. I deferred to him on all matters. An artist has to express what is inside. That is why it's so hard now. I'm on the blacklist again." She giggled, a wonderful lilting giggle.

"Blacklist?" asked Ben.

"I, too, have known unfair persecution." She giggled again. "Not *your* blacklist. When you were having yours, I was blacklisted because I was 'immoral.' Americans raged at me—at many Hollywood people—for whatever reason, as if I were evil. Now, it's a different kind of blacklist for me. I'm too old for the younger parts and too young for the older ones. There are no scripts being written for a woman my age." Then the irrepressible laughter bubbled up. "Maybe I can play one of the witches in *Macbeth* someday!" She giggled some more, breaking herself up. "I don't want to go around the world being honored at retrospectives!"

"But Ingrid," Ben said softly, "here we are. You've got a wonderful role. At least it will be perfect for you. I'm so glad we could meet." He turned his full charm on her. "I'm inspired to write for you."

No longer the mother, she was now very much the actress. "I don't think I can play a woman that old," she said. "How old is she?"

Ben thought fast. She obviously did not want to play a woman of fifty, which was what she was about to be.

"Well," he said, sparring for time, "if she left the village twenty years earlier, I guess she's got to be about forty-one or two."

"Even with the help of my marvelous makeup man, I don't know if I can really look that old."

Ingrid had liked Ben. Zanuck promptly signed him to write *The Visit*, the first of a five-picture deal, and invited us out to dinner with his current girlfriend, Irina Demick. They were waiting for us at his favorite place, Chez l'Ami Louis, near the Bastille. Zanuck was chipper and pleased with himself, and the lovely young woman opposite him glowed with happiness.

Irina Demick was not at all what I had expected. I suppose I thought she would look like a showgirl. Ben had briefed me. In Hollywood, Zanuck had been known for his insatiable sexual appetite. The expression "casting couch" had probably come into being because he kept a couch in an anteroom of his office, where, for the years of his tenure as founder-head of Twentieth Century Fox, starlets had their "screen tests." Psychoanalytically, the prevalent take on Zanuck was that, abandoned by his mother at an early age, he'd spent his life in a feverish conquest of women and competition with men.

During his long marriage to Virginia, a Mack Sennett bathing beauty, mother of his three children, he had never stopped having brief, passing affairs. In later years, in Europe, his liaisons lasted longer, usually ending because he tried unsuccessfully to give his mistresses a film career.[1]

The first of these was Bella Darvi, who gambled away a fortune of his money and eventually killed herself. We, and all Paris, were more interested in his second liaison, with Juliette Greco, a gamine-like existentialist chanteuse whose singing we'd admired at a Left Bank *boîte*. Greco was the only one of Zanuck's women who was independent and freethinking. She was also the only one who dumped him.

His ego had been terribly injured by being thrown over. Irina Demick had not only comforted him but given him a new lease on life. She'd been a model, was beautiful, and had the kind of cheekbones every woman yearns for. She wasn't actressy; she had an easy, open manner. I remember being able to relax with her, although I was still a little afraid of Zanuck.

They surprised us by speaking French to each other. Darryl's nasal French, like Ben's, was bad, he paid no attention to tenses, syntax, or gender, but was perfectly idiomatic. Even in French, Ben was a great raconteur but Irina saw to it that Darryl had the floor most of the time. Still, it was hard to hear their funny stories in French.

"*J'ai de la chance*—I'm lucky," Zanuck said. "I tried to get Brigitte Bardot for a cameo in *The Longest Day* as a female resistance fighter. I had lots of big stars playing tiny roles but Bardot wouldn't do it. That's when Irina turned up. She didn't want to be an actress. I think she just needed the money."

"*I* was lucky," she said beaming. "Without Zanuck, I would be nothing. I would be a cabbage."

I didn't have the feeling she was buttering him up. She seemed genuinely admiring of him as a filmmaker, exuded affection and good feeling. It was no wonder he was happy.

"The director's an old friend of yours, Ben," Zanuck said. "He told me he met you in Germany in 1949, that he almost worked with you on *The Devil's General*—Bernhardt Wicki. A wonderful guy. He directed the German parts of *The Longest Day*. I loved doing that film. You know, Ken Annakin,[2] the director, was great to work with. I'd always wanted to direct—and he let me direct whole scenes. I was thrilled."

Where was the angry, tyrannical, overbearing Zanuck I'd heard about? Maybe he was changing with age—or with his new love. Irina seemed like a loving daughter, glad of a fatherly guiding hand. How many women were like Sophia, who wanted a strong, wise, older man, a father figure!

Ingrid Bergman was not like that. She champed at the bit when anyone put her in an inferior position.

Irina was saying, "What exactly is the role you have in mind for me, Darryl?"

"Let Ben tell you."

"Ingrid plays a woman who comes back to the village that destroyed her youth. She was seduced and pushed into prostitution by an unscrupulous young man. The villagers were his accomplices. When Ingrid returns, he is the town's leading merchant. She is one of the wealthiest women in the world, and she promises a fortune to the townspeople if they will prosecute him, legally condemn to death the man who wronged her, and execute him. Dürrenmatt's point is that prostitution, legal or otherwise, is a matter of price." Then Ben added almost sweetly to her, "I can only describe your role this way. You play a beautiful and vulnerable young woman. Ingrid is hard and vengeful, but she is protective of you because you are her former self."

Irina gazed at Ben appreciatively. "*Ça fait du bien*—it does me good to hear you. What do you think, Darryl?"

Darryl took a big puff of his cigar, let out the smoke thoughtfully. I tried not to choke.

"I think," he pronounced, "that the part must be big enough and important enough for my Irina."

Nineteen sixty-three was also the year our daughter Luli turned seventeen and passed her first rac (the end of "high school"; she received the second baccalaureate a year later, after "Philo").

Perhaps because they were born in the States, I thought of our two eldest, Luli and John, twelve months apart, as "the American ones," and made an effort to give them an American education. In June, I brought Luli to Cambridge, Massachusetts, and enrolled her in Harvard Summer School. My dream was for her to go to Radcliffe as I had. With her good marks, the Bac, Harvard Summer School, and a mother who'd gone there, how could she fail to be accepted?

I stayed at the Hotel Commander, where Claude Shannon and I had first lived after we got married my junior year. For a few days, I helped Luli install herself in "digs" that we made cozier by doing what I had done at seventeen, buying an armchair, a throw, and cushions at The Coop on Harvard Square.

I said good-bye to Luli but remained in Cambridge an extra day ostensibly for my class reunion, my twenty-second. In truth I stayed over because I'd gotten in touch with Claude, who was teaching at MIT. He had decided to visit me surreptitiously.

February 28, 2001.

The obituary of my first husband, Claude Shannon, father of modern digital communications and information theory, lies next to me on my desk as I write this. Last night, on the radio, an MIT professor commented, "Perhaps Shannon is to the second half of the twentieth century what Einstein was to the first half."

The information content of a message, Claude theorized, consists simply of the number of 1s and 0s it takes to transmit it. Communications engineers adopted the idea and created the technology that led to today's Information Age. All communication lines are measured in bits per second, reflecting what Claude called "channel capacity." His theory made it possible to use bits in computer storage.

What is fascinating, at least to me, is that he did some of his most significant work in 1940 during our brief marriage. His master's thesis in electrical engineering, "A Symbolic Analysis of Relay and Switching Circuits," was largely motivated by the telephone industry's need to find a mathematical language to describe the behavior of the increasingly complex switching circuits that were replacing human operators, but the implications of the paper set out the basic idea on which all modern computers are built. At the same time, he received his PhD in mathematics from MIT and was awarded a National Research Fellowship, which brought us to Princeton's Institute for Advanced Study. My senior year at Radcliffe would have been 1940 to 1941. I didn't transfer to another college but worked as an economist for the League of Nations, housed in the Institute because of the war in Europe.

Claude's ideas spread beyond the field of communication into cryptology, the mathematics of probability, economics, biology, and genetics, where it has become routine to think of DNA replication in terms of information. He invented the machine that plays chess. I recall a mathematician friend of ours said to me once, "He's a genius, the only person I know whom I'd apply that word to."

But I like to remember Claude's whimsical side, how we spoke to each other in our own private intellectual-silly language, the way he loved words and repeated "Boolean" over and over for the sound of it. (He'd been inspired by a nineteenth-century mathematician, George Boole, who invented two-symbol Boolean logic.)

I can see Claude's elfish grin when he came home from his work at Bell Labs in the summer of 1940 when we lived in Greenwich Village, and told me with delight how he had ridden a unicycle up and down the lab corridors, juggling four balls, not five—his hands were too small.

In June 1963 in the Commander bar while I waited nervously for Claude, I thought of 1939, when he'd wooed me in the MIT room called "the differential analyzer," which used a precisely honed system of shafts, gears, wheels, and disks to solve equations in calculus. I thought, too, of his e. e. cummings–like verse, and the way he accompanied Bix Beiderbecke on his clarinet.

My father died on March 20, 1940, shortly after Claude and I were married. We lived in an apartment at 19 Garden Street, Cambridge. My sister phoned to tell us when to come down to New York for the funeral. Claude said, "I liked your father but you go alone. I hate funerals."

I sobbed. "Okay," Claude said. "I'll come on one condition, that the night of the funeral we spend at the Village Vanguard in Greenwich Village with Bobby Hackett on trumpet, Art Bernstein on bass, and Georgie Wettling on drums."

Claude appeared at the door to the hotel bar, putting an end to my reverie. He crossed to my table without hesitation, sat down. When I tried to say, "Hi, Claude," I found I'd lost my voice. He hadn't changed. He'd become more attractive, less boyish, surer of himself. He was still bony, his high cheekbones pronounced, his hair black. Brilliance shot out of his eyes. My stomach was doing flip-flops. I tried again to speak. Nothing came out.

"Why did you leave me?" he demanded, his voice trembling with fury.

I tried to answer but still nothing came out. Voiceless, I gestured for paper and pen, which he gave me. I wrote: "You were sick and wouldn't get help."

"You should have stayed!" he fired at me angrily.

I scribbled, "How are you now?"

"I have a nice wife, wonderful kids. I teach, do research. I have a collection of twenty-three cars. I tinker." He was still angry but could laugh at himself. "Tinker" made him laugh, a lovely laugh that lit up the somber brilliant face.

I put out my hand and smiled at him. He took it. First, he squeezed it between his two hands, then he took my hand to his mouth and pressed his lips ever so gently into the palm of my hand.

We went upstairs to my room and made love. My voice came back and we talked for hours.

"Are you happy?" he asked.

"Reasonably. And you?"

"Reasonably."

The next day, I attended my class reunion. My classmates were full of Betty Friedan. *The Feminine Mystique* had just been published.

Maurine said, "They took a survey of our class, the class of '41. Eighty-five percent of us started out wanting it all, husbands, children, career. After twenty years, most of us have two out of three: careers but no husbands, and we bring up our children alone. Others remain single or simply don't have children."

Kitty groaned. "College girls today just want husbands. They don't try to have careers. Fewer women are going to college than ever before."

"It's since the war ended," Maurine argued. "There's been this big concerted effort to get us back into the home. Our lovely consumer society wants women in the home so they'll buy the dishwashers."

"Not our consumer society," I corrected. "The big corporations."

Kitty and Maurine laughed. "We all know where you stand," Maurine said.

"Goodness!" said Kitty. "You're still pinko!"

Two or three weeks after my return to France, Ben and I received a letter from Luli saying she'd transferred to NYU Summer School. She'd met the charismatic son of our friends Joe and Rhoda Bellfort. Children of American progressives, brought up in France, interested in filmmaking, Luli and David Bellfort had much in common. Luli had sold the Harvard Coop decor and moved to New York. I couldn't help but compare her behavior with mine when I'd given up my senior year at Harvard to accompany Claude to the Institute for Advanced Study in Princeton. Why couldn't David Bellfort have moved to Cambridge, I asked myself.

Ben was struggling over two or three sets of screenplay pages interspersed with pink, pale blue, and yellow correction sheets whose margins were covered with Zanuck's cramped handwriting. "Too many cooks!" Ben grumbled. "Ingrid, Irina . . . !"

Zanuckia, Oasis for a Lost Bronstonian

The Visit could have been a stunning film. Instead, it was one of the worst failures of Ingrid's career. We shuddered when we finally saw it at Cannes. Bernhardt Wicki, the director, sat next to me, hiding his head on my shoulder. "I know, I know," he whispered. "I am heffy, heffy." "Heavy" with a German accent.

The film wasn't light and ironic. Those weren't the only things wrong with it. Tony Quinn said the worst mistake was that "Ingrid chose to play the part sympathetically. . . . It was Ingrid," Tony went on, "who taught me that you can tell an actress that she's a lousy cook and she will forgive you; you can tell her she's lousy in bed and she'll explain it away; but God forgive you if you question her acting . . ." [3] Quinn was frequently quoted on his Ingrid Bergman reflections. "I liked Ingrid so much that I seemed to lose my identity. I wasn't fighting for my identity. She was so dominant. She was too strong for the average man. She was even too strong for Mr. Lars Schmidt [her third husband]. I don't think Ingrid wanted to dominate but she was such an enormous personality that she dominated everything around her . . ." [4]

While *The Visit* was shooting in Rome, Darryl sent for Ben. This time, Ben took me along. The Ecumenical Congress was in session and we were appalled to learn that Zanuck had had a bishop dislodged from the Excelsior Hotel to make room for us.

At breakfast at Doney's on Via Veneto, Ben and Tony Quinn were reunited, having rarely seen each other since the days of *Back to Bataan* in 1945. Tony greeted me warmly, even flirtatiously. Full of machismo, he barely gave the time of day to a woman unless he judged her "fuckable." I felt he was an insufferable male chauvinist pig and my feelings would years later destroy an important project we had with him.

In 1963 at Doney's on Via Veneto, Tony Quinn was holding forth as if he were one of us. He too had had his run-ins with McCarthysim. "In Hollywood," Tony said, "Zanuck called me into his office and started asking me questions about my friends. I said, 'Are you asking me if I am a member of the Communist Party? The answer might as well be yes because I won't say any different.' Zanuck replied, 'Don't be a fool, Tony.

You don't have a contract. If there's any doubt about you, no one will hire you.' I took Katherine and the kids to New York," Tony said, "and got a part in a play."

Ben laughed. "Now Zanuck's proud he knows us."

Doney's. Via Veneto. The Excelsior. Ben and Lewis Milestone had stayed at the Excelsior and had left me at home with the children. For some reason, maybe because he was more successful, maybe because I was less of a threat, Ben was able to be nicer to me.

A car with driver spirited us out to Cinecittà, the studio where my picture *Finishing School (Luxury Girls)* had been shot a dozen years earlier.

The minute we were on the set, we could feel the heat, the passion, as Ingrid and Tony didn't play the love scene so much as they seemed to be ensnared in it. My God! The *chemistry* between them, his animal vitality, her exquisite beauty and strength. The *real thing.* Not Heston's ersatz gazing at Sophia adoringly, but over her left ear; Sophia's sensuality hiding her desire to clobber him. Ingrid and Tony were making love! Years later, Tony would say: "I fell in love with my sublime costar. It took the cocoon of a motion picture set to bring us together."

After the last take, Ingrid sidled by Ben, whispered to him, "Tony bit my nipple—"

Back at the Excelsior afterward, Ben remembered that everyone in Rome has afternoonsies and that when in Rome, one must do as the Romans do. We scurried up to our room, peeled off our clothes, jumped into bed like feverish youngsters—and made another baby, our last.

In the summer of 1963, with too many projects and too much everything, a cable came from the States. Ben's mother's doctor said if Ben wanted to see her alive, he better come at once. Ben applied to the U.S. consulate at Nice for a "visa of compassion." They checked with the Paris embassy, which refused, despite the fact that in a recent case similar to Ben's the U.S. Supreme Court had reinstated the naturalized citizen's American nationality, and our attorney Leonard Boudin had assured us that soon Ben would once again be a U.S. citizen.

Zanuckia, Oasis for a Lost Bronstonian

Ben did not wait for further news. He made a melodramatic, illegal crossing from Canada to the U.S. at a place where he judged he wouldn't be noticed, since a Canadian attorney warned him that he risked a sentence in an American penitentiary for illegal entry.

Ben was stopped at a lonely customs barrier. It was twenty below zero. An American customs official, who fortunately couldn't find his reading glasses, read Ben's name wrong, "Carsman?" he asked. Ben nodded. He made it back to Los Angeles to see his mother.

Mumma knew she was dying, Ben told me when he returned to France. On seeing him suddenly appear, she had smiled and said, "Now I don't care. I've seen you again." Then, with a shrug and another wan smile, "I know, I know. I've seen you. Big deal."

Ben told her about the aging Russian Cossacks who had become Paris taxi drivers, and she almost laughed. "Sometimes," she whispered, "life fools you. . . . Tigers become pussycats."

Ben had to sneak in and out of Hollywood to avoid being picked up for illegal entry. The only person he saw besides Mumma was Adrian Scott.

Adrian had married Joan in 1956 after he'd been released from jail. They were living in the San Fernando Valley in a tiny tract house. Ben had never met Joan. She was pretty, anxious, and anxious-making. Ben wondered why Adrian always chose neurotic women—Dorothy, Annie, Madeleine, and now Joan.[5] Ben wrote that he'd concluded that Adrian was "compassionate, not passionate," that although he appeared fragile, he needed to take care of someone.

However, at the time Ben sneaked in to see Adrian, Joan was working at Disney on her own as Joanne Court and was also fronting for Adrian on several television series.

Joan and Adrian were preparing to leave for England, where a friend had a job waiting for him. To Ben, they seemed to be comparatively happy to be leaving except that Joan had developed a real relationship with "Uncle Walt," was writing a feature for Disney, and had a future career assured if she remained.

While Ben was with them, Joan had a migraine, which often laid her low, she said, and Adrian was having his "usual belly pains." Adrian was not the man Ben had known twenty years before, the writer-producer with the promise of a stratospheric future. He was prematurely "old," bone-weary, but was still the same splendid human being.

Several months after the death of Ben's mother, two official registered letters arrived. The first, from the State Department, announced that after nine years of having been denied his American nationality, he was now, once again, a United States citizen. The letter didn't ask if he wished to be an American citizen, simply advised him he was.

The second letter was from the U.S. Internal Revenue Service asking for nine years' back taxes, from 1954 to 1963, during the period when Ben was stateless.

Ben and I composed a letter to the IRS stating that we did not believe anyone in their right mind would demand income tax from someone whose country had not facilitated their travel, nor provided public schools for their children, nor highways to drive upon. We added that we had happily paid income tax to France, which had provided us with all those things and much more. We sent a copy to our lawyer, and never heard any more about it.

31

The Blue Max

When Ben's American citizenship was restored, it meant we could consider visiting the States for the first time in fifteen years, and that Ben could work there. But 1964 was not the time to travel. In April, we had our seventh and last child, the girl we'd been waiting for, Suzo.[1] She was especially welcome since our only other daughter, Luli, was showing signs of flying the coop, which would have left us in a male, toilet-seat-up habitat.

Not only our new baby's arrival made travel impossible. Ben had another Sophia film to save and two Zanuck projects waiting. Luli and John would soon go to college in the States, but we still had an exciting set of children at home and their delightful Françoise, who stayed for almost ten years. Moreover, our home in Mougins, from 1964 to 1973, had become a center of the new international cinema, not just during the Cannes Film Festival.

We also returned frequently to our house in Paris, where we received the first Chinese film delegation, Wei-man Seto, head of Beijing Studio, and Lin Yi, a woman screenwriter with whom I remained friends for years. They took us to a twenty-three-course banquet at a Chinese restaurant on the Left Bank for which they had the food flown in from China. But most of the socializing was at Mougins at Sunday *déjeuner* on the terrace. Film historian Georges Sadoul, his wife, Ruta, and her daughter, Yvonne Baby, editor of the film pages of *Le Monde,* brought us Brazil's brilliant young director Glauber Rocha, whose *Antonio das Mortes* ushered in Third World Cinema. Also new film-makers like Uri Zohar of Israel, Lakhdar-Hamina of Algeria, Juan Bardem of Spain, and Michael Cacoyannis of Greece. Of course, the committed Italian directors, Basilio's friends, were always around—Elio Petri, Citto Maselli, Francesco Rosi, Mario Monicelli. And the "uncles" were constantly in attendance: Sidney Buchman, blacklisted screen-writer of some of Hollywood's most successful comedies (*Talk of the Town*) who'd headed Columbia during its best years; Basilio Franchina who collaborated with Ben throughout the 1960s and brought fabu-lous ice cream desserts from the most elegant *glacier.* The "honorary uncles" were film salesman Don Getz and his brother-in-law, producer Jules Buck.

I knew that from 1957 on, except for *Lawrence of Arabia,* Jules Buck had produced the Peter O'Toole films: *Becket, The Lion in Winter, The Ruling Class.* "Jules," I said one Sunday, "when Ben and I first arrived in London in 1949, we saw a play about World War I that wasn't very good. *The Long and the Tall and the Short of It.* But there was a mar-velous young actor with jet black hair and an enormous beak of a nose. His name was Peter O'Toole—"

Jules looked up and laughed. "That was him! The real McCoy! When I met him eight years later, he was jobless, in debt, and barely hanging on. I settled his debts, suggested he go blond and have his nose bobbed. We started a company together. Suddenly, I owned a star!"

Jules's charming wife, Joyce, obviously felt her husband had been indelicate, but by that time, those who wanted to avoid hearing Sidney Buchman's lecture on how to smoke a cigar were moving their seats nearer to Basilio, who was telling his utterly silly story of Sister Jes-selmina. Actually, we were all waiting for Sunil Dutt, India's foremost producer-director-actor, to bring forth the curry, which he'd spent the day cooking. Ben issued a loud huzzah as he spied Sunil carrying a steaming platter in our direction. Everyone scurried back to their places at table as Narghiz, Sunil's very young movie-star wife, known throughout the East for her attendance of international peace congresses, led the applause for him.[2]

At one of these luncheons, Ben, who always sat at the head of the long table, caught the eye of a teenage girl sitting far down at the other end next to Aaron. Ben squinted at her. "Do I know you?" he asked warmly with a charming smile.

"You know my father," she answered, "but I don't look like him. I look like his paintings."

Aaron, who had brought her, giggled. The girl giggled. "I'm a Picasso," she said.

It's difficult to describe Ben's charisma at this stage of his life. He had always been charming, like a magnet, drawing people to him to listen to his "raconting" skills. But something new had been added. In his castle, with his chatelaine, his princes and princelings, he was very much lord of the manor and looked it. It seemed appropriate that he was stocky, with enormously wide shoulders, broad chest, mustache, now well trimmed, distinguished, with a touch of gray at the temples.

He was on an Air France plane from Nice to Paris when the flight attendant approached respectfully, and bowed. "Your Highness, would you prefer to sit up front?" she asked diffidently, mistaking him for Prince Rainier, who took that flight almost daily.

"*Non, merci,*" Ben replied. "*Je suis bien où je suis.*"

Yes, those years in Mougins, in spite of bitterness, he was "well where he was." That period was filled with work, which was, of course, everything to him. When he was happy, he was ravishing. It was hard not to fall in love with him, but when I'd see him down at the end of the swimming pool with Basilio, under a parasol, talking story structure, I burned with frustration and jealousy. Why didn't I just close myself off and write? I don't know why I couldn't. There were a hundred reasons, and none.

At that time, aside from Louis Malle, who had Ben speak about the blacklist on his radio program, we weren't yet close to the emerging French New Wave, the celebrated *Nouvelle Vague* directors—Chabrol, Truffaut, and Godard. As early as 1959, we'd been *bouleversé,* thrown into an uproar by the New Wave when Betsy Blair phoned and asked: "Would you like to see *Hiroshima Mon Amour?*" Betsy and her French actor husband, Roger Pigaud, met us at a cinema on Avenue Wagram. We were not prepared for what we were to see. Betsy and I came out dazed. The four of us walked to the corner café. "Hiroshima," I said, "it's as if Resnais is crying out, 'How can people do that to people?'"

Betsy and I let the men know that something significant had happened to us, that we thought this film would launch a new era in filmmaking. Betsy proclaimed Marguerite Duras's screenplay, "Utterly free. Movies will never be the same."

Ben was subdued. He didn't like the movie but wasn't ready to argue.

"It's the way Resnais uses space and time," Betsy went on. "It's not like any movie I've ever seen."

"I don't exactly understand." I was puzzling it out. "Certainly time and space are treated as—something you can film."

"Although he has editors, Resnais does most of it himself," Ben said. "He's a great editor. The way he chooses images, frames them—the rhythm. But I don't particularly like this film."

"*Evidemment!* Of course not!" Roger agreed loudly. "It's not a good picture. It's didactic. It says 'War is bad. Atomic war is impossible.' But we know that!" His chair was perched precariously on the edge of a step. He waved his arms and he and the chair flew backward down the steps. Roger was hurt only mildly. "I'm an actor," he reassured us. "I know how to fall."

After *Hiroshima Mon Amour,* I paid more attention to the film journal *Cahiers du Cinema* and to what was going on in the film world, which led me to Agnes Varda, the director who really made the first New Wave film, *La Pointe Courte (The Short Point),* in 1954. Of course, she had the greatest film editor in the world, a young man named Alain Resnais, who, when he saw her footage, agreed to work for free.[3] I knew her only slightly until October 2000, when we met again at the Vienna

Film Festival, where I was invited to introduce a month of blacklist films. Varda's new film, *Les Glaneurs et La Glaneuse (The Gleaners and I)*, was one of the best documentaries I'd ever seen. In it, she meets with men and women along the roads of France who are gatherers, recyclers, treasure hunters. Out of necessity or choice, they deal with what others have discarded. "Who are these gleaners?" I asked her. "We are," she replied, "cineastes. We pick up everything others have discarded." I invited Varda to come along with a few writers and directors from the festival to see Vienna. "No," she said, getting out at the museum. "I need to see the Klees."

Our good friends Guy and Henrietta Endore, whom we hadn't seen since 1949, visited us in Mougins on their way back to the States after a disappointment. The film he was working on in Madrid for Phil Yordan, *Nightrunners of Bengal*, like so many projects, was never made.

Guy, a distinguished author of several novels, of which *King of Paris*, about the Dumas, *père et fils*, had been a Book-of-the-Month selection, was a blacklisted screenwriter who for no apparent reason never received a subpoena. I adored Guy. He was a close friend of my cousin Henry, had some of the same wit and whimsy, an oddball humor, and a lively interest in esoteric subjects like witchcraft. His curly ginger hair matched his fey personality. Guy ate only fruits and nuts and by the end of a meal, a mountain of peels and shells covered his plate. We felt he needed something more substantial like meat because his skin was translucent and he was cold to the touch.

His wife, Henrietta, had worked in nursery education as a teacher and principal. She was an expert in her field of child care but after years of parents coming to her for advice, she'd taken on the persona of a professional psychologist—which she was not. I admired Henrietta's plain folksy beauty, no makeup, long straight hair brushed back, tightly, severely, and large faded blue-denim skirts with aprons and hand-woven shawls.

I picked up the Endores at the airport and in the week that followed drove them to everything they wanted to see up and down the coast.

They wouldn't rent a car. American tourists frequently become like children. Not only could they not drive, they couldn't even make a phone call to English-speaking American Express, which meant that I was "on" all the time. Imagine my dismay when Henrietta said, "You don't give the children much time."

That was my first hint that Henrietta disapproved of me. Guy was adorable, seemed to love everything and enjoy his visit.

On Sunday, the day they left, Ben and I were driving to Sainte-Maxime to see Mike and Zelma Wilson but first we delivered Guy and Henrietta to the airport. I accompanied them to the gate, beyond which I could not go. Guy hugged me and was off. Henrietta grabbed my hands, looked into my eyes, and said, "Forgive me." Then she turned away and was gone.

When I returned to the car, Ben wasn't speaking to me, and wouldn't answer when I asked what was wrong. In the two-hour ride through Sunday traffic, I was finally able to ascertain the following: Henrietta had told Ben that I cared more about my Golden Bantam than I did about my children, to whom I no longer read at night, that I was a bad mother, and that he should get a divorce. She had spoken to him, he said, with the authority of a professional counselor. She had been convincing. Ben had accepted what she said. I couldn't make sense of it, finally deciding her behavior was that of a twisted, bitter woman. I tried to go over everything about their visit but only arrived at a guess, that perhaps Guy had been too admiring of me and of the way we lived. Ben admitted that Americans were set in their ways, and that everything had to be according to the latest in psychotherapy. We spoke about what we thought was wrong with the Endores. We never did discuss what was wrong with ourselves, and I never admitted to Ben that I felt frustrated and bitterly disappointed with my life.

The visit of Liz and Millard Lampell was in a class by itself. To this day I am still ashamed. Ben and I stood in the huge hallway downstairs while Millard, not drunk, batted Liz around the upstairs bedroom. I begged Ben to stop it. "It's none of our business," he said tightly, "and if you interfere, you'll probably get your teeth knocked out." I didn't know what to do and so we did nothing. Ben had never hit me, my father never hit me, but they did shout and rage, which was painful and scary in other ways.

The Scotts' visit was agonizing. I don't like to remember it. For many, the end of the 1960s meant the end of the blacklist. For Adrian and Joan Scott, their predicament worsened. The project that had brought him to England petered out. Though Adrian had another waiting for him in Hollywood, both he and Joan felt that, too, wasn't going to work out, which it didn't. The day they arrived in Mougins was sunny, teeming with children and laughter. It was as if *they* didn't belong there.

Joan was trying to look perky. She was small, pretty, with lavishly abundant hair. Her expression was pained. This was the first time I met her. Ben had told me about her migraines. After supper, she put on a tailored dressing gown and rejoined us. Something about her appearance had changed. She saw me staring at her. "You see the difference?" she asked. I nodded. "I had a wig on before," she said. "I hate my hair. You see how thin it is?"

She hated herself. "I can't get my hair to look nice," she went on explaining, "so I travel with a wig. My twin has the same hair but she looks okay. It's always been that way. For her, everything's great. She gets everything, she's always first. Zif—you know Zif—he was your analyst. Zif gave me something so I could remember way way back—intra-uterine. Jean, my twin, was first—she even came into the world first. But I gave her a kick." Joan didn't laugh. Adrian didn't laugh either. Afterward, she got a migraine and he had one of his bellyaches.

Adrian was utterly sad and hopeless. He had seemed forlorn when I first saw him sitting on our doorstep just after Ben and I were married. But two minutes later, we were jolly and laughing together. This time, he was despondent. We found no way to pull him out of it. He was going back to a Hollywood that had rejected him. The world had rejected him. That was the last time we saw him.

Besides the Endores, Lampells, and Scotts, a constant stream of houseguests poured into Mougins once our friends could obtain passports. Janet Stevenson, Lester Cole, my cousin Henry Myers, Lou and

Wilma Solomon's daughter, Dinah, and Al Levitt. Bobby and Jeannie Lees were a delight, so also the Hirsches and Bocours, but on the whole, these visits were depressing. What stands out in my mind was the 1973 New Year's visit of people we did not know.

For days, our sons Daniel, sixteen, and Paulo, fifteen, had ridden their bicycles up and down the Côte from Monte Carlo to Saint-Tropez, distributing leaflets announcing an anti–Vietnam War mass meeting. We'd been asked casually if we would *héberge*—put up at our house— the Vietnamese delegation to the Paris Peace Conference. Of course Ben and I said yes. We were thrilled. It was our first and only political act on foreign soil and I'm glad to say it was not "in the best interests of the United States" in their war against Vietnam.

What flashed through my mind? The Vietnamese baby alone in the middle of the road, crying for her dead mother. And then, there they were! The Vietnamese! The station wagon that had brought them from Paris climbed the long curved driveway, stopped in the middle of our carpark. I was the first to see them. Choked up, I precipitated myself toward them, Ben followed in a panting run, then the children, all except Suzo, who had the measles and watched from a window on the floor above.

The station wagon doors flew open. Four men and four women of all ages. A woman headed the delegation. I have never been so moved. I kissed and hugged them and wept. They kissed and hugged us and wept. Again and again, we embraced amid tears. Americans and Vietnamese!

That night, two thousand people in the Palais, home of the Cannes Film Festival, rose to their feet, cheering and applauding the eight Vietnamese who bowed and applauded back. I don't remember the speeches; I only remember the spirit. Two thousand French in the audience, mostly young, were saying *no* to the U.S. bombing of Hanoi a few days earlier.

After the meeting, we returned to the *mas,* feasted with our Vietnamese guests, and talked most of the night until we tucked them into bed in various parts of the house.

* * *

The Blue Max

Actually, during those years at Mougins, from 1963 to 1973, we had more than one impromptu, unscheduled visit, frequently unrewarding but once in a while, priceless.

In the latter category fell the visit of Lawrence Durrell, author of *The Alexandria Quartet*. Because Ben and Basilio were working on *Judith*, a vehicle for Sophia, based on an unpublished novella of his, Durrell had dropped in on us unannounced, bringing with him Peter Sellers and wife Britt Ecklund.

Durrell, a pleasant, sandy-haired Englishman who looked like a clerk, was unremarkable except that it was surprising to hear a distinguished world literary figure complain about needing money. He explained that his house in Provence still had an earthen floor, which I guess was why he'd written *Judith*.

Peter Sellers was so funny I almost fell in the pool. Ben, who'd just returned from a week at the New Delhi Film Festival, where he'd represented France, told Peter Sellers he'd been struck by the accuracy of his Indian and Pakistani stage accents. Peter, delighted, launched into a dialogue using the accents of a Pakistani student with an Oxonian accent and an Indian student with an Oxonian accent, explaining to each other the subtle differences between their accents. Then Peter regaled us with uproariously funny tales of how he had lived and died in L.A. and been brought back to life by four interns and a doctor at Cedars Intensive Care Unit. Irrepressible Peter proceeded to terrorize us by diving into our cold unheated pool, which, he explained afterward, could have hydrocuted him. Durrell talked a bit about *Judith* and the writing of it, didn't seem any more enthusiastic about it than we were. *Judith* was a cloak-and-dagger epic set in the first year of Israel's statehood. At every Cannes festival, year after year, we'd seen Kurt Unger, a lonely, unsmiling Israeli producer who'd never produced, wandering around with a toothpick in his mouth. Having convinced the head of Paramount, Karpf, a big wheel in the United Jewish Appeal, to back *Judith*, Unger finally made a deal with Carlo Ponti. Sophia was to play a Jewish concentration-camp survivor who comes to Israel to hunt for the Nazi husband who betrayed her. According to Carlo, the first screenplay of

Judith, by J. P. Miller, was so anti-Arab that the Arab world would have boycotted all of Sophia's movies. John Michael Hayes had rewritten, but many problems remained, which Ben was supposed to solve.

One of the perks for Ben's tackling the "horrendous" script of *Judith* was a movie job for Aaron, fifteen, who wanted to write and direct. Basilio subsidized his nephew and three other young Italian filmmakers to make a documentary about the making of *Judith,* and arranged for Aaron to go with them to Israel as assistant. That led to our friend Joris Ivens, the great Dutch documentary filmmaker, hiring Aaron as his assistant on *Le Mistral* the following year.[4]

After *The Visit* bombed, Zanuck, considerably weakened, did more and more work through Fox England. *The Longest Day,* the zillion-dollar film about D-Day, had given Zanuck his comeback. The reward to his old friend Elmo Williams, who gave him the strength to see it through, was to install him as chief of the London office and head of Fox Film Production in Europe.

Elmo Williams, about forty, a well-known Hollywood executive, had been working in movies since he was nineteen, principally in cutting rooms. Like Zanuck, he had a reputation for being able to fix anything. Ben liked Elmo, who was knowledgeable and energetic. Elmo found an early aviation epic, a Jack D. Hunter novel, *The Blue Max,* about a German World War I flying ace, and convinced George Peppard, at the height of his popularity, to play a German. This was not easy to do. With Ben's extremely long, full treatment of *The Blue Max,* Elmo interested John Guillermin, a rising young British director, and sent him down to us in Mougins to discuss it.

The English loved to hold meetings on the Côte d'Azur. Guillermin showed up around noon.[5] Ben had told me to stick around. I served Bloody Marys. Guillermin, in his cold, stiff-lipped manner, began by saying it was ghastly to have to do a picture that showed how lovely the Germans were—even if we were talking about the Germans of 1914 to 1918, twenty years before Hitler.

"It's a question of class," Ben explained. "The Junkers, the landed aristocracy in Prussia, had some of those qualities we associate with the

Nazis, but not the people. Many Germans were socialist then, warmly disposed to their brothers, the French workers, and did not want war."

Guillermin was not happy. He said, "I have only one difficulty with your treatment."

"What's that?" Ben asked.

"How can you make a film about someone who's not sympathetic? The hero, George Peppard, is not sympathetic."

"That's because he's a Junker, a landed aristocrat, a forerunner of a Nazi. He's not supposed to be sympathetic."

"The audience won't stick with it, an unsympathetic hero. I tell you what," said Guillermin, suddenly very British. "You don't need to think so hard. It's easy to make him sympathetic. Just give him a little dog."

"Just give him a little dog" became our shorthand for a phony way of dealing with a story problem. Some of Ben's contempt in that meeting must have showed. The result: he received only story credit.

In the spring of 1965, Suzo was a year old and could travel. Ben said, "Now." I knew what he meant: rent a house in Beverly Hills for the summer. I wrote Anne Shirley (Annie Scott, now Mrs. Charlie Lederer), who lived on Beverly Drive. Although I hadn't forgiven her for what she'd done to Adrian, we still corresponded. Her reply was: "You can have Rory Calhoun's house at the corner of Sunset and Bedford. It's enormous, room for all seven children."

It was expensive but I figured we could rent Mougins to offset the cost. Almost immediately, Alex North called. "My houseguest, Judy Prince, is looking for a house to rent around here for the summer. Can I send her down to you?"

Judy was a delight. Daughter of our friends Ethel Tyne (wife of black-listed actor Buddy Tyne) and film composer Saul Chaplin, Judy was married to Broadway's hottest young producer, Harold Prince. Judy was enthralled with the *mas*. "Just what we want," she cried enthusiastically, "a farmhouse, no pretensions, acres and acres to run around in, the tennis court, the pool—and that darling little gatekeeper's cottage where we can put friends."

I apologized for its being rather simple and not well kept up, but she was all for it. "It's perfect for summer when you want to relax. Hal will love it." As for price, I told her it had to cover the rent we were going to be paying at the other end.

Fine, fine. Great, great. We had long-distance phone calls from Hal, confirming all this. Then we took off, Nice to Paris. Paris to New York.

At U.S. Customs at La Guardia, we presented our fresh green passports and Françoise her new navy-blue French one. We were stopped. "She," said the customs official, pointing to Françoise, "may pass. I'm afraid *you* may not," he said, looking us all over. "And the baby stays." Françoise was carrying Suzo.

"I stay," said Françoise, her large blue eyes staring at her first American official.

"But I was born in New York City," I said. "I was just here two years ago. What's the problem?"

"You are here with your family," he replied.

"But that's silly," I replied. "We're all U.S. citizens except Françoise."

"You are on a list. Until there is an okay, you'll have to stay in there—and wait." He pointed to a tiny glass cubicle.

The sweat was pouring down me. It was a steamy hot New York June. He marched us toward the glass cubicle. On the way, I saw, over the side of a railing, in a milling throng of people, a gyrating man, waving his arms wildly. Joe Hirsch. He was trying to signal "V." I thought V for Victory, but then he fashioned an "O." He had difficulty making an "R," and an "S." "T," he could manage. V O R S T. My favorite New York restaurant. Then he mimed being a fish, swimming in water, and with his arms, made lots of "O's," little round things. SHAD ROE. My favorite dish that time of year. He'd reserved a table for dinner at Vorst's and they were saving us shad roe. His charade made the more than two-hour wait in the cubicle, standing up, without water, more bearable.

At last, the official said, "We've got the okay. Now, just a few questions. Where can we reach you at all times? And how long are you staying?"

Ben was quiet.

"We're not international spies," I said. "We're U.S. citizens coming home. You don't have a right to ask us that. I'm going to report all this."

"The sooner you answer," he said coldly, "the sooner you'll be out of here."

"Aren't you ashamed frightening these children?" I demanded. Daniel, Paulo, and Marco looked at him as if he were from another planet. Aaron tried to look aloof. Fortunately, Luli and John were already in America. "What must they think?" I went on. "This is their introduction to the United States."

"Madam," he said, "all I'm asking is your address."

"The whole summer we will be living in Rory Calhoun's house," I replied, certain this jerk would be familiar with the name of a top western star. "603 North Bedford at the corner of Sunset Boulevard, Beverly Hills." He said nothing.

After sixteen years, we came back to Los Angeles and found it burning! By chance, we had hit the very moment when the black community was fed up. Summer 1965.

Ben had planned to show the children where we'd lived, the *Examiner* building at Olympic and 11th where I'd worked, the studios, Chinatown, Japantown, the Latino district, and the black neighborhoods. "In the old days," he told the kids, "blues singers would try to out-sing each other at weekly sessions at the clubs. Afterwards, they—and I—gorged ourselves on gumbo."

But smoke choked the air all the way to Hollywood. Cars appeared, their fenders busted, their windshields smashed. Frightened drivers warned us to go no farther.

The terrifying violence of Watts had exploded. Officially, over thirty-five people died. Whole blocks were burned or destroyed. A friend of Ben's, an Army doctor, said he hadn't seen wounds as savage even in the South Pacific. From then on, all summer, we didn't dare leave Beverly Hills.

Our French children considered that privileged part of Beverly Hills, and Rory Calhoun's particularly select section of it, a slum. All that open grass in front of it like public gardens, not properly fenced or walled as

French villas are, and separated only by a driveway from the house of our neighbor Johnny Green, the composer.[6] When Green's teenage daughter came over, graciously welcomed us in French, and asked if there was anything they could do to help us, our children didn't understand. In France, people don't come into your house that way, unless invited.

Included in the rent was a maid who curtsied and a housekeeper who showed us over the house, its three wet bars, its projection room, while repeating endlessly that the Calhouns were simple people who lived simply. Luli, just starting at UCLA Film School, shot the house with the housekeeper's voice-over. Luli's student film was called *Them*.

Soon after our arrival, Hal Prince phoned from our house in Mougins. He'd been trying to reach us while we were still in New York. "I have nothing nice to say," he began.

"What's the matter?" I cried.

"Your place is run-down. How can one entertain? There isn't enough pool furniture."

I stopped him. "Go buy what you need at our outdoor-furniture store. Charge it to us."

"But it's so primitive!"

"Hal," I said. "Judy saw it and loved it. It's a summer place. It doesn't have satin walls. It's a farmhouse with a pool and tennis court. If you don't like it, go. The agency can still get summer renters."

"I don't want to go anywhere," he said petulantly. "I just want you to know your house stinks!"

We had a few more calls like that. After a while, it simmered down but the aftermath was horrendous. Not the hundreds of dollars of outdoor furniture he charged to us—I liked what he'd chosen. But he left us with a two-thousand-dollar phone bill that he said was fair because he had paid too high a rent. We heard that, when they got back to New York, Hal Prince made fun of us at dinner parties. Even that, I didn't mind so much.

Ben taught me some fine Yiddish words, several of which have crept into the English language. A useful one is *chutzpah*. Ben defined chutzpah this way: a young man who kills his mother and father pleads with the court for mercy on the grounds that he's an orphan. In our little gatekeeper's cottage, where Hal Prince kept his houseguest, Tony Perkins, Hal had run up a wall between the tiny kitchen and living-dining area because Tony was sensitive to cooking odors! Hal Prince had chutzpah.

We gave a party for the Party, that is, for the old comrade-friends left behind. Some didn't attend because they didn't dare to cross the city. Violence was everywhere, not just in Watts. Most of our friends showed signs of wear and despair, of energy and courage, and some even of hope. Al and Helen Levitt, who were writing TV together, seemed happy, Bobby Lees was pleased that Jeannie had created a terrific store called Town and Travel, Adrian and his wife, Joan Scott, were in England. Janet Stevenson and her new lovely husband, Benson, glowed with sun-and-sea-glazed color from a sailboat trip around the world, which she later wrote about in *Woman Aboard.*[7]

Ben went to see Sammy Weisbord at the William Morris office to remind him that many of the films he'd done in Europe were festival pictures. It was clear that Sammy thought of Ben as a European screenwriter, just as Joe Losey had become a European director. "The blacklist is over," Sammy explained. "But they think you're out of touch."

One of the reasons we stayed in New York for a few days after our return from California was to take John to Harvard. He had been accepted. And here John was, dyspeptic about the whole thing, unwilling to speak English. We drove with fellow Harvard students Jim Lardner and Timmy Hunter, sons of blacklisted Ring Lardner, Jr., and Ian Hunter, left John Barzman in Cambridge to *débrouiller*—to cope—and went on our way.

On our return to France, we discovered that Zanuck was anxious for Ben to compress all four volumes of Durrell's *Alexandria Quartet* into one film, *Justine,* the title role to be played by Elizabeth Taylor, and waif-like Melissa by Irina Demick.

Ben knew it was going to be a ballbreaker but he'd become philosophical. He had no more illusions since his meeting with Sammy

Weisbord about working in Hollywood—even though *The Blue Max* was "socko at the B.O."

Ben had to do spade work to condense the four novels, but he was lucky. Though many people had the beautifully bound four volumes on their bookshelves, I was one of the few who'd read them all and could spare Ben some of the work, though it was too difficult a task, finally, to deal with the complexity of characters, plots, themes, settings that should have been in four films.

Several screenwriters after Ben had a stab at it. *Justine* was eventually made with Anouk Aimée and Anna Karina. It was an awful flop.

Nine months later, my Radcliffe classmates were gathering in June 1966 for our twenty-fifth reunion. At the same time, I could see how John was getting on at Harvard.

On the way to Cambridge, I stopped in New York to see my dear friend Ruth. After her divorce from Joe Hirsch, she had married a wonderful man, a manufacturer of artists' materials, Leonard Bocour. A frustrated painter, Lenny liked to help poor artists. He gave them brushes and paints. They gave him their paintings. Leonard and Ruth had one of the most outstanding private collections of contemporary art. Their immense Riverside Drive apartment overwhelmed with Mark Rothkos, Jackson Pollocks, Morris Louises, Philip Gustons, Helen Frankenthalers, Frank Stellas, Roy Lichtensteins. One of the pleasures of New York was staying with them. That was my first time, but from then on over three decades I visited them dozens of times, living with art as you cannot in a museum.[8]

While at Ruth's, I telephoned John to tell him when I'd be arriving. I hadn't seen him for one whole year, not since Ben and I had dragged him to Cambridge, not knowing whether he was able or willing to speak English, which he hadn't spoken since he was four. All year his letters (in French) described the university, the curriculum, his professors, said nothing about himself.

I rang the number he'd given me. "May I speak to John Barzman?" I asked.

The Blue Max

A voice as American as apple pie answered. "Hi, Mom."

Goose prickles worked their way up my arms, around to the back of my neck. "John!" I asked, "How are you?"

"Fine. When are you coming?"

"John," I said again, "is it all right—Harvard? I mean, can you stand it there? I always told you, if at the end of the year, you didn't like it, you could transfer wherever you wanted, France, England." When he didn't reply, I asked, "Do you like it?"

Pause. "I don't like it," he answered. "But I have a role to play."

It was the late 1960s. Vietnam. Student unrest. He meant he had a political role to play.

The evening I arrived at the Hotel Commander in Cambridge, I was handed a message. It read: "Let's have dinner. Meet me in the dining room at seven. Claude." He'd been so stressed about lying to his wife two years earlier that I wasn't sure he would want to see me again. We started with two dry martinis. Halfway through dinner, he said, "Should we waste time?"

I wasn't certain how I felt. To talk, to get reacquainted didn't seem like wasting time to me. But perhaps it was different with a man.

We made love and it was as exciting and as marvelous as it had been two years before. Suddenly, he laughed a horrendous laugh and sat bolt upright.

"What?" I asked.

"Don't you see? We could never have been together anyway."

"I don't understand."

"They would never have let us. You, with your ideas. Me, top-secret. Don't you realize what I was working on? They could never have permitted it. We were lucky to have ended it so early. Later on, who knows? They might have felt obliged to kill you." I shivered. I felt as if I were seeing a bad movie.

The next day was filled with reunion events. I sat with Maurine and Kitty at the luncheon.

"I know you live in Europe," Maurine began, "and you're practically never here—"

Kitty interrupted, "But you've got to be a part of what's happening. Remember two years ago, we were talking about Betty Friedan?"

"Well, because of her and others, state commissions investigated the status of women in America and found we were going backwards."

"We're losing ground. There are fewer women in the professions. Women earn sixty percent of what men earn and almost all the women who work are in the bottom jobs."

Then Maurine announced in a formal tone, "We're forming an organization. NOW. The National Organization for Women. At the conference in Washington, we'll draw up a statement of purpose. Here's part of it, just to give you an idea—" She put on her glasses and read aloud from a paper: "We reject the current assumptions that a man must carry the sole burden of supporting himself, his wife, and family, and that a woman is automatically entitled to lifelong support by a man upon her marriage, or that marriage, home, and family are primarily women's world and responsibility, hers to dominate, his to support. We believe a true partnership between the sexes demands a different concept of marriage, an equitable sharing of the responsibilities of home and children . . . proper recognition should be given to the economic and social value of homemaking and child care. We believe the current state of 'half-equality' between the sexes discriminates against both men and women, and is the cause of much unnecessary hostility between the sexes." Maurine took off her glasses.

"That's great," I said. "I'm all for it. What do you want me to do?"

Kitty smiled at me. "Give us a check for one hundred dollars made out to 'NOW.' We'll put you on the mailing list and keep you informed."

I took out my checkbook. "I'm glad somebody is doing something about something."

Maurine and Kitty were impressed when my handsome nineteen-year-old son, John, came by. I said good-bye to them and joined him. "Do you want to see *The Blue Max*?" he asked me.

The Blue Max was the successful movie Ben had written the treatment for; the Blue Max was also the German World War I medal with which the flying ace is decorated in the picture. And, just before I left Mougins, Ben had received a package. Inside a purple velvet satin-lined box nestled a replica, or the real item, we weren't sure, the most distinguished decoration other than The Iron Cross, the blue and silver Blue Max with a card, "Affectionately, Darryl."

What other Blue Max was there?

As John opened the door of his blue Volkswagen Bug for me, he said, "*My* Blue Max."

32
Nyet

In July 1966, we were in the pool when our phone rang. I ran dripping through the cypresses and caught it in time. "*Les Etats Unis,* the United States calling," the operator announced. "It's Joe!" he said when the operator connected us. "Joe Hirsch. I'm in New York. Gen and I are going to the Soviet Union. We've just found out we have to have another couple with us to qualify as 'de luxe tourists' with a car and an interpreter. Will you come with us?"

Ben, overweight, puffing, right behind me, had the receiver to his ear. "Say yes!" he cried.

"August tenth from Paris. We'll meet you there. Send passports to the Soviet embassy in Paris. They'll have your visas, we'll have your tickets."

We'd been back to the States. But we'd never been to the Soviet Union! It was about time.

The Aeroflot plane was modern, not like the one with tassels on its window shades that brought us back from Czechoslovakia. But Ben was pale, panicked. "I don't know if the plane will stay in the air," he whispered.

"What do you mean?" I asked, horrified.

"Look at the sleeve of the hostess when she passes." (We didn't yet say "flight attendant.") "Just look. There's a big hole at the elbow. They don't make inspections."

Joe and Gen laughed nervously.

Once airborne, I excused myself, opened the lavatory door. Two handsome blond Red Army officers were making love passionately, one seated on the toilet, the other standing. I slammed the door shut, staggered back to my seat.

Joe, Gen, Ben stared at me. I couldn't speak.

"You better tell us," Joe said.

I shook my head.

"Norma," said Ben.

"You know I have nothing against homosexuality," I spluttered. "*You* do, Ben, and I don't. It's not that. But I feel—nauseated. I don't know what's making me sick. Red Army officers? Because we're in a plane? Because the door wasn't locked?" I began to cry. "On a Soviet plane?" I was completely undone.

On the way from Moscow airport to the Hotel Metropole, we saw dozens of vehicles, mostly trucks, abandoned by the side of the road. I actually tried to explain the wrecks away by saying something like, "They have so many new trucks, they don't know where to put the old ones."

Olga, our interpreter, had no use for the Tretyakov Museum. She didn't think Impressionists worth looking at. The Tretyakov turned out to be crammed full of the best Cézannes, Renoirs, Monets I'd ever seen anywhere.

Soon after we arrived, a young cousin of Ben's, Natasha, his mother's sister's daughter, came to our hotel, bearing the traditional three stems of welcome gladioli. She proceeded to scold us. "You tried to get in touch with Cousin Elizaveta at her office." Natasha was stern. "You frightened her. She works at the Plan. They'll think she has contact with Americans. *Never* call her! We'll have her to lunch Sunday. You're invited."

We were excited to see the inside of a Soviet home. We made our way through a shabby part of town to the two-room apartment in a dilapidated building where Natasha, her father, her brother, Zachary, and her mother, Ben's aunt Sonya, lived. Cousin Elizaveta had been too frightened to come.

At one point, Ben asked, "People say there's anti-Semitism?"

Aunt Sonya, who looked remarkably like her sister, Mumma, cut him off quickly, "No more synagogues," she said in Yiddish, "but who needs them? Eh, Natasha?"

Sonya's husband said, "No. No anti-Semitism."

"Can Natasha and Zachary prepare for whatever careers they wish?" Ben asked.

The parents nodded.

"I shall become an interpreter," Natasha said.

"And your brother? What does he want to do?" I asked.

"Zachary wants to be an engineer," Natasha replied.

"Does he go to engineering school?" Ben asked.

"Jews can't get into the engineering schools but it's all right because they can go into the army and learn engineering. That's where Zachary is now."

"There is no anti-Semitism," repeated her mother, who brought out a tin box decorated with a picture of the Kremlin on the lid. She opened the box. The same cookies that Mumma baked! Of course. The sisters had learned from their mother. I couldn't help it. A big fat tear ran down the side of my cheek.

We were called to a meeting at the Writers Union. Twelve men and one woman. The men were screenwriters, the woman, a translator. I said I was a screenwriter. "Why are no women screenwriters present?" I asked. Looking vague, they scratched their heads, turned to each other, mumbled. I caught a name. "Vera Panova!" I repeated. "I know who that is. I read her novel *The Factory.* She wrote the screenplay. I saw the film in Paris. But don't you have any women screenwriters?"

They brushed that off, lashed back with what *they* wanted to know: How did residuals work? What percentage of the profits did American screenwriters get? How much were they paid? All practical dollar-and-cents questions, no curiosity about content, theory, technique.

In August, Moscow broiled. Occasional showers failed to cool. In the big department store, GUM, I bought an expensive, ugly umbrella, which, when I opened it, flew inside out. The streets were filled with people dressed for hot summer, the women in unremarkable thin dresses, the men in unremarkable lightweight pants and short-sleeved sport shirts. The following week in Leningrad, the people in the street, the women in thin dresses, the men in lightweight pants and sport shirts, were chic. The department store windows, unlike Moscow's GUM, were eye-catching and colorful. Leningrad was Paris, Moscow was Lyon. Leningrad had a tradition of beauty and culture.

Unfortunately, on arrival, Ben came down with 105-degree flu. A woman doctor put him on an antibiotic that made him deathly ill. She examined the medicines Ben had with him, one for hypertension, one for sinusitis. She cried out in glee, "We have that! We have that!"

Ben stayed in bed, Joe, Gen, and I regaled ourselves with the Hermitage. Joe took three steps at a time, calling back to us, "I'm at the Danae!" For years, he'd planned this pilgrimage to one of Rembrandt's rare nudes. Gen and I spent two or three hours going through the museum, which lived up to its reputation, then went back and found Joe still staring at the Danae's belly. "I'll have to come back tomorrow," he murmured.

While Ben was ill, I tried to visit a summer camp. Our Olga—the interpreters were Olgas in both cities—said "Nyet!," the one word of Russian I'd learned, "No!" Wherever I turned, I met a big fat "Nyet!" "No" to phoning long distance from your room, "No" to staying in the store an extra five minutes. "Nyet," Olga repeated for emphasis. "You would have had to apply for permission a year ago."

My mother would not have taken "nyet" for an answer. I had worked my ass off for the American-Soviet Friendship Society. I took myself to the Friendship Societies Building, where I was passed along from one dour woman to the next, each with her own unique way of bestowing authority on "nyet." Where was the smiling face of socialism put forth to the world in colorful publications like *Soviet Union Today* and *Soviet Woman*?

I shouted, "I want the most high-up person!"

That got results. He was a man of course.

"I shall not leave the Soviet Union," I told him, "until I have seen something of Soviet education and child care, which I've heard so much about."

"I like your spirit!" he chuckled. "But you come at a most dif—"

"It's always a difficult time."

"No," he replied. "The schools are closed for the holi—"

"I want to see *summer* camps, *summer* schools—"

Now he laughed. "I see why they sent you to *me*. All right. You shall see our finest summer camp on an island in the Neva. Here—" He handed me three official documents, which he signed with a flourish.

Worth fighting for, the camp was better than anything in the United States or Israel, where child care was pretty damn wonderful. The children exuded happiness. They were doing all the things children should be doing, freely and yet well observed. The sleeping, eating, play areas were impeccable, well equipped, well staffed. Olga had never known anyone who'd been there. "It's for the children of—" she made an upward gesture with her thumb. Already in bad with the powers-that-be because she'd taken her little boy out of day care and given him to her mother, she seemed afraid of saying too much.

"Why did you take him out?"

"Too crowded, bad care."

As soon as Ben was better, we called Volodya's cousin. He had the same name, Vladimir Pozner, and he was head of Lenfilm. He showed us over the modern, well-equipped studios. Then we took the hydrofoil on the Neva to Peter the Great's summer palace, and saw young couples getting married at the wedding palace.

In summer, as in the Scandinavian countries, the midnight sun makes the evenings last forever. After a brilliant performance of the Kirov Ballet's *Don Quixote,* music by Prokofiev, we walked home from the theater to the Hotel Europa. As we approached an intersection, we saw crossing a large square, a man leading a horse and a boy leading a donkey, Don Quixote's horse, Sancho Panza's donkey, being taken back to the stables. That scene, as in a dream, lit by the magic midnight sun, always stayed with us.

Nyet

On the wall near the hotel elevators, someone had tacked up a poster of an icon exhibition held months previously. I asked the concierge if I could buy it. The answer, of course, was "Nyet."

"I could take it for you easily," Joe Hirsch whispered.

"Oh, no, you couldn't!" Gen snapped. "An American was held in prison for months for far less!"

Miserable and saddened by this trip, Ben and I returned to Mougins just as Ben's classmates from Reed College, Eleanor and "Mac" Maccoby, arrived. At Stanford, she headed the developmental psychology department, he the Institute of Communications. The Maccobys, progressive in their youth, told us many of their friends in academe had been fired because they wouldn't sign the loyalty oath. Mac and Eleanor had weathered McCarthyism "by keeping their noses clean," but maintained that the university could not be free while the military-industrial complex controlled research funding.

Every day for a month, we played doubles and each day Mac trounced Ben at singles. The Maccobys left September 30. Ben had always reminded me that his father had died of a heart attack at fifty-four, and warned that he too might die before his fifty-fifth birthday, which was coming up October 11. Ben had a heart attack on October 1! Bad diet, lack of regular exercise, stress had nothing to do with it! He preferred to believe it had been triggered by seeing the Soviet Union—and the United States—in a clear light.

Ben's heart attack frightened me and made me realize how much I really deep down cared for him. He came home from the hospital in time for a glorious American Thanksgiving. From the Victorine Studios in Nice, where Romain Gary's *Promise at Dawn* was shooting, came Julie Dassin, who was directing it, Melina who was starring, and Bob Lawrence, our old friend the editor of *El Cid, The Fall,* and *Fiddler on the Roof,* who was cutting it. I managed to get all the fixin's, cranberry sauce, sweet potatoes, chestnuts. Julie, looking sicker than Ben, had tripped at the studio, fallen, slipped a disc. He had to eat lying flat on the floor. Melina didn't eat much, smoked endlessly.

It took almost a year for Ben to recuperate from the heart attack. Just as he was beginning to feel himself, a charming, progressive young producer named Henry Lange who for years had promoted projects that never saw the light of day, brought us the files on a crime that had rocked France. A Moroccan, Ben Barka, leader of the Third World Independence Movement, was kidnapped on Boulevard Saint-Germain, right in front of Brasserie Lipp, tortured, and put to death. That a man could be seized in broad daylight amid throngs of Parisians and his killers could get away was a scandal. Rumor had it that the king of Morocco's Minister Oufkir had wanted to get rid of what was for Morocco an embarrassment—a revolutionary leader with a huge following—but Oufkir thought it too dangerous to commit the crime at home.

Ben and I read the news clips and articles, agreed it could make an important film. But another country doing its dirty work in France made it "delicate." Yvon Guézel, the producer, a hardheaded Breton, refused to be intimidated even after the French IRS threatened to audit ten years of his taxes if he made the film.

After winning the Cannes award for Best First Film with this *Le Vent des Aurès*,[1] our Algerian friend Mohammed Lakhdar-Hamina. (See photo insert). invited us to Algiers. He said he thought a vacation would do Ben good. We had no illusions. Lakhdar wanted Ben to supervise the film the Algerians were making about their struggle for independence.

The Hotel St. Georges in Algiers was luxurious. Our first night, Lakhdar and his French wife took us to a fine restaurant on the port, with his friend Jamal and the head of the Algerian film industry. We were six. One unbelievably enormous lobster, like a sci-fi beast, con- structed in a studio, only *real,* the size of a calf, on a silver platter was placed in the middle of the table, more than enough for six—and deli- cious! Lakhdar laughed his wild laugh, "On this side of the Mediter- ranean," he said, "everything is bigger and better."

The next night, we had dinner at Jamal's. Jamal, a boy-hero of the Algerian revolution, turned out to be second to President Boumedienne. Jamal's mother, with other ladies, prepared the *mechoui,* baby lamb with couscous. The president, who loved movies, dropped by unexpectedly. Jamal's guards at the front door signaled his approach. The ladies, including Jamal's mother, hurriedly took away wine bottles and glasses. The president was a teetotaler in a country of teetotalers.

Like Casablanca, Algiers has a casbah, and on our third night there, we explored it. On the way, we passed a huge square where people were busily erecting stands and discovered that *Salt of the Earth* was to be projected outdoors in the square. Made in 1953 in New Mexico, brainchild of Herbert Biberman and Adrian Scott, who'd just gotten out of jail, and of Paul Jarrico, who became the producer when Adrian was too ill, *Salt of the Earth* was, as Paul said, "our chance to really say something in film, because we had already been punished, already been blacklisted." Paraphrasing Gilbert and Sullivan, he went on, "We wanted to commit the crime to fit the punishment. . . . It was unequivocally pro-labor, pro-minority, pro-women."[2] Biberman directed and Michael Wilson wrote the screenplay, the story of a mining strike and the development of union consciousness and feminist consciousness by the Mexican-American men and women strikers. " . . . In a remarkable campaign of guerrilla ingenuity and doggedness, they made a movie, against the coordinated opposition of studios, unions, labs, and the federal government, which went as far as to have the leading lady deported midway through shooting."[3]

Ben and I had seen *Salt of the Earth* in Paris in 1956 when it opened in the Latin Quarter to double lines around the block. Here it was in Algiers, ten years later, to be shown on the first night for men, the second night for women! The women of Algiers had heard about *Salt of the Earth*. They weren't going to be put off. It was easy in the dark to fool people with men's caftans and draped headgear. They climbed over the fences early and filled the stands. When the men arrived, there were no more seats. The women stayed and saw the film. At the end, they rose as one and cheered! The next day, the women's exploit was the talk of Algiers.

Lakhdar drove us to the lush, hilly part of Algeria, where he'd shot his prizewinning film. On the way back, Ben told him about the Ben Barka project. Lakhdar almost lost control of the wheel. "That's what we've been searching for, an Algerian-French coproduction. We'll supply all the below-the-line. You've got a deal!"

Ben and Basilio were hurrying to finish the script on Ben Barka when a screenplay from Paris arrived by special delivery with a note from Costa Gavras. On the cover of the script was just one letter, "Z." Ben didn't know what it was.

"It's about the Fascist colonels taking power in Greece," I said. "I liked the book. Hats off to Costa for daring to do it."

We were acutely aware of the Greek exiles in France. The most distinguished, Nikos Kazantzakis, was the author of the novel *Christ Recrucified*, made into the film *He Who Must Die*, written by Ben, directed by Julie Dassin.

Ben and I read the screenplay Costa sent. We were upset. It was, as Ben said, "just not very good." Costa phoned. "May we come over?"

Costa was a good-looking bundle of turbulent energy; Jacques Perrin, a darling actor, was taking an ever bigger role—in production; and Eric Schlumberger, scion of the steel family, was a large, dark, heavy young man.

I went up to my room. After a few minutes, Ben came running upstairs. "What'll I tell them?"

"What did you say so far?" I asked.

"I made small talk, how wonderful to do a film that might bring down the colonels. What'll I say about the script?"

"You can say, it was a wonderful book, it had a documentary quality that made it exciting. That's what the film needs to be."

Ben went down. They talked for a long time. Ben asked them to stay to lunch.

Costa, happy, turned to me, "Your Ben has solved it for us."

During the period that Ben was ill, Sophia, who had a charity appearance in Monte Carlo, made it her business to go out of her way to see him. She really cheered him up. As she had on her other visits, she took me aside to keep me posted on her baby-having progress.

Nyet

When we celebrated Sophia's receiving the Cannes Palme d'Or for her performance in *Two Women,* she'd told me she wanted a large family. "I'm Neapolitan," she said. "It's the badge of being a real woman. Carlo and I have had so many problems with marrying that I didn't worry as much as I might have. " She lowered her voice. "In spite of not using birth control, I haven't gotten pregnant." She had visited us in Paris in February 1962 on our son Daniel's sixth birthday, brought him a leather-and-gold-bound notebook, inscribed: "Write in this. It will become a book. Baci, Sophia." She had a big feeling for children and liked to be in the midst of my brood. Then, alone with me, she said it was time to start if she was to have the big family she wanted. In 1963, when she'd had her first miscarriage, I tried to cheer her up by telling her I'd miscarried before my first child and it hadn't kept me from having a big family. She brought it up again when she was showing us the Pontis' fabulous triplex apartment on Avenue George V, which they'd bought so that the French authorities would give them citizenship and Carlo a proper divorce that would permit them to marry legally. "You see," she said, "we're respectable married folk, only I can't seem to make a baby." Her enormous eyes overflowed. Wherever and whenever I saw her—on the set of *Lady L* in Nice; when she was president of the Cannes Jury; when they received us in Marino during the Olympic Games in Rome—she would give me a look and I understood.

In January 1967, I received a panicky call from Basilio, who was with her in Rome. She'd just had a second miscarriage. She was terrified and hopeless and blamed her Italian obstetricians. I called Dr. Michael Sacks of the World Health Organization in Geneva, where he'd settled after spending the McCarthy years in India. His answer: Sophia should see Dr. Hubert de Watteville. She flew to Geneva and had all the tests. The doctor told her there was no reason she shouldn't have a normal pregnancy. "But don't get pregnant right away. Wait at least four months," which they did. But still she had not gotten pregnant. She flew to Geneva. Dr. de Watteville ordered her to stop worrying. "Just relax and let nature take its course."

Then, Basilio phoned at last to say Sophia was happily pregnant and de Watteville was coming to Rome to take her back to Geneva with him. Carlo had booked a suite for her in the Intercontinental Hotel. Under the doctor's supervision, she had regular estrogen injections to strengthen the lining of the uterus, and sedatives to keep her from having anxiety that could cause a miscarriage. She was to stay in bed for nine months.

Basilio, with Ines, Sophia's secretary, were in constant attendance. I phoned from time to time. Sophia was still angry with her Italian obstetricians for her miscarriages. Because of them she would have to have a cesarean, which limited the number of children she could have. She was sad she'd never have a large family.

During the many months she was incarcerated in the Intercontinental, Dr. de Watteville let her get up for a couple of hours each day, during which she cooked with Ines and Basilio and began writing her book, *Cooking with Love*.

In December at Christmas break, I drove Daniel, twelve, and Paulo, eleven, to ski camp in Switzerland. We stopped off in Geneva to pick up the Sackses' son. I left the three boys in an alpine resort and returned to Geneva for Christmas. Mike, his wife, Barbara, and I had dinner at the Richemond, one of the world's great hotels. My turkey and Barbara's were tender and excellent, but we watched Mike in consternation trying to cut his and chewing for dear life when he did manage to hack off a piece. Barbara and I complained on his behalf. The maître d' said, "We have two turkeys. We always serve the ladies off the tender one."

I thought that was funny and told it to Sophia on the phone. She laughed and told me to come over. When I arrived, I found Carlo and Basilio and Ines all waiting around for the arrival of Cipi (Carlo, Jr.). Sophia kissed me, pinched my cheek, and said, "And *you* have them so easily. It's not fair. I can't even put on my slippers."

I helped her put on her slippers, and suddenly she began to laugh. As she moved her great bulk with much difficulty through the hallway, her laughter became uncontrollable. She, who constantly teased others, also laughed at herself. And her laughter was infectious. I giggled and as we approached the living room, Basilio, who was setting up an electronic high-tech game to amuse her, hee-hawed as he made a face like a donkey. Carlo looked up from the Geneva-Milano plane schedule and beamed. Sophia, still laughing, put her arms protectively around her enormous belly and sank into a wide armchair.

I pondered. First, I could see how fortunate I was to have seven bright healthy children. Second, even if she put baby-having above all else, she'd established her career before she had children, something I now consider essential for every career-minded young woman. Third, nothing she'd achieved was without struggle.

How could someone deprived as a child of all that psychologists consider indispensable have matured into one of those rare phenomena, a happy woman? Career. Love. Family. Children. Sophia's choice was to have it all.

33

May '68

For Americans, May '68 was just a student revolt. It did begin that way, first against the American war in Vietnam, then against the antiquated French educational system, but it became "a revolution of the whole of French society," said France's biggest weekly, *L'Express*. "Capitalism doesn't satisfy us but socialism as practiced in the East has failed. The problem for the French, and all Europeans, is to invent something new."[1] According to British historian David Goldey, "Student demonstrations triggered off a massive general strike, and the combination of the two seemed ready to bring down the impressive facade of the French State. In the heady atmosphere of May, students moved from trying to reform their universities to attempting to revolutionize society. . . . "[2]

Our son Aaron, a screenwriter who today lives with his wife and three children in Paris, was, in 1968, a first-year student at Nanterre, a university in the suburb where the May '68 revolt began. The first sit-in was March 1967 in the women's dormitories as a protest against restricted visiting hours. To pacify the students, a swimming pool was built, but by this time, their satisfaction had become linked with wider political issues. After breaking the American Express windows to protest the Vietnam War, a Nanterre student was arrested. He, like Aaron, was part of the Trotskyist *Jeunesse Communiste Revolutionnaire,* or JCR, the Revolutionary Communist Youth. Students occupied the university and closed it down. Student leader Daniel Cohn-Bendit was called before the disciplinary committee at the Sorbonne, where thousands of students massed. The police pulled in hundreds, including Aaron, whose arrest was only the first of several. Then, their parents, professors, the neighborhoods, and a large part of the nation joined the students' protests.

In Mougins, Ben and I knew only what we read in the papers but soon there were no newspapers, no television. Everything was on strike and at a standstill. According to Aaron, and to Johnny and Luli, who arrived late from their American colleges, Paris had become different from the Paris we knew. Farmers sent food into the city; carpools replaced buses and *métro;* shops let you put your purchases on a tab, since banks were closed. People were nice. Parisians were *nice!*

At the Cannes Festival, French cineastes were as excited as the students. Truffaut, Godard, and Chabrol climbed up on the stage of the Palais des Festivals, crying: "Close the festival! For a people's cinema!" Fresh from their success in getting our friend Henri Langlois, head of the Paris Cinemathèque, reinstated after being summarily dismissed, directors, screenwriters, and actors felt ready to oppose the small, tight, reactionary administration of the French film industry. Henry Lange, the young producer of the *Ben Barka* project, who was staying with us, thought we should all go up to Paris "to be part of the most exciting time in France since 1789!"

By staying in the south, we had missed seeing our three eldest on the barricades, and being witness to many weeks of creative debate by the "*Etats Généraux,*" the Revolutionary Committee, set up to inquire into the potential of cinema. Enthusiastic progressives applauded direct participatory democracy in action. There were meetings on university reform, marathon teach-ins, happenings in the Sorbonne courtyard. The walls of Paris were covered with posters and slogans like "Imagination Is King!" or "Be Realistic. Demand the Impossible!"

The strike spread to the Renault, Peugeot, Citroën factories, but the

Communist-led CGT, the industrial unions, would not declare a general strike although gradually it was becoming exactly that. In the center of Paris, the tough CRS, the special riot police, brutally arrested the students and kept four in jail. Twenty thousand students marched down the streets crying "Free our comrades" and singing the International. This was the moment of the greatest sympathy of the population but still the Communist Party remained aloof, refused to support the workers who were united with the students.

Toward the end of the "Events of May," Ben and I drove up to Paris, our Citroën station wagon packed with jerricans of gasoline, since it was impossible to buy gas.

On arrival, our son Aaron, busy with the battle, presented himself briefly, handed us a leaflet of the March 22 Movement to help us understand what was happening, and was gone. I have only just found a copy:

> There are 10% of workers' sons in higher education. Are we fighting so that there should be more of them, for a democratic reform of the university? This would be better, but this is not the most important thing. . . . There are students who, on leaving the University, do not find a job. Do we fight so that they may get one, for a good employment policy for graduates? This would be better but it is not the essential. . . . When a worker's son becomes a student, he leaves his class. When the son of the bourgeoisie goes to the university, he may learn the true nature of his class. . . . We want to build a classless society. . . . Your struggle is more radical than our legitimate demands because it not only seeks an improvement of the worker's lot within the capitalist system, but it implies the destruction of that system. Your struggle is political . . . you are *not* fighting to replace one prime minister by another, but to deprive the owner, the boss, of his power in the factory and in society: the appropriation of the means of production and of the power of decision by the working people.

My kids had grown up in France, which had no Beat generation, no hippies or flower children. Our son John, newly arrived from Harvard, exploding with its own student unrest mainly in opposition to the war in Vietnam, explained to us that French youth assumed, perhaps because of France's tradition, that society could be changed, that it was possible to fight for socialism. (John is now professor of history at a French university.)

From the moment we arrived in Paris, not at our house but at the Gilberts' François Ier apartment that they'd lent us, the excitement was palpable. Ben came alive. After all, we had just returned from depressing visits to the repressive USSR and the inegalitarian U.S. of Watts, violence, and women struggling not to go backward. Ben was revitalized by his children's activity and by hope for the world. In Paris, in the midst of May '68, when I was forty-seven and Ben fifty-seven, I fell in love with him all over again.

Ascribe it to the headiness of *les événements*—the events. Blame it on my light-headedness in the face of what I saw as the corroboration of everything I'd believed and wished for, that human beings would make a better world. Or, if you prefer, mark my falling in love with Ben down to what is more likely: Glowing with appreciation of his children's participation in "our fight," and with an easy, good-natured responsiveness to his discovery that he had Trotskyist sons, Ben became irresistibly attractive to me, and brought forth in me waves of love and emotion.

He adored the wall slogans no less than I and made up a few of his own. The children didn't have time for us, but we talked to the people next to us at cafés and restaurants. With his warmth, wit, and newfound good humor, Ben charmed them and those who picked us up in the street and gave us a lift.

By the time we returned to Ruth Gilbert's dark green, velvet-draped, translucent pink "shell room," I seduced him. I had never wanted to be with anyone else. At moments like this, I knew why.

Our bliss was short-lived. The Communists attacked the students and the workers who joined them, empowering de Gaulle to disappear mysteriously for two days to go by helicopter to Baden Baden in Germany to ask the NATO generals for help in putting down the insurrection. Why didn't the Communist Party support the strike? Because, according to them, the students would lead the revolution into an "irresponsible leftist direction." The CP was surely afraid of not being in the forefront of the revolution. "The working class will make its own revolution," they said.

We should not have been surprised. The CGT, or *Confédération du Générale Travail* (Confederation of Labor), the Communist-dominated union, and the Communist Party had always had an aura of being more revolutionary by their image than by their acts, more by what they stood for than by what they did. One reason the French Communist Party was so conservative during May '68 was that they were institutionally wedded to the French state. Like the British Labour Party, they were a de facto loyal opposition.

For Ben and for me, the Party's position was untenable. We felt betrayed, as if they were aiding and supporting de Gaulle.

Nineteen sixty-eight was more than a little late for disillusionment with the Communist Party and the Soviet Union. In 1956, after the Soviets put down the Hungarian Revolution, the French Communist doctors left the Party in a body.[3]

Ben loved his doctors, all Communists, recommended to us on our arrival in France. They never let us pay for their services. When we begged to pay, their replies were, "We cannot take money from you. You stood up against American Fascism."

Like me, Ben had never been a member of any political organization after we left the United States but we had developed political and emotional closeness to European Communists. On our return from the Soviet Union in 1966, we began to have doubts, but although I didn't like the way the French Party backed up whatever the Soviet Union did, I was keenly aware that the Italian Party had managed to maintain its independence and I hoped the French Party would learn to do likewise.

When I look back at the American Party, with which I eventually became disgusted because of its subservience to the Soviet Union, I still cannot help but be proud of its fight against Fascism, its support of workers and labor unions, its pioneering struggle for women, minorities, and for all civil rights.

Part of the reason I hung in for so long, I suppose, is my nature—my optimism, my hopefulness, which led me to believe that Communists would once again fight for what they always stood for: freedom for all peoples and a better life for everyone.

A second weekend of violence, the cessation of city services like garbage pickups, and a general strike frightened the people into the arms of the government, which, since de Gaulle's visit to NATO, was showing increased vigor. The revolt was soon over. The events of May had led to a vast conservative Gaullist majority in the elections. There was no choice. The only alternative was civil war. "But for five weeks, French society vibrated at all levels, experienced an earthquake which didn't bring down the walls, but which left them cracked, without plaster to hold them together. The walls can still hold for a long time, but they are not the same as they were."[4]

On the heels of the Gaullist victory, Soviet tanks rolled into Prague and stamped down the Czech movement for "socialism with a human face." The end of May was the nadir of our long years of exile, and it bankrupted any hopes we might have had that socialism could be democratic, at least in our lifetime. The significance of May '68, for me and for many, was the spirit of it, the delirium of being free to express hopes for the future. I talked about it with friends, about the Party's betrayal, about our commitments to a new and truly free people's revolution, which had nothing to do with the Party or the Soviet Union. Ben would have none of it, slipped into his deepest depression.

What had it really meant, May '68? Daniel Singer, for many years European correspondent for *The Nation*, writes in his book *Prelude to Revolution:* "In reviving such concepts as class struggle, the intervention of the masses in the historical process, and revolution from below, the young students and workers of France have given a new impetus to man's unending, if sometimes slow and subterranean struggle for mastery over his fate."

I guess when you know you must engage in the struggle and don't yet have the guts, you stall, or you get sick. Back in Mougins, I got sick. Hepatitis. The bad kind. The kind you die of. Months in bed. I was unable to attend Luli's Los Angeles wedding to a young documentary filmmaker. Harold and Grace Robbins, in Hollywood at the time of the wedding, took care of everything. Grace organized the reception; Harold gave away the bride.

I told myself that the hepatitis virus had hit me because I was in a weakened condition. I *was* in a weakened condition. In 1949 when I left the U.S., I'd stopped being political; in 1955 I was cut off from my nascent writing career. But the brush with death made me say, as Ingrid had, "I don't want just 'Beloved Wife and Mother' on my epitaph." In bed, I read all of Sartre and de Beauvoir. Temporarily, I became an existentialist: everyone has a choice, even the armless, legless man in Trumbo's *Johnny Got His Gun* who urges that his armless, legless trunk be exhibited to warn of the horrors of war.

I had a choice.

Though I did not yet know it, I was recuperating from massive betrayal and self-delusion. It would take time for me to act.

But whenever I felt weak or afraid, I would remember that when student leader Daniel Cohn-Bendit was expelled from France, tossed over the border into Germany by the French government, thousands of Parisians, young and old, in solidarity with him, thundered: "*Nous sommes tous des Juifs Allemands.*" "We are all German Jews."

I could visualize that terrible June 1 when de Gaulle was back in power. Yet students and workers, by now maybe only 30,000, their red flags flying, bravely marched down Montparnasse, chanting the slogan that will stay with me forever: "It's only a beginning. . . . Let us continue the struggle."

34

You Can Go Home Again

May '68 waked me out of a twenty-year stupor.

I slammed into activity, suddenly aware of the needs of our four young ones still at home: I had handed Suzo over for the first nine years of her life to lovely Françoise; I had not been a mother to Marco, or to Paulo, who was in a group of Cannes *drogués,* or to Daniel, who needed to prepare seriously for university.

The French cinema was *en crise* but Ben had a growing conviction that he wasn't getting jobs because he was too far from the action. Accordingly, I didn't renew the lease of the renters in our Paris house, and moved the family back.

How could I have guessed what we would find? The house was literally collapsing, a perfect metaphor for our life in France.

Our beloved city of Paris had illegally built the foundations of one of their nursery schools right up against our foundations. "No, no," they insisted, "the nursery school has nothing to do with your house sinking. Underground streams run all through that part of Paris, making the soil unreliable."

We countered that from 1920, when the house was constructed, until the 1960s, when they built the school, the house had suffered not so much as a crack. Instead of responding to our entreaties, the city informed us that in the near future they would declare the house uninhabitable.

Fortunately, I was full of energy. I met over and over again with geologists, architects, engineers, city officials, and lawyers, while trying to take my parental responsibilities seriously. I succeeded in convincing the best art school in Paris to take Paulo, attended Marco's parent-teacher meetings, and, remembering Henrietta Endore's admonitions, read to Suzo at bedtime.

What amazes me is that I was suddenly and mysteriously able to write. I began to develop my play idea, *May '68,* about two old radicals (based loosely on Sartre and de Beauvoir) who lead the uprising but are completely outdistanced by the radical youth movement.

For the moment, Ben had no commitments. Costa informed Ben that the cast was assembled and *Z* was ready to shoot. Would Ben permit him to substitute *Z* for *Ben Barka* and allow him to use the production deal Ben had in Algiers? Ben struggled with Costa's demand, but, incredibly, he felt he couldn't refuse. He said it was like naming names—there had never been a choice about that for us. In this instance, I thought it foolish to yield, but had to admire Ben's sacrificing his personal desires for what he thought more important, ridding Greece of the Fascist colonels.

Jorge Semprun, who wrote the screenplay of *Z*, didn't want adaptation credit to go to Ben. Worse, permitting Costa to shoot *Z* in Algeria, using Lakhdar's production setup, delayed Ben's own project, *Ben Barka*. But that's what he agreed to. *Ben Barka,* called *L'Attentat* or *The French Conspiracy,* was shot in Paris by another young friend of ours, Yves Boisset, with a terrific cast—Michel Piccoli, Jean-Louis Trintignant, and Jean Seberg. Ben and Basilio had screenplay credit. Semprun took adaptation credit. The film opened to excellent reviews and full houses, may even have helped topple the de Gaulle government, but has been viewed as "an imitation *Z*."

Ben, at loose ends, decided to write the *May '68* play with me. Surprisingly, we discovered that we had a ball working together. I can still hear our hysterical laughter as we hurled young-radical double-talk at each other. Often, we played out the parts, he a grumpy Sartre, me an all-wise de Beauvoir. Nevertheless, despite Ben's enjoyment in the work, he frequently bemoaned his "situation": no film to write, no money coming in.

Ben became so unhappy that I tried to promote a project for him. I told Marta András, head of Martonplay Agency, who had wanted to hire me, of a Heinrich Bölle novel, *Group Portrait with Lady*. I was sure it would make a wonderful film and suggested our Yugoslav friend, Aleksander Petrovich, to direct. I gave the book to Ben and to Petrovich. They both liked it. Marta set up a meeting with Bölle. Unfortunately, Ben fought with Petrovich all the way from Paris to Munich, where, at least, I met the Great Man, Heinrich Bölle, who was very *sympa* even though he was trying to stop smoking.

Group Portrait with Lady fell through, but as a result, its would-be German producer, Arthur Brauner, engaged Ben to write *Korszak,* a German-Polish coproduction to be directed by Aleksander Ford,[1] who'd made many of the great Polish film classics.

Ben and I dropped the play for a while, read the reams of material from the Warsaw Ghetto uprising, and worked out a way of dramatizing the story. Once again, I was dismayed to find myself thrown in as "researcher" although I don't recall minding it so much this time. Ben wrote a moving screenplay about the doctor-educator who walked into the Nazi ovens with his orphan charges rather than take the escape route planned for him.

Ben and I were on our way to Warsaw when a telegram arrived: "KORSZAK POSTPONED. DO NOT COME." Shortly thereafter, at our front door, Aleksander Ford, his American wife, and three children appeared, looking hunted and haunted. A Warsaw pogrom had chased Jews from the film industry. Ford, head of Film Polski, had been forced to run for it with his family. With a slap, we remembered all the warnings of Zuka and Louis Mitelberg when they'd returned from Poland. We saw the Fords off to Israel, where, we never knew why, Aleksander committed suicide.[2]

We returned to our play, finished it. Pleased with ourselves, and thinking she'd be great as the Simone de Beauvoir character, we sent it to Simone Signoret.

She invited us to her Paris home in Place Dauphine. The French are usually very polite and well behaved. Once Ben lost an arbitration because he wouldn't shake hands with his adversary, whom the arbiters had judged in the wrong. I was astonished at Simone's manner. She breathed fire. She snarled, "How dare you Americans write about *our* May '68? About Sartre and de Beauvoir? You cannot understand our culture no matter how long you live here!"

We sent our play to our New York agent, who showed it to several Broadway producers. They didn't know what to make of it. "You are too French," wrote one of them. "No one here will understand what you are talking about."

Ben, feeling rejected by the French, was once again moaning about his "roots" (he hadn't arrived in Los Angeles until he was twenty-eight). Since his heart attack, he'd also worried about his health, not sufficiently to diet or exercise but enough to wonder if American medicine was better than French.

Around that time, in 1976, when I was fixing up our Mougins house to rent and staying with another novelist friend, Robert Littell,[3] Harold Robbins took me to dinner at a tiny restaurant on Cannes' Suquet, the high, picturesque hill with the ancient square-towered abbey where the old Cannois families lived.

Grace was away and he was lonesome. He may have been on something. He talked incessantly about his life, being an abandoned orphan; running away from his adopted parents; riding freight trains at fifteen during the Depression; becoming successful at twenty by buying options on farmers' crops and selling them to canning factories; losing everything and heading West; his beginnings as an accountant in Hollywood. He spoke practically without stopping, except to swallow his food and sip his wine, and was still telling me about himself as we walked down the steep Suquet, drove back past Mougins to Bob Littell's house in Castellaras. Harold said a warm good night, I thanked him for dinner, and he drove off.

You Can Go Home Again

I let myself in, descended to the *rez-de-jardin*, the basement guest room, which was cold and damp. I went to bed, wheezing. I hadn't had asthma in twenty years. I didn't sleep all night, *une nuit blanche*, a white night, as the French call it. The *entire* plot of a novel came at me. An antihero like Harold, a zillionaire writer of steamy best-sellers who lives like the characters in his books, and whose values boomerang. His life is threatened.

By morning, I had the story completely worked out. When Bob returned from taking his young sons to school, I told it to him. "It's a best-seller," he said. "You've got to write it as fast as you can."

Two months later, Bob drove to Paris in his little orange Volkswagen Bug, and parked in front of our door. "How far along are you?" he asked. I told him I'd outlined it and written the first chapter. I thought that was pretty damn good. "Not fast enough. Let me see it." After he'd read it, he said, "It's good, but you've got to hurry up. It's going to be a big fat book like Harold's books. What would you say to writing it with the Old Pro?"

"Ben?"

"It's a big undertaking. I wouldn't say this except you guys are going to make a mint if you get it out fast."

Bob Littell, an ex-*Newsweek* editor, was a close friend. He and his wife, Deanna, a successful fashion designer, had exiled themselves, not because of McCarthyism, not because they were on the Left, but because a murder was committed in Central Park near where their two little boys were playing. New York was dangerous. They emigrated to find a safe and pleasant atmosphere. Bob first came to our house shortly after they arrived in France. Did we know a good pediatrician? Where could they get American products? But he really wanted us to read his first novel, *The Defection of A. J. Lewinter*, which his American agent and an American editor had characterized as "no good—why don't you go back to *Newsweek*?" We read it, loved it, passed it on to publisher Marcel Duhamel. We didn't hear from Marcel and finally called him. He said, simply, "Of course, it's very good! We are publishing it." *Lewinter* came out first in French, published by Gallimard. From then

427

on, Bob's subsequent books were published in the States. In 2002, his novel *The Company,* about the CIA, was on the best-seller list.[3]

So, Bob called in Ben, who didn't have a commitment, and told him, my story. Ben thought *The Writer* (as I titled it) sounded like fun. We wrote it from 1977 through 1979 between our work on movie projects.

Of course, after our novel was published in 1982, Harold wouldn't talk to us, and kept our daughters, Suzo and Adréana, who were good friends, apart. It wasn't until he was near death in 1997 that he telephoned me. He spoke low, haltingly. "It's okay . . . babe. It's . . . a good story."

It *was* a good story and we wondered when we started writing it whether, after thirty years in France, we'd be able to write the American-speak of the characters, another reason why we returned to the States.

On the family front, Luli had become a doctoral student in film, Johnny a doctoral student in history, both at UCLA, and Daniel, who had attended one year of French university, wanted to transfer to UCLA, too. And, after Paulo, eighteen, the artist, was injured in a car crash and spent the year immobilized in our crumbling house, Luli brought him to Los Angeles, which meant that four of our seven were in L.A. She ceded to Paulo her job as Jean Renoir's literary secretary, which became full-time every day for the last three years of Renoir's life. If his father, Pierre-Auguste, were alive, Renoir told Paulo, he would be a film director, not an artist. Thereupon, Paulo decided to give up painting and become a film director.

Our friends Ruth and Milton Roemer,[4] hearing we might want to return, offered us their Brentwood home while they went on a mission to Asia. In 1951, Dr. Milton Roemer had been on the staff of the fledgling World Health Organization. Under the pressure of McCarthyism, the U.S. government withdrew approval of his appointment. Fired, he was brought to the Canadian province of Saskatchewan, where he implemented the first social insurance plan for hospital care—in effect the start of Canada's program of socialized medicine.

Although most of the 1970s were spent in a house that was tottering, Ben and I were more solidly together than we'd been in a long time.

Whether Ben was weaker or I stronger, I was less overpowered. My affairs had always been for a reason: to fill emptiness when I'd been beaten down, shut out, frustrated—without work.

Pieces of the house were falling. Scaffolding barely held it up. It was time to leave. I found a great jurist who assured me that I had done a good job, that from that point on, whether I was there or not, we would win in the courts. What he said came to pass. We recovered hundreds of thousands of dollars for the extraordinary engineering feats necessary to rescue the building and restore it; in addition, hundreds of thousands to indemnify us for years of misery, which came in handy to start off life in America.

Our Paris house is now the embassy of the tiny Central African Republic. On my trips to Paris to visit the children, I never fail to pass our house and salute the unfamiliar flag that flies over it.

Ben liked nothing about California except the sun and his daily swim in the pool. He was depressed, took sleeping pills, did nothing to improve his health. The inevitable happened, except that his second heart attack, July 4, 1979, was massive. It kept him in UCLA's intensive-care unit for a record period. (Ben was afraid of being alone. For two and a half months, I slept in the ICU.) The cardiologists said there was "nowhere to bypass to" and released him in September, telling me that he would not live until Christmas. He lived for ten years, very medicated, and very diminished. We rented a house in Westwood near UCLA Hospital. As soon as Ben was well enough, he and I finished the Harold Robbins novel. We gave the first draft to literary agent Bert Briskin, husband of novelist Jacqueline Briskin. They read it. Next thing we knew, Bert called from New York. "I've got a deal," he said. "Warner Books. $200,000 advance. Okay?" We were flabbergasted. America!

I made numerous trips to New York to meet with our charming two-martini-lunch editor, Bernie Shir-Cliff, who helped us get the novel in shape. We were happy. The book was exactly what we thought it should be, a satire of the big Harold Robbins sex-money-power novels that people were snapping up in every language including Swahili. Unfortunately, the head of Warner Books, Howard Kaminsky, believed satire was what closes Saturday night. He wanted readers to think it was just another Harold Robbins kind of book, talked us out of our title *The Writer* and into a computerized title, *Rich Dreams*. Next, he wanted us to give up hardcover and let them bring it out in paperback right away.

I flew to New York and flounced into Howard's office. "Do you realize what we'd be giving up if we did that?"

"We're into this for a lot of money," Howard replied. "You two don't have a name. But it'll sell like a hotcake if it's an original paperback."

I glared at him. "You're asking us to give up reviews. This book needs reviews. People need to know what it is."

"I'll pay you for whatever you give up." He took out his checkbook, started writing. "Here's ten thousand dollars."

"You can keep it."

"Okay, okay," he cut in. "I'll be generous. I'll double it."

"Forget it. Hardcover means too much to us."

"Nobody'll buy it. It doesn't have Harold Robbins's name on it."

"It's not for Harold Robbins readers," I retorted. "The only way people will buy it is if reviews tell them it's a satire of today's commercial shit-fiction. Then they'll know it's funny and laugh. We've got a contract for *hard*cover."

"It's *hard* on us," Howard punned.

"A lawsuit would be harder. If you want us to settle for paperback, offer something possible."

"This is the highest I can go," he said. "This is it." He pulled out his desk drawer, handed me a check already made out. "Thirty thousand. That's a lot of money. You already have two hundred thousand."

"Ben and I would never accept thirty," I said, pushing away the check. "We've already discussed it."

Howard looked at his watch. He was sweating. It was a cold night. "I'm a commuter. I have to catch a train."

"Then run along. We don't need the money."

"Okay," he said. "I'll put in some of my own money. Forty thousand. But let me catch my train."

"Go ahead. Catch your train. We wouldn't accept a penny under $50,000." I turned toward the door.

"You're a tough cookie. Here's your fifty thousand!" He hurled another check at me. "Now let me out of here!"

A quarter of a million dollars for a book in 1982 wasn't bad, but we were right, *Rich Dreams* needed reviews. Sophia gave us a quote: "I loved it!" Annie and Art Buchwald praised it. In Hollywood, where there was a demand for it when the publicity hit, Warner Books didn't have enough copies in bookstores. Anyway, the romantic cover design showed a window through which you saw a man and woman kissing. It looked like something it wasn't.

The following year, it was published in French by one of France's top publishers, Presses de la Cité, and received excellent reviews. *Le Monde* and *Figaro Littéraire* pointed out that it was a satire. Titled *Convoitises (Cravings)*, it went into three editions and was sold to a book club.

Subtly, our relationship, Ben's and mine, underwent a metamorphosis. The heart attack had greatly weakened him but it wasn't just that. I had earned my half of both the $250,000 and the French royalties. I was also responsible for winning our claim against the city of Paris. But there were other reasons. In thirty years, the atmosphere in America had changed. I went up in a Saks elevator with four young black women who were laughing and enjoying themselves with abandon. What a fine feeling! It seemed as if a whole society was liberating itself, especially women. I could see and feel the results of the women's movement—women doctors, lawyers, producers, professors. For a fleeting second I heard Ben's, "You *cannot* take that job!" and knew at once that that could not happen today.

Working changed the way I felt, looked, behaved. Sometimes, I was afraid I was developing into "too tough a cookie." But not often.

By chance, Ben ran into Tony Quinn at the Beverly Wilshire Hotel. Over a drink, Tony confided that he wanted very much to play Picasso. Ben said, "But you're so big."

Tony replied, "I will make myself small."

Ben came home, excited. What could one do with Picasso? Anything written would bring suit from someone in the Picasso family.

"Not if it's fantasy," I said. "Not if you don't say Picasso really did any particular thing."

"What do you have in mind?"

"We're in a fortunate position," I replied. "We actually spent two days with Picasso celebrating his eightieth birthday. We could call it *Picasso's Birthday*, stick to what we know happened in those two days, and just let ourselves go with his fantasies."

Ben and I worked hard. Tony loved it and got his favorite producer, Frank O'Connor,[5] to take an option on it.

When I had been a bedable young woman, Tony was charming to me. Now I was Ben's collaborator and it was my story. Tony behaved differently toward me. For example, at story conferences, when I was speaking, Tony's eyes found Ben's as if I wasn't there.

Frank O'Connor died unexpectedly while we were making a deal with Société Française de Production. As we came out of the memorial services at the Catholic Church in Santa Monica where a nice young Irish priest said Frank had gone to a better place, Tony accosted us. "I've got an idea, Ben," he said, looking straight at him. "We'll meet."

The three of us met at Tony's Burton Way apartment in Beverly Hills. "I've got it solved!" he announced. "I've talked to some people and they'll go with it. A Broadway musical. *Picasso's Birthday*. I've got the guys to do the book, the music, the lyrics—"

"Hold on, Tony," I said. "It'll take a few years to get that going. We can get a deal on the picture right now."

Tony focused on Ben. "I'll dance—" He began dancing the *Zorba* dance. "I'll sing about my Blue Period!"

I could see that it would be wonderful but I couldn't bear his commandeering my idea and our project in such a high-handed manner. He didn't even have the courtesy to offer us the book of the show to write. If we were lucky, the credits would read, "From an idea by Ben and Norma Barzman."

I leaped to my feet. Ben was too feeble to fight me but I could see that he was horrified by my stance. "I'm afraid not, Tony," I said. "If you don't want to play in the film, we'll get someone else." I knew as I said it, the project would collapse. *Picasso's Birthday* would never be made. But I had reached a point in my life where I would no longer allow anyone to appropriate my ideas and my work.

Ben was not the only brilliant, powerful, talented figure disintegrating because of the blacklist, exile, rejection, and of course, age. During the early 1980s, we had three visits from Joe Losey. One was in March 1980 when he was in L.A. to negotiate a picture with a Chicago background (he wanted so much to make a film in the U.S.). *Silence,* Joe told us, was about the love of a young black girl and an older white doctor in the midst of a race riot. The musical score would be Chicago blues.

In October 1981, Joe returned to L.A. for further talks, discovered the film had been "postponed," i.e., canceled. He was in a foul drunken mood. I tried to distract him, asked him what he thought of our mutual friend Karel Reisz's picture, *The French Lieutenant's Woman.*

"Didn't see,' he slurred.

"You what?"

"I didn't see it—"

"C'mon," I said. "There's a screening tonight."

I dragged him, and sitting next to him, observed him watching it. It hurt him. Every once in a while he'd bend toward me and whisper, "That's not how I would have done it." Suddenly, he nudged me hard, "I would have cut to the servants' faces," Joe rasped, "and stayed on them as their eyes follow Meryl Streep."

In 1983, a year and a half later, he was in L.A. again. The BBC project that he was going to shoot in Dallas, Dennis Potter's *Track 29!* had collapsed. Joe was in collapse too. He took my hand for comfort, squeezed it hard. "I don't know how much more I can stand," he wheezed. "If I can keep on. . . . Last time I was here, you told me about a screenplay you and Ben were writing about Nazis in America. I'll read it on the plane."

A Walk in the Night, the story of a Jewish child adopted by a Gestapo officer and his wife, now respectable members of the Beverly

Hills community, excited Joe. He was able to interest two producers and sent us a breakdown of the script with budget. He was planning on doing it and was still writing copious notes for changes in the spring of 1984 when he was dying.[6]

No matter how great were their careers in Europe, Joe Losey and Ben Barzman hugged their bitterness to them. Ben and Joe were both named Chevalier of Arts and Letters by the French Ministry of Culture, and in 1984 Ben was the first screenwriter to have a retrospective of his work. Costa Gavras arranged for a week of Ben's films to be shown at the Paris Cinemathèque. But even after that, the very same year, Ben told Larry Ceplair: "During the blacklist and exile, I felt cheated and victimized. I experienced resentment, humiliation, and rage. The feelings of exclusion, alienation, and uprootedness never really left me. As a writer, I felt circumscribed, a writer needs to be steeped in the mainstream of the culture he is writing about. I did not feel I was a part of the French community."[7]

Sammy Weisbord, new head of the William Morris Agency, handed us over to a sweet young agent, Mike Peretzian, who found a succession of well-paid jobs for Ben and me. I actually had a contract and received my share of the money! Producer Gail Stayden sent me alone to Portugal to do the research for *The Man from Lisbon*. Ben was not able to do much of the work. I was writing screenplays and feeling guilty and ashamed when the pictures were never made. Later, of course, I found out that only one out of every twenty films in development is ever made.

The summer of 1985, Ben and I were invited to teach screenwriting at Chateauvallon, a French festival near Toulon. Our brightest, best student was Dai Sijie, fresh from China, who would write the international best-seller *Balzac and the Little Chinese Seamstress*.

In an outdoor amphitheater, we saw a pageant about the Renaissance, *Springtime*, by a professor of philosophy, Denis Guénoun. The festival head, Gérard Paquet, found the money for us to collaborate with Denis on a film adaptation of his spectacle. We let our film students experience the process by which we adapted *Springtime* for the screen. They were wild with enthusiasm, and it was exciting for us.

At the end of the summer, Denis, to whom we had become close, came to California and worked with us. Paquet, the producer, had gotten European financing, but when they finally read our lengthy treatment and realized the film would cost $40 million, they backed off. Today, it would cost $100 million.

At Chateauvallon, Ben Barzman and Jean-Luc Godard debated "*le scénario.*" Godard, of course, in the *Cahiers du Cinema* tradition, lambasted Ben and his ilk from Hollywood who had ruined cinema with "their well-constructed screenplay." Ben defended himself valiantly and lit into Godard's formless, incomprehensible films.

Toward the end, I put up my hand, still shyly in front of these French intellectual hotshots, and demanded, "Isn't there room for both kinds of film?"

By the spring of the following year, 1986, Ben was almost unable to travel. However, we wanted very much to be on hand when our screenwriter son Aaron's first feature film, *Salômé,* opened the Cannes festival in the new "palais" that looked like a fortress. *Salômé,* a weird, exotic film, did not do well with critics or audiences. Since then, Aaron has written principally movies of the week for French television.

During the festival, we were informed that my sister had been taken to the Pope's Hospital with incurable cancer. We flew to Rome. When we saw she had no television set, we went out and bought one. Imagine our astonishment when we turned it on to Rai Tre, Channel 3, where *Fanciulle di Lusso,* my film *Luxury Girls,* was being shown in Italian!

We stayed with my sister after she got out of the hospital until Ben insisted that if he remained in Rome, he too would die right then and there. We hastily left for the States. Ben wanted to be near his doctors and UCLA Hospital.

At that moment, another event severed our connection with Europe. A gang of teenagers burglarized our Mougins house. They took every last stick of seventeenth-century Spanish furniture, in fact all the furniture, paintings, household equipment, Le Creuset blue casseroles, copper pots, forged-iron chandeliers and wall appliqués, cupboard doors, and more important, all our scripts, photographs, and papers. Our long sojourn in France was really over.

Once home, Ben seemed to be on a downhill spiral. As he became more and more ill, I did less and less. One day, our son Daniel said to me harshly, "What are you going to do? Just sit there watching him die? Do something. I know you can't cook or sew. What *can* you do?" Daniel is the practical one, the vice president of an HMO in California.

"I'm a newspaper person," I told him. "That's the only thing I really know. I could write a column about what L.A. was like when we left compared to now, thirty years later."

"Write it," he commanded. "Take it to the editor of the *Examiner*."

I wrote three funny sample columns about the changes in L.A. and took them to Sheena Paterson, editor. She chortled as she read. "Smashing!" she exclaimed. I thought I was in. She handed them back to me. "Too bad we have so many columns about L.A."

Daniel had told me, if she doesn't take your columns, ask what she does need.

"What *do* you need?"

She thought a moment. "A column on aging."

Sheena, now my friend, says I turned chartreuse. She thought I was going to throw up on her carpet. I sidled toward the door, thanked her, and disappeared. But, on my way from downtown, I saw everyone was aging, even the toddlers. By the time I got home, I raced to the typewriter, wrote three sample columns on aging, which I titled "The Best Years," and sent them to Sheena. The next day she called. "We didn't know what we wanted but that's exactly it. You're hired." I wrote the column every week for three years until the *Examiner* folded, November 1, 1989. Fan mail told me that my upbeat attitude toward aging had inspired many readers to go out and start new lives. That gave me a lot of satisfaction. I was starting a new life, too.

• • •

Ben died in December 1989. The preceding ten years had been a long, slow, agonizing preparation but the last months of deterioration were shocking.

"We've had a pretty good life together," he croaked in an unrecognizable voice.

"You forgive—?"

"The affairs?" he interrupted softly. "They meant nothing."

"Then you forgive me?"

"No."

"What don't you forgive me for?"

"For not letting Picasso use our studio." Hoarsely, "He and I would have become close."

Ben knew he was dying and was very frightened. Often, I just sat and held his hand in silence. He had given me to understand that when you don't believe in God or a hereafter or have any kind of hope for the world, dying is difficult.

"Pollyanna," he teased me, barely audible. "*You* . . . believe . . . if heaven doesn't exist, there's something . . . better . . . "

Ben was aware his pessimism had prevented him from having as good a life as he could have had. There were moments when he had almost experienced the complete insane rapture of being alive, but for him mortality took away the wonder of life itself. I had a hard time with that. Fortunately, we could both laugh. Humor and our ability to laugh at ourselves made it possible for us to stay together for forty-seven years.

And so I told him one of his favorite jokes: "The optimist and the pessimist," I said and paused. "Their mother consults a shrink who counsels, 'Christmas morning, fill the pessimist's room with everything a child could possibly want. The optimist, it doesn't matter; just put some shit in his room.' Christmas morning arrives. The pessimist's room is loaded with everything F. A.O. Schwartz has to offer. The parents open his door. The pessimist is sitting in the midst of all the toys, crying his eyes out.

"The parents go to the optimist's room. He's laughing and chortling and shoveling shit at a great rate. 'What are *you* so jolly about?' his mother asks.

"The boy looks up, his eyes shining gleefully. 'With so much shit,' he says, 'there must be a pony!' "

The suggestion of a smile played about Ben's lips. I had to lean my head close to hear him: "You still can't tell a joke," he whispered.

Epilogue

This is the story of a young couple, both screenwriters, who because of their left-wing idealism, were, with their small children, uprooted and forced to face exile. But as destructive as the blacklist was for many, for these two, it opened up the world.

The story is not over.

For six months after Ben's death, I wrote features for the *Times* syndicate and continued to write my column for the *Los Angeles Times* after the *Examiner* folded. But I wasn't happy. I don't mean that I was grieving. I just wasn't happy. I asked myself Daniel's question, "What *do* you need? What *do* you want?"

I wanted to write a novel and I knew exactly the novel I wanted to write. The one I'd done with Ben had been a satire of the popular contemporary novel just as Jane Austen's first, *Northanger Abbey,* had been a satire of the Gothic novel of her time. She had gone on to write what she thought a novel should be. Now I wanted to write what I thought a novel should be.

I headed for Cremona, Italy, where seventeen years earlier, I'd spent four days with my cousin Henry Myers, researching his historical novel about one of the great violin makers of all time, Giuseppe Guarneri del Gesù.

When I began writing the novel about those four days, I made the "I" character a travel writer, forty-three, a married woman with college-age children, but still an incurable romantic.

In Cremona, she sees her idol for what he is, a writer prepared to distort history to meet his needs. At the Scuola, the school where violins are made as they were in the time of Stradivarius, she discovers that violin making, although artisanal, can be "art." In the course of her research on Guarneri, she gets caught up in a mystery: why were the world's greatest violins made in Cremona? Feeling her way into a maze of intrigue, she finally solves the age-old mystery. My heroine plummets to earth, rids herself of a lifetime of romantic fantasy. Cremona dramatizes how easy it is to romanticize life; how difficult, how necessary, and how rewarding it is to face reality.

Not even Yehudi Menuhin, eager to know the answer to the mystery, ever learned the truth, which he would so have loved. I may be the only one who has dug out the real story.

During Ben's long illness, it became clear that I would have to fight to save myself. I worked hard, never stopped, except for a trip to Cuba for the twentieth anniversary of the revolution. There, I met a professor from an American university who was, in my daughter Luli's words, "perfect for the role he was to play."

For more than fifteen years, three or four times a year, I took two-week vacations with him. He was my age, a reformed Old Lefty, tall, muscular, in good shape physically, attractive, knowledgeable, with a New York Jewish background. Sound like an ad from the personals?

We attended world congresses in Mexico City, Barcelona, Madrid, Stockholm; I accompanied him to universities all over the world, from Berkeley to Germany's oldest, Tübingen, where he lectured and gave papers; we vacationed at Tahoe, Palm Springs, Carmel, Santa Barbara; explored New England, saw plays in New York. The relationship kept me alive when Ben was no longer there for me.

Right after Ben's death, indecently quickly, the professor turned up. "Now we can get married," he said. I said *no.* "We don't have to marry," he said, "we can live together." I said *no.* "We don't have to live together," he said. "I can get an apartment down the street from you."

I continued to travel with him for another five or six years. He didn't understand why we couldn't be together all the time. "You can write," he said. "You don't have to do anything. I'll cook. I'll do everything— except the windows."

Yes, he even had a sense of humor. And he was a feminist. My friends thought he was lovely. I asked my old psychologist friend, Mac, Dr. Nathan Maccoby, head of Stanford's Institute of Communication, why I hadn't said yes. "It's simple," Mac said. "You want to be alone."

I was writing. I was alone. I was happy. I'd almost forgotten about the blacklist.

Epilogue

Then Paul Jarrico, whom I hadn't seen since Europe, told me of his struggle in the Writers Guild to restore credits to blacklisted screenwriters who'd worked under assumed names or with fronts. But Paul didn't stop there. Nineteen ninety-seven was the fiftieth anniversary of the 1947 HUAC hearings in Washington that had resulted in the imprisonment of the Hollywood Ten. Historically, the Academy had wanted no part of the growing movement to *condemn* the blacklist, but nonetheless gave its Samuel Goldwyn Theatre for the exciting 1997 event. The four Hollywood unions—the Writers, Screen Actors, and Directors Guilds and AFTRA (American Federation of Television and Radio Artists)—apologized formally for having supported the blacklist. Paul Jarrico, who engineered the apologies, was honored for his tireless efforts on behalf of the blacklistees.

That morning Paul had taken part in the inauguration of the USC memorial monument to the blacklisted; he attended the Academy event and reception that night, and the following day's Writers Guild luncheon. On the way home to Ojai, about seventy-five miles north of Los Angeles, weary from the triumph of the long, good fight, he fell asleep at the wheel of his car, crashed into a tree, and was killed instantly.

Two days later, I got a call from the Writers Guild. As a newspaper person, could I help them? The *Los Angeles Times* refused to print anything about the Academy meeting of eleven hundred persons or about Paul Jarrico's death the following day. I phoned John Lindsey, then managing editor of the *Times,* who spent twenty minutes explaining why they couldn't run the story. The *Times* calendar section, he said, had devoted much good space to the fiftieth anniversary of the blacklist. That was it! Not one word more! Paul would have a Sunday obit.

I maintained that all four unions and the Producers Association had admitted they'd been wrong to blacklist and *that* was national and international news. Furthermore, when I was a young feature writer, I would have given my eyeteeth for the story of a man who righted a wrong and died a hero. It should be on page one.

"Okay," he gave in finally, "but not page one."

Next morning, I walked down the driveway and picked up my *Times*. There it was on page one, pretty much as I'd dictated it.

That night, the phone rang. John Lindsey. "Norma," he said, "I'm calling to thank you. It was a great story. I got a lot of praise for it. Any time you have something to tell me, call. Don't hesitate."

In March 1999, ten years after Ben's death, the Writers Guild restored screenplay credit to Ben for *El Cid* and solo original screenplay credit ("Written By") to me for *Luxury Girls*. At that same moment, the Academy announced their intention to bestow an honorary Oscar on Elia Kazan. Along with Abe Polonsky, Bernie Gordon, Jean Butler, Bobbie Lees, and the other surviving blacklistees and their offspring, I was goosed into action. I'd been comparatively quiet, attending blacklist retrospectives, promoting *Tender Comrades* at bookstores and universities. But I was energized once again. I collected money for ads in *Variety* and *The Hollywood Reporter;* picketed outside the Dorothy Chandler Pavilion with my grandson, Matthew, Daniel's son; spoke on radio and TV. A big demonstration greeted Oscar-goers, most of whom did not stand or applaud Kazan.

The Academy, severely criticized by many of its own members as well as the press, was feeling vulnerable. I wanted to take advantage of the moment. I asked President Bob Rehme to "do something for us." I proposed a retrospective of blacklist films, discussion panels, a poster show, a lecture series. I believe it was my sixth proposal to which he agreed: an exhibit to examine the history of the Hollywood blacklist. Further, the Academy accepted my suggestion to hire Larry Ceplair, coauthor of *The Inquisition in Hollywood,* as curator. Larry did a bang-up job. The exhibition, well attended during February, March, and April 2001, made the front page of the *Los Angeles Times* and drew worldwide attention to the blacklist period.

Ben once had confided to Larry Ceplair, "Living through the blacklist and exile was like having gone to war—it was a rich and rewarding experience, but I wouldn't want to go through it again." That, in turn, recalled to me the words of Salka Viertel: "No matter how hard it is for

Epilogue

a man to face exile, it is always doubly hard for the woman who must hold it all up, keep the ship from sinking, the wife, mother who must also buoy up the spirits of a neurotic artist-husband." Salka could have been talking about me or any of the wives of the blacklisted.

Despite Ben's brilliant film career in Europe, he was bitter. I could have been bitter. My writing career was nipped in the bud. But so much came to me. Perhaps it's harder for a woman to have a successful career but easier for her to have a fulfilling life. Perhaps the important skills are the ability to adapt and not to be too fixed on a single goal.

Right now, for example, I have more than one goal. At Vienna's Jewish Museum, I came across a Marcuse quote urging us to remember the effects of the Holocaust on our culture. All at once, I realized it could apply to the blacklist. We need to inscribe on our memory tablets the humanist contributions made to our culture by the progressives of the thirties and forties, and be mindful of how the blacklist and the fear it engendered mutilated and degraded our culture for generations. At the retrospective in Vienna, I was surprised to see a film of the early 1940s, *Smashup,* written by "rigid" John Howard Lawson, head of the Hollywood section of the Communist Party. I felt it could have been written by a young feminist woman writer today!

In 1999, along with all the other blacklisted writers, I received a Lifetime Achievement Award from UCLA's graduating screenwriting class. They explained: In the light of the Academy's honoring Kazan, the students felt that whether we, the blacklisted, wrote B films or Oscar-winning ones, we deserved an award for the way we lived our lives, for the choice we made, not to destroy others to save our own careers, and for our own small victories.

This memoir is one woman's personal history of those small victories.

Notes

Chapter 1. Boy Meets Girl

1. Sol Barzman was a lyricist who collaborated with Ben. After being drafted into the Army, Sol returned to New York City at the end of the war where he wrote *The First Ladies* and other books.

2. Lardner would win an Oscar again in 1970 for *M*A*S*H*.

3. Betsy Blair was later nominated for Best Actress in *Marty* in 1955.

4. Biberman directed several films, including *One Way Ticket* (1935) and *Meet Nero Wolf* (1936), before directing *Salt of the Earth* in 1953.

5. The University of Southern California was organizing a film department.

6. I accompanied Claude to Princeton, where he worked with Einstein, Von Neumann, and Weyl at the Institute for Advanced Study, while I worked for the Economic Section of the League of Nations. Dr. Claude Shannon died February 24, 2001.

7. Agent Harold Hecht married another Norma, founded Norma Productions a few years later with star Burt Lancaster. Eventually, Hecht became an informer during the HUAC hearings in the late 1940s.

Chapter 2. Girl Gets Boy

1. For the most comprehensive treatment of Hollywood politics of the thirties and forties, see *The Inquisition in Hollywood,* by Larry Ceplair and Steven Englund, Univ. of Calif. Press, 1979, soon to be registered by Univ. of Illinois Press.

2. Ceplair and Englund, pp. 18–20. "A company-formed union called the Academy of Motion Pictures. . . . "

3. Television residuals began to be paid in 1953. In 1948, two companies began paying residuals for theatrical films, but residuals did not come into general practice until 1960.

4. In the fall of 1947, Adrian Scott, Edward Dmytryk, Alvah Bessie, Herbert Biberman, Ring Lardner Jr., Lester Cole, John Howard Lawson, Albert Maltz, Sam Ornitz, and Dalton Trumbo were subpoenaed to appear before the House UnAmerican Activities Committee in Washington, D.C. When they refused to answer questions about their political beliefs or affiliations, they were declared in contempt of Congress, which the courts upheld. They were sentenced to prison for six months to one year, and blacklisted by the film industry.

5. Director John Berry died November 29, 1999, at eighty-two, while editing the film he shot in South Africa, Athol Fugard's *Bozman and Lina,* with Angela Bassett and Danny Glover. John Berry—Jack—was one of our closest friends during the thirty

years we lived in France. He came to France shortly after we arrived, remained for fifty years, acting and directing.

6. Patrick McGillan and Paul Buhle, *Tender Comrades*, St. Martin's Press, p. 334. "We had some of the best-run mass organizations in the country, and they were manned— if I may use the wrong word—by women. The women were so remarkable in their organizational skills that many of them went on to become successful organizers in bourgeois enterprises after the Party was no longer a force in Hollywood."

7. The branches of the C.P. were, whenever possible, related to a guild or union. Actors' branch, writers, directors, technicians, and a branch for wives.

8. Leo and Pauline Townsend later became informers for HUAC.

9. *The People's World* was a West Coast Communist newspaper similar to *The Daily Worker*.

10. Dan and Lilith James collaborated on *Bloomer Girl,* based on Lilith's idea, which became a hit musical on Broadway the following year, 1944. Many years later, I discovered a best-seller, *Famous All Over Town,* written in the first person by Danny Santiago, a young Latino. When I visited the Jameses in Carmel, Dan confessed that he was "Danny Santiago." The book had been, in fact, authored by Dan James, who, with Lilith, had spent more than twenty years as a benevolent social worker in the *barrio.*

11. George Sklar is best known for the interracial drama *Stevedore.* He cowrote *Merry Go Round* with John Howard Lawson. Sklar was never very successful as a screenwriter (*City Without Men, First Comes Courage*). In later years, he wrote some first-rate novels.

12. Salka Viertel, *The Kindness of Strangers,* Holt, Rinehart and Winston, 1969.

13. When HUAC issued Sidney Buchman a subpoena, Harry Cohn, head of Columbia, who said he loved him "like a son," unsuccessfully tried to "arrange" things for him. Nonetheless, Sidney was thrown out of his job and blacklisted. He managed car parks until he was able to obtain a passport and join us in France.

Chapter 3. Girl Gets Job

1. Ben Barzman's journals.

2. Mike Gordon would inform late in the game in order to make the movie *Pillow Talk.*

3. Howard Fast served a prison sentence for contempt of Congress when he refused to give the names of members of the Civil Rights Congress of which he was an officer. Ten years later he left the Party.

4. Arbit Blatas died at age ninety in 1999. He is remembered for his bas-reliefs of the Holocaust that are placed at the entrance to the Historical Ghetto of Venice.

Chapter 4. Feudal Lords

1. John Paxton wrote the screenplays of three other films Adrian produced and Dmytryk

directed: *Cornered* (1945), *Crossfire* (1947), and *So Well Remembered,* in England, 1946. Paxton never joined the Communist Party but was gray-listed anyway. After years of not being able to work, he and his wife, Sarah Jane, joined us in France. Later he wrote the screenplay of *On the Beach.*

2. Edward Dmytryk, *Odd Man Out,* Southern Illinois Univ. Press, 1996, p. 5.

3. Sara Holmes, *Julia Morgan, Architect,* Abbeville Press, 1995.

Chapter 5. The Honeymoon Is Over

1. Anthony Quinn died in May 2001.

2. I interviewed the psychotic young woman backstage before she was taken away to a mental institution. She was a dancer with an obsession. Later, when I visited her apartment, I discovered every wall was pasted with photographs of Toscanini or of drawings she'd made of him, many obscene.

Chapter 6. Reel Life

1. For a biography of Abe Polonsky, see Paul Buhle and Dave Wagner, *A Very Dangerous Citizen,* Univ. of California Press, 2001. *Force of Evil,* which he wrote and directed, is considered one of the best of the blacklist films.

2. Ceplair and Englund, *The Inquisition in Hollywood,* p. 233.

3. I. A. L. Diamond became Billy Wilder's principal screenwriter.

4. In 1999, John Garfield's daughter, Julie, helped me with the anti-Kazan campaign when the Academy awarded Kazan an Oscar for lifetime achievement. Julie is an actress and beautiful like her mother.

5. Constancia de la Mora, author of *In Place of Splendor,* Harcourt Brace, 1939.

6. Lee J. Cobb became an informer for HUAC. He was named by Larry Parks in 1951 but resisted the Committee for two years. During that time, he ran out of money, could get no work. His wife, actress Helen Beverly, was institutionalized for alcoholism. On June 2, 1953, in room 1117 of the Hollywood Roosevelt Hotel, testifying in executive session, Lee J. Cobb became an informer. Not long after he testified, he had a massive coronary but survived. His career went forward after his informing. See Victor S. Navasky, *Naming Names,* Viking, 1980, pp. 268–73.

7. Ceplair and Englund, pp. 233–34.

8. Ceplair and Englund, pp. 233–5

9. I met Gerda Lerner and her husband, Carl, a film editor, in the 1940s. Gerda said she'd known Albert well, and thought his recanting was a result of being convinced, as she and most of us were, that Party unity was more important than the theoretical correctness of Marxist literary criticism. "I think we all felt, as Albert said finally himself,

that at that time 'the Party *was* the best hope of mankind,' and nobody would have risked expulsion and isolation." In the 1960s, Gerda went back to school and became one of the most distinguished historians of our time. A pioneer in women's studies, she gave women back their history—*The Creation of Feminist Consciousness, The Creation of the Patriarchy.* She is professor emerita of history at the University of Wisconsin, Madison. Temple University Press published her memoir, *Ironweed,* a political autobiography, in 2002.

10. Janet Stevenson's screenplay credits include *The Law vs. Billy the Kid, Dramma nella Kasbah,* and *Counter-Attack* from her and her husband Phil Stevenson's play. She had more success as an author, one of her best-known books being *The Ardent Years.*

11. Tammy Gold, a blacklisted screenwriter, is the daughter of Sonya Levien, one of Hollywood's early and highly paid screenwriters. Tammy has written a novel, *Among the Survivors,* biographies of George Sand and John Reed, and a history of the construction of the Paris *métro, Paris Underground.*

Chapter 7. Galileo

1. John Barzman, magna cum laude Harvard, PhD UCLA. Professor of history, University of Le Havre. *Longshoremen, Metalworkers and Housewives,* published in France, 1999.

2. Lester Cole, *Hollywood Red.* Ramparts Press, 1981.

3. Johnny Weber, Bernard Vorhaus, and Ben formed a company, Riviera Films, that produced *Stranger on the Prowl* and *Luxury Girls* in Italy, 1951–1952, both distributed by United Artists.

4. Navasky, *Naming Names,* Viking, p. 131.

5. Ibid.

6. Many years later in Paris, Ben and I saw the East German Berliner Ensemble production with their distinguished actor Ernst Busch in the title role. He also resisted Brecht's condemnation of Galileo. "How are we supposed to condemn a man," Busch asked, "who weakened his eyes at the telescope, almost went blind in defiance of the Church, copying a book extremely useful to mankind; whose quest for truth drove him into increasing danger and finally to the loss of his freedom?"

7. Faith Hubley died in 2001.

Chapter 8. The Shit Hits the Electric Fan

1. One month later, eleven of the nineteen were called to the witness stand. Only one, Berthold Brecht, answered the committee's questions, denied ever being a Communist, and left immediately for East Germany. (Joe Losey accompanied him to Washington and saw him off.) All of the Ten who refused to cooperate with HUAC, citing

Notes

the Bill of Rights, were our friends: John Howard Lawson, Dalton Trumbo, Ring Lardner, Jr., Herbert Biberman, Sam Ornitz, Alvah Bessie; four of them, Adrian Scott, Eddie Dmytryk, Albert Maltz, and Lester Cole, close friends. They'd been to dinner at our house, we to theirs; we'd given each other gifts when our babies were born.
2. Ceplair and Englund, p. 135

Chapter 9. Not Enough Jeopardy
1. Ceplair and Englund, p. 329.
2. *Pacific Film Archive,* April 1993.
3. Alfred lewis Levitt, blacklisted screenwriter, died Nov. 16, 2002.
4. From Ben Barzman's journals.

Chapter 11. A Bit Soupy, eh Guv'ner?
1. Phil Brown later played Luke Skywalker's uncle in *Star Wars.* More recently, he made a career by touring *Star Wars* events throughout the country. Brown was never in the Party but was gray-listed because of his friendships with Communists.

Chapter 12. For King and Country
1. Charlotte and Sam Wanamaker's daughter, Zoe, became a leading actress of the contemporary London stage. In 1998, New York acclaimed Zoe's *Electra.* However, she lost the Tony to Judy Dench, who'd just received an Oscar.
2. J.R. Mulryne and Margaret Shewring, *Shakespeare's Globe Rebuilt,* Oxford Univ. Press, 1997, p. 11.
3. *Christ in Concrete* was called *Give Us This Day* in England and at the festivals, where it won "Best Picture"—Karlovy Vary, Vichy, and Venice. Its title in France was *Donnez-Nous Aujourd'hui* and in the United States, where it was given a limited run, *Salt to the Devil.*
4. In 1986, *Christ in Concrete* opened the Toronto Film Festival under its original title to glowing reviews. Paul Buhle, professor of American civilization at Brown University, included *Christ in Concrete* as one of the best films of the blacklisted in his book, *Radical Hollywood* (The New Press, 2002). Ownership problems have kept *Christ in Concrete* from being shown on television. There is a movement afoot to restore the film.

Chapter 13. April in Paris
1. From Ben Barzman's journals.
2. Ceplair and Englund, pp. 340–350.
3. Pop's son and his wife and granddaughter turned up in the 1960s, found by the Red Cross.

4. Karnow, Stanley, *Paris in the Fifties,* Times Books, 1977, pp. 40–41. Karnow won the Pulitzer for his book *In Our Image: America's Empire in the Philippines.*

Chapter 14. Dépaysés—Uncountried

1. In 2000, I attended Ruth Gilbert's ninetieth birthday celebration. I'd once written a column about her for the *L.A. Examiner,* "Late Bloomer."
2. Larry Adler died August 7, 2001, in London.

Chapter 16. Paris in October

1. Roger Boussinot died May 2, 2001.
2. Zuka Mitelberg's work was given a Paris exhibition in April 2001.

Chapter 17. Shalom

1. Ben wrote an excellent screenplay but he'd been right. Leytes's direction made the children seem painfully amateurish. *Faithful City* had a limited distribution.

Chapter 19. The New Man

1. I could not have guessed it would take forty-nine years to be granted solo original screenplay credit for my work.
2. Patrick McGilligan and Paul Buhle, *Tender Comrades,* interview with John Berry, St. Martin's Press, 1997, pp. 76–77.

Chapter 20. Finishing School

1. After the hearings and his testimony, Dmytryk was hired by the King Brothers to make a low-budget feature. Later, he made a four-picture deal with Stanley Kramer.
2. Instead of Bernard's name and mine, Piero Museta and Ennio Flaiano appeared on the credits until corrected by the Writers Guild in March 1999.
3. Johnny Weber died two months later, May 17, 2001.
4. Secretary of State Dean Acheson announced in May 1952 that passports were being withheld from alleged Communists, from anyone whose "conduct abroad is likely to be contrary to the best interests of the U.S." *Inquisition,* pp. 355–56.
5. We never knew whether the loss of my passport was a result of the 1951 HUAC hearings. Of the people we knew, I was the first to get my passport lifted, and after that anyone foolish enough to go into the embassy also lost his/her passport. Therefore, people stayed out of embassies and waited for their passports to expire. They got a few extra years in foreign countries that way.

Notes

Chapter 21. The Herring Barrel

1. Dr. Michael Sacks had a distinguished thirty-year career with the World Health Organization. In 1953 in India, he initiated antimalaria and clear-water programs. In 1978, as senior adviser to the UN Development Program, he concentrated on the HIV-AIDS epidemic. He died at eighty-four in May 2000.

2. Hannah Weinstein produced *The Adventures of Robin Hood* (1955), *The Buccaneers* (1956), *The Adventures of Sir Lancelot* (1956), *Sword of Freedom* (1957), and *Four Just Men* (1959), all television series. She also produced *Claudine* in 1974 (Jack Berry directed), *Greased Lightning,* and *Stir Crazy.*

3. I also wrote the English dialogue for three Italian films, among them Marcello Mastroianni's first, *Sunday in August.*

4. Ben Barzman's journals.

5. A replica of the caves, with copies of the murals, was built for tourists to visit from then on.

6. Stanley Karnow, *Paris in the Fifties,* Times Books, 1997, pp. 188–98.

7. *A Walk in the Night* was scheduled to shoot when Joe Losey died.

Chapter 22. Home Sweet Home

1. *Ananas rêve,* pineapple dream: sponge cake, fresh pineapple, caramel, chocolate and whipped cream.

2. Daniel Barzman, MSPH, Public Health, UCLA, presently a vice president of an HMO in the U.S.

3. Jules Dassin married Melina Mercouri and lived with her in Athens.

4. *Tender Comrades,* p. 220. Dassin said he did not invite me because it had been such a hassle even to get Ben invited.

5. Ibid.

6. Yves Allegret, director of many films such as *Riptide, The Cheat,* and *The Proud and the Beautiful.* His daughter, with Simone Signoret, is Catherine Allegret, an actress.

7. John Sanford, author of *The People from Heaven* and *A Man Without Shoes,* whom the *Los Angeles Times Book Review* called "one of the least known, most distinguished literary figures in America," was ninety-five when he telephoned me after Dmytryk died. Sanford's wife, blacklisted screenwriter Marguerite Roberts (*True Grit, Honky Tonk, Ivanhoe*), died in 1989. Sanford's comment: "I can't forgive any of the stool pigeons. Not after the way Maggie was made to suffer. They killed her. . . . "

8. Paulo—Paul Barzman, French TV Director, wrote and directed feature film *Time is Money* with Max von Sydau and Charlotte Rampling.

9. The idea for *Salt of the Earth* came from Adrian Scott and Herbert Biberman.

10. David Caute, *Joseph Losey,* Oxford Univ. Press, 1994. p.134. The *New York Times* recommended *Blind Date,* 11/29/60.

11. Ben Barzman's journals.

Chapter 23. Be Your Sylph

1. *Los Angeles Times,* December 5, 2000.

2. Navasky, p. 178. Zero Mostel played the actor who killed himself in *Guilty by Suspicion.*

3. Paul Robeson, after many years of being deprived of a passport, had, like us, just been granted one.

4. Ben's book, *Out of This World,* was published in the U.S. by Putnam, under the title *Twinkle, Twinkle Little Star* and then in paperback, as *Echo X.*

5. Ted Allan cowrote *The Scalpel and the Sword,* a biography of Norman Bethune, the Canadian doctor who first used blood plasma on the battlefield in the Spanish Civil War. Allan, a Montreal Jewish writer, had success with his play and film, *Lies My Father Told Me.*

6. *By a Stroke of Luck,* the autobiography of Donald Ogden Stewart, Paddington Press, 1975, p. 299.

7. Ibid.

8. Ibid.

9. Ceplair and Englund, p. 102.

10. Ella and I never finished *Be Your Sylph.*

11. After he returned to America with his French wife, Geneviève, Joe Hirsch and I corresponded.

12. *Blind Date,* an original and not very good Eric Ambler script, adapted from a novel by Leigh Howard. The film was also known as *Chance Meeting.*

13. Caute, p. 131. The incident around Losey's letter is mentioned also in Ben Barzman's journals.

14. Millard Lampell, lyricist and singer of folk music with Pete Seeger and Woody Guthrie. *Saturday's Hero* was his novel, which he adapted to the screen.

15. *Variety,* 1960.

16. Caute, who cites the October 29, 1960, *New York Times* reference.

17. My sister and brother-in-law, dubbing Italian films into English, thought they hadn't received the proper remuneration from Riviera Films (Barzman, Vorhaus, Weber), and complained to the Italian *guestura* who, in turn, gave the information to the U.S. embassy.

Chapter 24. La Mamma

1. Today, a picture like *El Cid* would cost a hundred million to make.

Notes

Chapter 25. Cold Pasta

1. My description of how Bronston operated during this period comes from many conversations with Ben and from Ben's journal.
2. Charlton Heston, *The Actor's Life Journals,* 1956–1976. Dutton, 1976, p. 110.
3. Colasanti and Moore were nominated for Oscars for art and set direction.

Chapter 26. The Fall

1. Charlton Heston, p. 109.
2. Ibid., p. 114. In 1993, Martin Scorsese pushed for making a new print of *El Cid,* which he considers one of the greatest epics ever made. He is not alone. The world press hailed *El Cid,* which was a huge box office success as well.
3. Heston, p. 114.
4. Alex North, a talented composer of many film scores including *A Streetcar Named Desire,* received an honorary Oscar in 1985, after having been nominated fifteen times but never winning the award.
5. David Caute, *Joseph Losey, p. 143,* quoting John Francis Lane's *Films and Filming.* September 1962. In France, posters advertising *The Damned* noted "Screenplay by Ben Barzman."
6. Caute, quoting Philip French, *The Observer,* May 19, 1962.
7. Marc Barzman, PhD Berkeley in Biologic Control, Chief of Projects in Vietnam, Latin America, Bangladesh. Univ. of California, Davis, supervisor California Central Valley Project. Currently agricultural economist with the European Union.

Chapter 27. Bronstonia

1. Pidal, the historian, told us that when Isabella's Jewish doctor had been unable to save her teenage son from a dire illness, she became wildly angry and let the Inquisition have its way. In 1492, she expelled Jews who would not convert, and later Moors.
2. In 1999, the Writers Guild restored Ben Barzman's screenplay credit for *El Cid.*

Chapter 28. The Kiss of Death

1. The *New Yorker,* Current Cinema, 2000.
2. Gordon, Bernard. p. 190.
3. Arthur Cohn produced many features. He also won Oscars for the feature documentaries *The Sky Above, the Mud Below* (1961) and *American Dream* (1989).
4. Luli Barzman MFA, UCLA. Her original screenplay about Louis Braille, the creator of Braille, was bought recently by a French production company. She is presently making videos for French television.

Chapter 29. Heavy Water

1. Excerpted from Ben Barzman's journals.
2. *Spartacus,* directed by Stanley Kubrick, screenplay by Dalton Trumbo, adapted from the novel by Howard Fast.
3. *Heroes of Telemark:* the composer was Malcolm Arnold (*The Bridge on the River Kwai, I Am a Camera, The Thin Red Line*). Ivan Moffat also got screen credit for his work on the script. Besides Kirk Douglas, Richard Harris, Ulla Jacobsson, and Michael Redgrave also played in it.
4. Citroën Model DS—*déesse*—goddess—that looked like a whale. The cheaper model was the ID-*idée*—idea. Everyone loved the puns.

Chapter 30. Zanuckia, Oasis for a Lost Bronstonian

1. Ben Barzman's journals.
2. Ken Annakin, director of *Battle of the Bulge, Swiss Family Robinson.*
3. Quinn, Anthony. *One Man Tango,* HarperCollins, 1995, p. 324.
4. Leamer, Laurence. *As Time Goes By.* Harper & Row, 1986, p. 274.
5. Ben Barzman's journals.

Chapter 31. The Blue Max

1. Suzo, our youngest, attended American College in Paris. Photo-news journalist, assistant to Candice Bergen and then to Mira Sorvino for five years.
2. Ben and Basilio's project with Sunil Dutt, *Taj Mahal,* never materialized.
3. In 1961, Varda's *Cleo—5 à 7* had an enormous impact on me, as did her *Le Bonheur* (1964).
4. Aaron Barzman writes movies of the week for French TV. *Salômé* is, so far, his only feature film.
5. John Guillermin, director, *Waltz of the Toreadors, Bridge at Remagen, The Towering Inferno.*
6. Johnny Green, *Body and Soul, The Inspector General,* among many other films as composer or musical director.
7. *Woman Aboard* by Janet Stevenson, Crown Books, 1969. Other books of hers include: *Sisters and Brothers, Weep No More, The Ardent Years, Departure, The Undiminished Man.*
8. Ruth Hirsch Bocour died in September 2000. The art collection was bequeathed to St. Mary's College, Maryland.

Notes

Chapter 32. Nyet

1. *Le Vent des Aurès* should have been called *The Mother.* The film is his mother's search for his father, who was taken away by the French.

2. *Tender Comrades,* p. 342.

3. Ring Lardner, Jr., *I'd Hate Myself in the Morning,* Nation Books, 2000, p. 194.

Chapter 33. May '68

1. *L'Express* Special Supplement, May 1968.

2. Philip M. Williams, *French Politicians and Elections,* Cambridge Univ. Press, 1970. Monographs by David Goldey.

3. Doctors' letter to *Le Monde.*

4. Jean-Pierre Jeancolas, *Le Cinema des Français,* Stock, 1977, p. 52.

Chapter 34. You Can Go Home Again

1. Aleksander Ford was a writer-director: *The Five Boys of Barska Street, Eighth Day of the Week, Black Cross.*

2. In 1991, I was shown a film, *Korszak,* written and directed by Andrzej Wajda. It was remarkably similar to Ben's screenplay except for the distasteful ending. With me at the projection was Louis Mitelberg, a Warsaw Jew. He commented, "Wajda portrays the Jews like Polish peasants. The Warsaw Jews were probably more sophisticated culturally than any Europeans at the time."

3. Bob Littell's best-seller *The Company: A Novel of the CIA,* has been purchased for films. Known as the American Le Carré, he has written more than a dozen suspense novels set in Washington and the USSR during the Cold War: *The Debriefing, The October Circle, The Defection of A. J. Lewinter. The Amateur* was the only one made into a movie.

4. Dr. Milton Roemer, dean of UCLA's Graduate School of Public Health, died in 2001.

5. Frank O'Connor, producer of the television classic *The Grey Goose.*

6. Joe Losey died June 22, 1984.

7. Ceplair and Englund, p. 402.

Index

Index

Index

Index

Index